PATH OF THE ASSASSIN

Lifelong Friends, with the Same Dreams,
Striving to Grow into a Rising River.

story
KAZUO KOIKE

art
GOSEKI KOJIMA

DARK HORSE MANGA™

translation
NAOMI KOKUBO
with assistance by **JEFF CARLSON**

lettering and retouch
SNO CONE STUDIOS

publisher
MIKE RICHARDSON

editor
TIM ERVIN

book design
DARIN FABRICK

art director
LIA RIBACCHI

Published by Dark Horse Comics, Inc.
in association with Soeisha Inc.

Dark Horse Comics, Inc.
10956 S.E. Main Street
Milwaukie, OR 97222
www.darkhorse.com

First edition: October 2006
ISBN-10: 1-59307-504-9   ISBN-13: 978-1-59307-504-0

1 3 5 7 9 10 8 6 4 2

Printed in Canada

To find a comics shop in your area, call the
Comic Shop Locator Service toll-free at 1-888-266-4226

半蔵の門 COMPARISON OF A MAN

by **KAZUO KOIKE**
& **GOSEKI KOJIMA**

VOLUME
3

"A tiger of a father and a wolf of a brother . . . sandwiched between the two, I wonder what my tomorrow holds."

In the first year of Eiroku (Year 1558), Matsudaira Motonobu (Ieyasu) successfully captures Mikawa Terabe Castle using both the tactics of surprise and Hattori Hanzō's ninja techniques. It is a fantastic outcome for his first battle. This victory earns him the trust of Imagawa Yoshimoto, and Yoshimoto grants him permission to change his name to Motoyasu. Meanwhile, Oda Nobunaga foresees Yoshimoto's move against the capital and strives to block his ambitions. How slim are Motoyasu's chances if he must go to war as a member of Imagawa forces?

半蔵の門 PATH OF THE ASSASSIN

TABLE OF CONTENTS

Chapter On Relinquishing Factions

No. 5: It Rains at Home, and it Rains on the Battlefield, Part 2

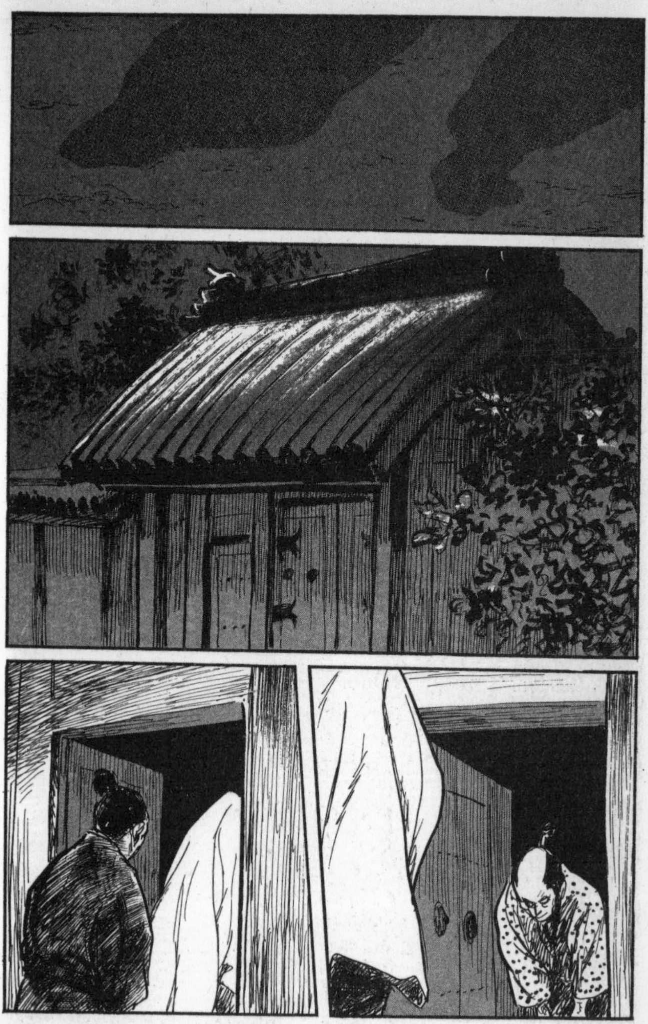

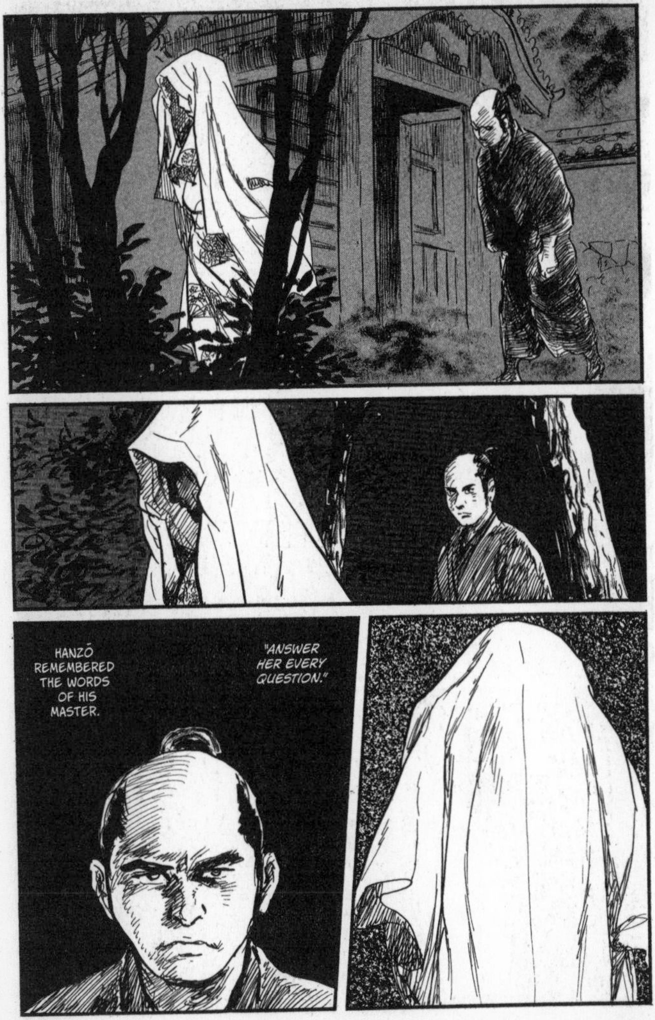
"ANSWER HER EVERY QUESTION."
HANZŌ REMEMBERED THE WORDS OF HIS MASTER.

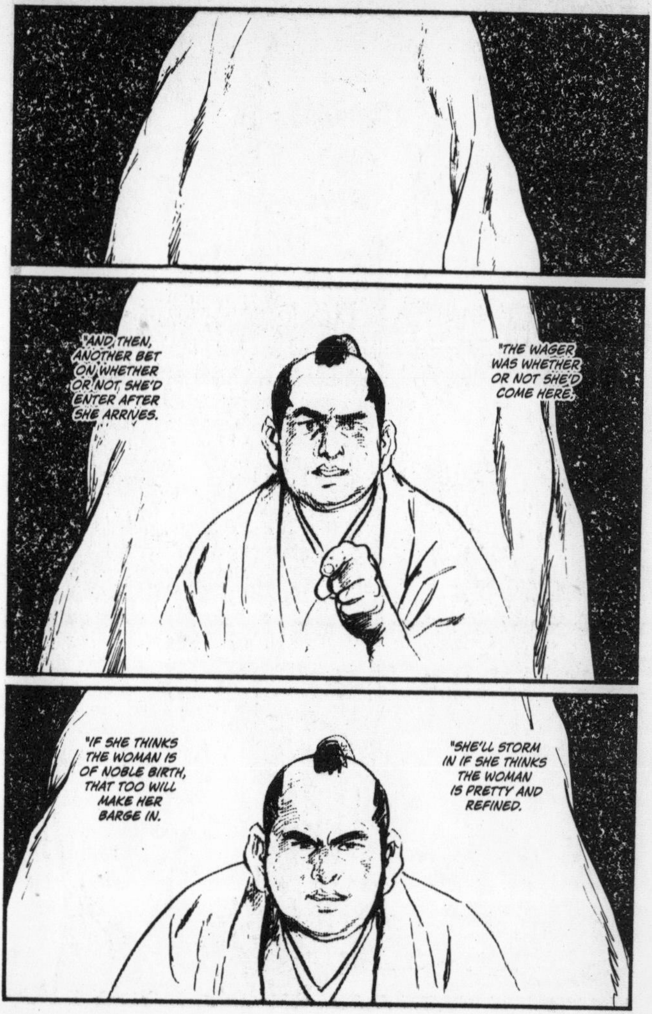
"THE WAGER WAS WHETHER OR NOT SHE'D COME HERE.
"AND THEN, ANOTHER BET ON WHETHER OR NOT SHE'D ENTER AFTER SHE ARRIVES.
"SHE'LL STORM IN IF SHE THINKS THE WOMAN IS PRETTY AND REFINED.
"IF SHE THINKS THE WOMAN IS OF NOBLE BIRTH, THAT TOO WILL MAKE HER BARGE IN.

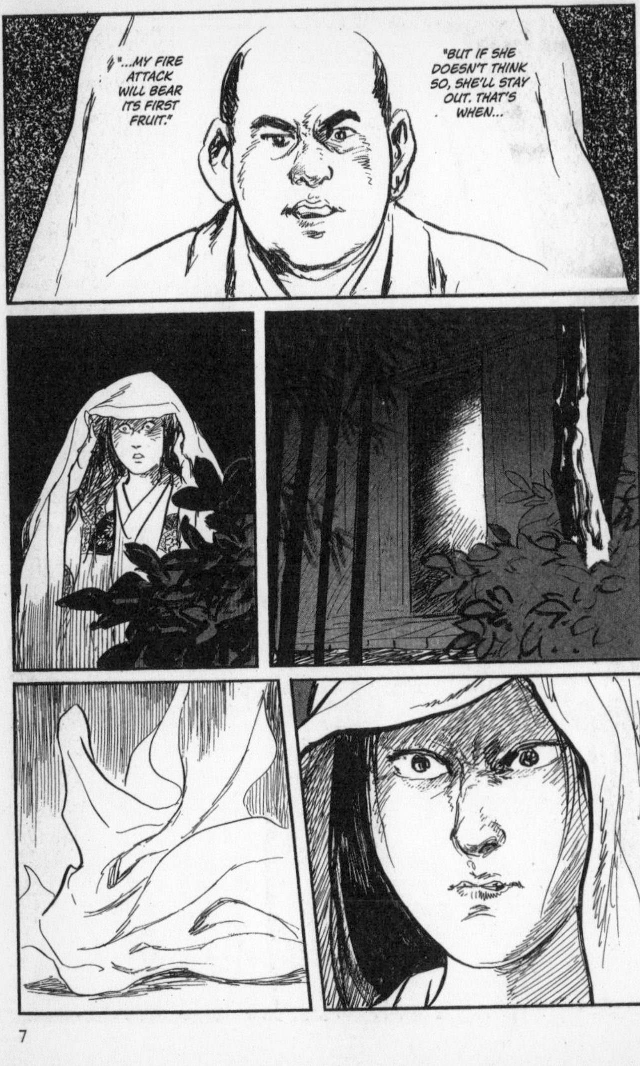
"BUT IF SHE DOESN'T THINK SO, SHE'LL STAY OUT. THAT'S WHEN...
"...MY FIRE ATTACK WILL BEAR ITS FIRST FRUIT."

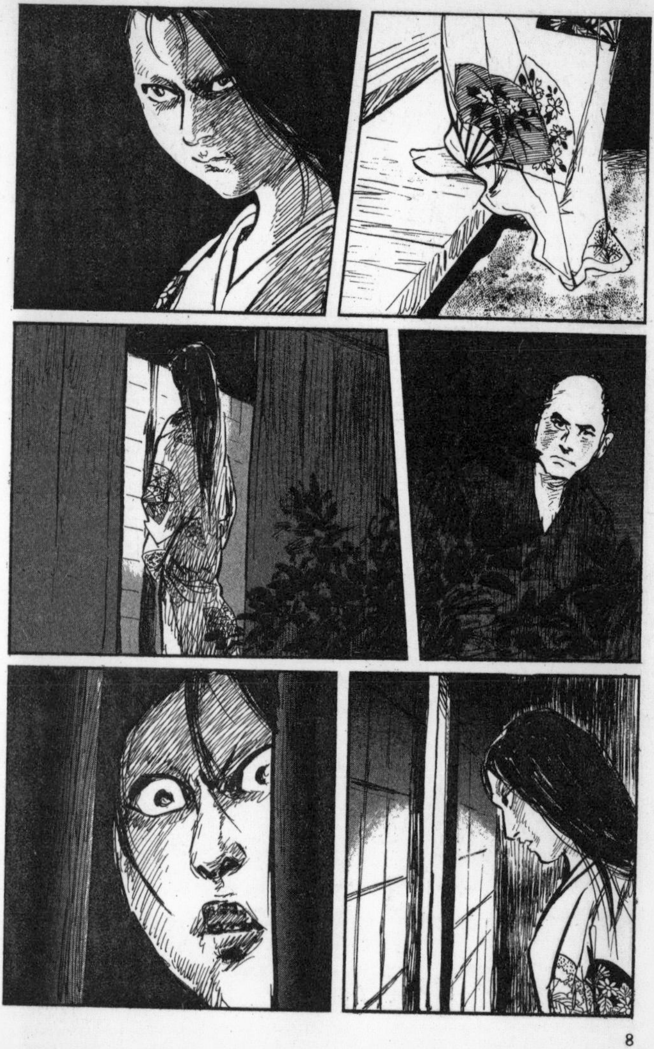

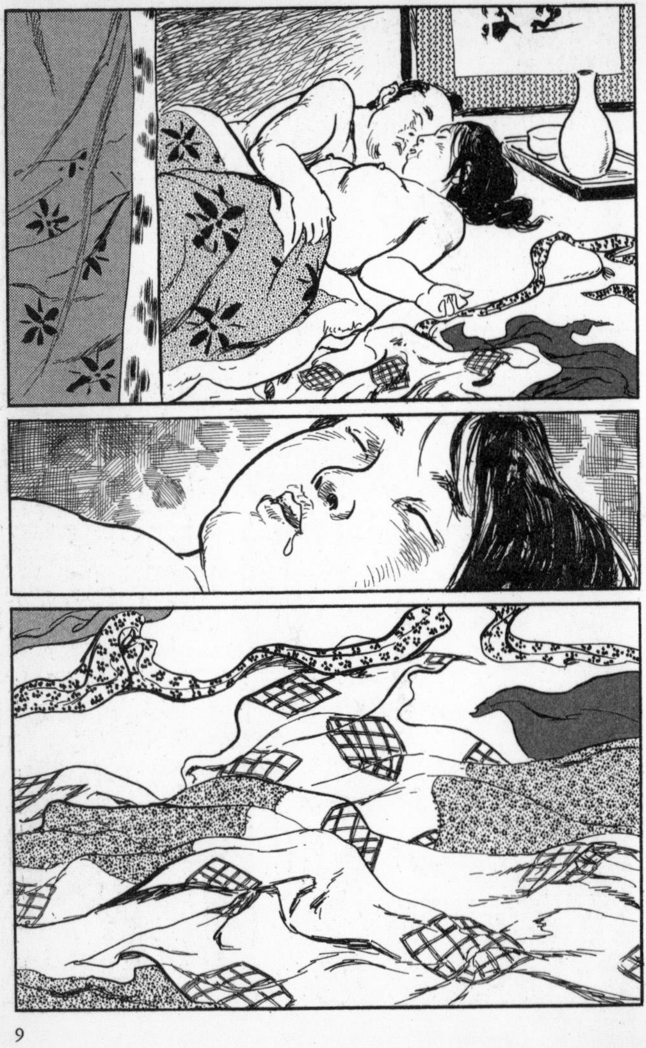

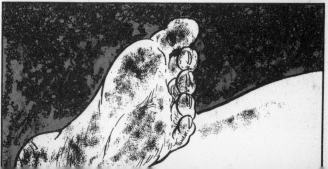

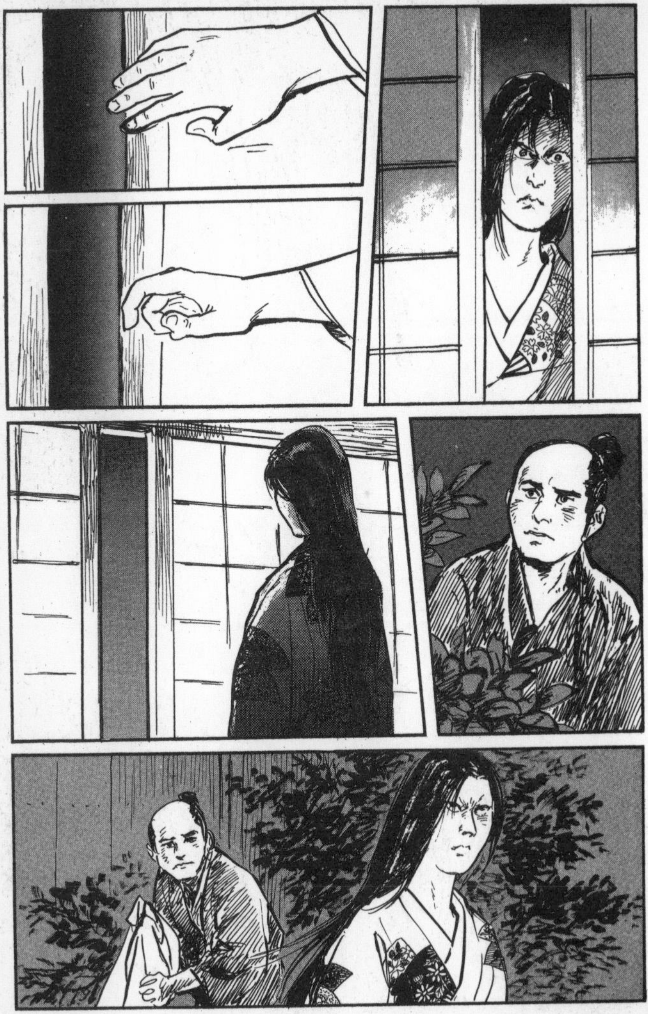

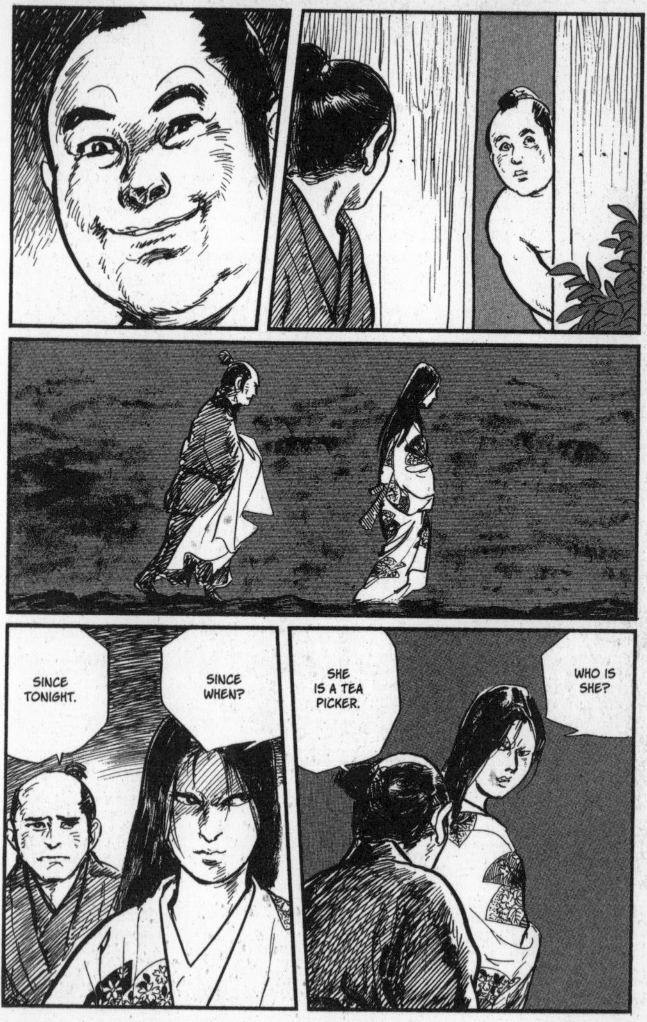
WHO IS SHE?
SHE IS A TEA PICKER.
SINCE WHEN?
SINCE TONIGHT.

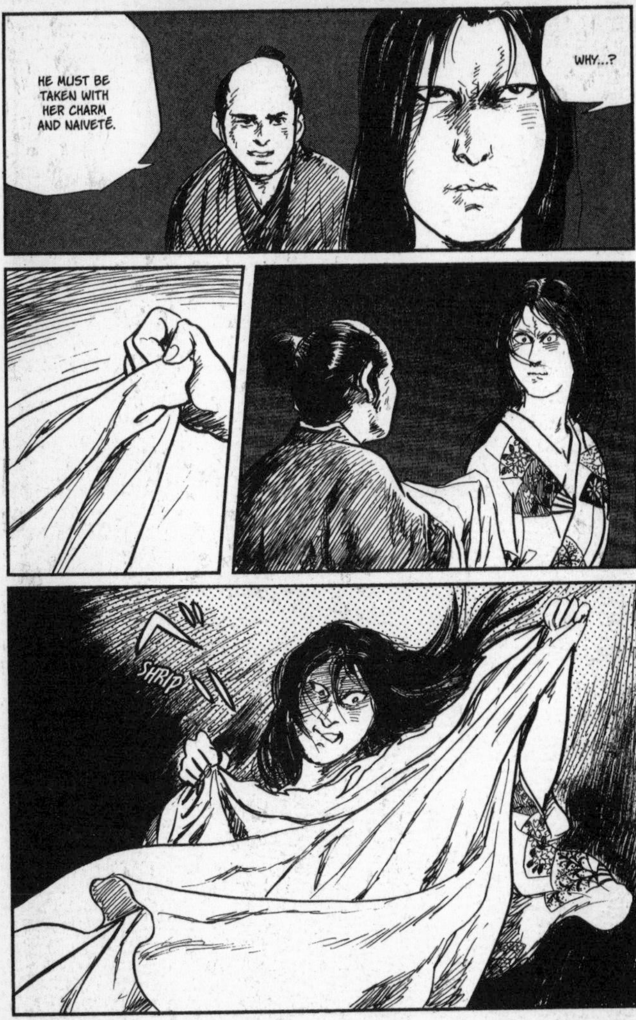
WHY...?
HE MUST BE TAKEN WITH HER CHARM AND NAIVETÉ.
SHRIP

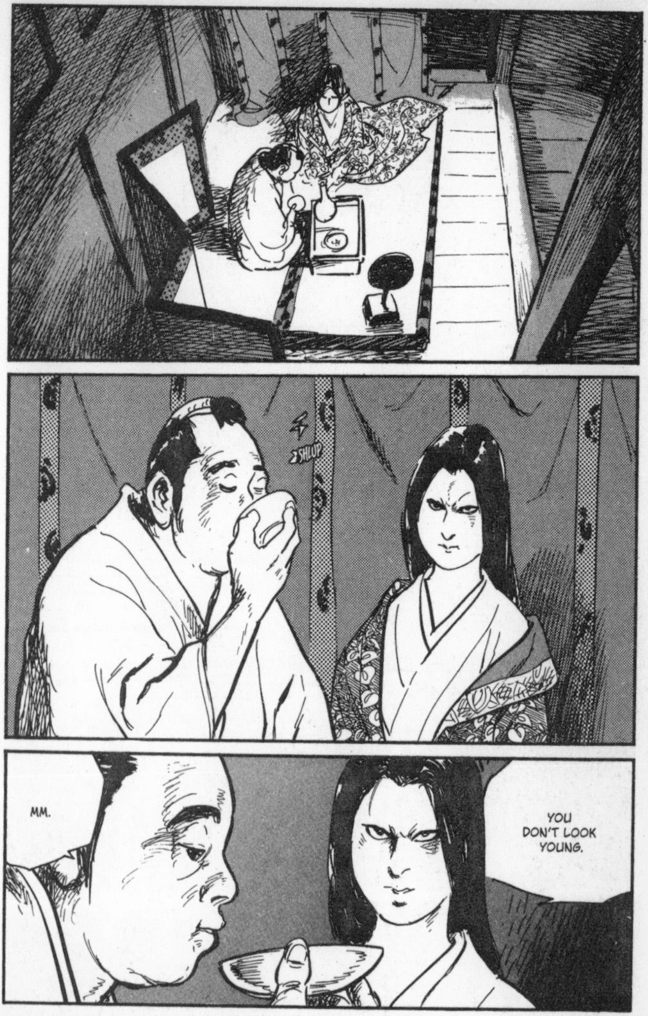
SHLUP
YOU DON'T LOOK YOUNG.
MM.

SAY SOMETHING!
SURE.
THERE'S NOTHING YOUTHFUL ABOUT YOU AT ALL.
NO LUSTER. NO SPIRIT OR VIGOR!
HM, NOT AT ALL, EH?

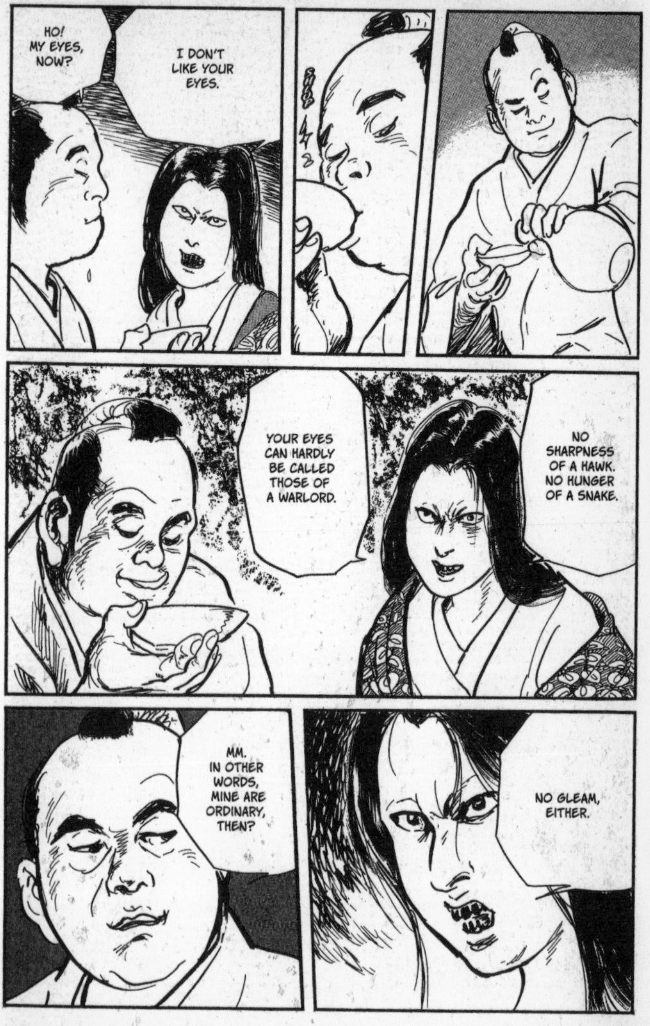
SHUP
I DON'T LIKE YOUR EYES.
HO! MY EYES, NOW?
NO SHARPNESS OF A HAWK. NO HUNGER OF A SNAKE.
YOUR EYES CAN HARDLY BE CALLED THOSE OF A WARLORD.
NO GLEAM, EITHER.
MM. IN OTHER WORDS, MINE ARE ORDINARY, THEN?

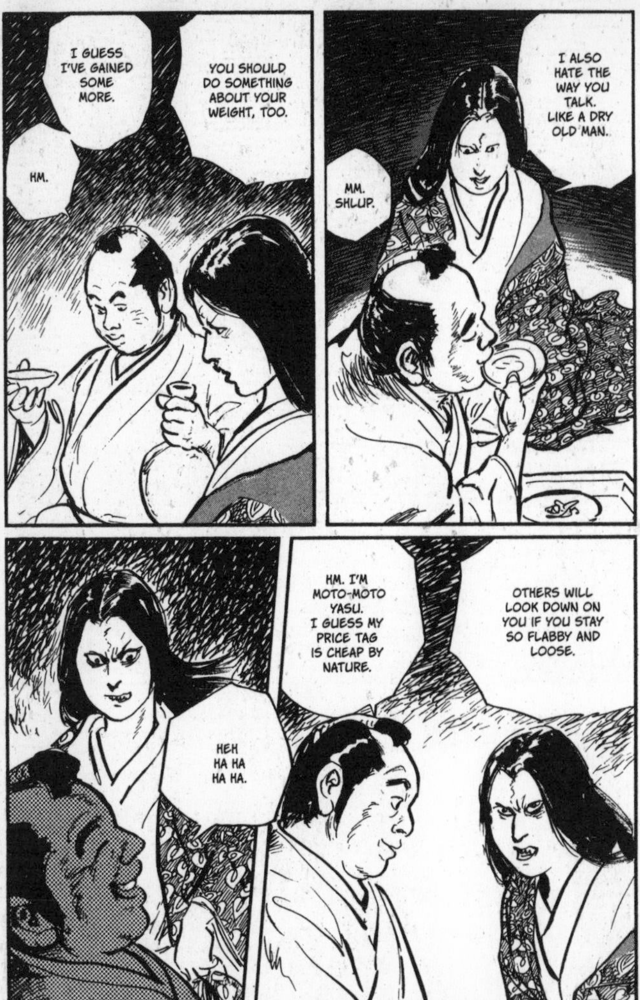
I ALSO HATE THE WAY YOU TALK. LIKE A DRY OLD MAN.
MM. SHLUP.
YOU SHOULD DO SOMETHING ABOUT YOUR WEIGHT, TOO.
I GUESS I'VE GAINED SOME MORE.
HM.
OTHERS WILL LOOK DOWN ON YOU IF YOU STAY SO FLABBY AND LOOSE.
HM. I'M MOTO-MOTO YASU. I GUESS MY PRICE TAG IS CHEAP BY NATURE.
HEH HA HA HA HA.

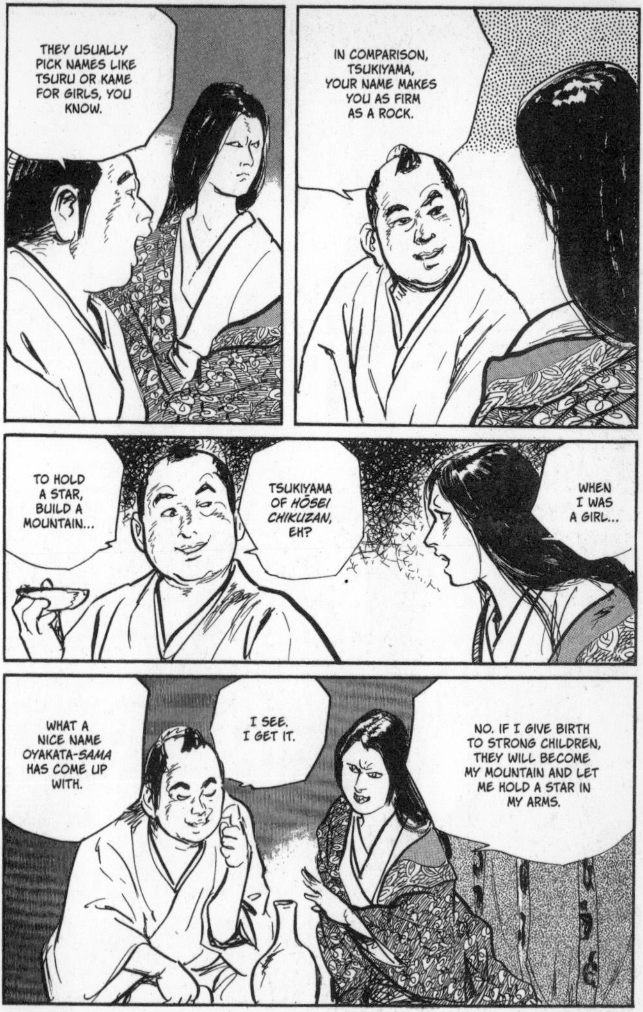
IN COMPARISON, TSUKIYAMA, YOUR NAME MAKES YOU AS FIRM AS A ROCK.
THEY USUALLY PICK NAMES LIKE TSURU OR KAME FOR GIRLS, YOU KNOW.
WHEN I WAS A GIRL...
TSUKIYAMA OF *HŌSEI CHIKUZAN*, EH?
TO HOLD A STAR, BUILD A MOUNTAIN...
NO. IF I GIVE BIRTH TO STRONG CHILDREN, THEY WILL BECOME MY MOUNTAIN AND LET ME HOLD A STAR IN MY ARMS.
I SEE. I GET IT.
WHAT A NICE NAME OYAKATA-*SAMA* HAS COME UP WITH.

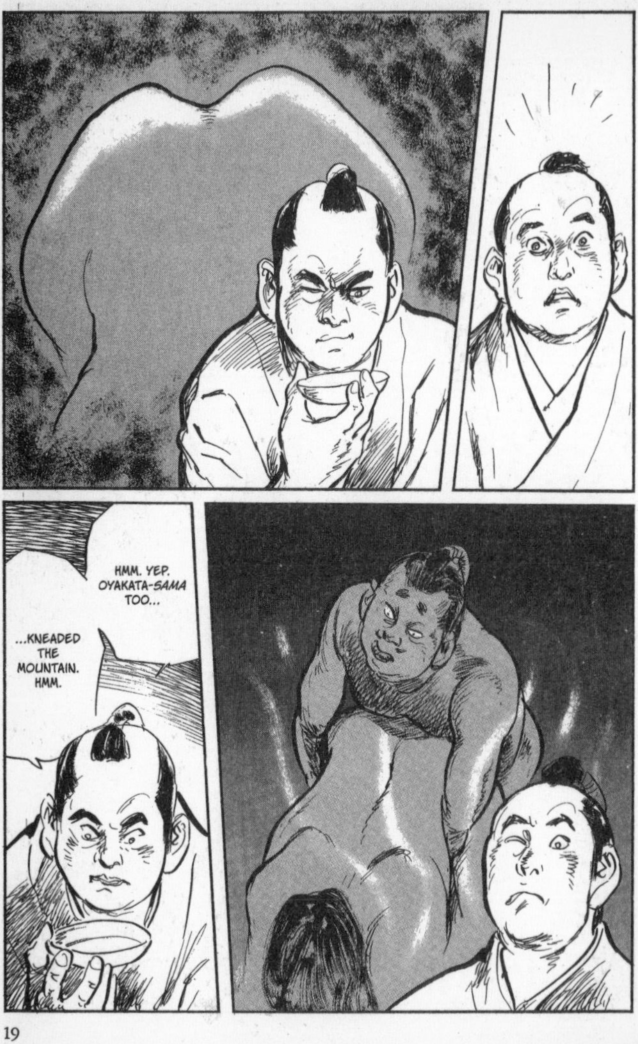
HMM. YEP. OYAKATA-SAMA TOO...
...KNEADED THE MOUNTAIN. HMM.

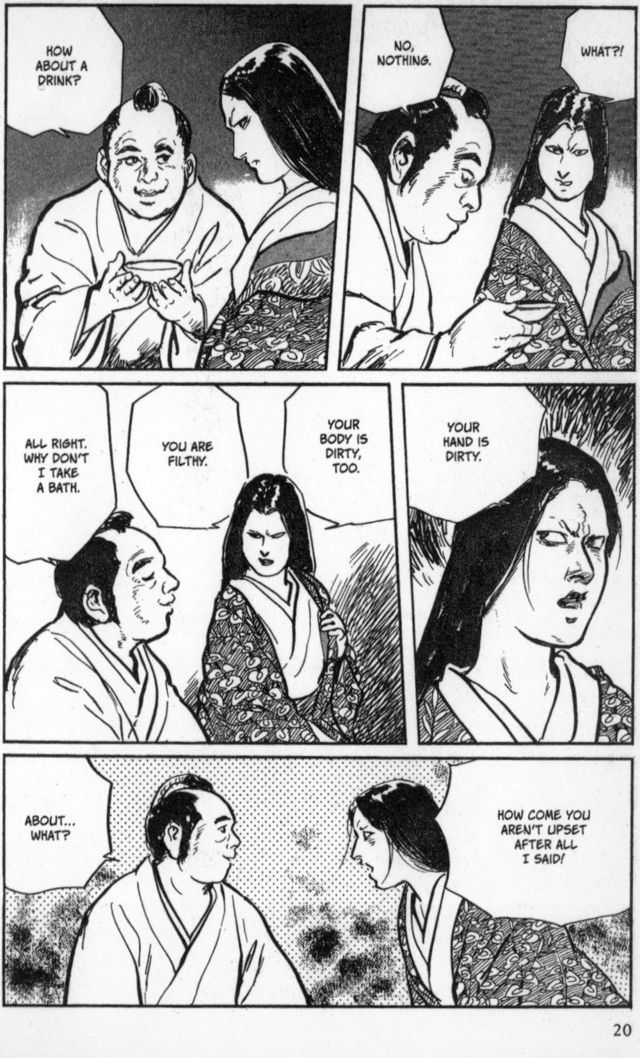
WHAT?!
NO, NOTHING.
HOW ABOUT A DRINK?
YOUR HAND IS DIRTY.
YOUR BODY IS DIRTY, TOO.
YOU ARE FILTHY.
ALL RIGHT. WHY DON'T I TAKE A BATH.
HOW COME YOU AREN'T UPSET AFTER ALL I SAID!
ABOUT... WHAT?

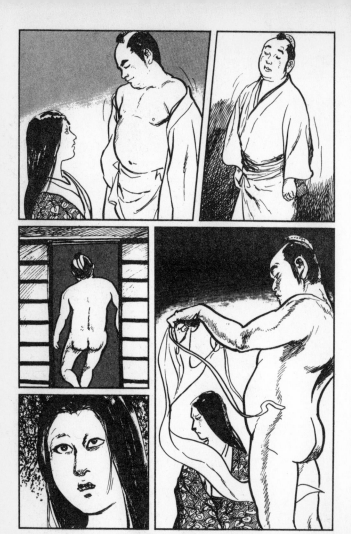

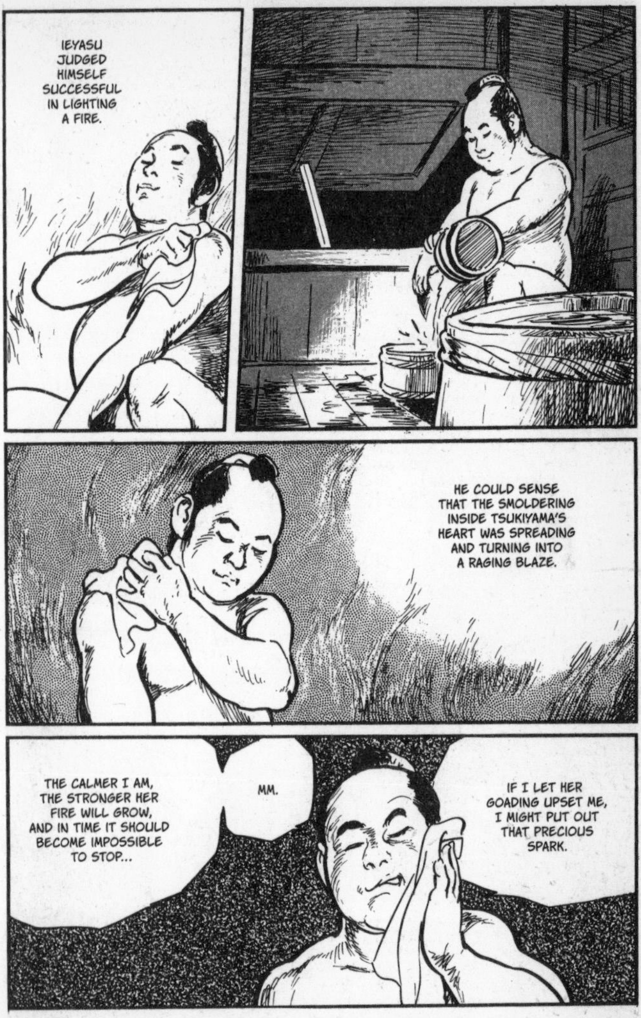
IEYASU JUDGED HIMSELF SUCCESSFUL IN LIGHTING A FIRE.
HE COULD SENSE THAT THE SMOLDERING INSIDE TSUKIYAMA'S HEART WAS SPREADING AND TURNING INTO A RAGING BLAZE.
IF I LET HER GOADING UPSET ME, I MIGHT PUT OUT THAT PRECIOUS SPARK.
MM.
THE CALMER I AM, THE STRONGER HER FIRE WILL GROW, AND IN TIME IT SHOULD BECOME IMPOSSIBLE TO STOP...

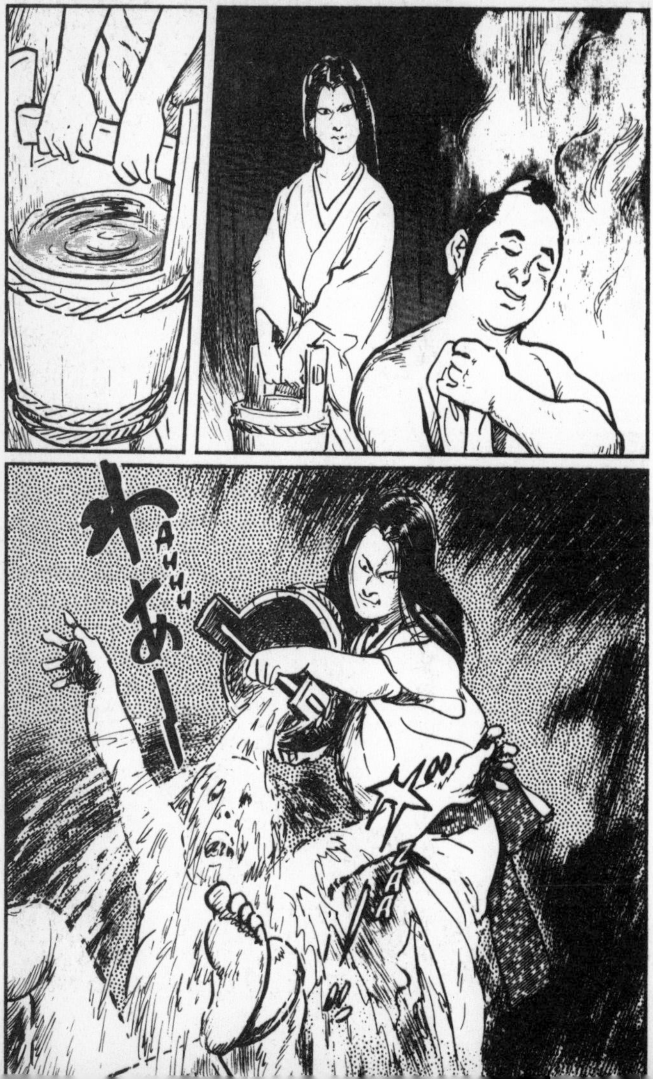
わあー
AHHHH
ZAAA

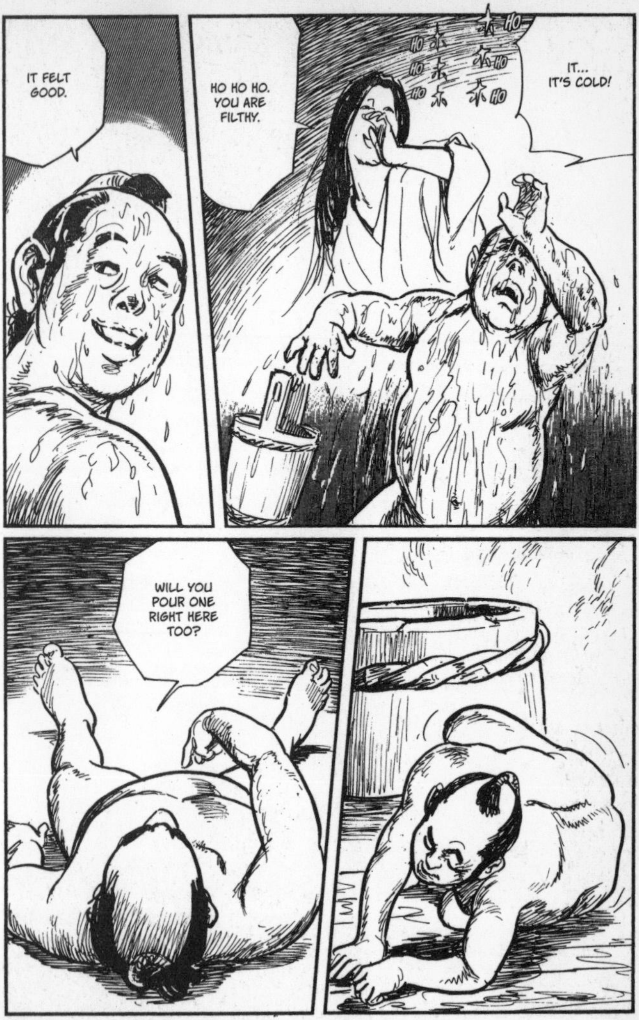
HO HO HO HO HO HO HO
IT... IT'S COLD!
HO HO HO. YOU ARE FILTHY.
IT FELT GOOD.
WILL YOU POUR ONE RIGHT HERE TOO?

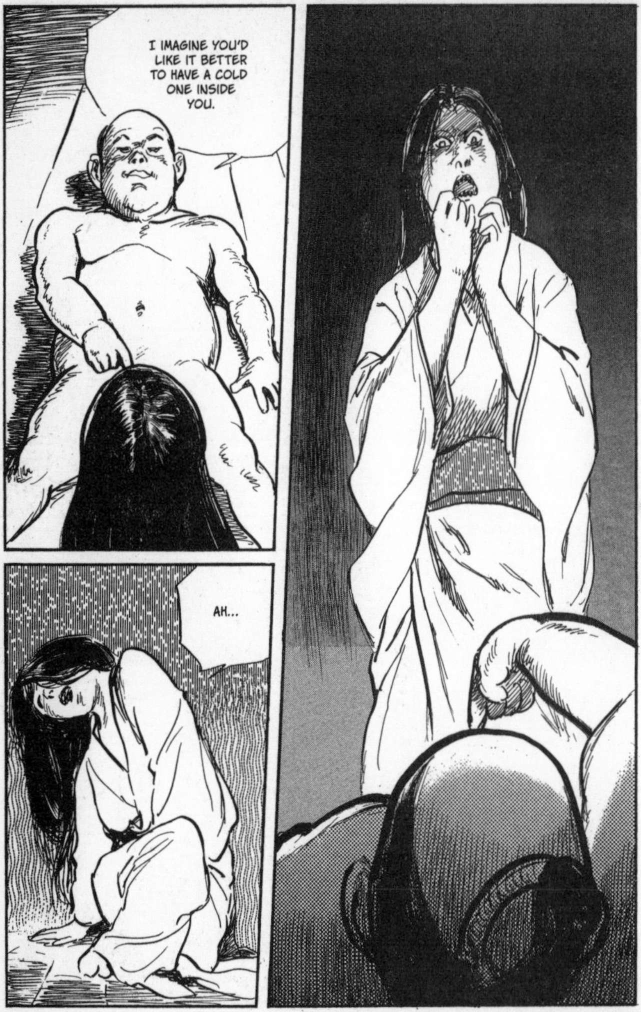
I IMAGINE YOU'D LIKE IT BETTER TO HAVE A COLD ONE INSIDE YOU.
AH...

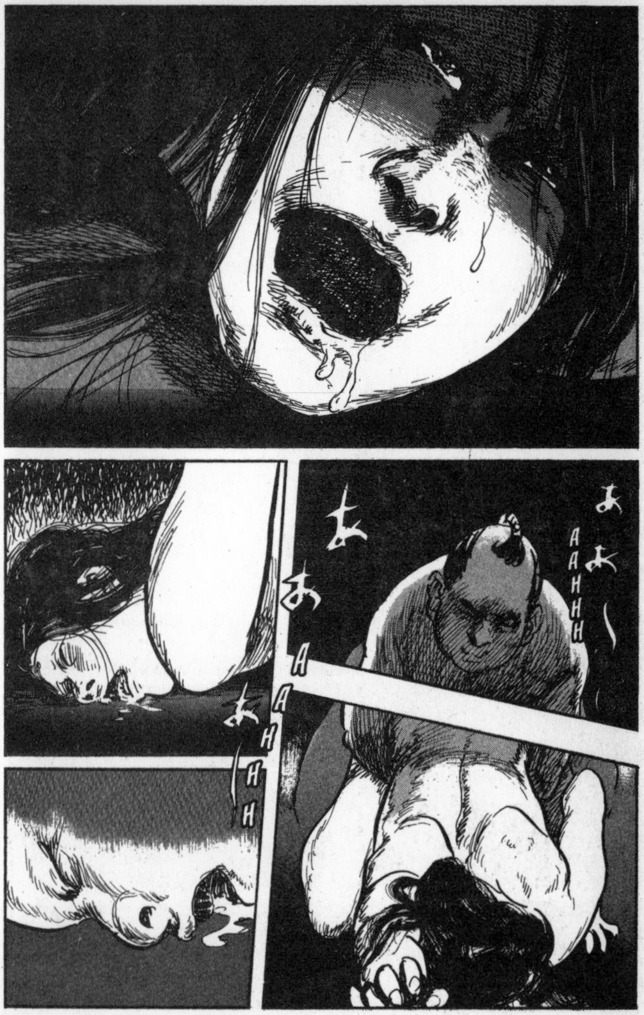
AAHHH
AAHHHH

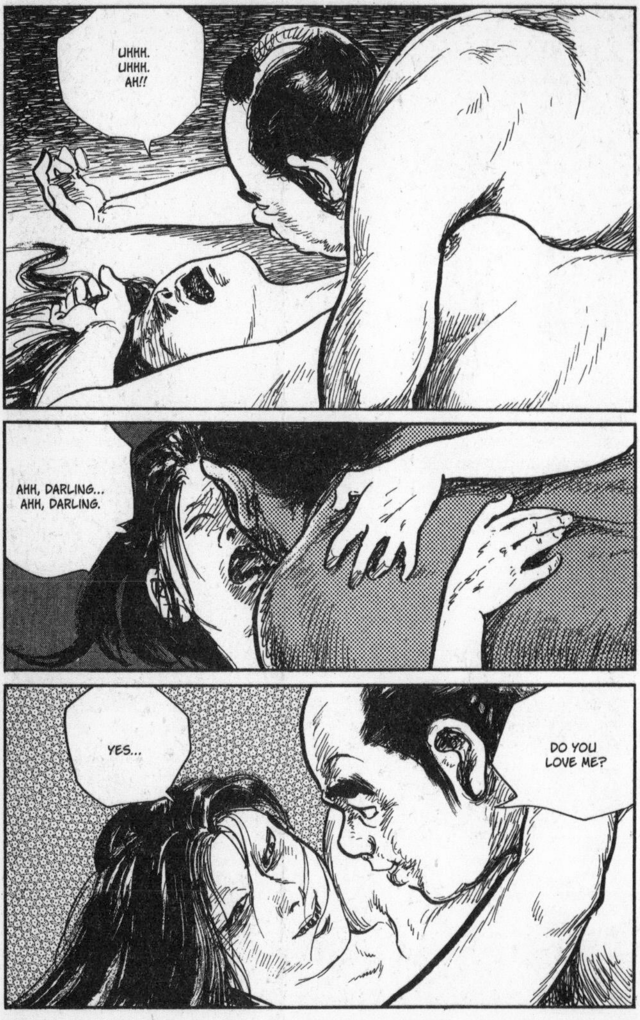
UHHH. UHHH. AH!!
AHH, DARLING... AHH, DARLING.
DO YOU LOVE ME?
YES...

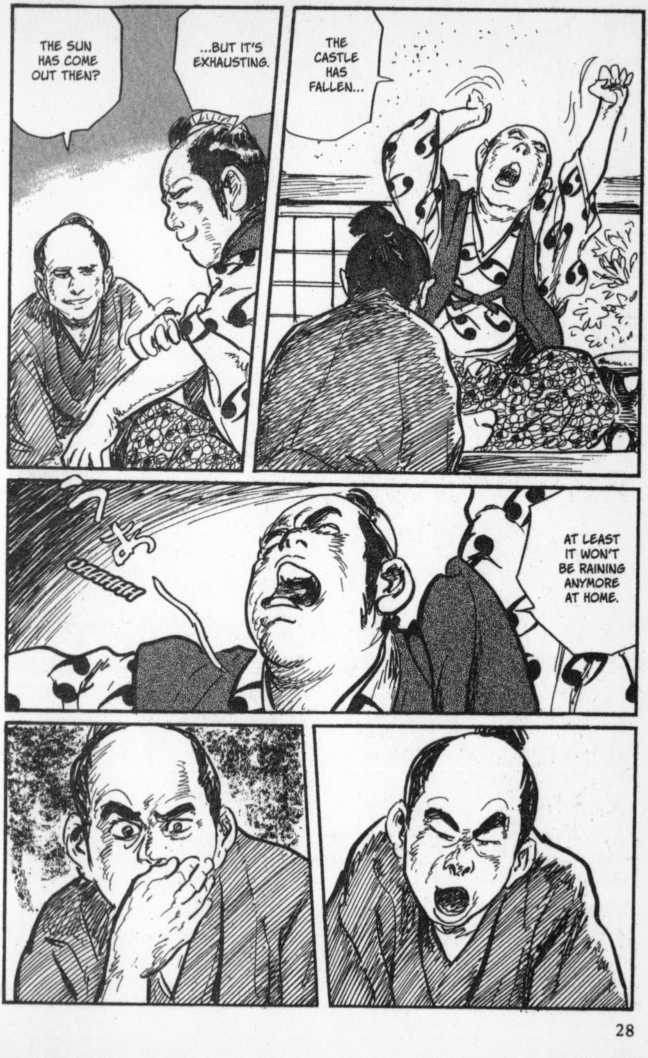
THE CASTLE HAS FALLEN...
...BUT IT'S EXHAUSTING.
THE SUN HAS COME OUT THEN?
AT LEAST IT WON'T BE RAINING ANYMORE AT HOME.
UAAHHH

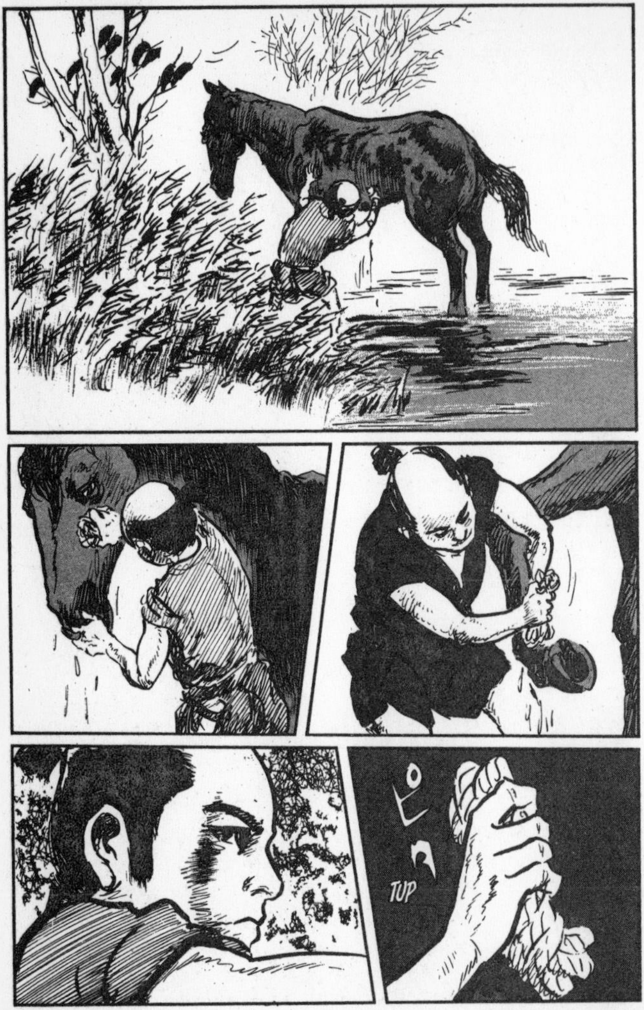
ピト
TUP

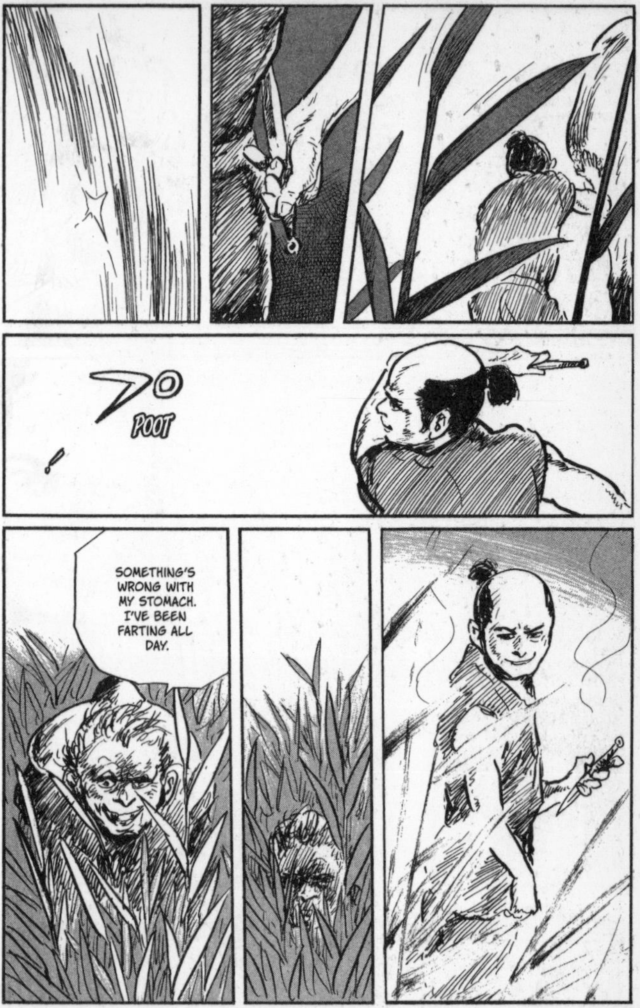
POOT
SOMETHING'S WRONG WITH MY STOMACH. I'VE BEEN FARTING ALL DAY.

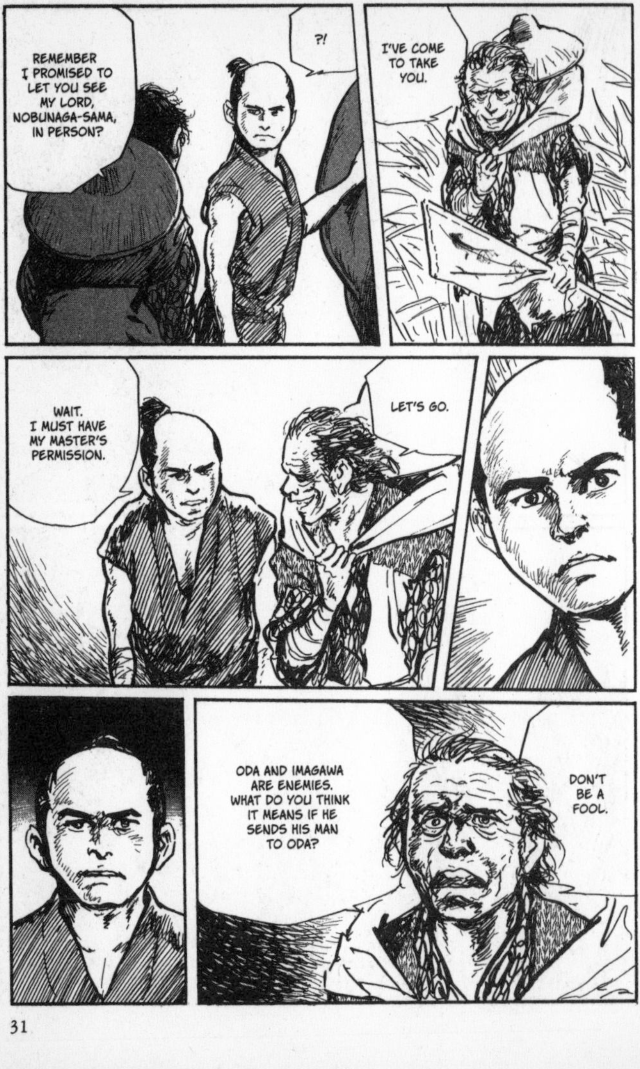
I'VE COME TO TAKE YOU.
?!
REMEMBER I PROMISED TO LET YOU SEE MY LORD, NOBUNAGA-SAMA, IN PERSON?
LET'S GO.
WAIT. I MUST HAVE MY MASTER'S PERMISSION.
DON'T BE A FOOL.
ODA AND IMAGAWA ARE ENEMIES. WHAT DO YOU THINK IT MEANS IF HE SENDS HIS MAN TO ODA?

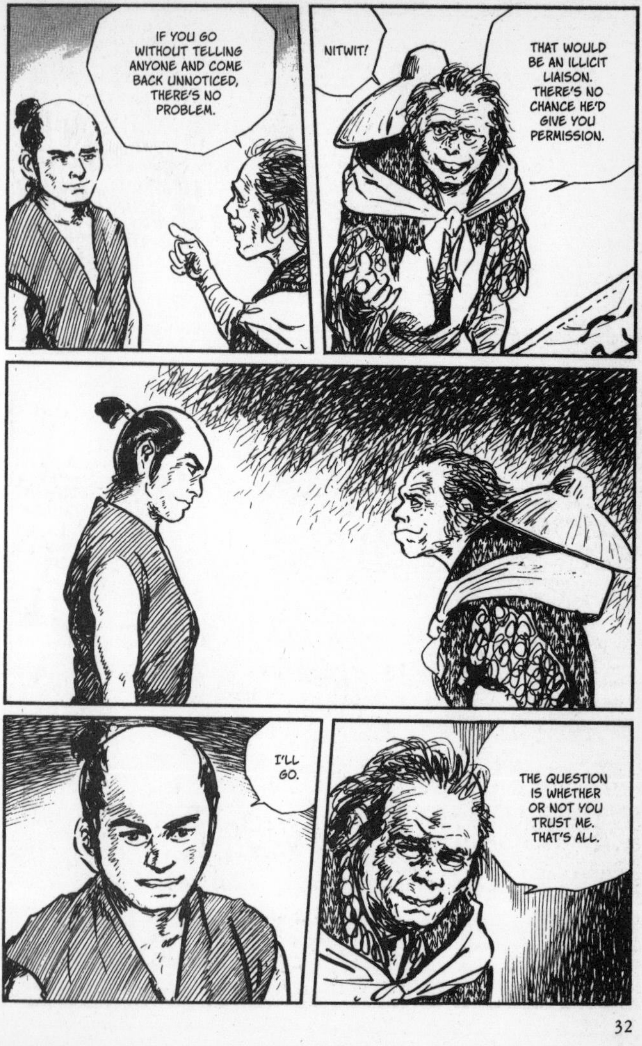
THAT WOULD BE AN ILLICIT LIAISON. THERE'S NO CHANCE HE'D GIVE YOU PERMISSION.
NITWIT!
IF YOU GO WITHOUT TELLING ANYONE AND COME BACK UNNOTICED, THERE'S NO PROBLEM.
THE QUESTION IS WHETHER OR NOT YOU TRUST ME. THAT'S ALL.
I'LL GO.

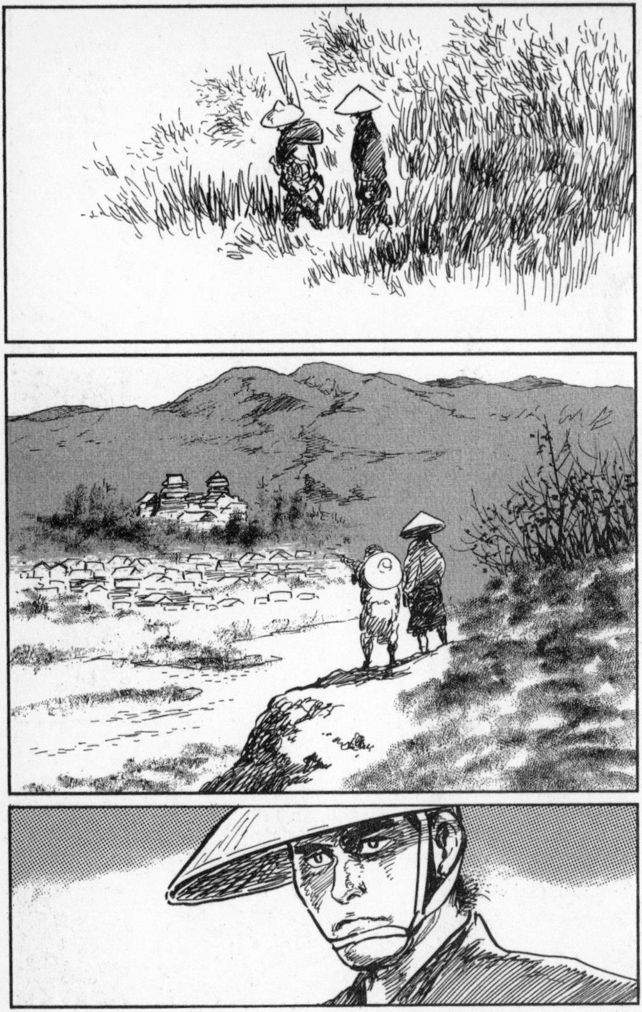

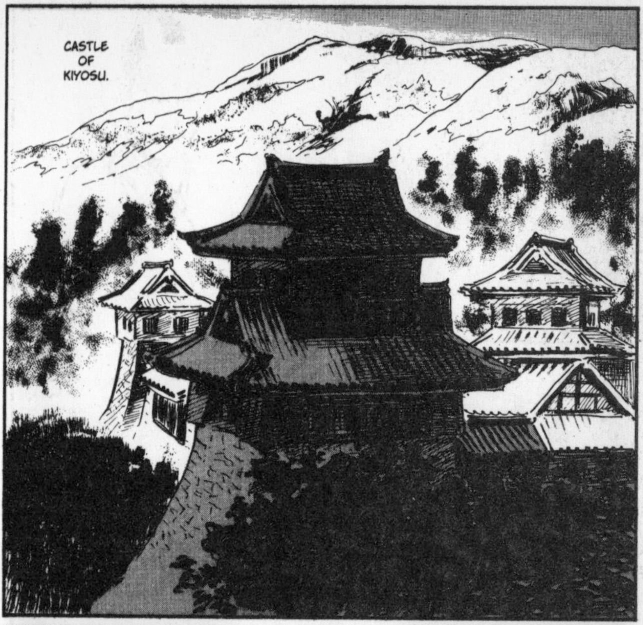
CASTLE
OF
KIYOSU.
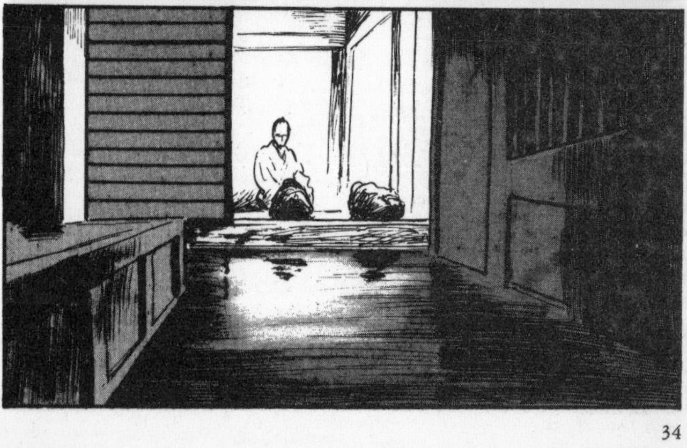

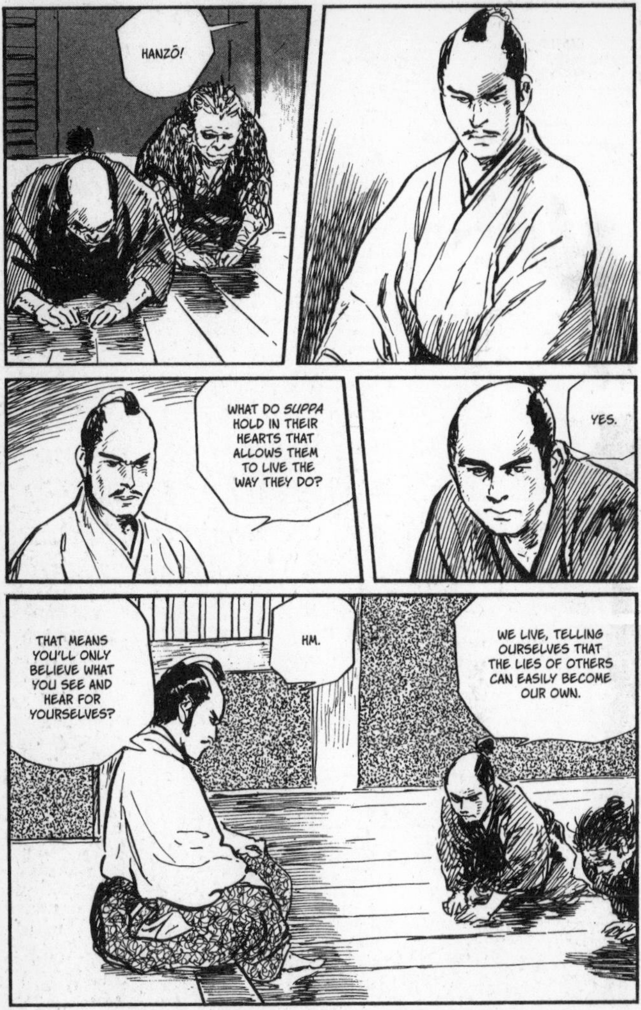
HANZŌ!
YES.
WHAT DO *SUPPA* HOLD IN THEIR HEARTS THAT ALLOWS THEM TO LIVE THE WAY THEY DO?
WE LIVE, TELLING OURSELVES THAT THE LIES OF OTHERS CAN EASILY BECOME OUR OWN.
HM.
THAT MEANS YOU'LL ONLY BELIEVE WHAT YOU SEE AND HEAR FOR YOURSELVES?

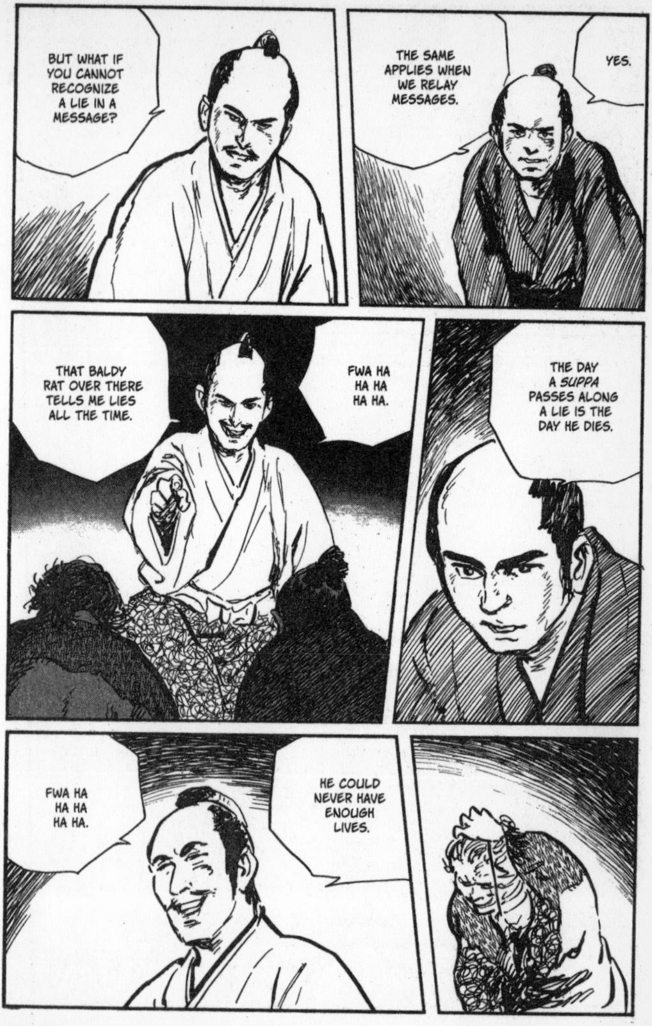
YES.
THE SAME APPLIES WHEN WE RELAY MESSAGES.
BUT WHAT IF YOU CANNOT RECOGNIZE A LIE IN A MESSAGE?
THE DAY A *SUPPA* PASSES ALONG A LIE IS THE DAY HE DIES.
FWA HA HA HA HA HA.
THAT BALDY RAT OVER THERE TELLS ME LIES ALL THE TIME.
HE COULD NEVER HAVE ENOUGH LIVES.
FWA HA HA HA HA HA.

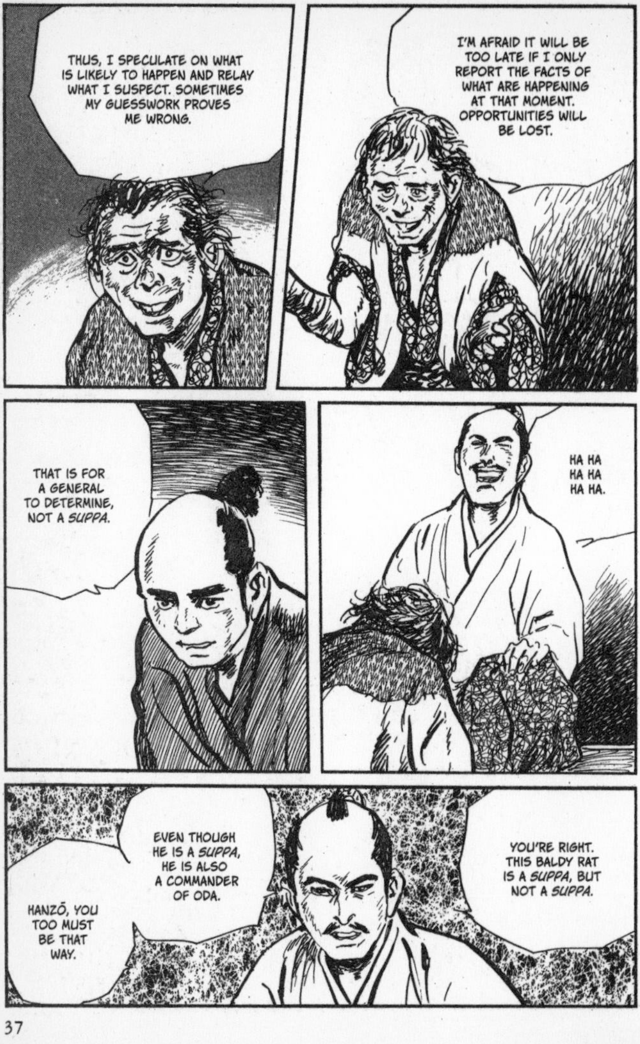
I'M AFRAID IT WILL BE TOO LATE IF I ONLY REPORT THE FACTS OF WHAT ARE HAPPENING AT THAT MOMENT. OPPORTUNITIES WILL BE LOST.
THUS, I SPECULATE ON WHAT IS LIKELY TO HAPPEN AND RELAY WHAT I SUSPECT. SOMETIMES MY GUESSWORK PROVES ME WRONG.
HA HA HA HA HA HA.
THAT IS FOR A GENERAL TO DETERMINE, NOT A *SUPPA*.
YOU'RE RIGHT. THIS BALDY RAT IS A *SUPPA*, BUT NOT A *SUPPA*.
EVEN THOUGH HE IS A *SUPPA*, HE IS ALSO A COMMANDER OF ODA.
HANZŌ, YOU TOO MUST BE THAT WAY.

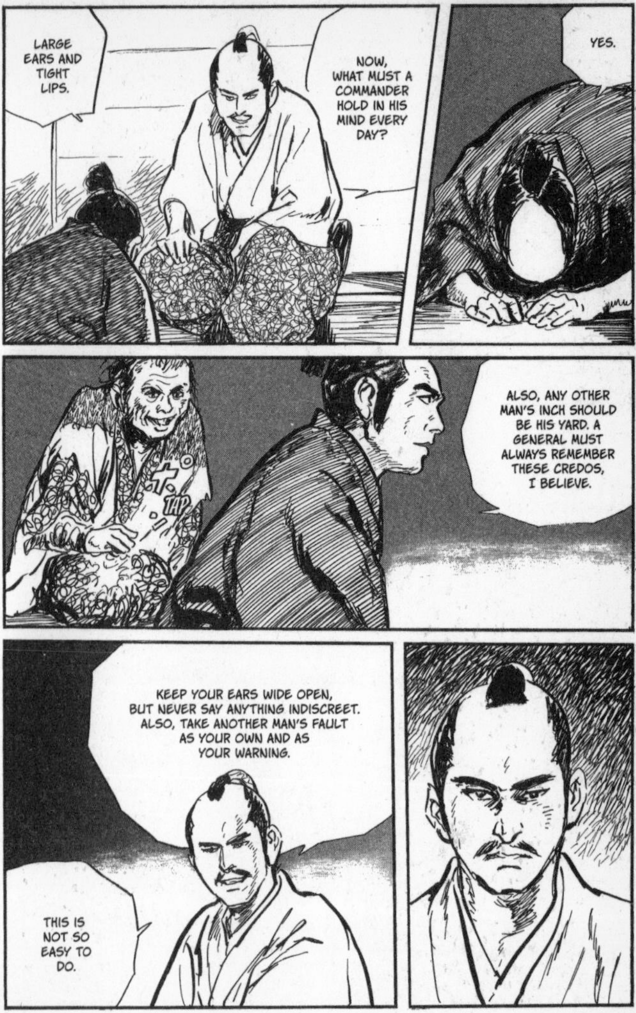
YES.
NOW, WHAT MUST A COMMANDER HOLD IN HIS MIND EVERY DAY?
LARGE EARS AND TIGHT LIPS.
ALSO, ANY OTHER MAN'S INCH SHOULD BE HIS YARD. A GENERAL MUST ALWAYS REMEMBER THESE CREDOS, I BELIEVE.
TAP
KEEP YOUR EARS WIDE OPEN, BUT NEVER SAY ANYTHING INDISCREET. ALSO, TAKE ANOTHER MAN'S FAULT AS YOUR OWN AND AS YOUR WARNING.
THIS IS NOT SO EASY TO DO.

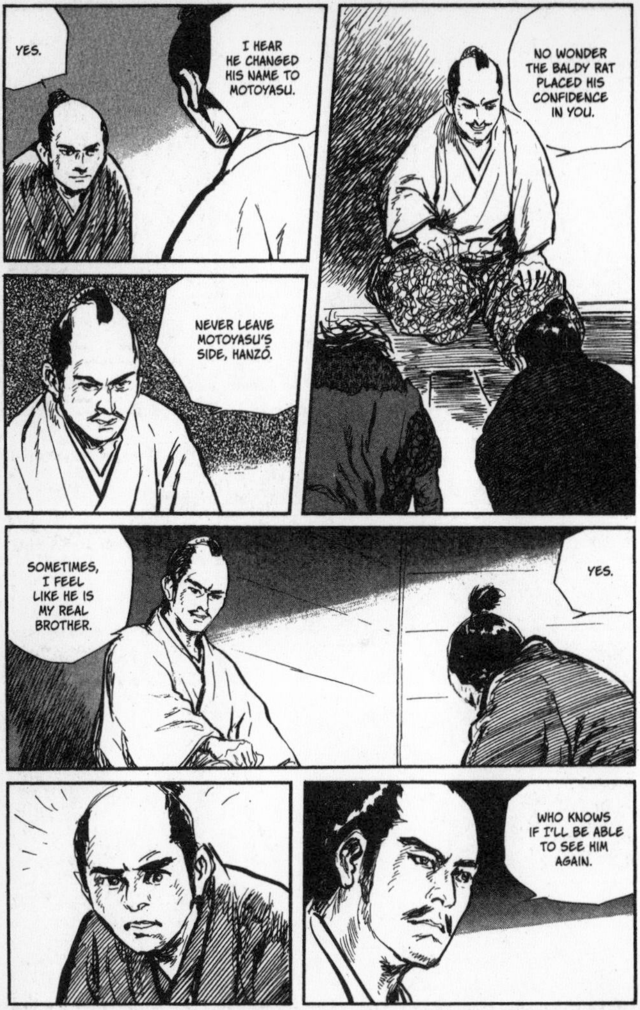
NO WONDER THE BALDY RAT PLACED HIS CONFIDENCE IN YOU.
I HEAR HE CHANGED HIS NAME TO MOTOYASU.
YES.
NEVER LEAVE MOTOYASU'S SIDE, HANZŌ.
YES.
SOMETIMES, I FEEL LIKE HE IS MY REAL BROTHER.
WHO KNOWS IF I'LL BE ABLE TO SEE HIM AGAIN.

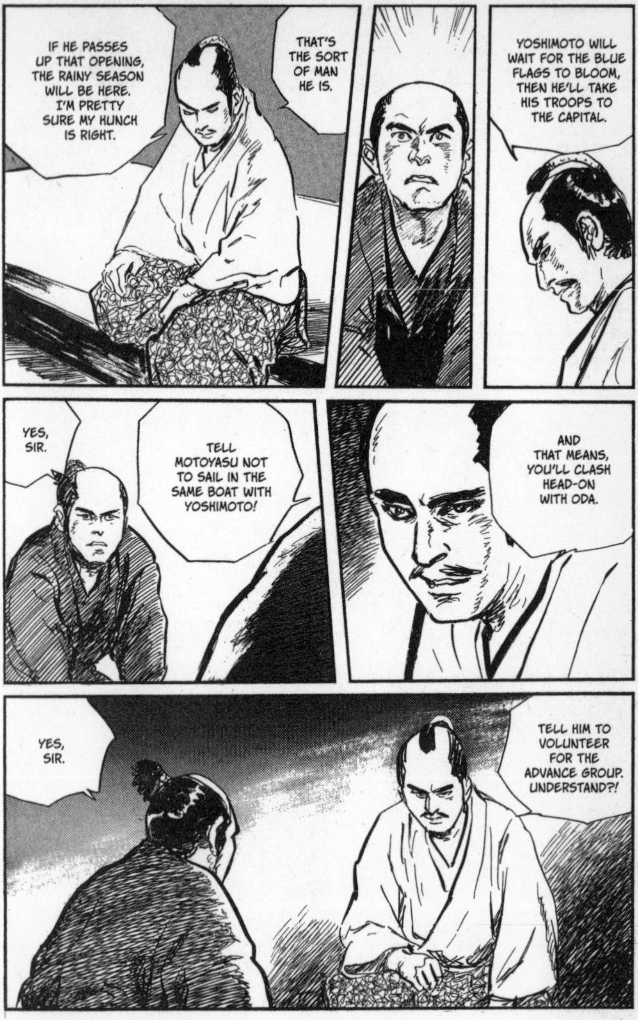
YOSHIMOTO WILL WAIT FOR THE BLUE FLAGS TO BLOOM, THEN HE'LL TAKE HIS TROOPS TO THE CAPITAL.
THAT'S THE SORT OF MAN HE IS.
IF HE PASSES UP THAT OPENING, THE RAINY SEASON WILL BE HERE. I'M PRETTY SURE MY HUNCH IS RIGHT.
AND THAT MEANS, YOU'LL CLASH HEAD-ON WITH ODA.
TELL MOTOYASU NOT TO SAIL IN THE SAME BOAT WITH YOSHIMOTO!
YES, SIR.
TELL HIM TO VOLUNTEER FOR THE ADVANCE GROUP. UNDERSTAND?!
YES, SIR.

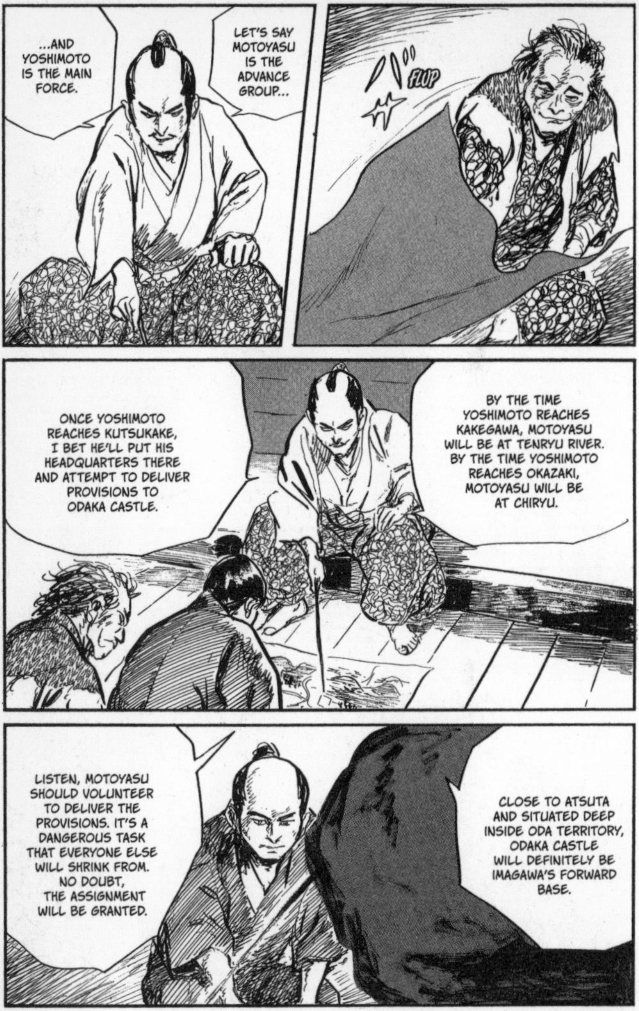
FLUP
LET'S SAY MOTOYASU IS THE ADVANCE GROUP...
...AND YOSHIMOTO IS THE MAIN FORCE.
BY THE TIME YOSHIMOTO REACHES KAKEGAWA, MOTOYASU WILL BE AT TENRYU RIVER. BY THE TIME YOSHIMOTO REACHES OKAZAKI, MOTOYASU WILL BE AT CHIRYU.
ONCE YOSHIMOTO REACHES KUTSUKAKE, I BET HE'LL PUT HIS HEADQUARTERS THERE AND ATTEMPT TO DELIVER PROVISIONS TO ODAKA CASTLE.
CLOSE TO ATSUTA AND SITUATED DEEP INSIDE ODA TERRITORY, ODAKA CASTLE WILL DEFINITELY BE IMAGAWA'S FORWARD BASE.
LISTEN, MOTOYASU SHOULD VOLUNTEER TO DELIVER THE PROVISIONS. IT'S A DANGEROUS TASK THAT EVERYONE ELSE WILL SHRINK FROM. NO DOUBT, THE ASSIGNMENT WILL BE GRANTED.

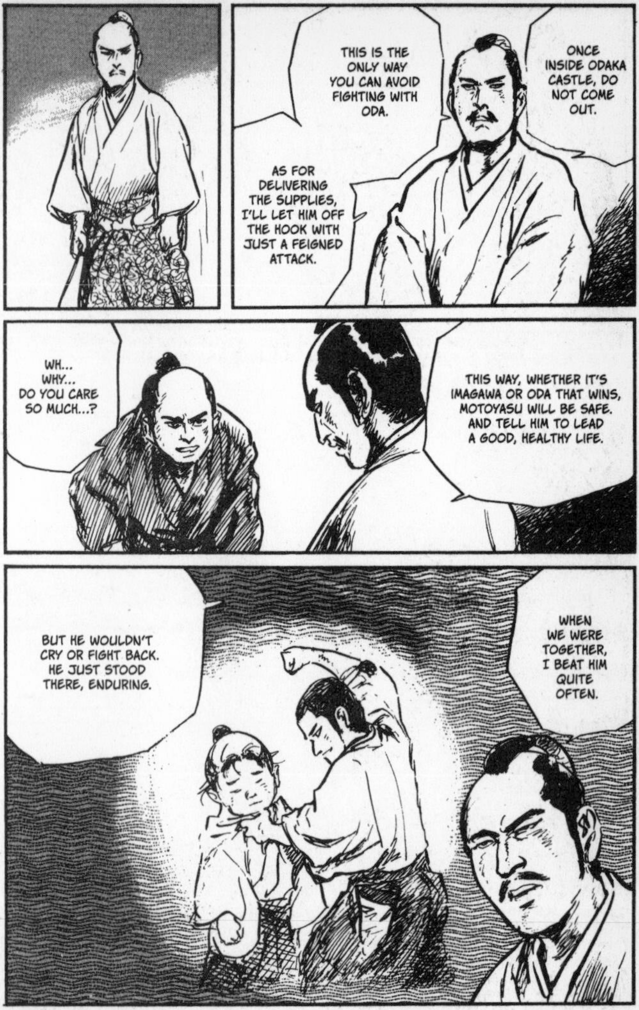
ONCE INSIDE ODAKA CASTLE, DO NOT COME OUT.
THIS IS THE ONLY WAY YOU CAN AVOID FIGHTING WITH ODA.
AS FOR DELIVERING THE SUPPLIES, I'LL LET HIM OFF THE HOOK WITH JUST A FEIGNED ATTACK.
THIS WAY, WHETHER IT'S IMAGAWA OR ODA THAT WINS, MOTOYASU WILL BE SAFE. AND TELL HIM TO LEAD A GOOD, HEALTHY LIFE.
WH... WHY... DO YOU CARE SO MUCH...?
WHEN WE WERE TOGETHER, I BEAT HIM QUITE OFTEN.
BUT HE WOULDN'T CRY OR FIGHT BACK. HE JUST STOOD THERE, ENDURING.

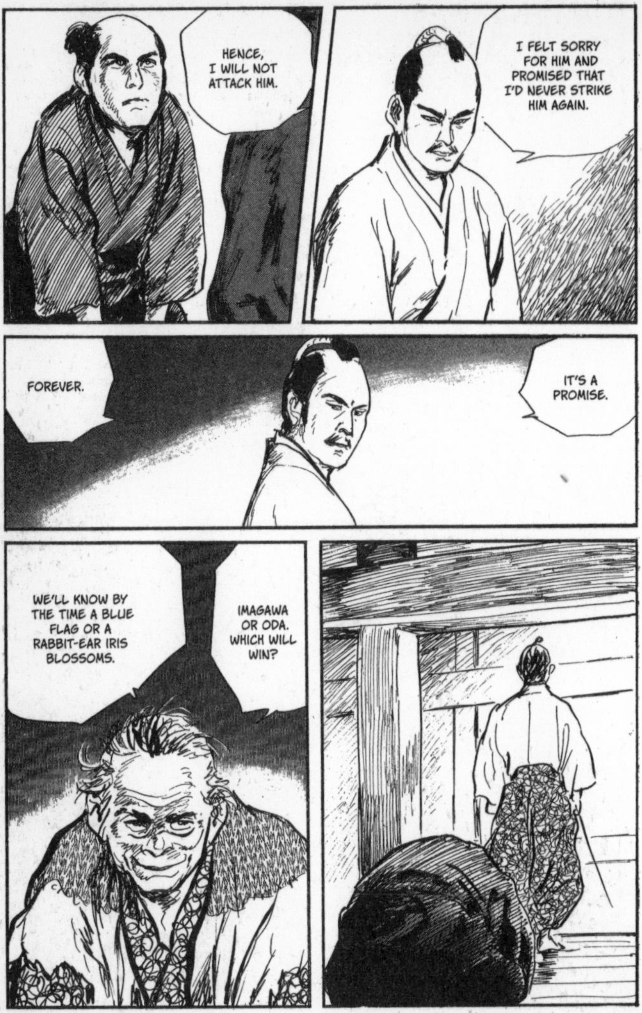
I FELT SORRY FOR HIM AND PROMISED THAT I'D NEVER STRIKE HIM AGAIN.
HENCE, I WILL NOT ATTACK HIM.
IT'S A PROMISE.
FOREVER.
IMAGAWA OR ODA. WHICH WILL WIN?
WE'LL KNOW BY THE TIME A BLUE FLAG OR A RABBIT-EAR IRIS BLOSSOMS.

Chapter On Relinquishing Factions

No. 6: Blue Flag and War

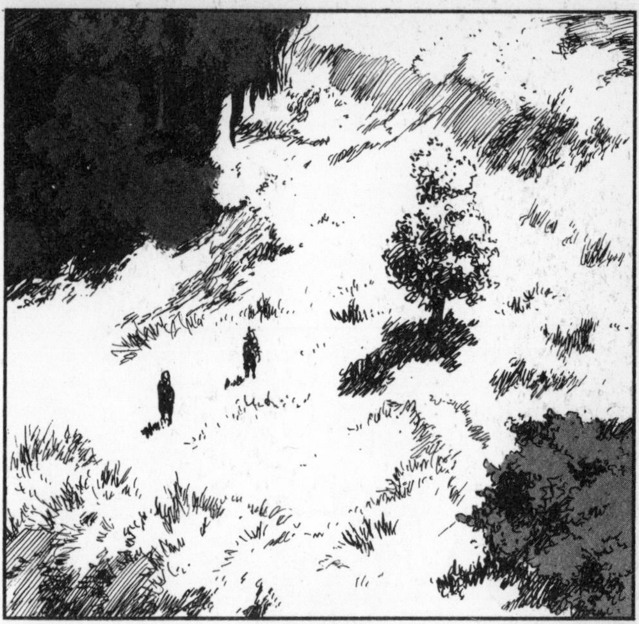
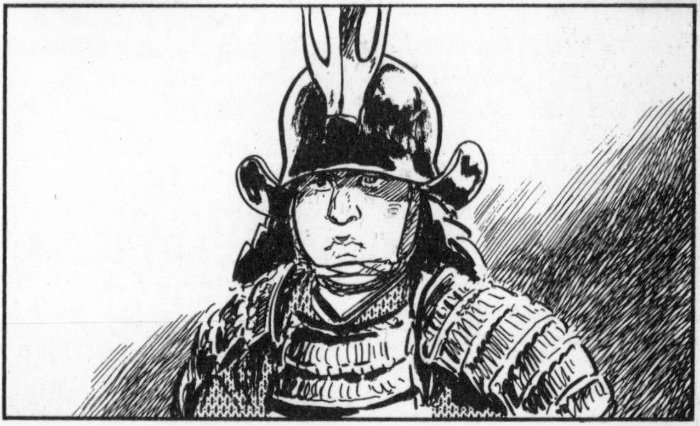

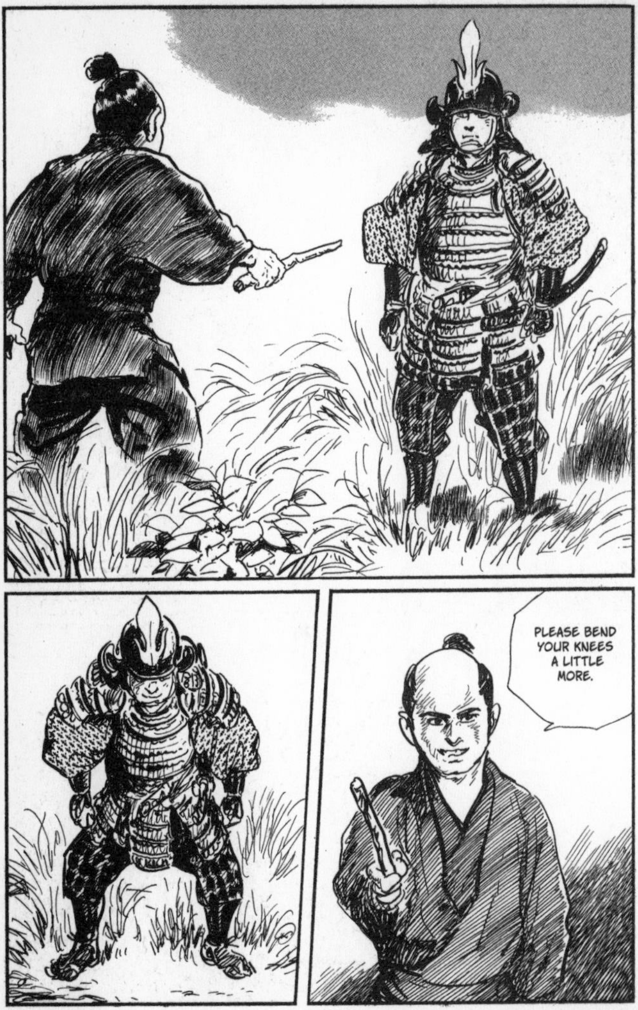
PLEASE BEND YOUR KNEES A LITTLE MORE.

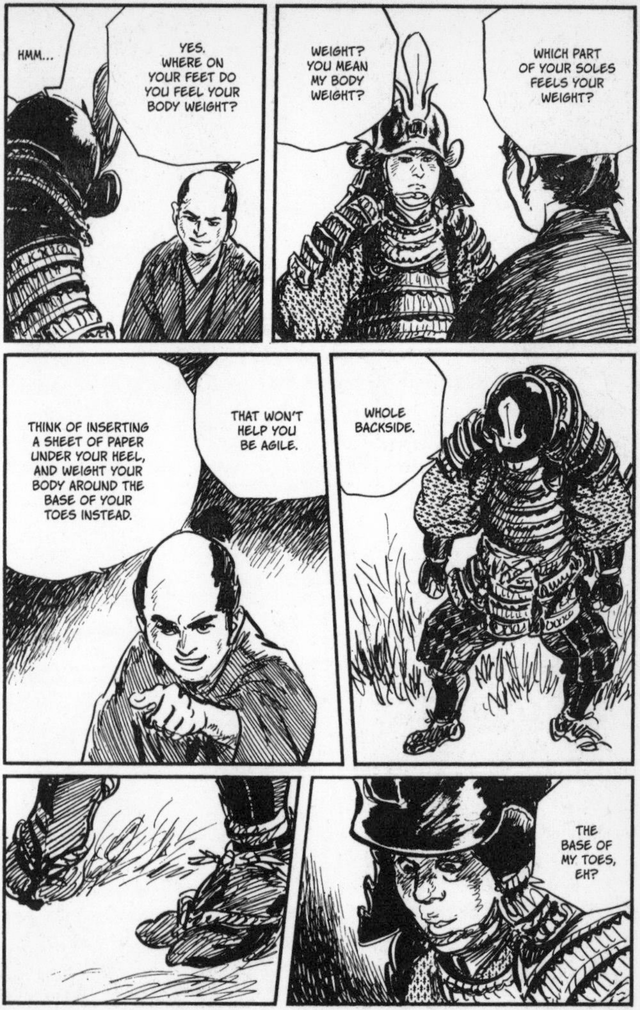
WHICH PART OF YOUR SOLES FEELS YOUR WEIGHT?
WEIGHT? YOU MEAN MY BODY WEIGHT?
YES. WHERE ON YOUR FEET DO YOU FEEL YOUR BODY WEIGHT?
HMM...
WHOLE BACKSIDE.
THAT WON'T HELP YOU BE AGILE.
THINK OF INSERTING A SHEET OF PAPER UNDER YOUR HEEL, AND WEIGHT YOUR BODY AROUND THE BASE OF YOUR TOES INSTEAD.
THE BASE OF MY TOES, EH?

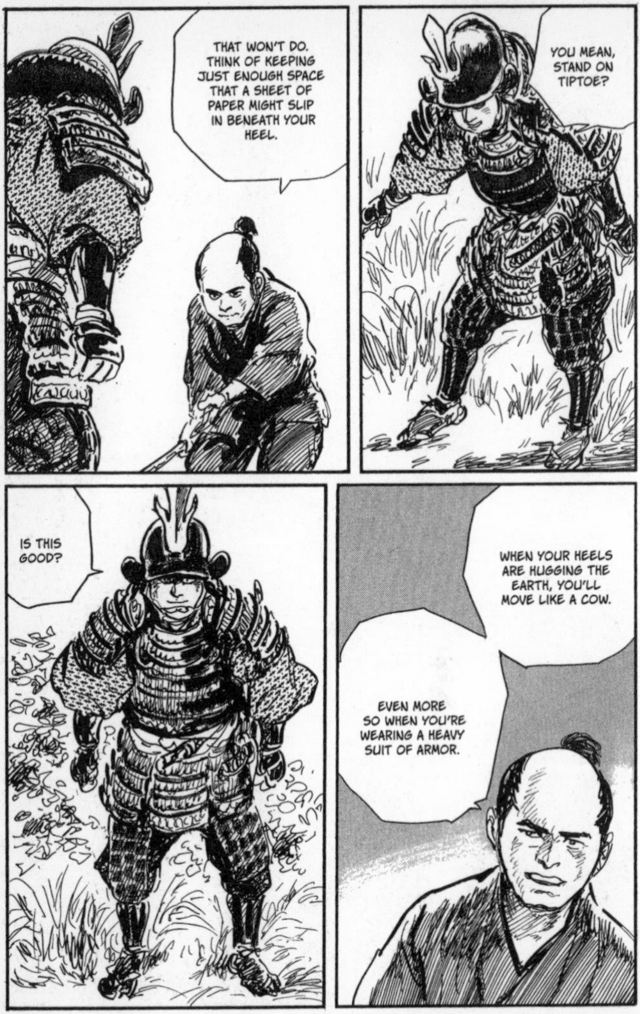
THAT WON'T DO. THINK OF KEEPING JUST ENOUGH SPACE THAT A SHEET OF PAPER MIGHT SLIP IN BENEATH YOUR HEEL.
YOU MEAN, STAND ON TIPTOE?
IS THIS GOOD?
WHEN YOUR HEELS ARE HUGGING THE EARTH, YOU'LL MOVE LIKE A COW.
EVEN MORE SO WHEN YOU'RE WEARING A HEAVY SUIT OF ARMOR.

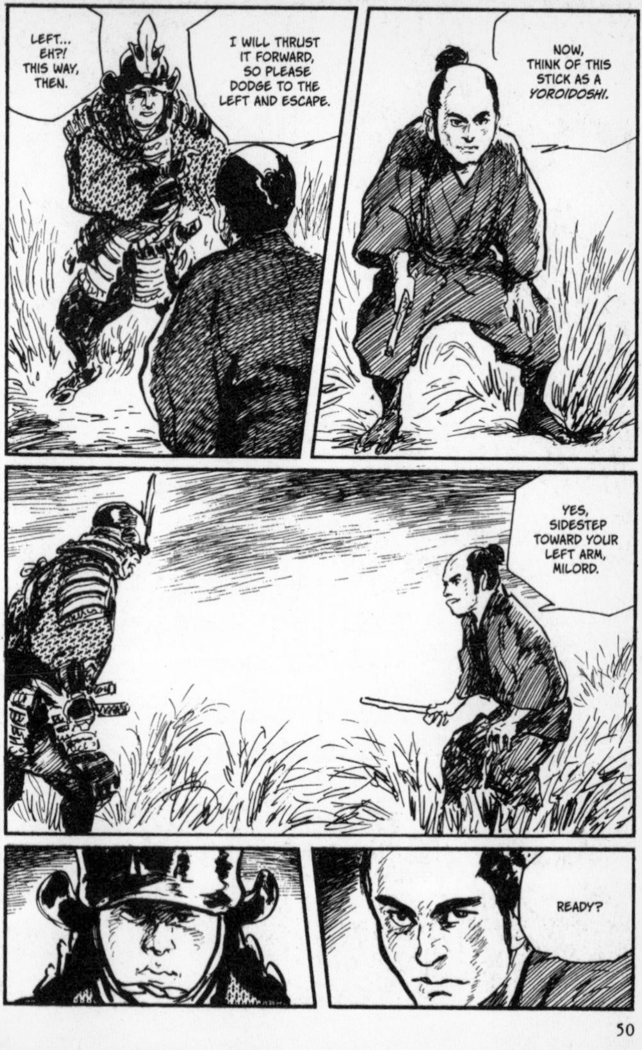
NOW, THINK OF THIS STICK AS A *YOROIDOSHI.*
I WILL THRUST IT FORWARD, SO PLEASE DODGE TO THE LEFT AND ESCAPE.
LEFT... EH?! THIS WAY, THEN.
YES, SIDESTEP TOWARD YOUR LEFT ARM, MILORD.
READY?

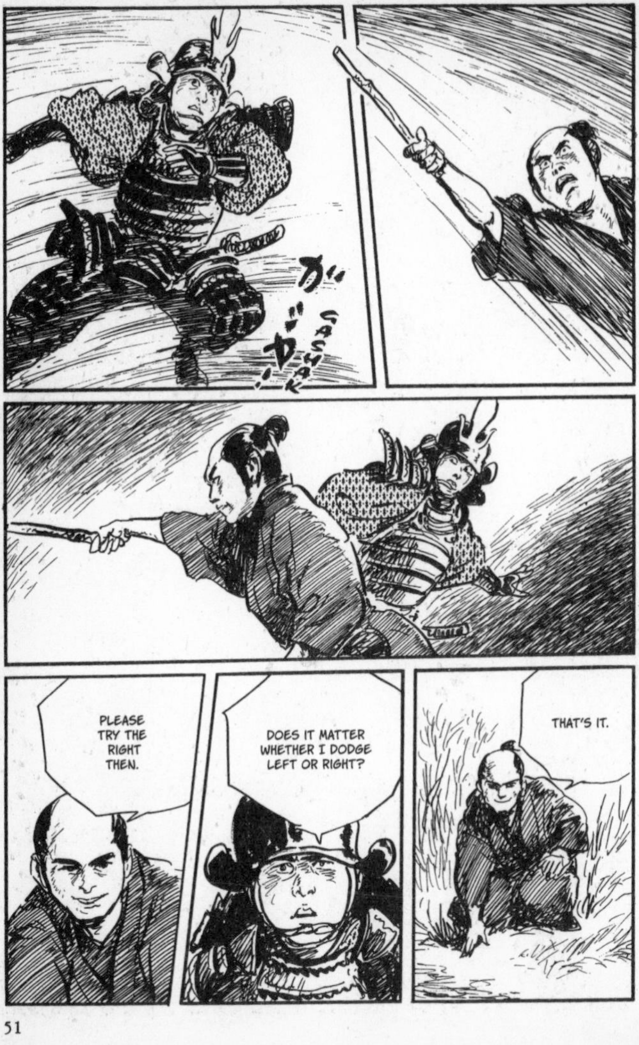
GASHAK
THAT'S IT.
DOES IT MATTER WHETHER I DODGE LEFT OR RIGHT?
PLEASE TRY THE RIGHT THEN.

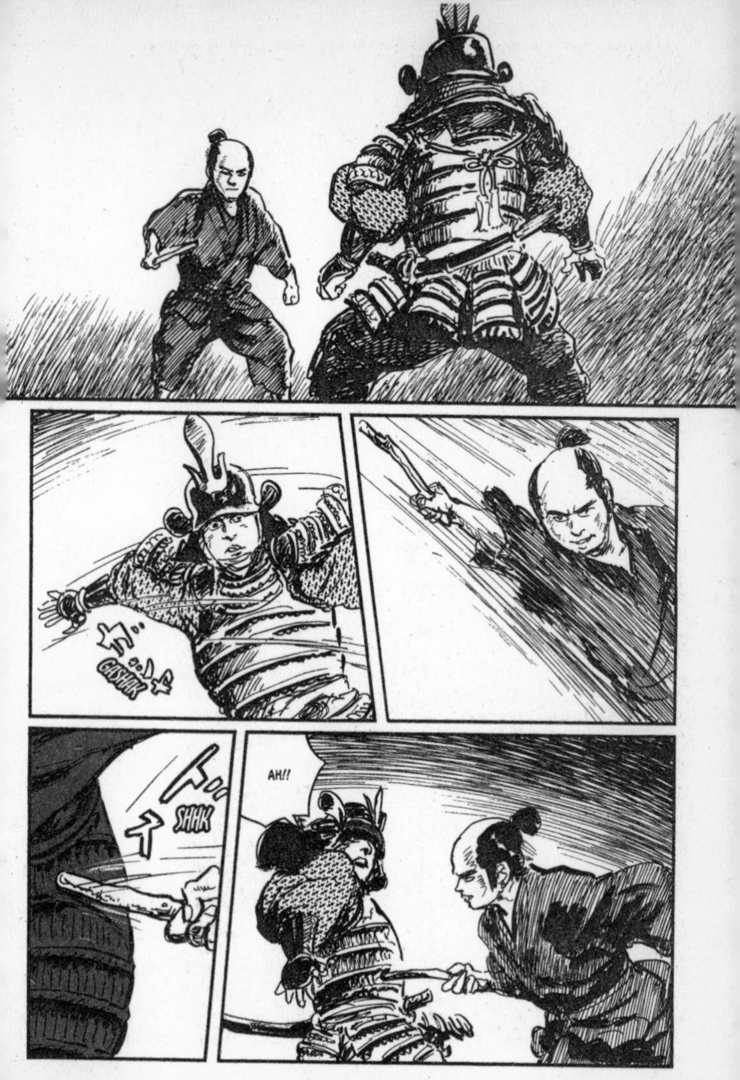
GASHAK
AH!!
SHHK

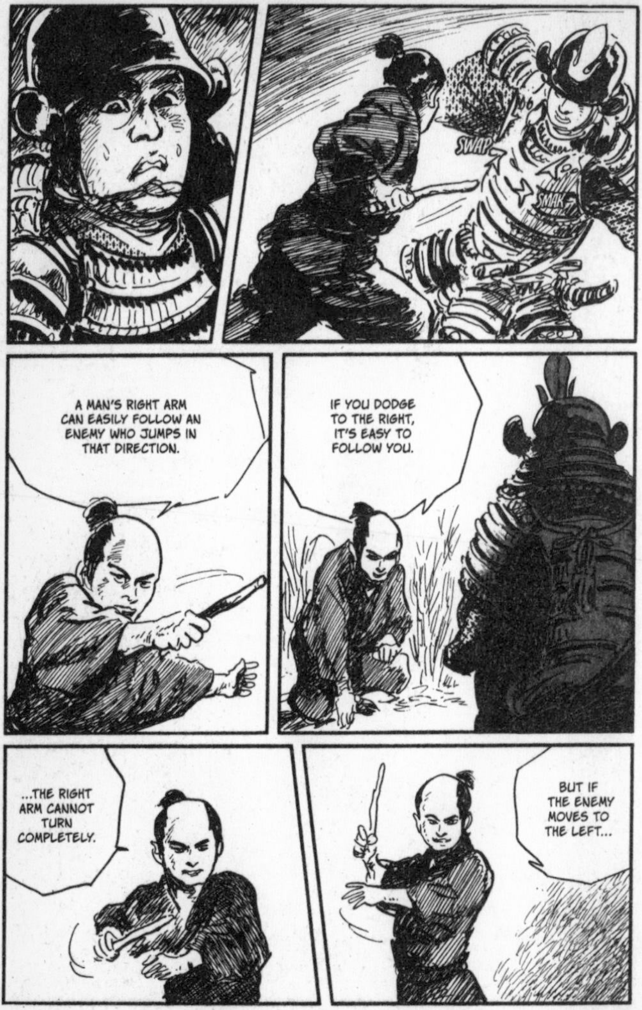
SWAP
SMAK
IF YOU DODGE TO THE RIGHT, IT'S EASY TO FOLLOW YOU.
A MAN'S RIGHT ARM CAN EASILY FOLLOW AN ENEMY WHO JUMPS IN THAT DIRECTION.
BUT IF THE ENEMY MOVES TO THE LEFT...
...THE RIGHT ARM CANNOT TURN COMPLETELY.

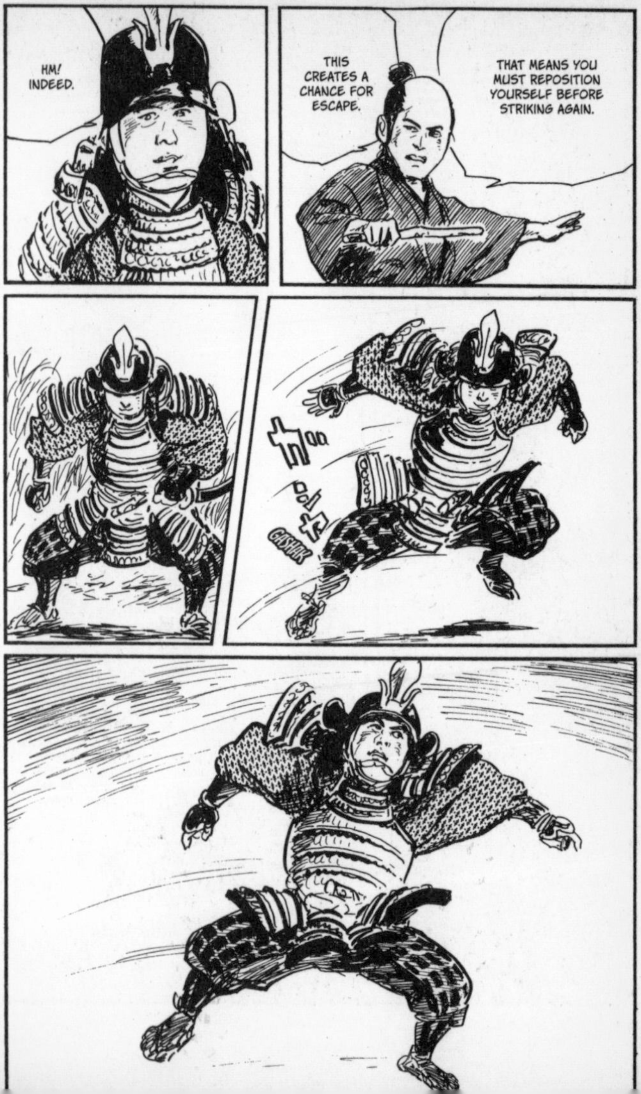
THAT MEANS YOU MUST REPOSITION YOURSELF BEFORE STRIKING AGAIN.
THIS CREATES A CHANCE FOR ESCAPE.
HM! INDEED.
GASHIK

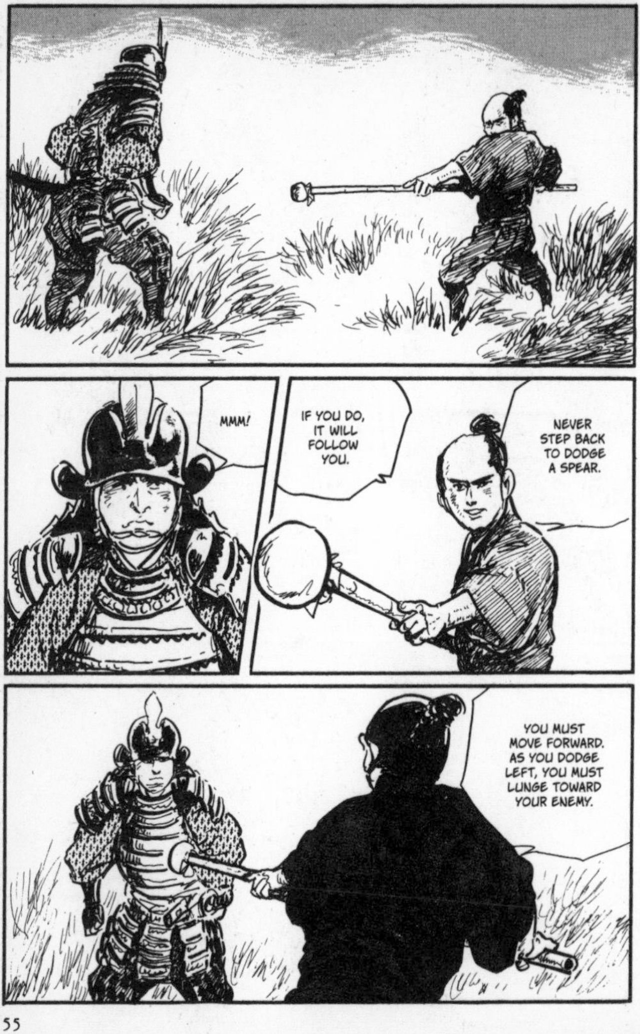
NEVER STEP BACK TO DODGE A SPEAR.
IF YOU DO, IT WILL FOLLOW YOU.
MMM!
YOU MUST MOVE FORWARD. AS YOU DODGE LEFT, YOU MUST LUNGE TOWARD YOUR ENEMY.

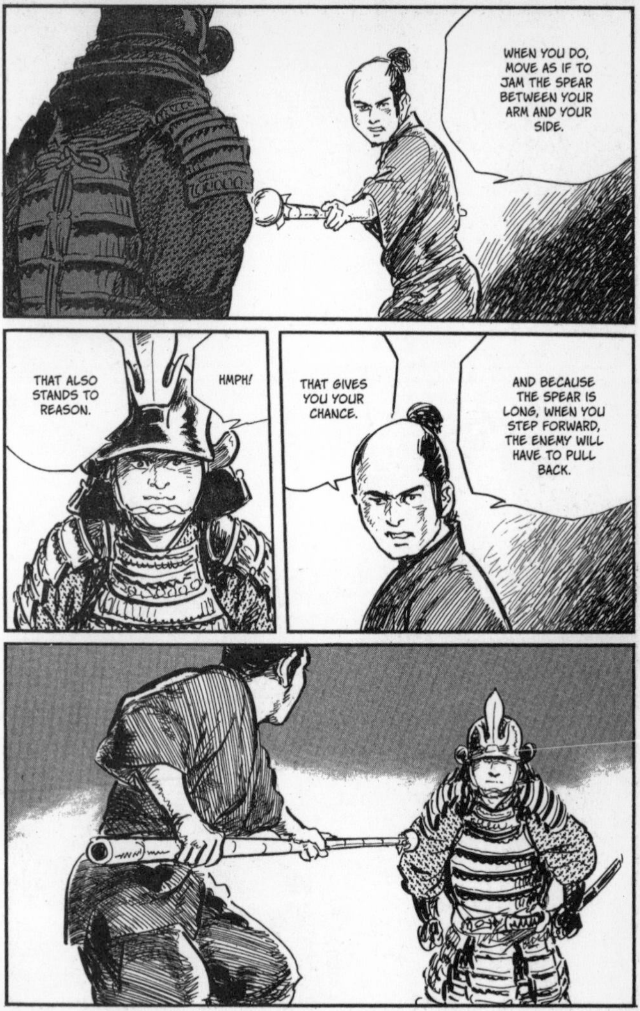
WHEN YOU DO, MOVE AS IF TO JAM THE SPEAR BETWEEN YOUR ARM AND YOUR SIDE.
AND BECAUSE THE SPEAR IS LONG, WHEN YOU STEP FORWARD, THE ENEMY WILL HAVE TO PULL BACK.
THAT GIVES YOU YOUR CHANCE.
HMPH!
THAT ALSO STANDS TO REASON.

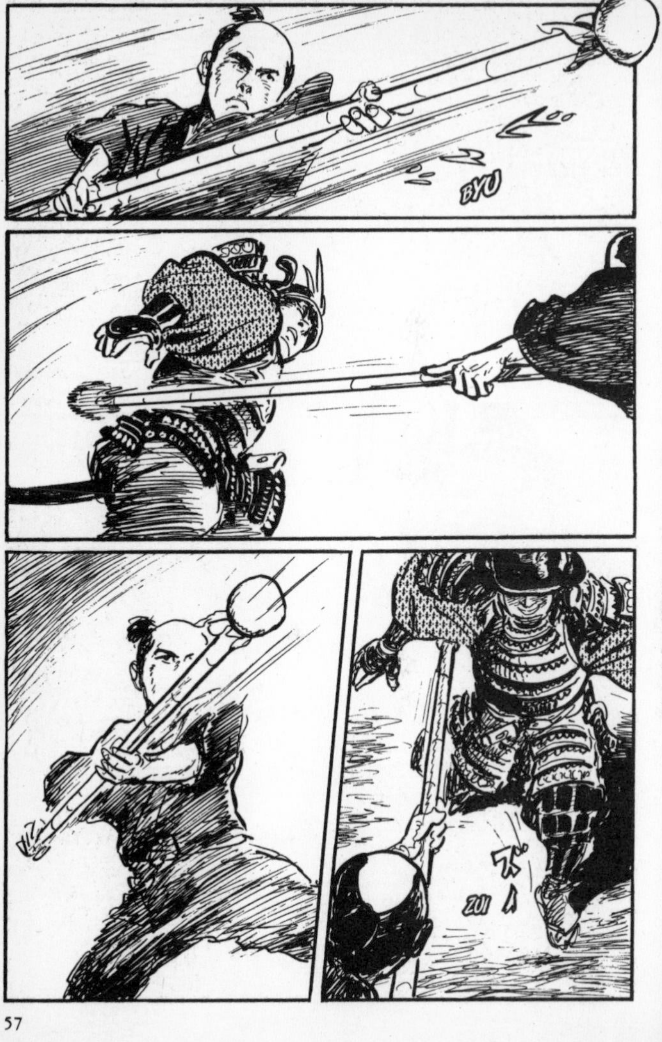
BYU
ZUI

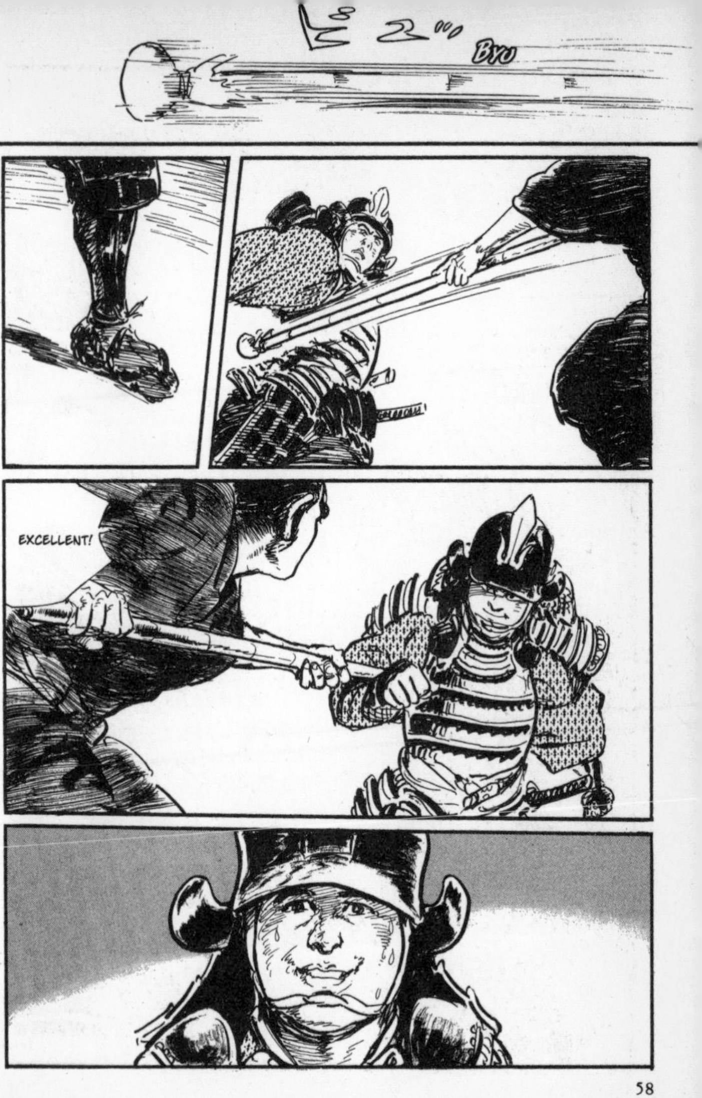
BYU
EXCELLENT!

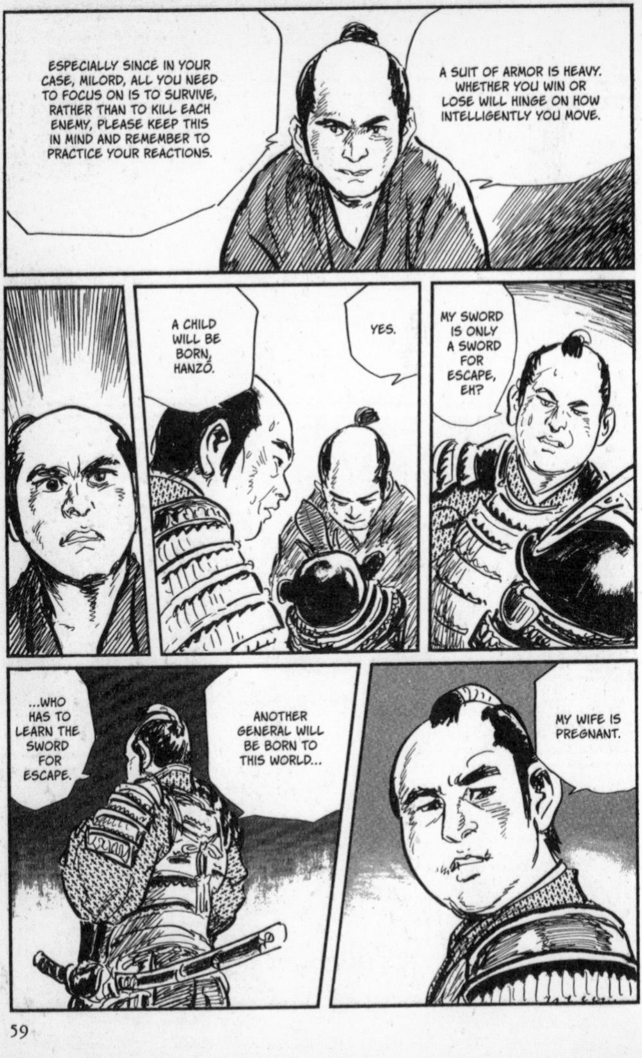
A SUIT OF ARMOR IS HEAVY. WHETHER YOU WIN OR LOSE WILL HINGE ON HOW INTELLIGENTLY YOU MOVE.
ESPECIALLY SINCE IN YOUR CASE, MILORD, ALL YOU NEED TO FOCUS ON IS TO SURVIVE, RATHER THAN TO KILL EACH ENEMY, PLEASE KEEP THIS IN MIND AND REMEMBER TO PRACTICE YOUR REACTIONS.
MY SWORD IS ONLY A SWORD FOR ESCAPE, EH?
YES.
A CHILD WILL BE BORN, HANZŌ.
MY WIFE IS PREGNANT.
ANOTHER GENERAL WILL BE BORN TO THIS WORLD...
...WHO HAS TO LEARN THE SWORD FOR ESCAPE.

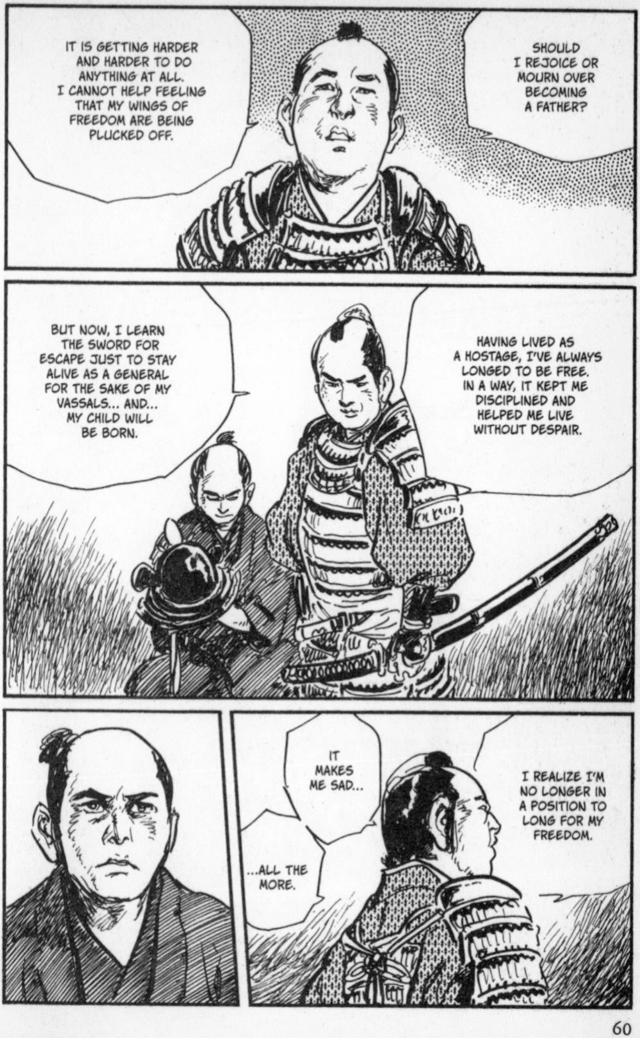
SHOULD I REJOICE OR MOURN OVER BECOMING A FATHER?
IT IS GETTING HARDER AND HARDER TO DO ANYTHING AT ALL. I CANNOT HELP FEELING THAT MY WINGS OF FREEDOM ARE BEING PLUCKED OFF.
HAVING LIVED AS A HOSTAGE, I'VE ALWAYS LONGED TO BE FREE. IN A WAY, IT KEPT ME DISCIPLINED AND HELPED ME LIVE WITHOUT DESPAIR.
BUT NOW, I LEARN THE SWORD FOR ESCAPE JUST TO STAY ALIVE AS A GENERAL FOR THE SAKE OF MY VASSALS... AND... MY CHILD WILL BE BORN.
I REALIZE I'M NO LONGER IN A POSITION TO LONG FOR MY FREEDOM.
IT MAKES ME SAD...
...ALL THE MORE.

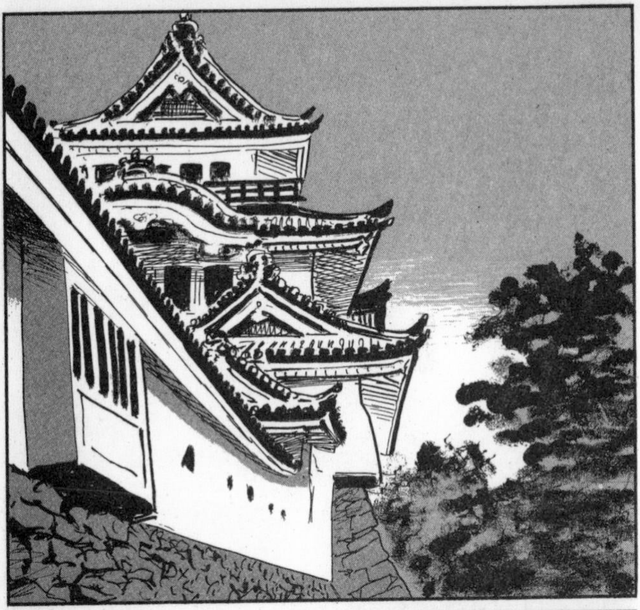

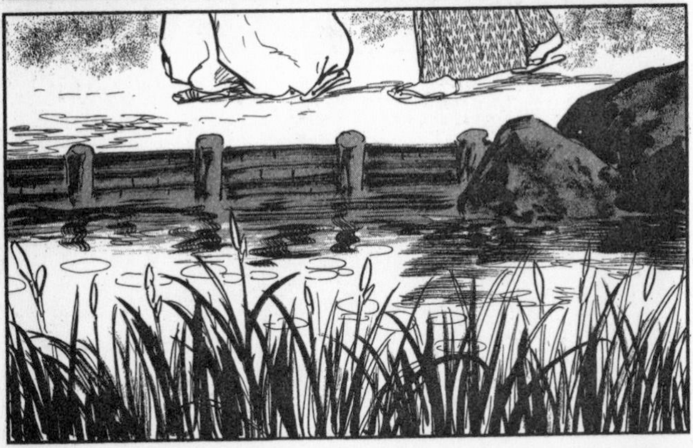

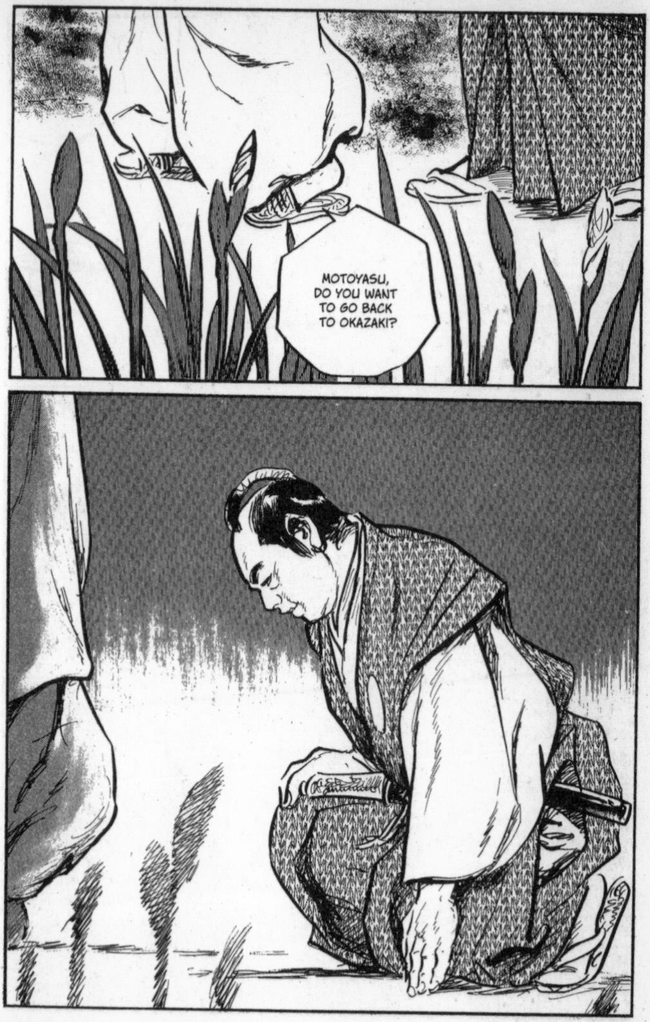
MOTOYASU, DO YOU WANT TO GO BACK TO OKAZAKI?

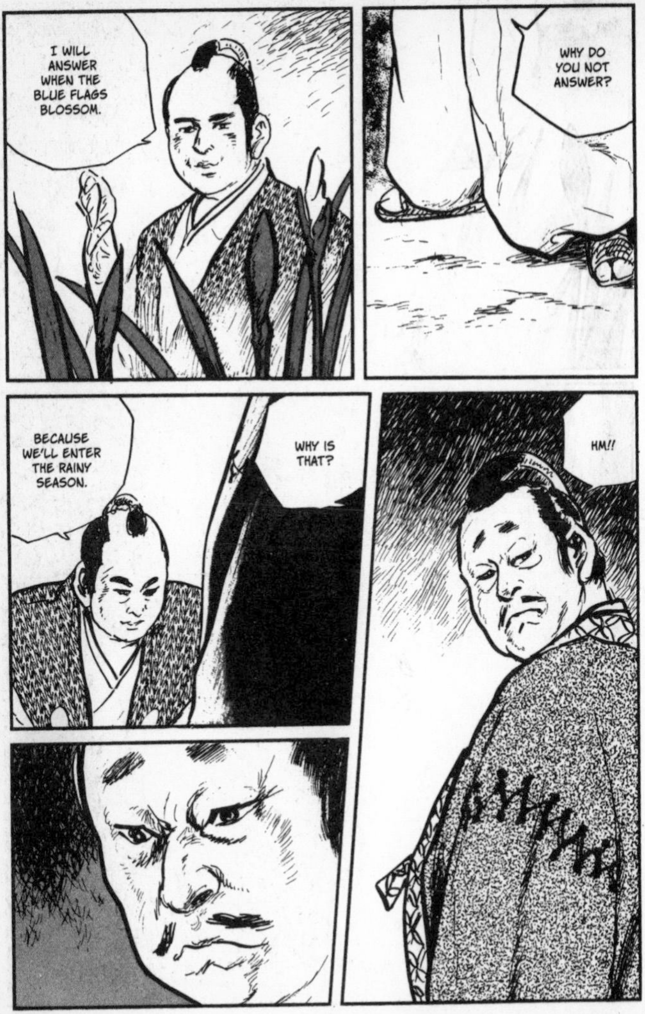
WHY DO YOU NOT ANSWER?
I WILL ANSWER WHEN THE BLUE FLAGS BLOSSOM.
HM!!
WHY IS THAT?
BECAUSE WE'LL ENTER THE RAINY SEASON.

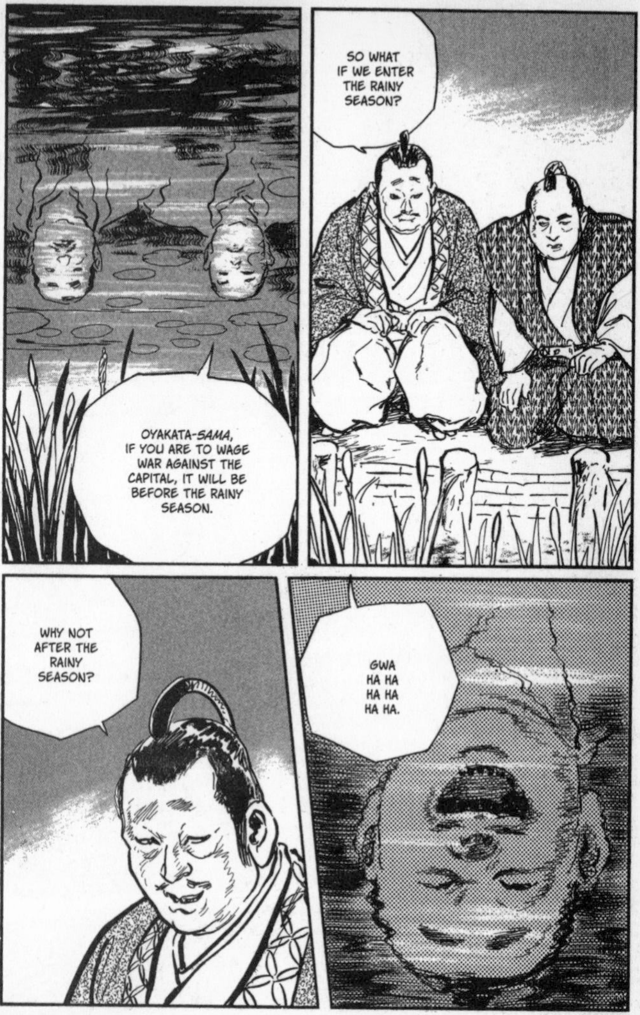
OYAKATA-SAMA, IF YOU ARE TO WAGE WAR AGAINST THE CAPITAL, IT WILL BE BEFORE THE RAINY SEASON.
SO WHAT IF WE ENTER THE RAINY SEASON?
WHY NOT AFTER THE RAINY SEASON?
GWA HA HA HA HA HA HA.

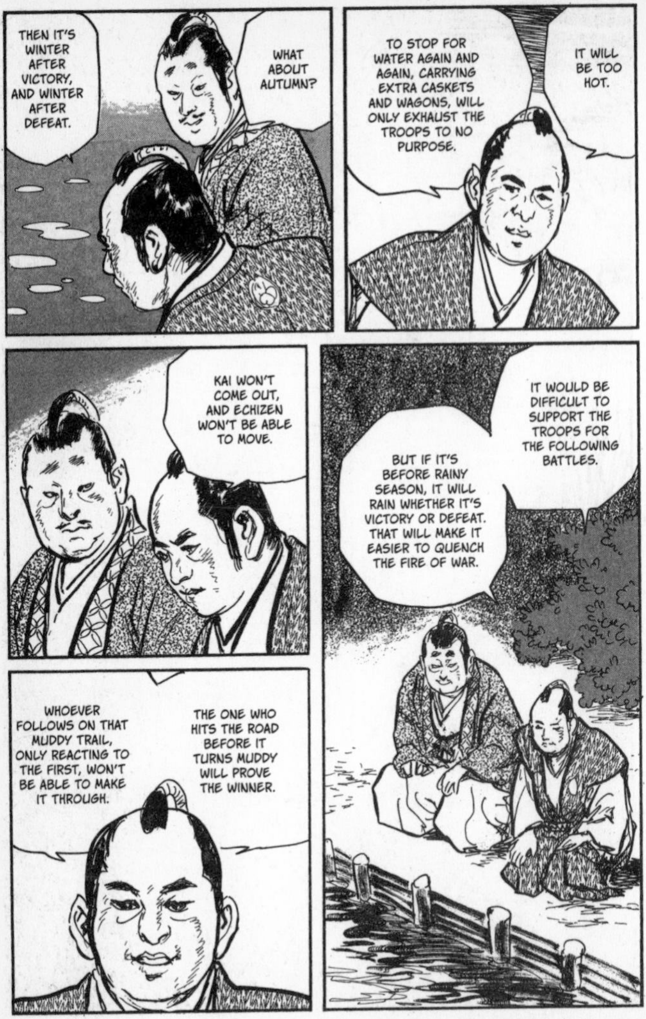
IT WILL BE TOO HOT.
TO STOP FOR WATER AGAIN AND AGAIN, CARRYING EXTRA CASKETS AND WAGONS, WILL ONLY EXHAUST THE TROOPS TO NO PURPOSE.
WHAT ABOUT AUTUMN?
THEN IT'S WINTER AFTER VICTORY, AND WINTER AFTER DEFEAT.
IT WOULD BE DIFFICULT TO SUPPORT THE TROOPS FOR THE FOLLOWING BATTLES.
BUT IF IT'S BEFORE RAINY SEASON, IT WILL RAIN WHETHER IT'S VICTORY OR DEFEAT. THAT WILL MAKE IT EASIER TO QUENCH THE FIRE OF WAR.
KAI WON'T COME OUT, AND ECHIZEN WON'T BE ABLE TO MOVE.
THE ONE WHO HITS THE ROAD BEFORE IT TURNS MUDDY WILL PROVE THE WINNER.
WHOEVER FOLLOWS ON THAT MUDDY TRAIL, ONLY REACTING TO THE FIRST, WON'T BE ABLE TO MAKE IT THROUGH.

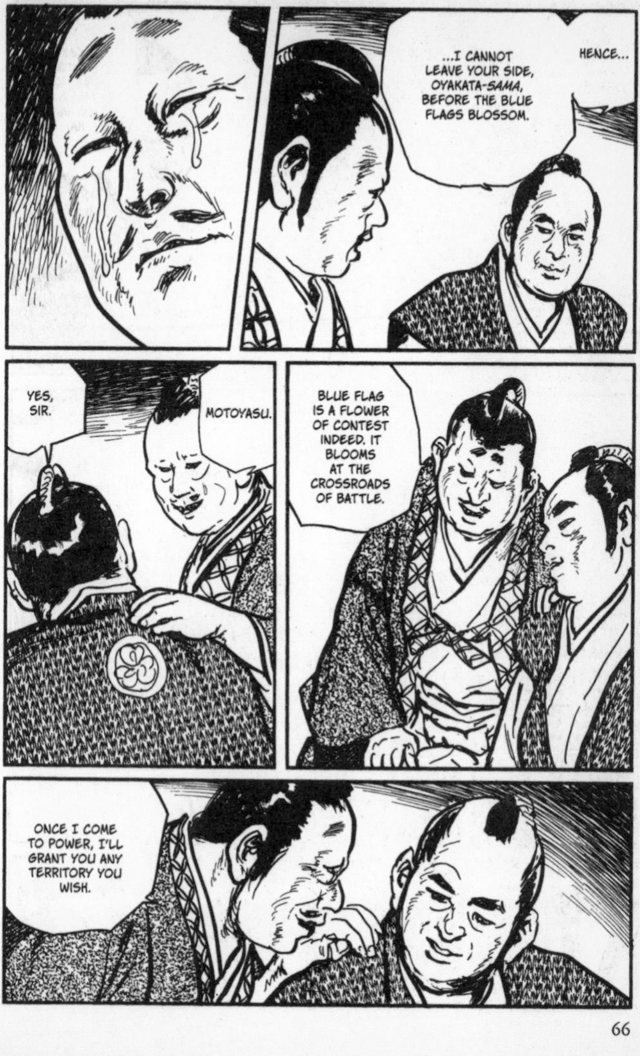
HENCE...
...I CANNOT LEAVE YOUR SIDE, OYAKATA-SAMA, BEFORE THE BLUE FLAGS BLOSSOM.
BLUE FLAG IS A FLOWER OF CONTEST INDEED. IT BLOOMS AT THE CROSSROADS OF BATTLE.
MOTOYASU.
YES, SIR.
ONCE I COME TO POWER, I'LL GRANT YOU ANY TERRITORY YOU WISH.

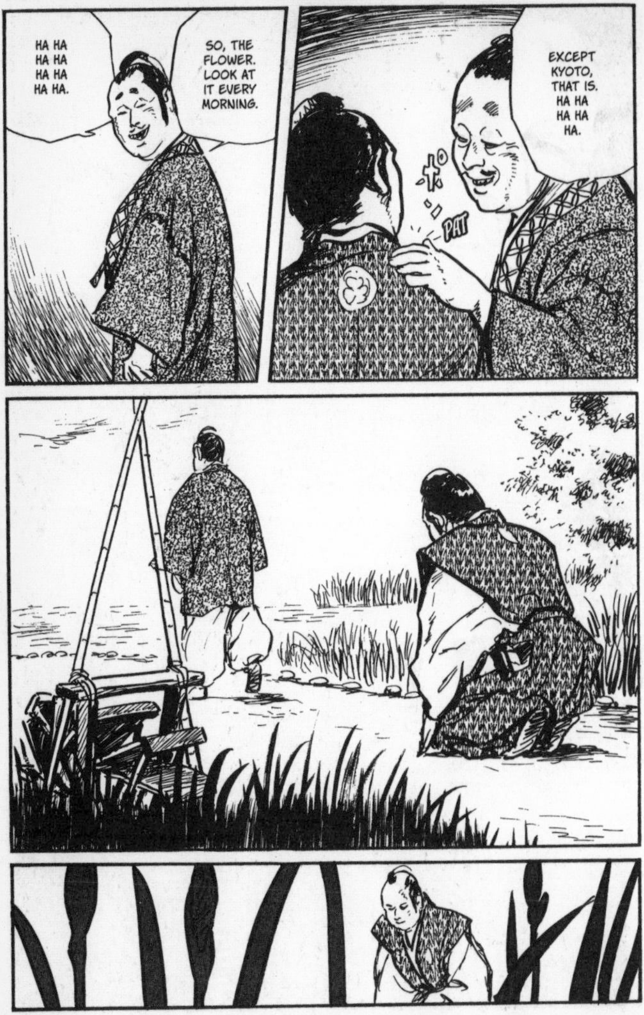
EXCEPT KYOTO, THAT IS. HA HA HA HA HA.
PAT
SO, THE FLOWER. LOOK AT IT EVERY MORNING.
HA HA HA HA HA HA HA HA.

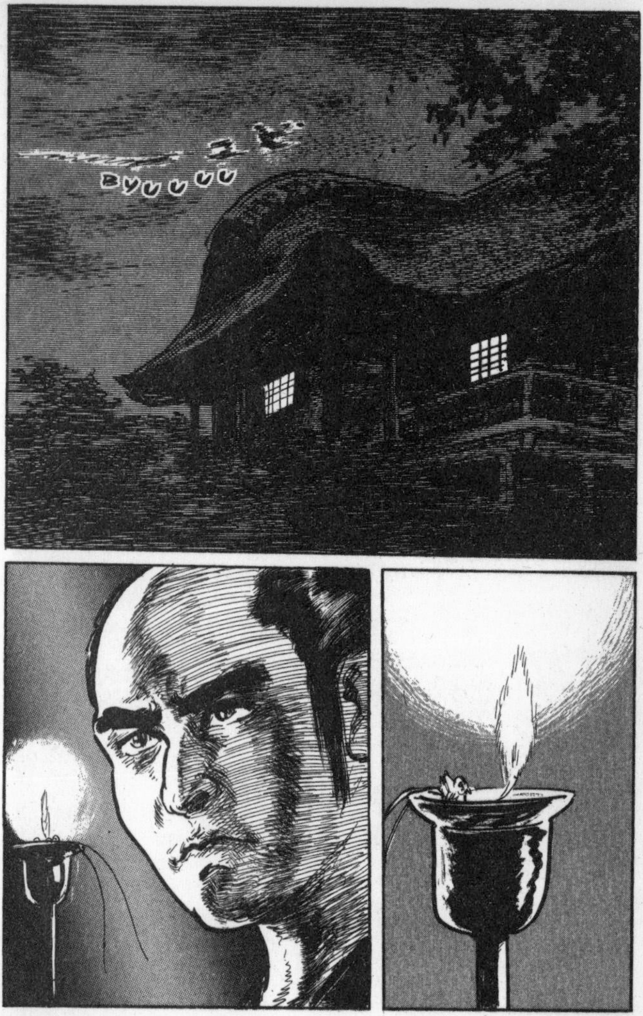
BYUUUU

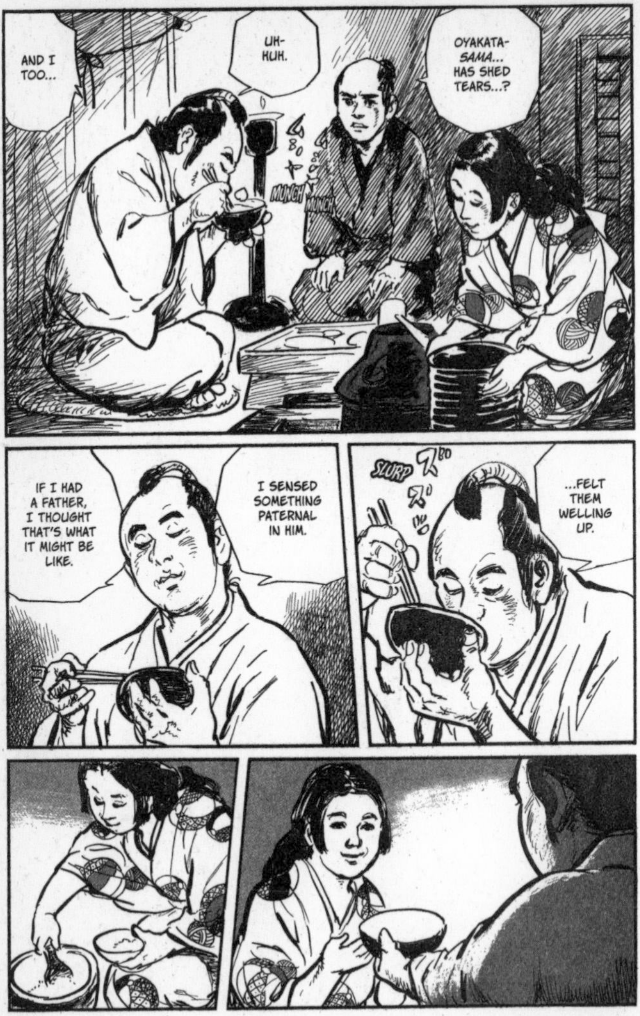
OYAKATA-SAMA... HAS SHED TEARS...?
UH-HUH.
AND I TOO...
MUNCH
MUNCH
SLURP
...FELT THEM WELLING UP.
I SENSED SOMETHING PATERNAL IN HIM.
IF I HAD A FATHER, I THOUGHT THAT'S WHAT IT MIGHT BE LIKE.

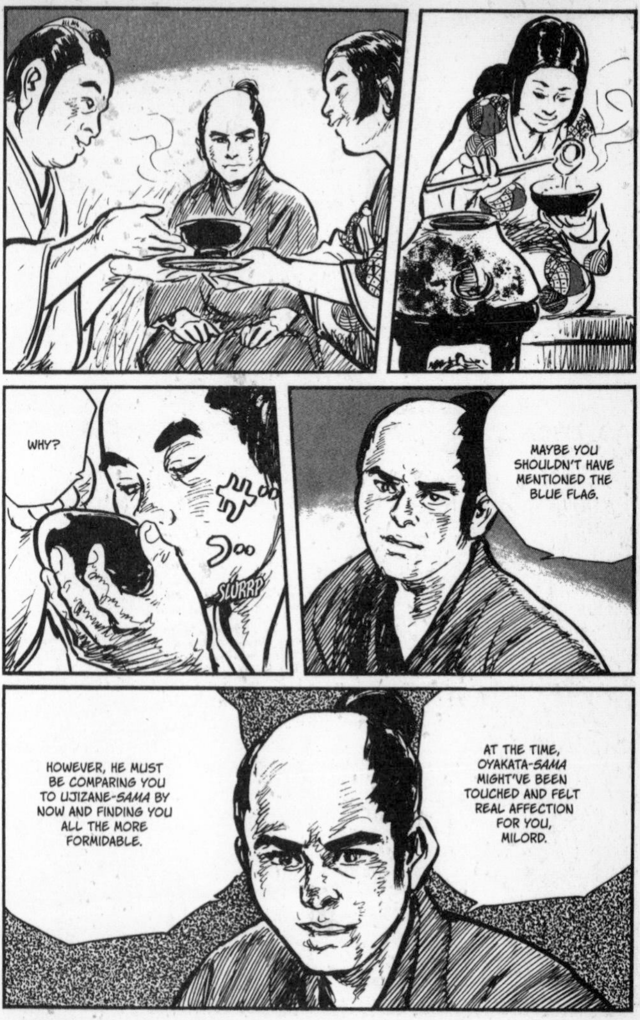
MAYBE YOU SHOULDN'T HAVE MENTIONED THE BLUE FLAG.
WHY?
SLURRP
AT THE TIME, OYAKATA-*SAMA* MIGHT'VE BEEN TOUCHED AND FELT REAL AFFECTION FOR YOU, MILORD.
HOWEVER, HE MUST BE COMPARING YOU TO UJIZANE-*SAMA* BY NOW AND FINDING YOU ALL THE MORE FORMIDABLE.

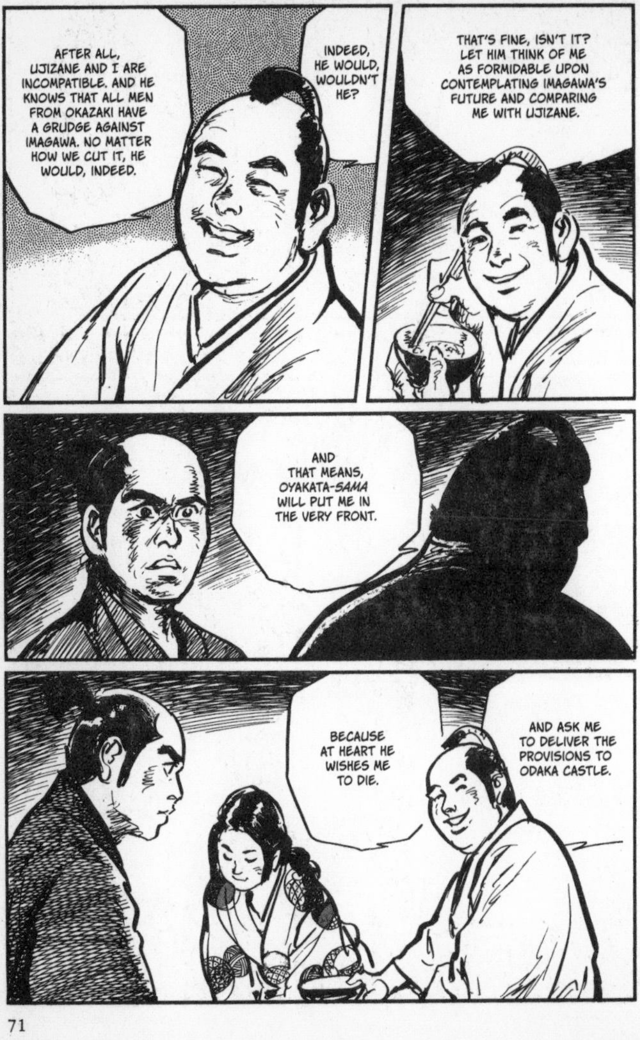
THAT'S FINE, ISN'T IT? LET HIM THINK OF ME AS FORMIDABLE UPON CONTEMPLATING IMAGAWA'S FUTURE AND COMPARING ME WITH UJIZANE.
INDEED, HE WOULD, WOULDN'T HE?
AFTER ALL, UJIZANE AND I ARE INCOMPATIBLE. AND HE KNOWS THAT ALL MEN FROM OKAZAKI HAVE A GRUDGE AGAINST IMAGAWA. NO MATTER HOW WE CUT IT, HE WOULD, INDEED.
AND THAT MEANS, OYAKATA-*SAMA* WILL PUT ME IN THE VERY FRONT.
AND ASK ME TO DELIVER THE PROVISIONS TO ODAKA CASTLE.
BECAUSE AT HEART HE WISHES ME TO DIE.

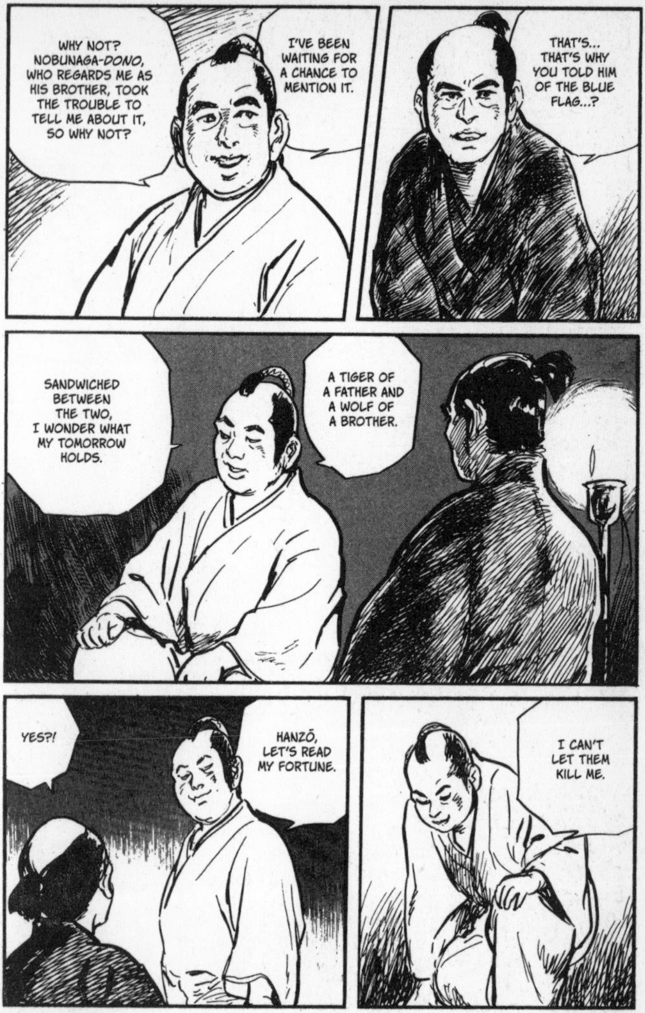
THAT'S... THAT'S WHY YOU TOLD HIM OF THE BLUE FLAG...?
I'VE BEEN WAITING FOR A CHANCE TO MENTION IT.
WHY NOT? NOBUNAGA-*DONO*, WHO REGARDS ME AS HIS BROTHER, TOOK THE TROUBLE TO TELL ME ABOUT IT, SO WHY NOT?
A TIGER OF A FATHER AND A WOLF OF A BROTHER.
SANDWICHED BETWEEN THE TWO, I WONDER WHAT MY TOMORROW HOLDS.
I CAN'T LET THEM KILL ME.
HANZŌ, LET'S READ MY FORTUNE.
YES?!

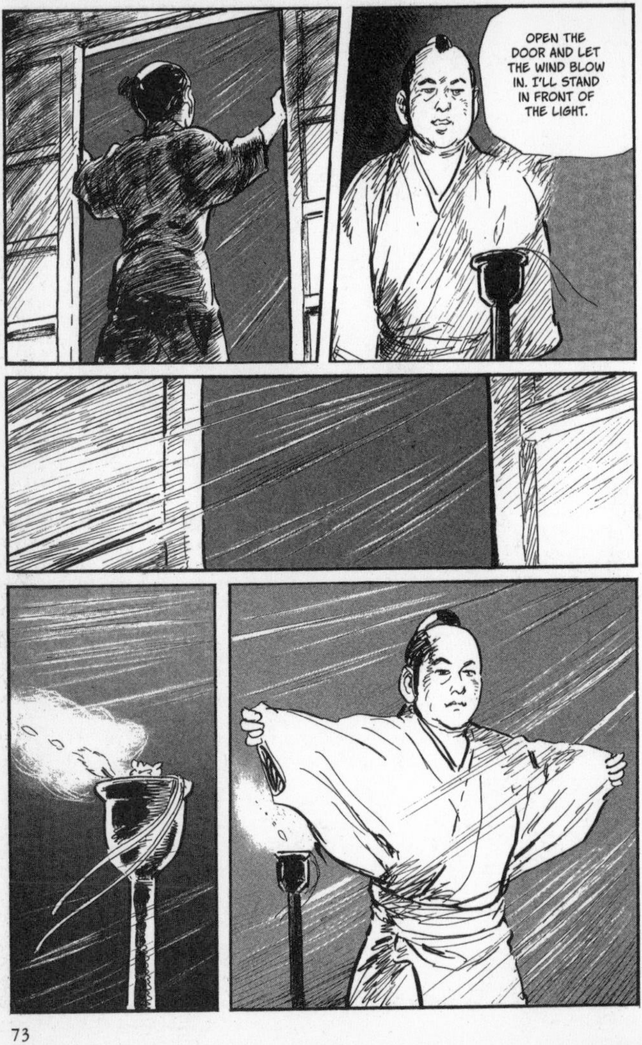
OPEN THE DOOR AND LET THE WIND BLOW IN. I'LL STAND IN FRONT OF THE LIGHT.

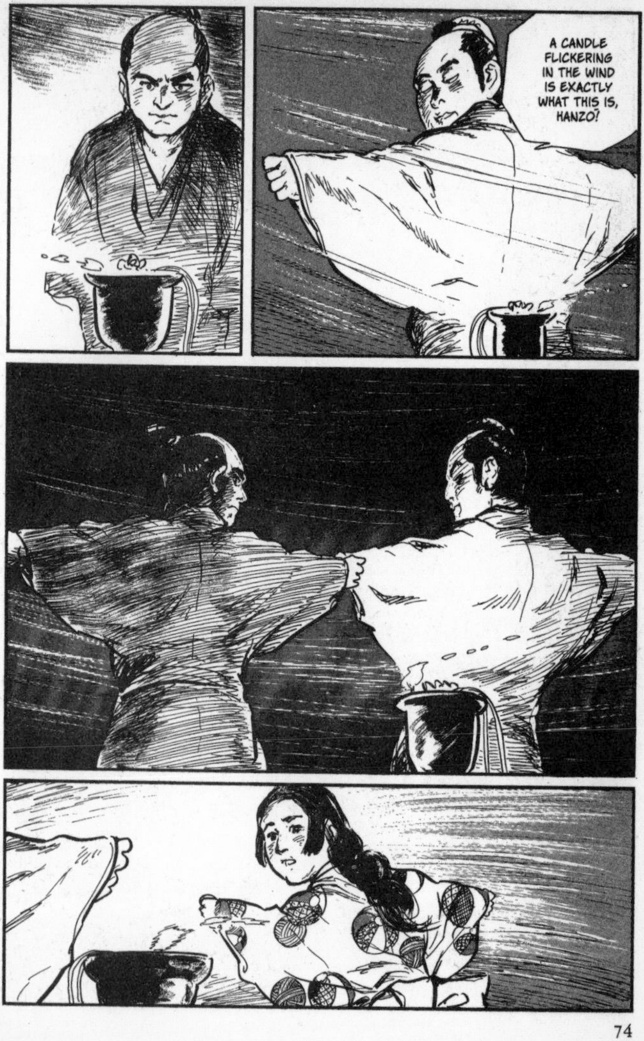
A CANDLE FLICKERING IN THE WIND IS EXACTLY WHAT THIS IS, HANZO?

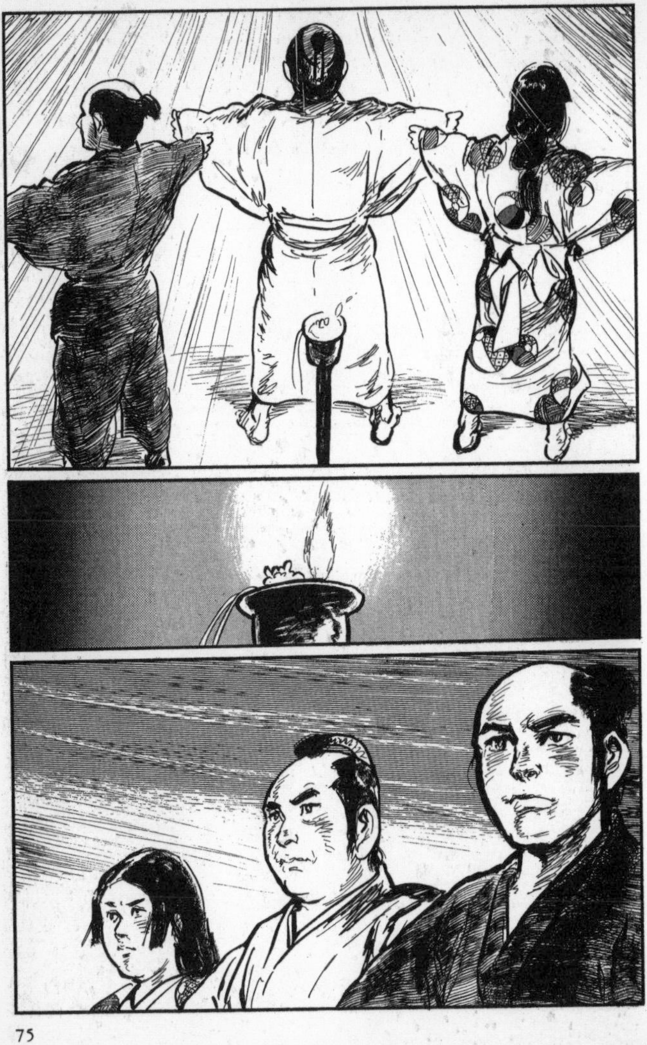

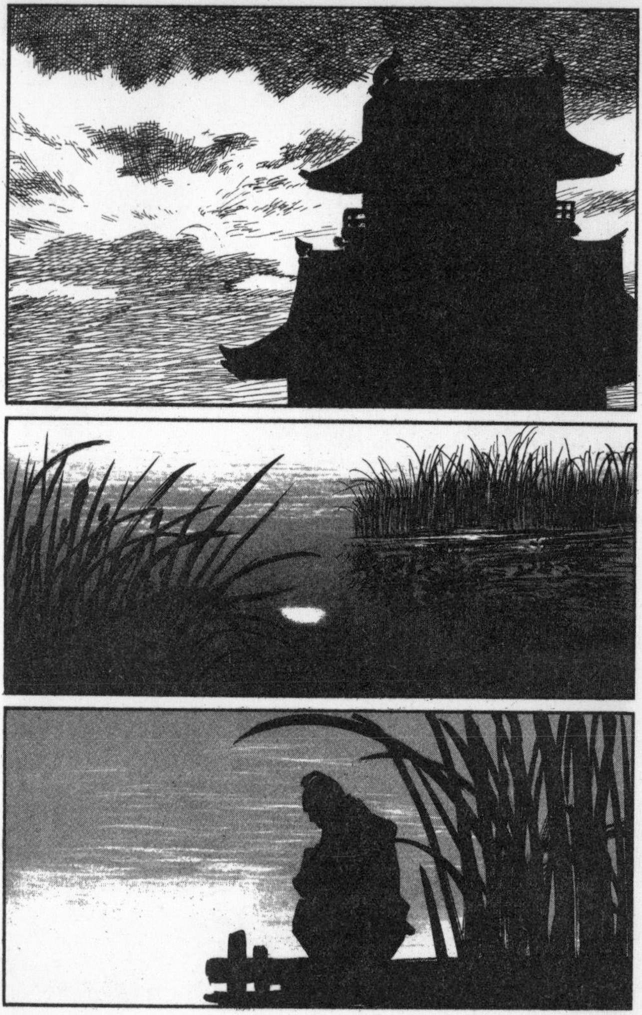

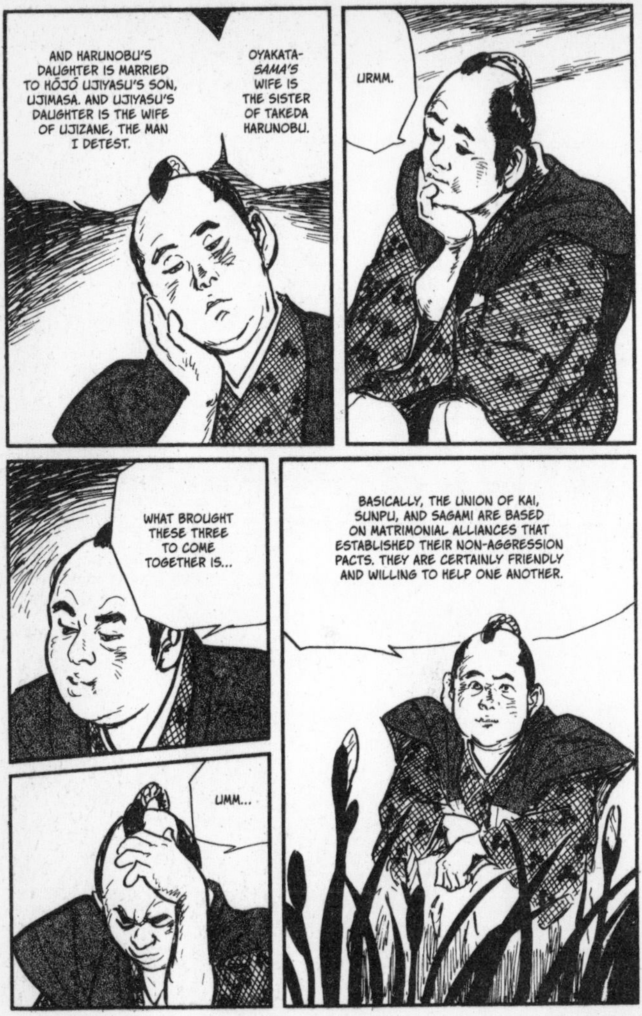
URMM.
OYAKATA-SAMA'S WIFE IS THE SISTER OF TAKEDA HARUNOBU.
AND HARUNOBU'S DAUGHTER IS MARRIED TO HŌJŌ UJIYASU'S SON, UJIMASA. AND UJIYASU'S DAUGHTER IS THE WIFE OF UJIZANE, THE MAN I DETEST.
BASICALLY, THE UNION OF KAI, SUNPU, AND SAGAMI ARE BASED ON MATRIMONIAL ALLIANCES THAT ESTABLISHED THEIR NON-AGGRESSION PACTS. THEY ARE CERTAINLY FRIENDLY AND WILLING TO HELP ONE ANOTHER.
WHAT BROUGHT THESE THREE TO COME TOGETHER IS...
UMM...

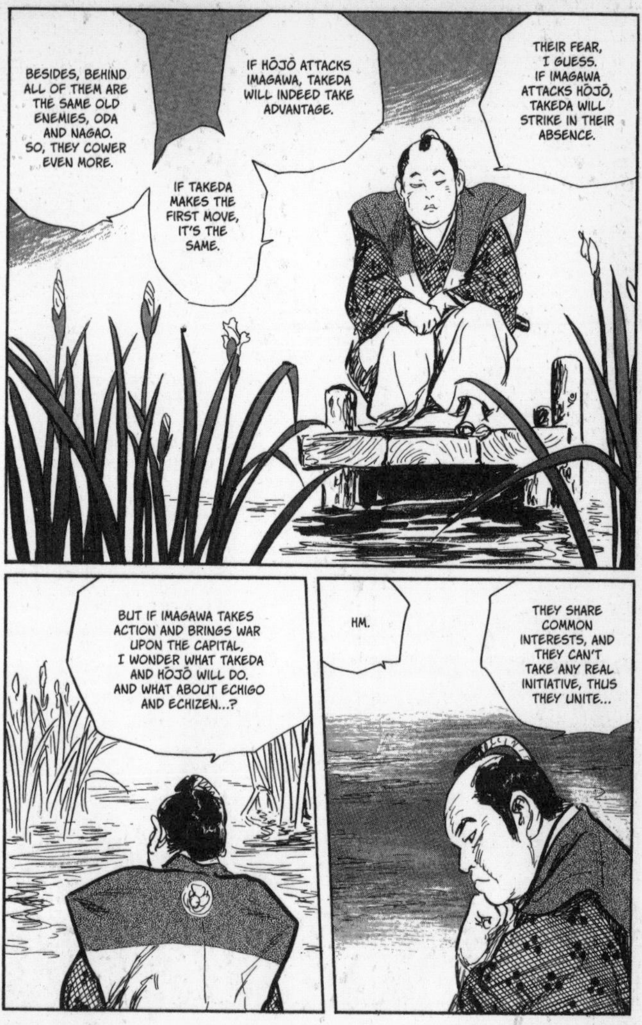
THEIR FEAR, I GUESS. IF IMAGAWA ATTACKS HŌJŌ, TAKEDA WILL STRIKE IN THEIR ABSENCE.
IF HŌJŌ ATTACKS IMAGAWA, TAKEDA WILL INDEED TAKE ADVANTAGE.
IF TAKEDA MAKES THE FIRST MOVE, IT'S THE SAME.
BESIDES, BEHIND ALL OF THEM ARE THE SAME OLD ENEMIES, ODA AND NAGAO. SO, THEY COWER EVEN MORE.
THEY SHARE COMMON INTERESTS, AND THEY CAN'T TAKE ANY REAL INITIATIVE, THUS THEY UNITE...
HM.
BUT IF IMAGAWA TAKES ACTION AND BRINGS WAR UPON THE CAPITAL, I WONDER WHAT TAKEDA AND HŌJŌ WILL DO. AND WHAT ABOUT ECHIGO AND ECHIZEN...?

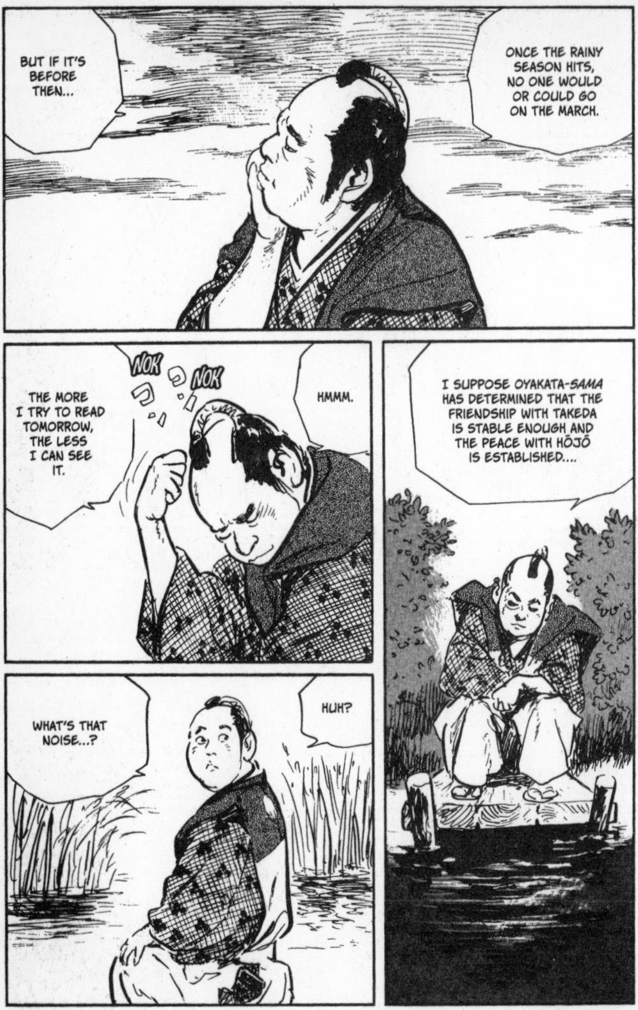
ONCE THE RAINY SEASON HITS, NO ONE WOULD OR COULD GO ON THE MARCH.
BUT IF IT'S BEFORE THEN...
I SUPPOSE OYAKATA-*SAMA* HAS DETERMINED THAT THE FRIENDSHIP WITH TAKEDA IS STABLE ENOUGH AND THE PEACE WITH HŌJŌ IS ESTABLISHED....
HMMM.
NOK
NOK
THE MORE I TRY TO READ TOMORROW, THE LESS I CAN SEE IT.
HUH?
WHAT'S THAT NOISE...?

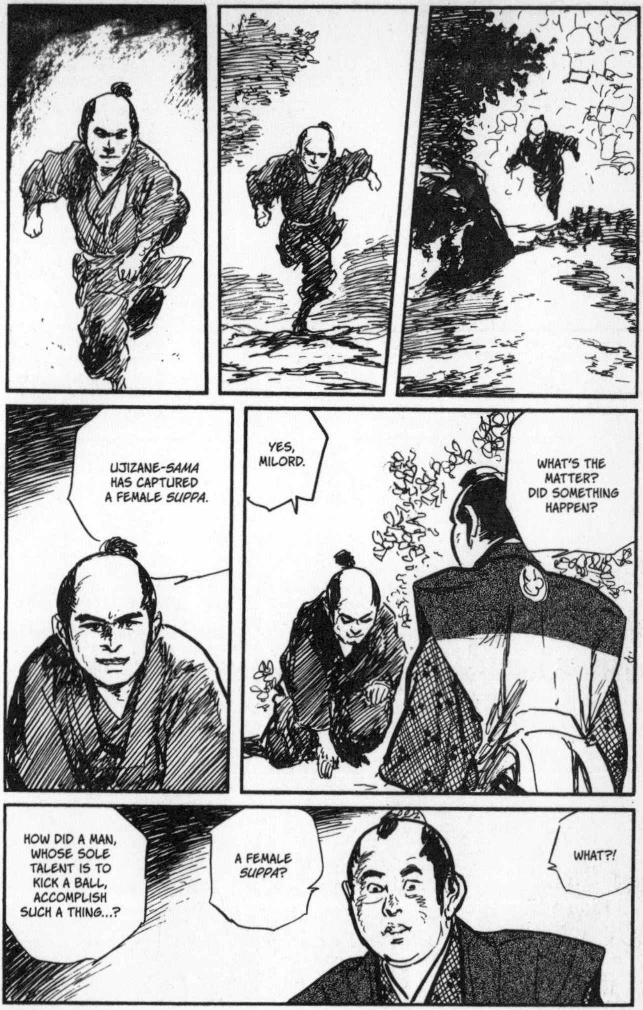
WHAT'S THE MATTER? DID SOMETHING HAPPEN?
YES, MILORD.
UJIZANE-SAMA HAS CAPTURED A FEMALE *SUPPA*.
WHAT?!
A FEMALE *SUPPA*?
HOW DID A MAN, WHOSE SOLE TALENT IS TO KICK A BALL, ACCOMPLISH SUCH A THING...?

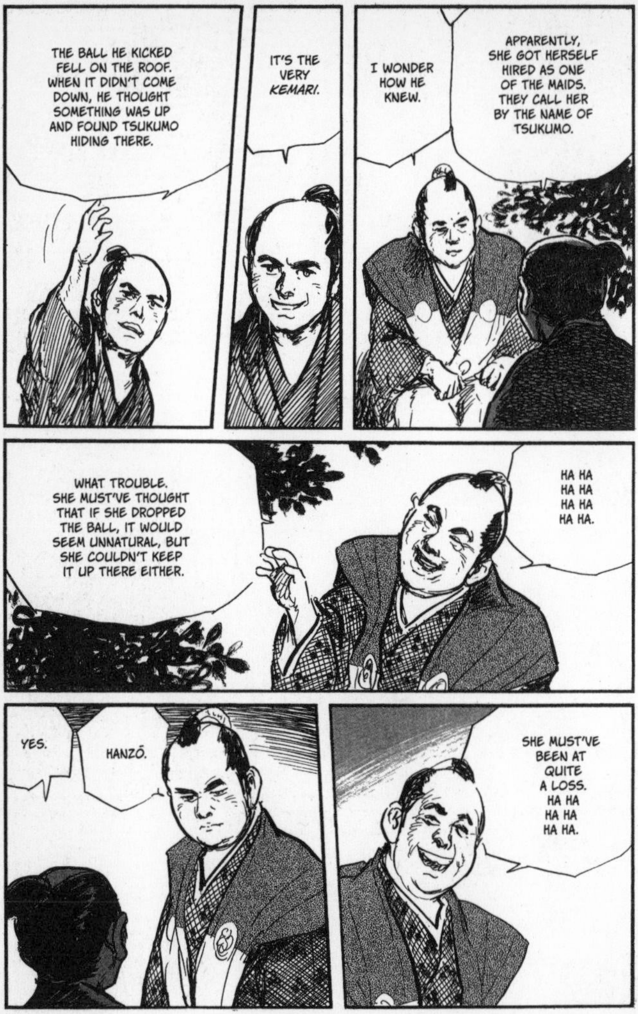
APPARENTLY, SHE GOT HERSELF HIRED AS ONE OF THE MAIDS. THEY CALL HER BY THE NAME OF TSUKUMO.
I WONDER HOW HE KNEW.
IT'S THE VERY *KEMARI*.
THE BALL HE KICKED FELL ON THE ROOF. WHEN IT DIDN'T COME DOWN, HE THOUGHT SOMETHING WAS UP AND FOUND TSUKUMO HIDING THERE.
HA HA HA HA HA HA HA HA.
WHAT TROUBLE. SHE MUST'VE THOUGHT THAT IF SHE DROPPED THE BALL, IT WOULD SEEM UNNATURAL, BUT SHE COULDN'T KEEP IT UP THERE EITHER.
SHE MUST'VE BEEN AT QUITE A LOSS. HA HA HA HA HA HA.
HANZŌ.
YES.

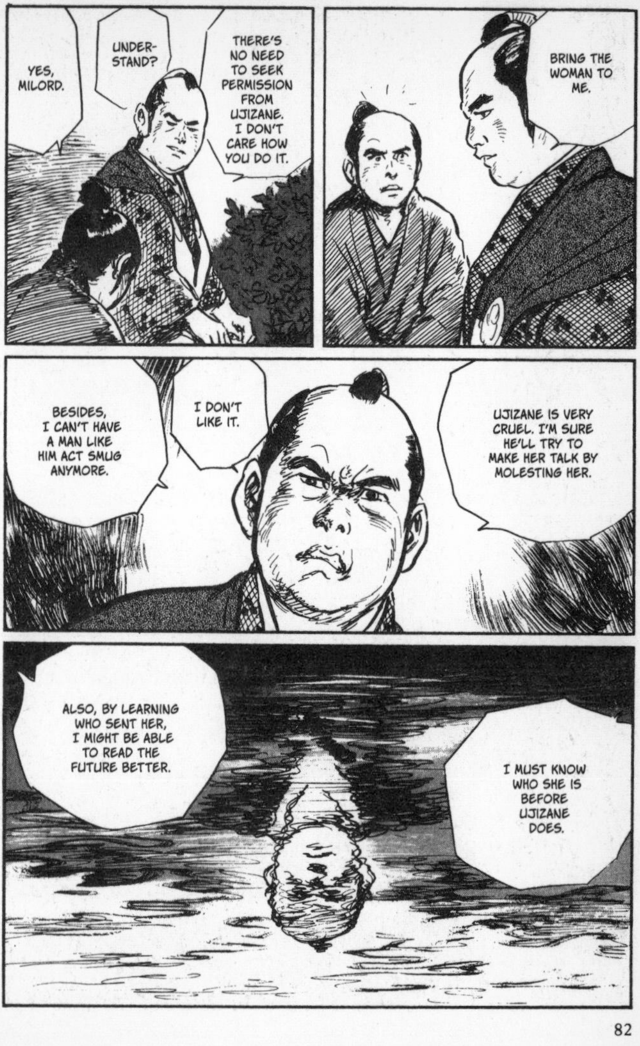
BRING THE WOMAN TO ME.
THERE'S NO NEED TO SEEK PERMISSION FROM UJIZANE. I DON'T CARE HOW YOU DO IT.
UNDER-STAND?
YES, MILORD.
UJIZANE IS VERY CRUEL. I'M SURE HE'LL TRY TO MAKE HER TALK BY MOLESTING HER.
I DON'T LIKE IT.
BESIDES, I CAN'T HAVE A MAN LIKE HIM ACT SMUG ANYMORE.
I MUST KNOW WHO SHE IS BEFORE UJIZANE DOES.
ALSO, BY LEARNING WHO SENT HER, I MIGHT BE ABLE TO READ THE FUTURE BETTER.

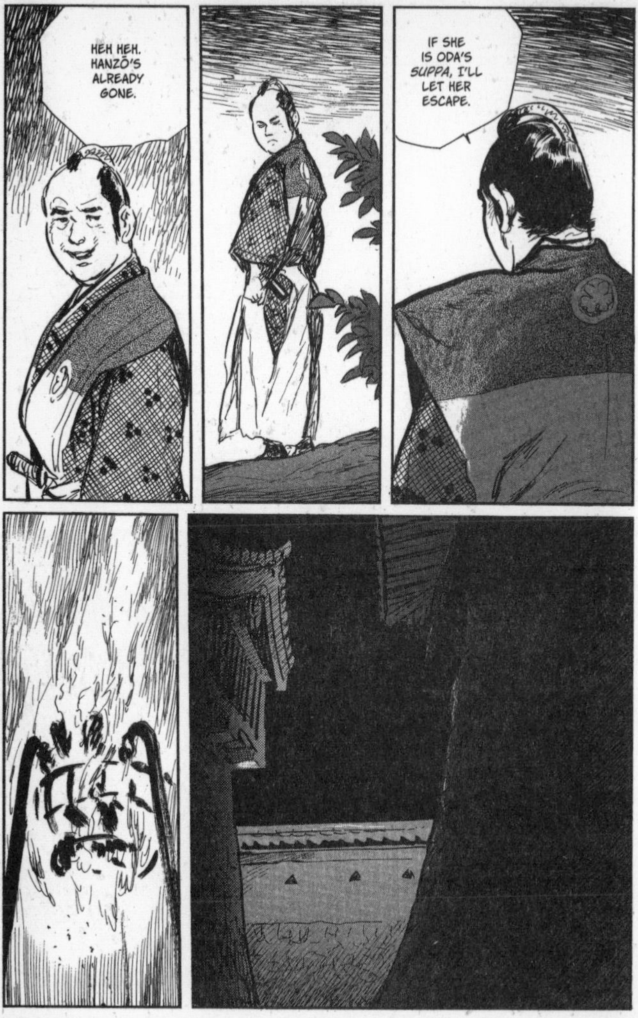
IF SHE IS ODA'S *SUPPA*, I'LL LET HER ESCAPE.
HEH HEH. HANZŌ'S ALREADY GONE.

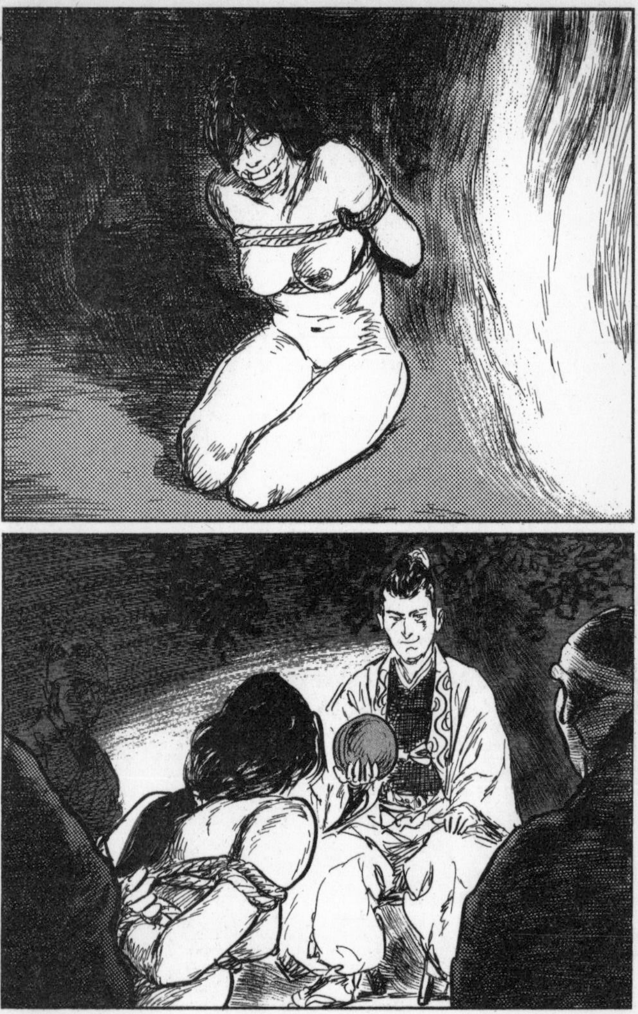

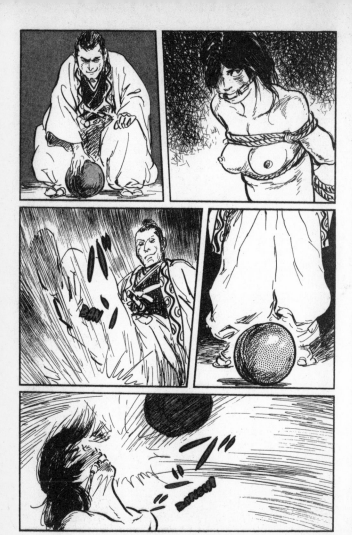

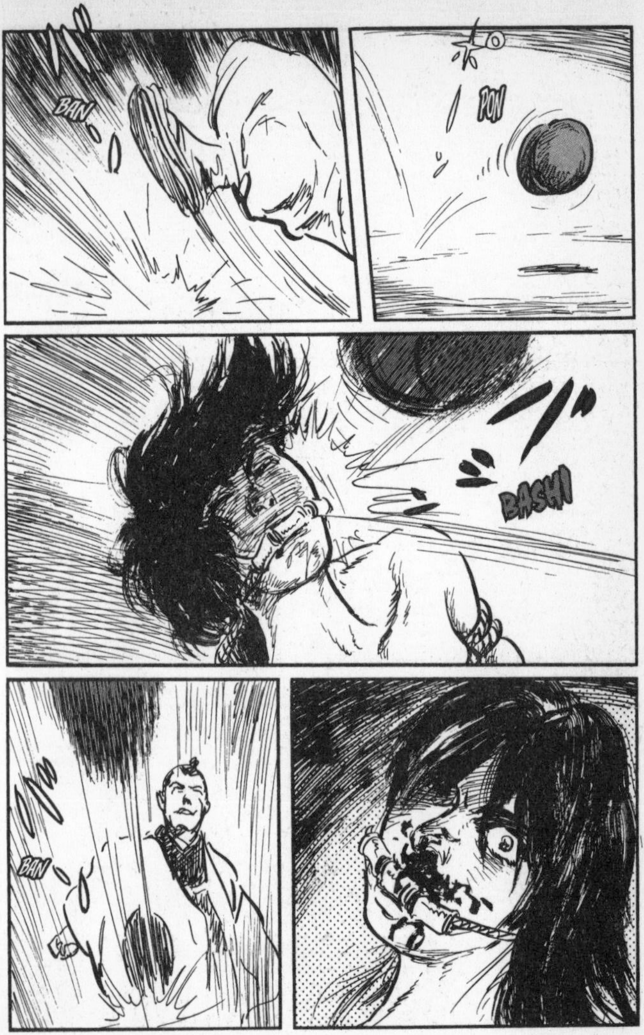
PON
BAN
BASHI
BAN

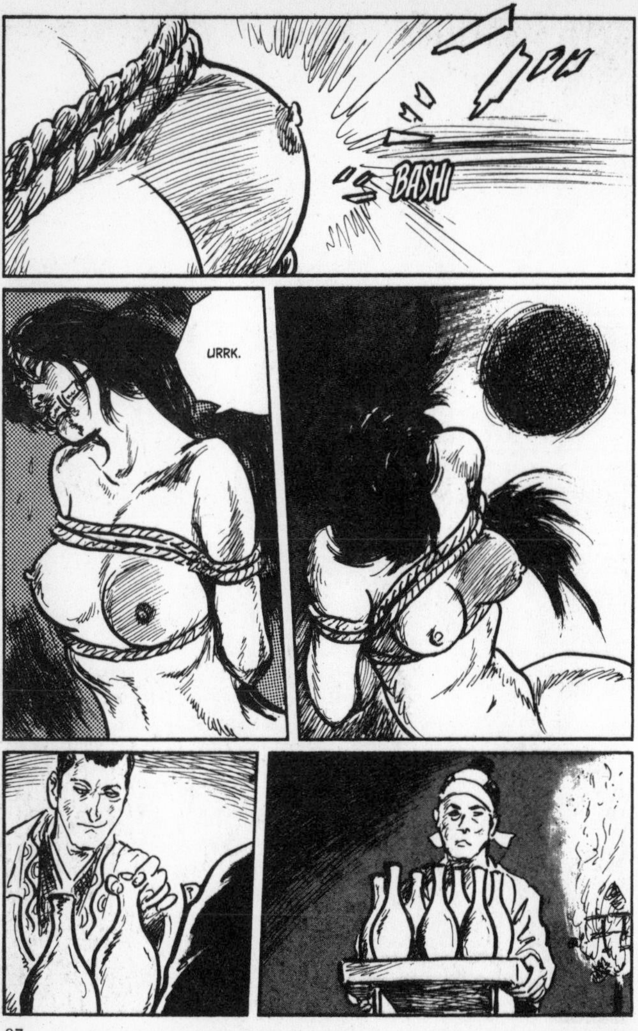
BASHI
URRK.

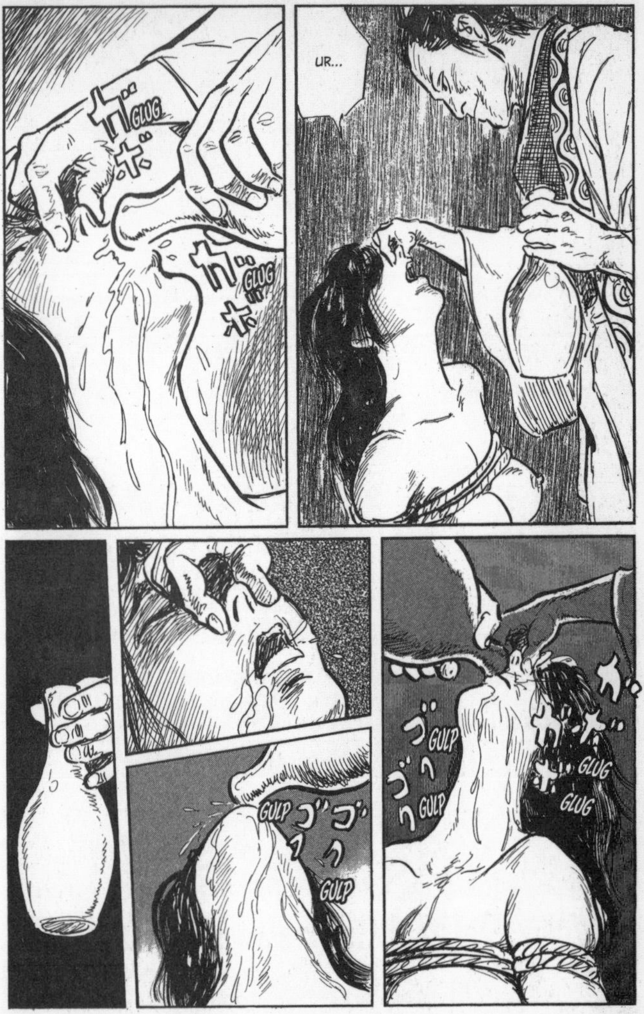
UR...
GLUG
GLUG
GULP
GULP
GLUG
GLUG
GULP
GULP

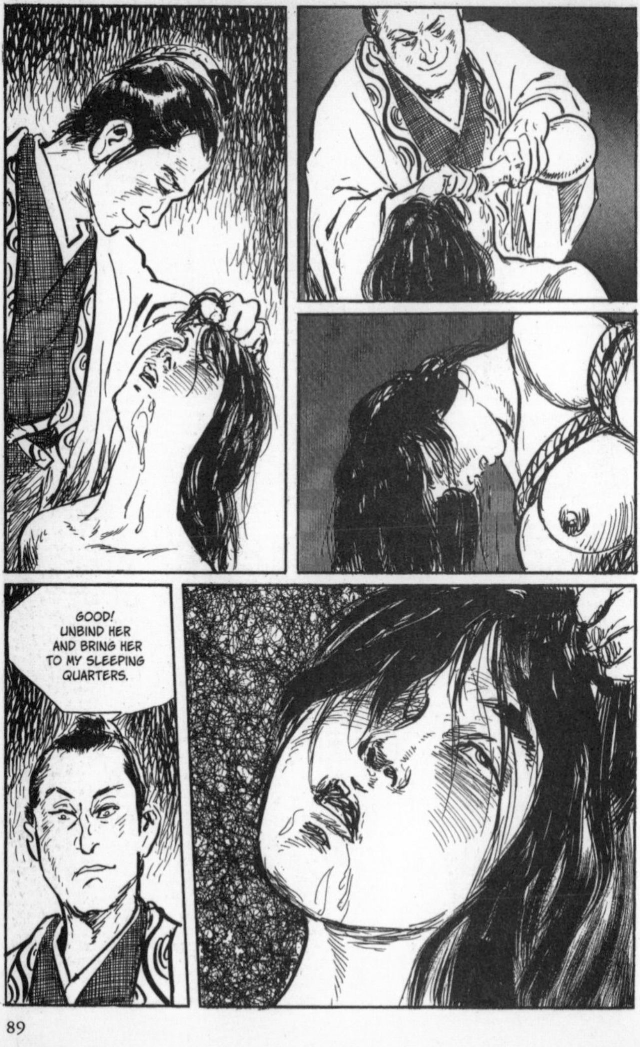
GOOD! UNBIND HER AND BRING HER TO MY SLEEPING QUARTERS.

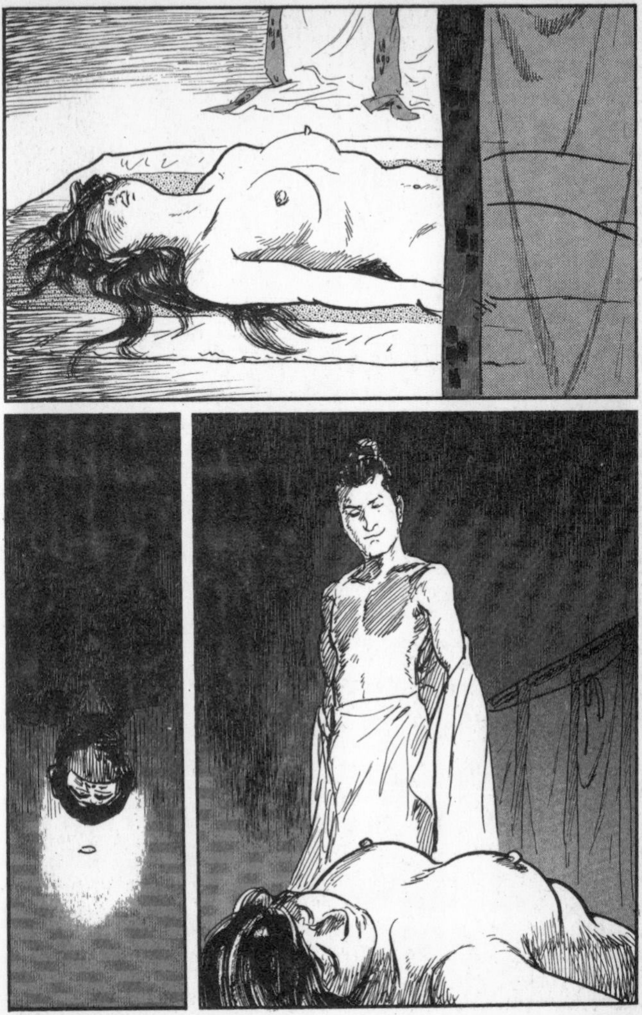

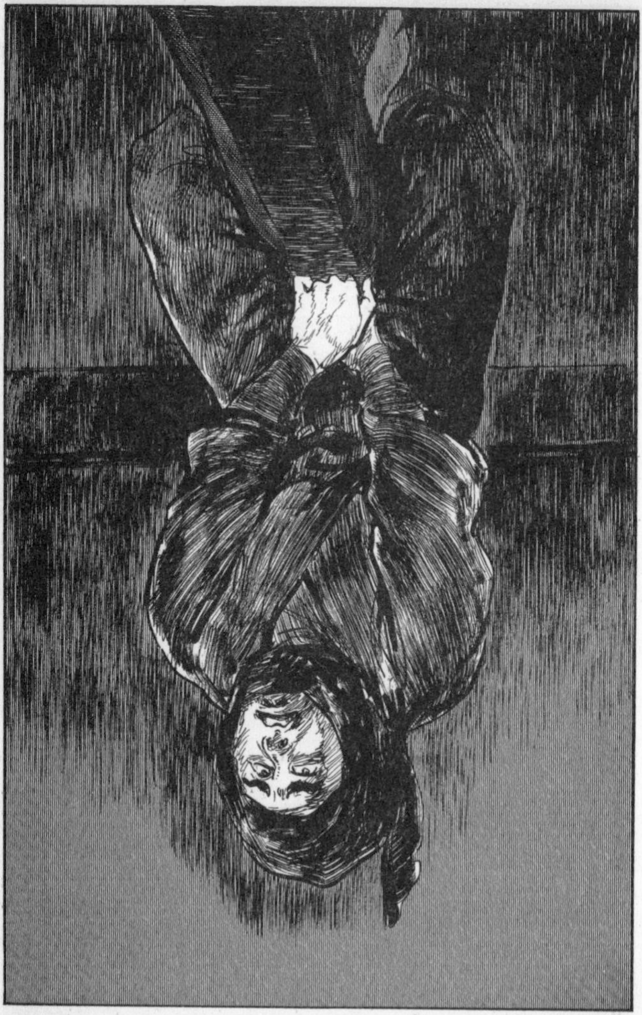

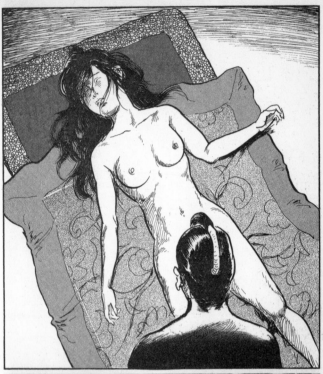

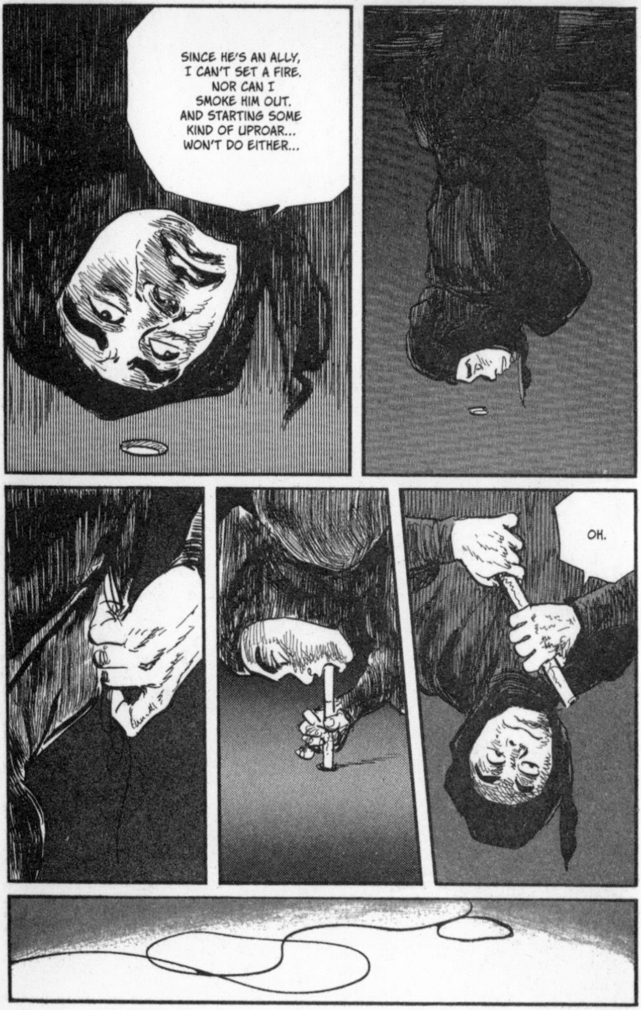
SINCE HE'S AN ALLY, I CAN'T SET A FIRE. NOR CAN I SMOKE HIM OUT. AND STARTING SOME KIND OF UPROAR... WON'T DO EITHER...
OH.

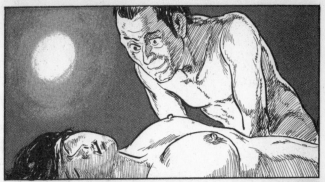

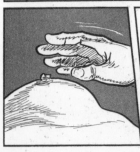

HEH
HEH
HEH.

WHAT
BEAUTY
FOR A
SUPPA.

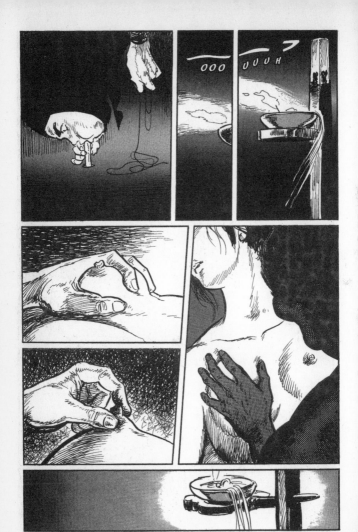

OOO UUUH

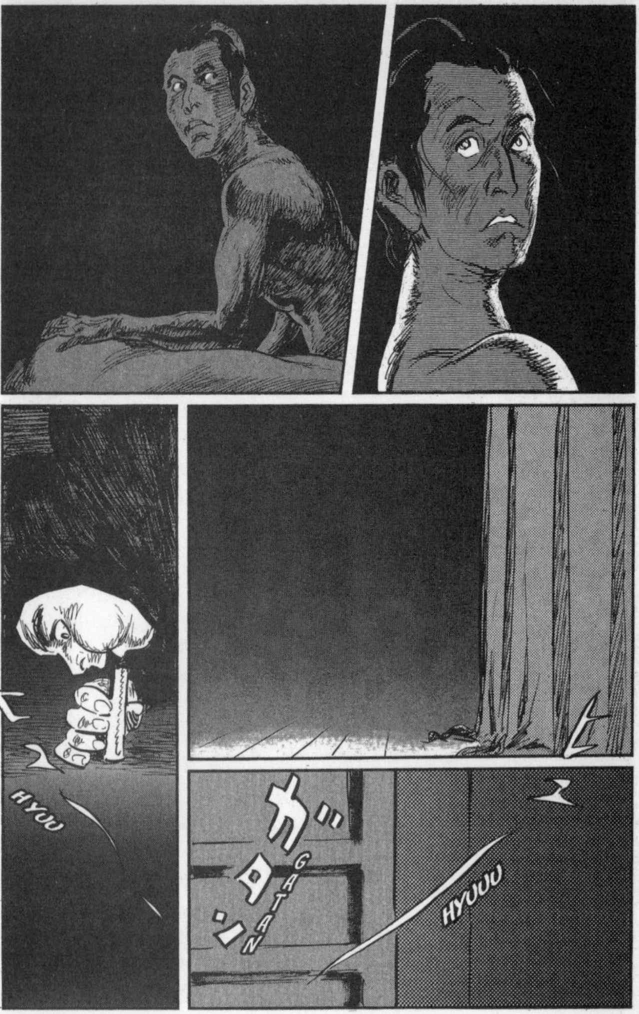
ガタン
GATAN
HYUUU
HYUU

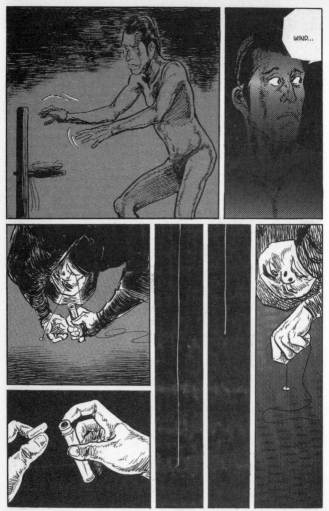

WIND...

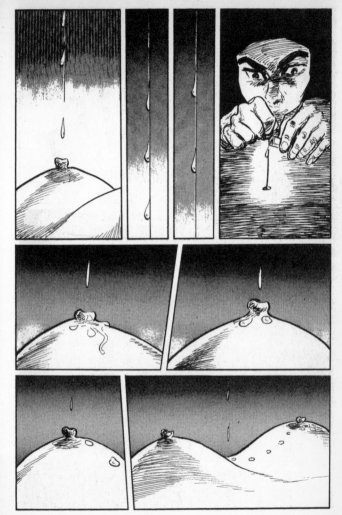

98

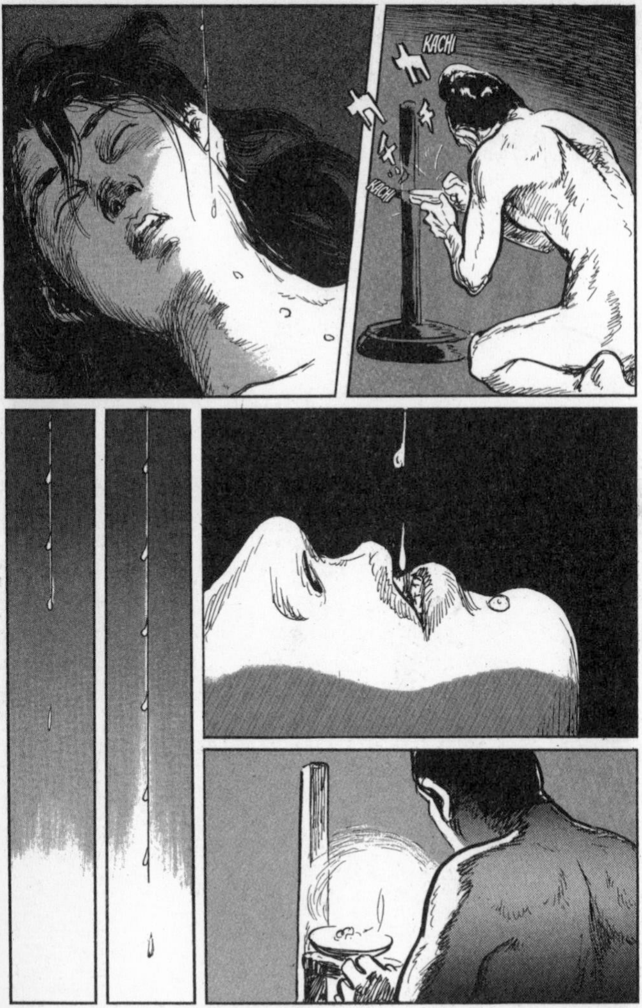
KACHI
KACHI

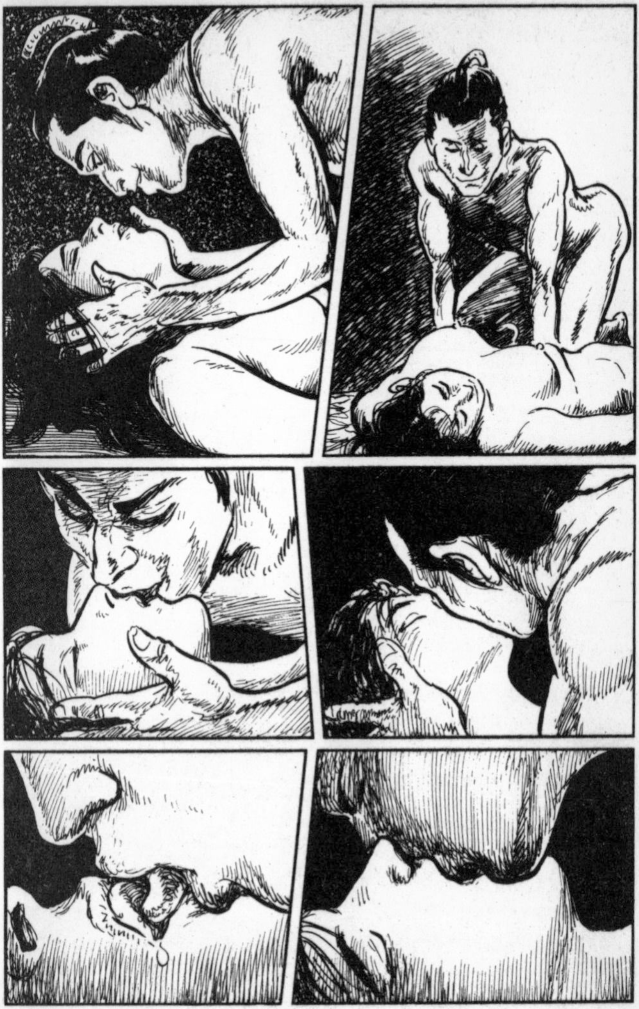

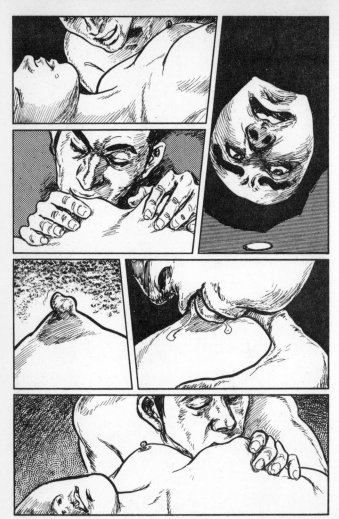

101

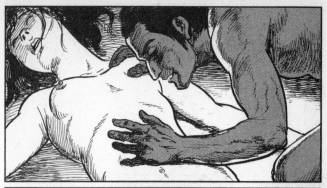

HMMM...

THIS IS THE
SORT OF SKIN
THAT BELONGS
TO A KID.
SHE'S TRAINED
JUST ABOUT RIGHT.
SLENDER AND
PRETTY.

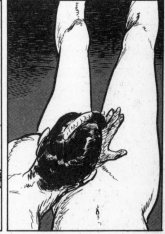

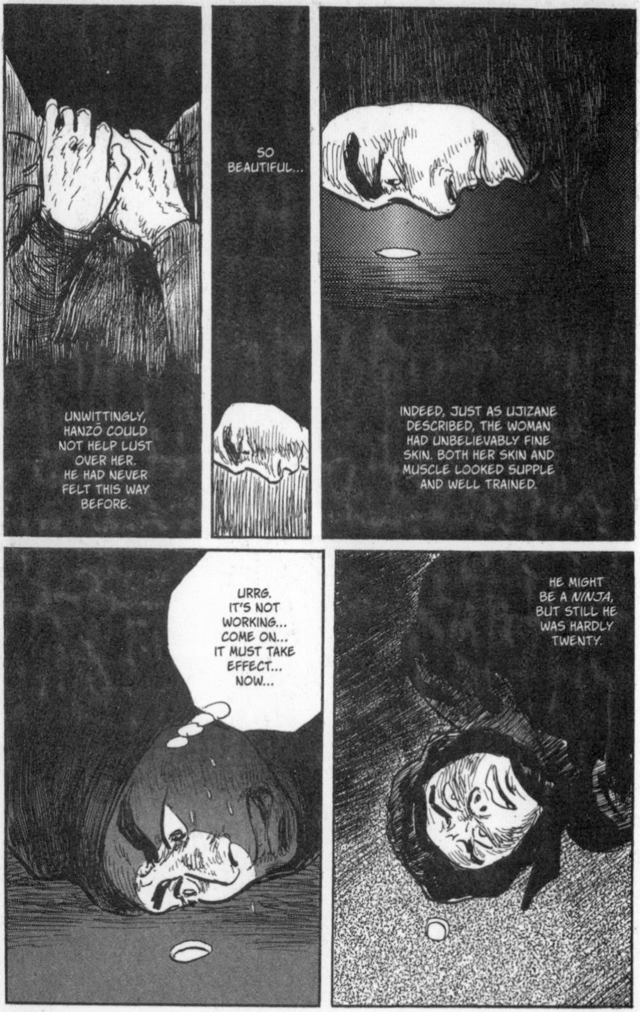
INDEED, JUST AS UJIZANE DESCRIBED, THE WOMAN HAD UNBELIEVABLY FINE SKIN. BOTH HER SKIN AND MUSCLE LOOKED SUPPLE AND WELL TRAINED.
SO BEAUTIFUL...
UNWITTINGLY, HANZŌ COULD NOT HELP LUST OVER HER. HE HAD NEVER FELT THIS WAY BEFORE.
HE MIGHT BE A *NINJA*, BUT STILL HE WAS HARDLY TWENTY.
URRG. IT'S NOT WORKING... COME ON... IT MUST TAKE EFFECT... NOW...

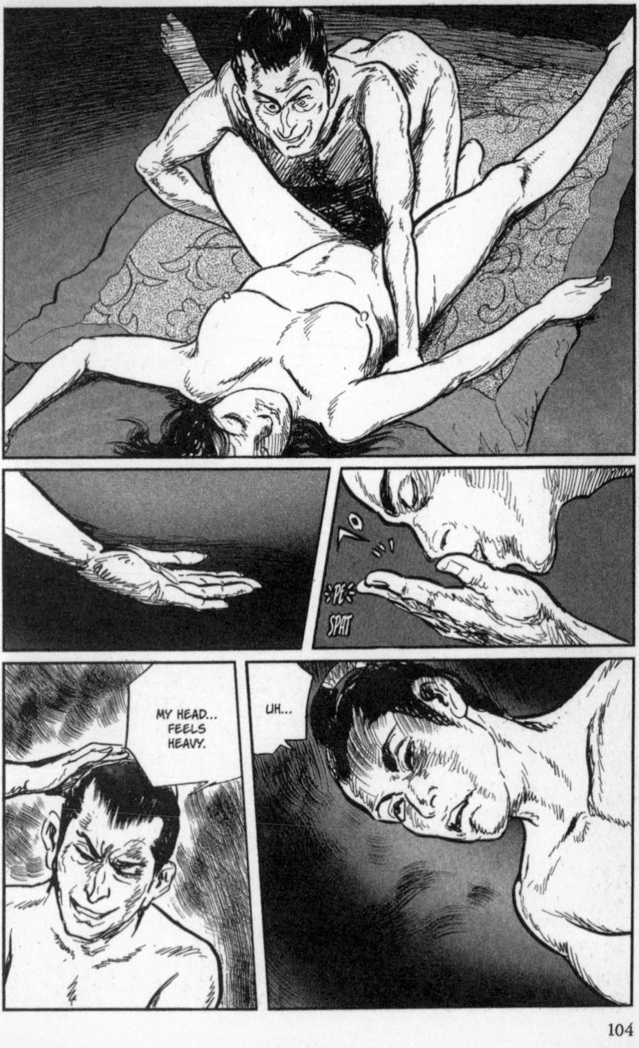
PE
SPAT
UH...
MY HEAD... FEELS HEAVY.

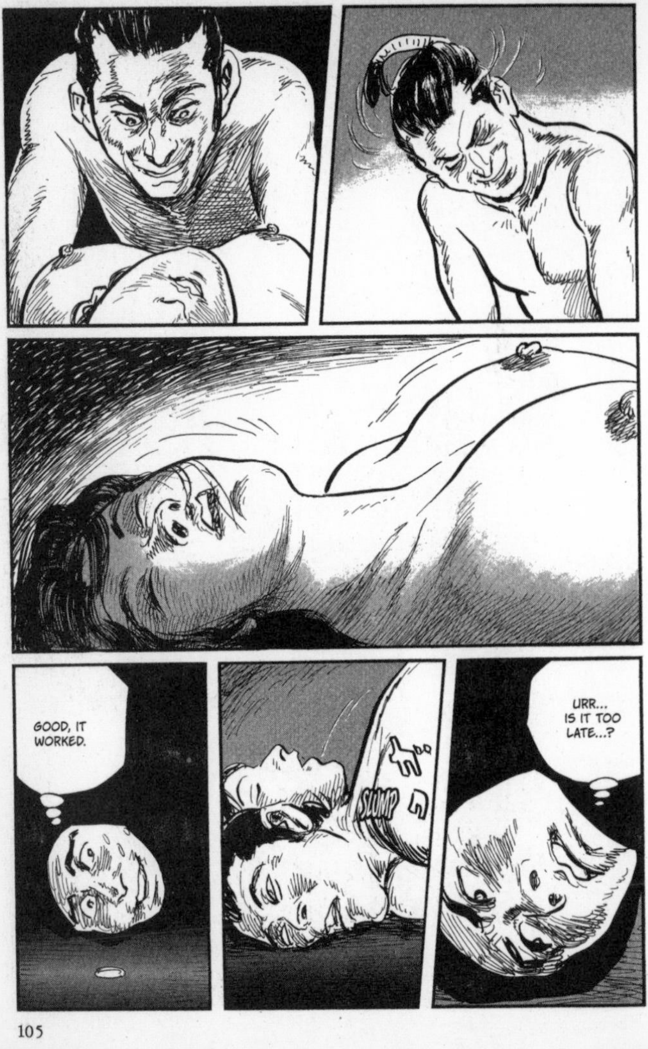
URR... IS IT TOO LATE...?
SLUMP
GOOD, IT WORKED.

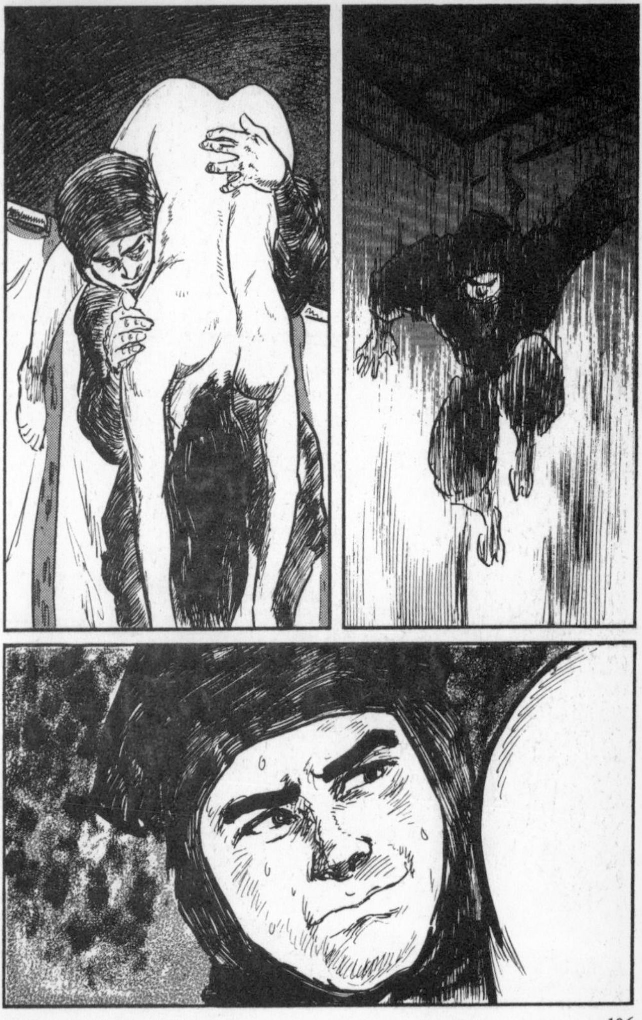

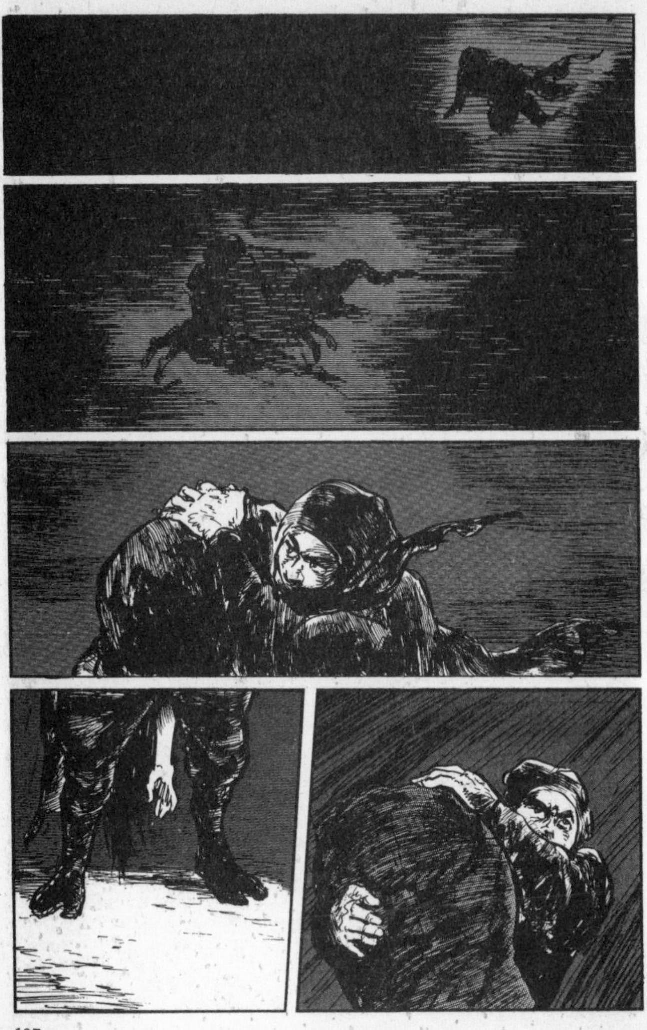

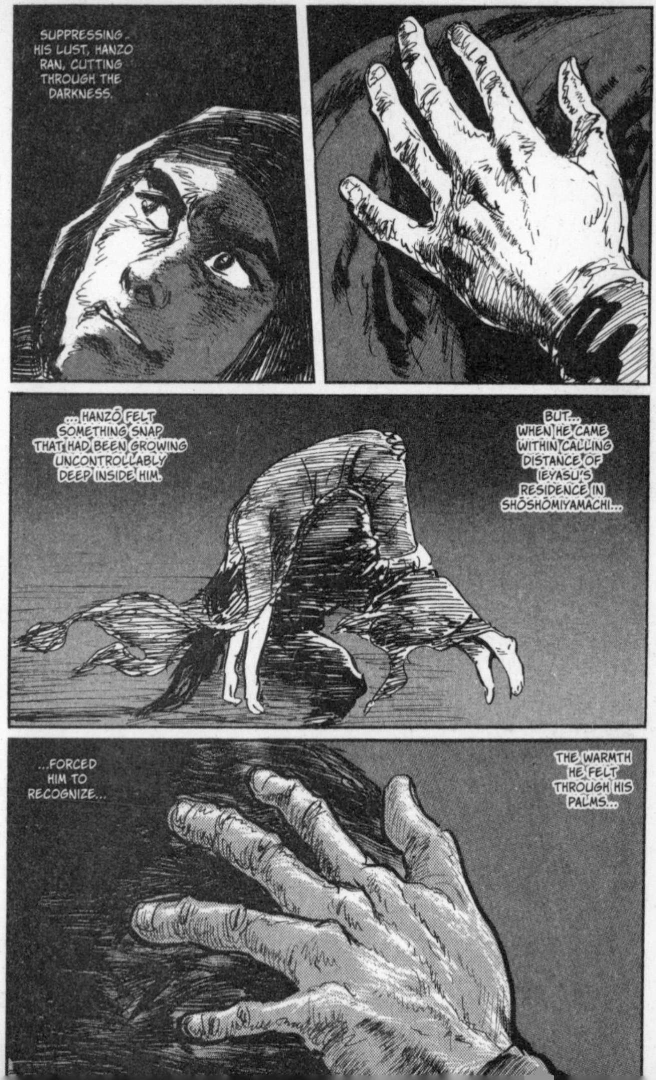
SUPPRESSING HIS LUST, HANZO RAN, CUTTING THROUGH THE DARKNESS.
BUT... WHEN HE CAME WITHIN CALLING DISTANCE OF IEYASU'S RESIDENCE IN SHŌSHŌMIYAMACHI...
...HANZŌ FELT SOMETHING SNAP THAT HAD BEEN GROWING UNCONTROLLABLY DEEP INSIDE HIM.
THE WARMTH HE FELT THROUGH HIS PALMS...
...FORCED HIM TO RECOGNIZE...

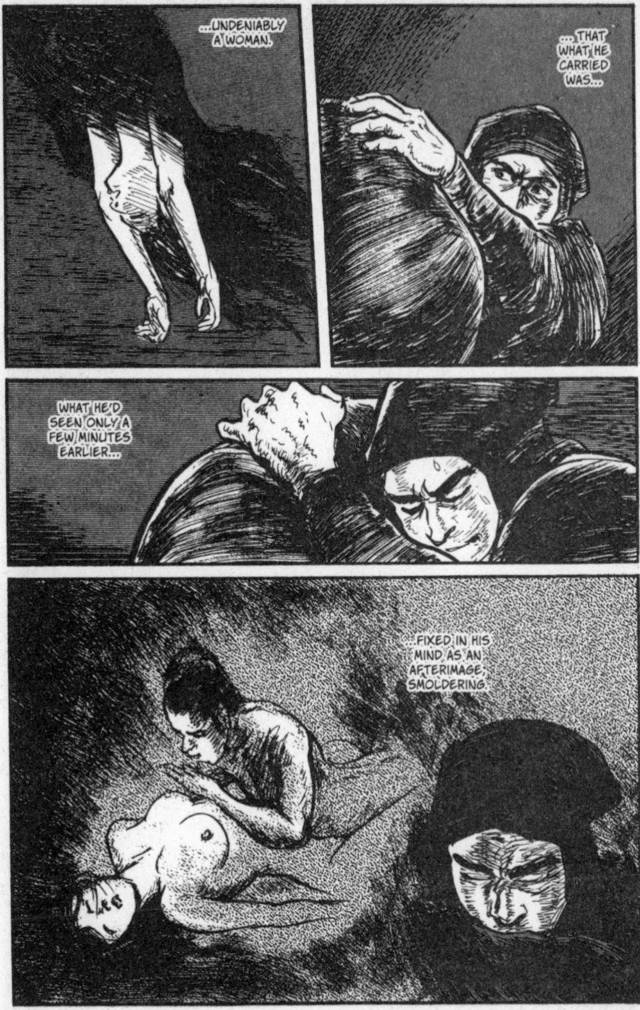
...THAT WHAT HE CARRIED WAS...
...UNDENIABLY A WOMAN.
WHAT HE'D SEEN ONLY A FEW MINUTES EARLIER...
...FIXED IN HIS MIND AS AN AFTERIMAGE, SMOLDERING.

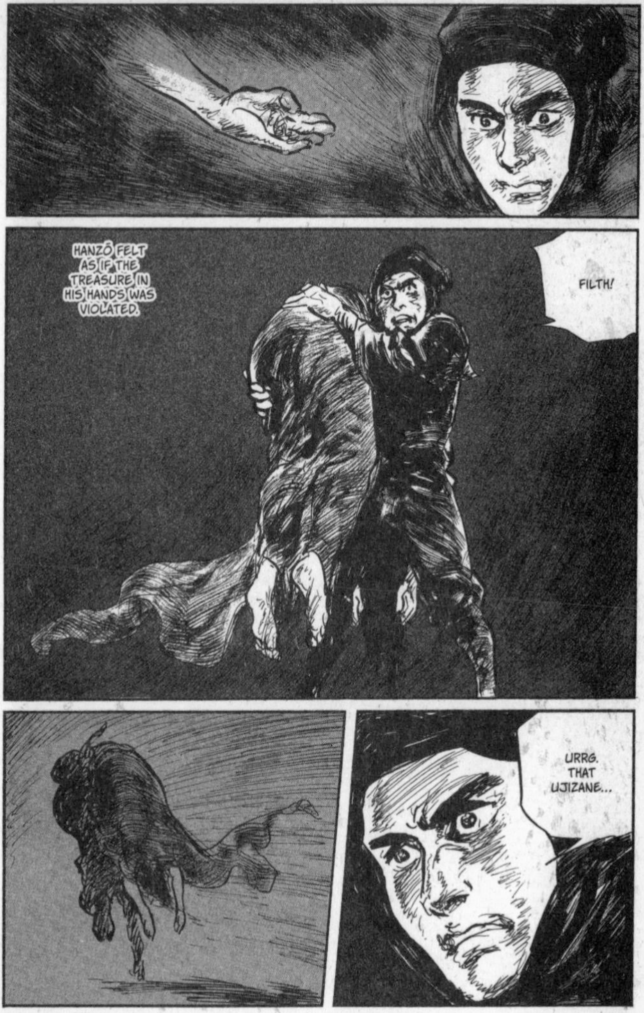
FILTH!
HANZŌ FELT AS IF THE TREASURE IN HIS HANDS WAS VIOLATED.
URRG. THAT UJIZANE...

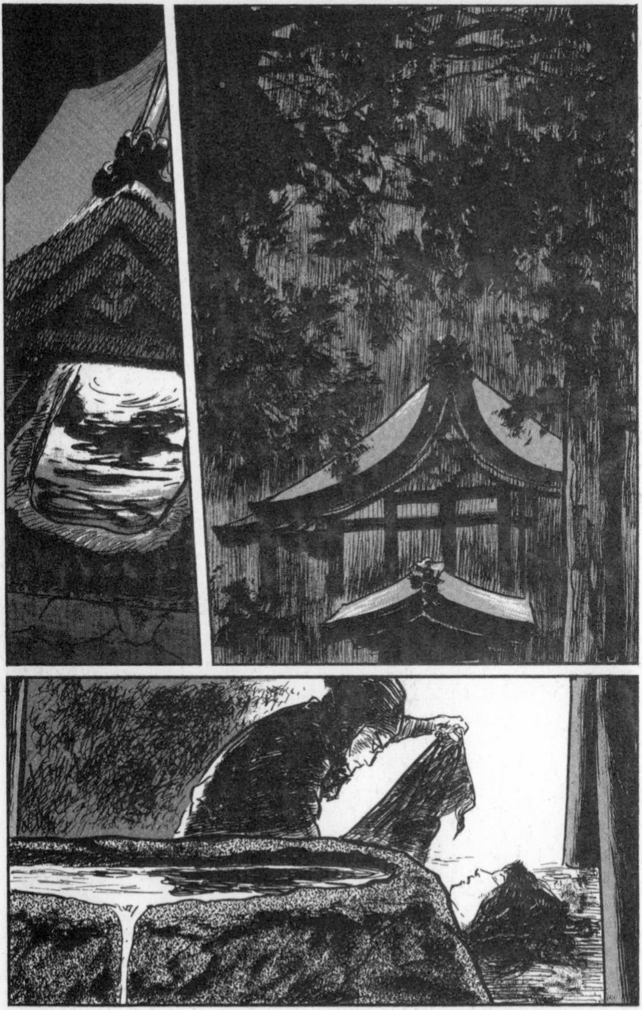

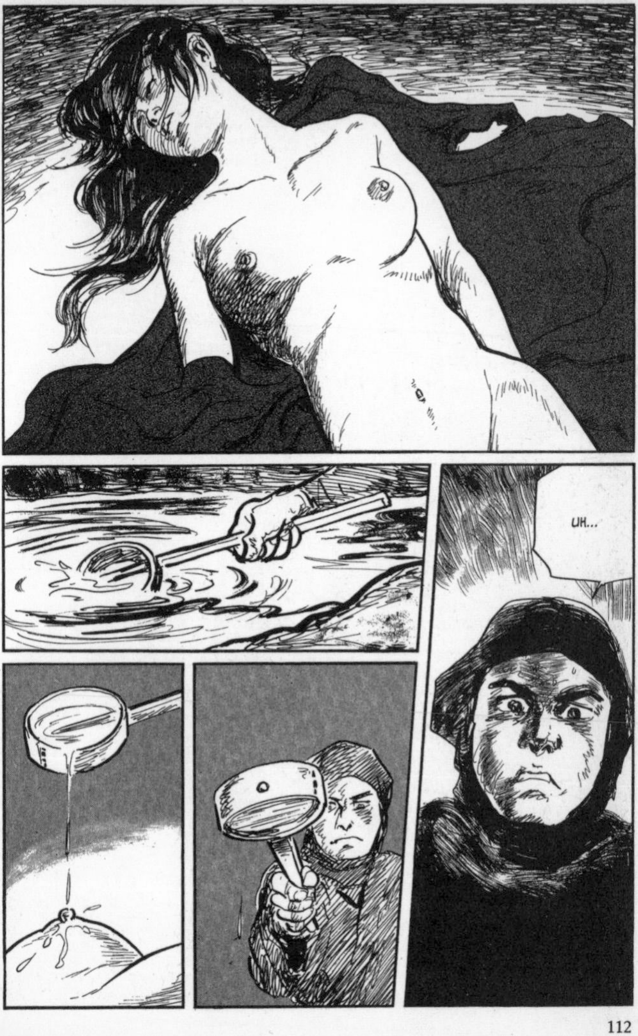
UH...

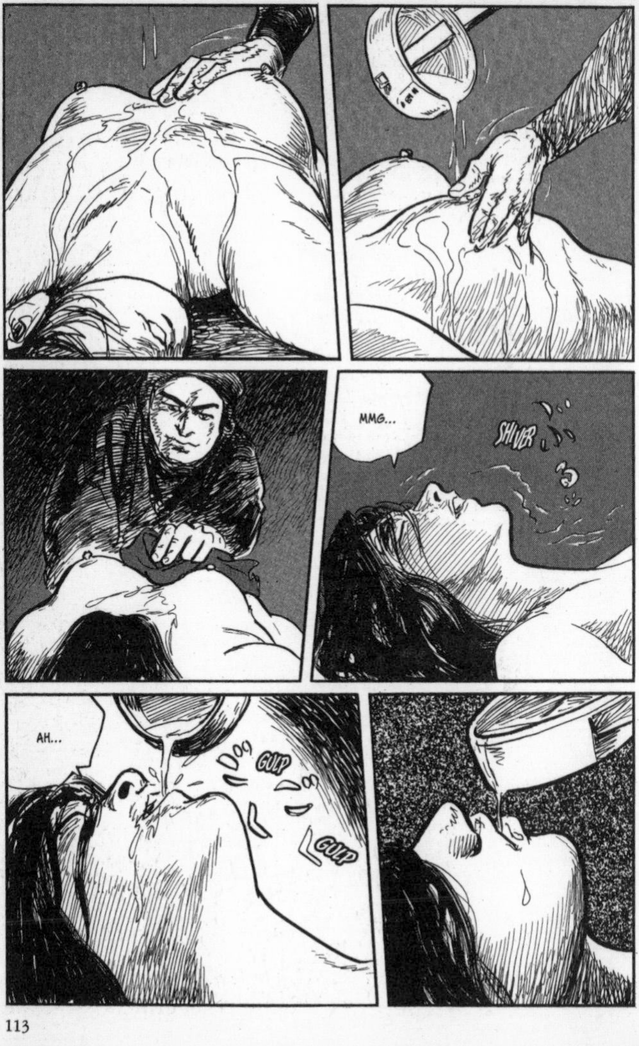
MMG...
SHIVER
AH...
GULP
GULP

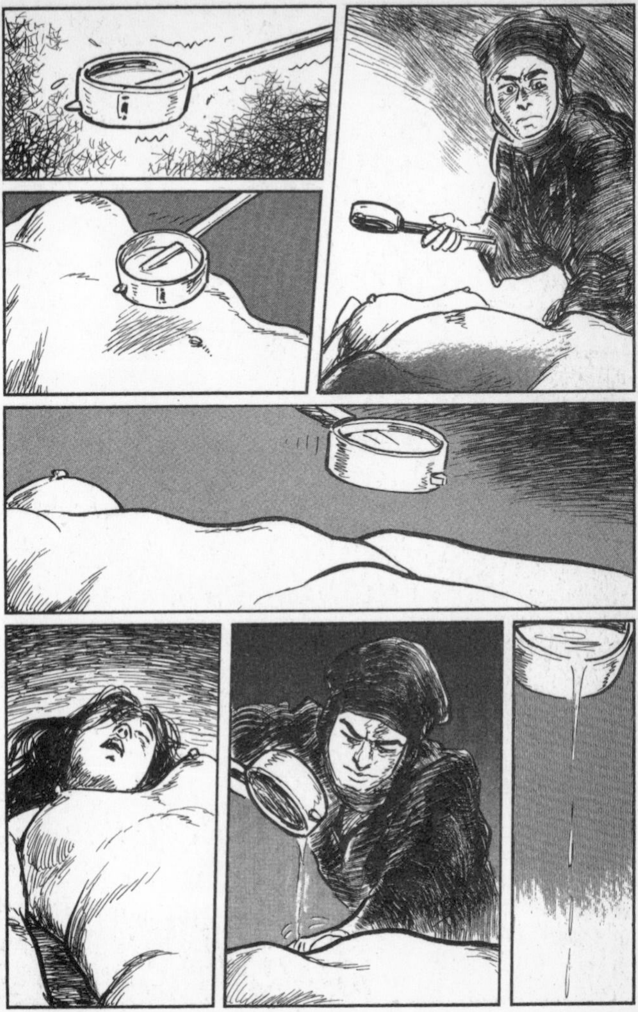

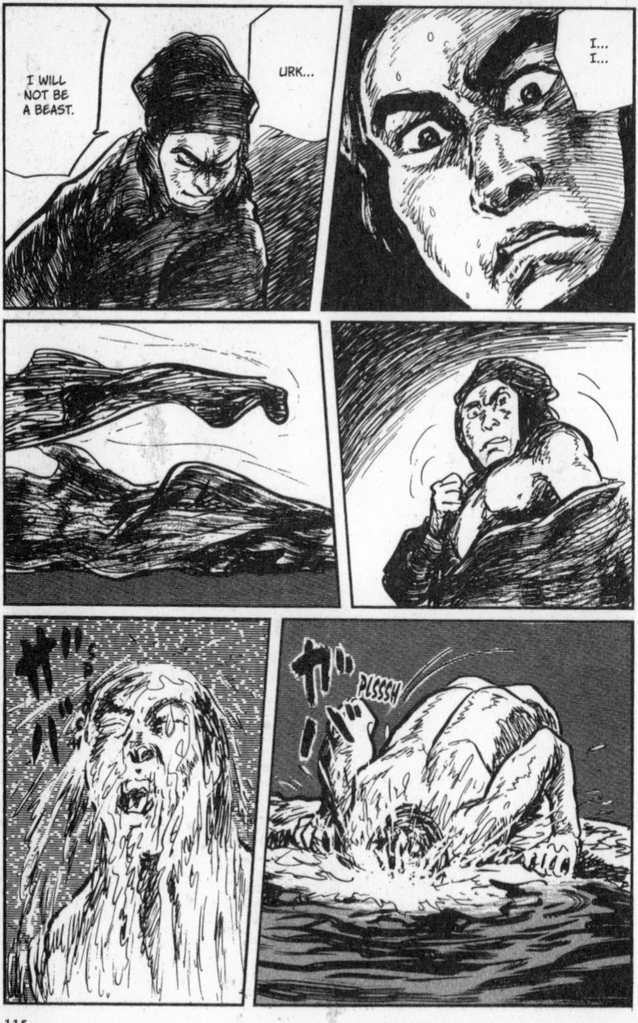

I...
I...
URK...
I WILL NOT BE A BEAST.
PLSSSH

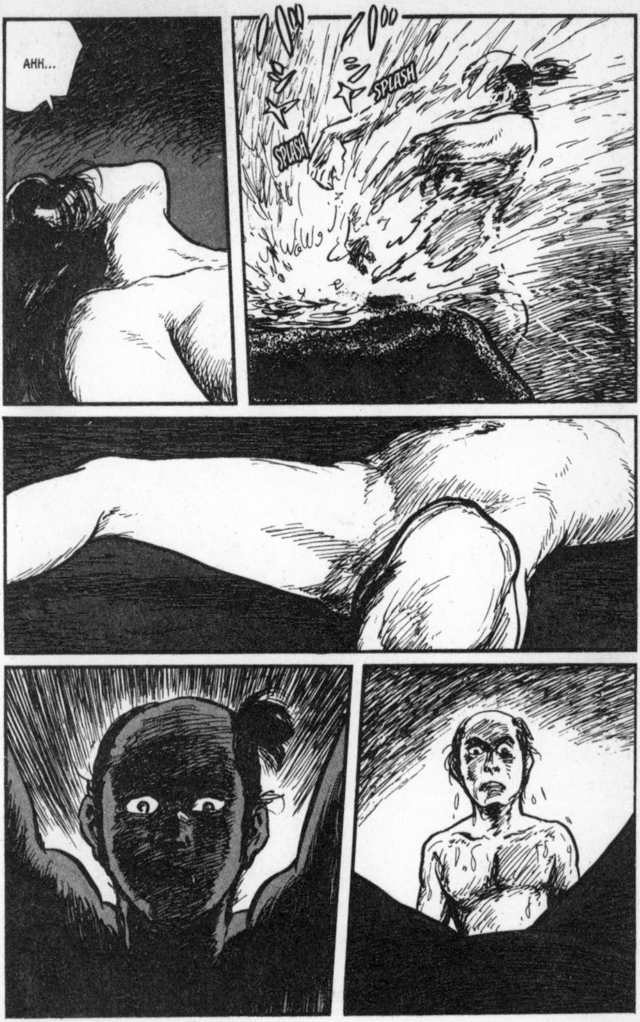
SPLASH
SPLASH
AHH...

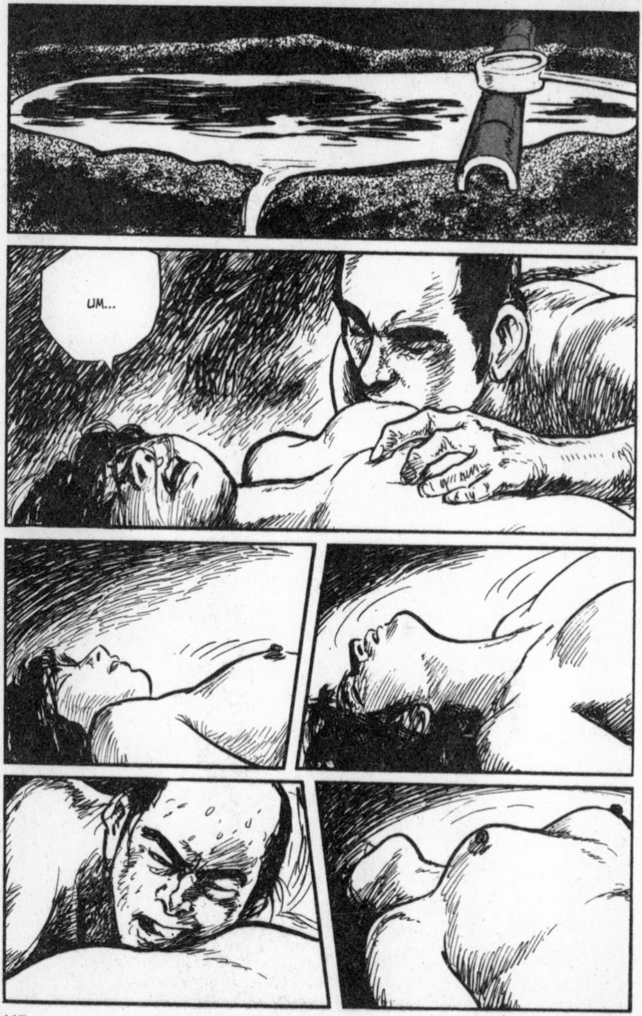
UM...

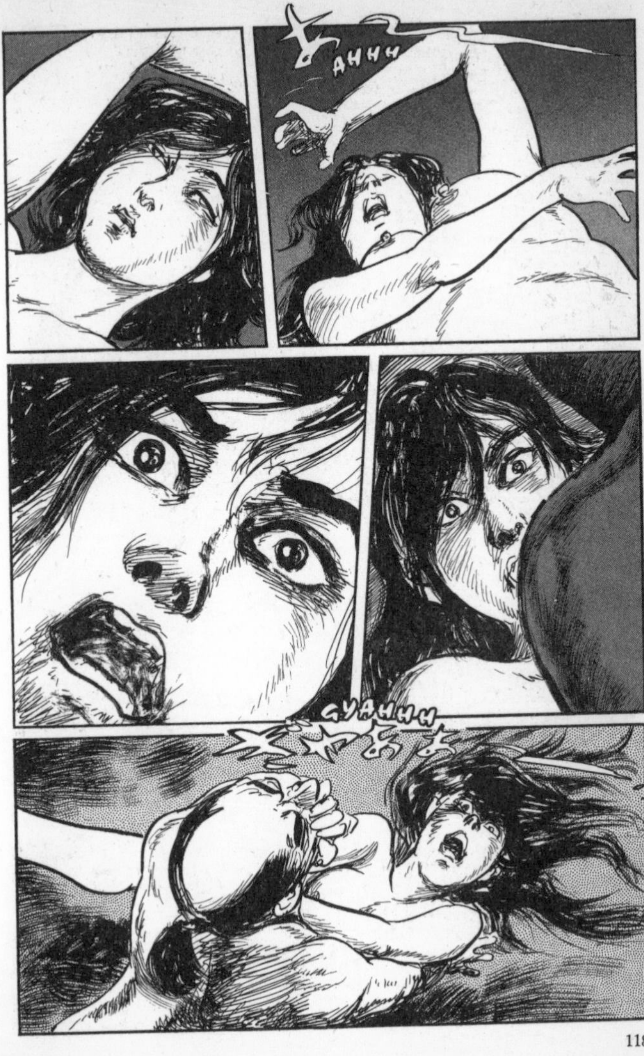
AHHH
GYAHHH

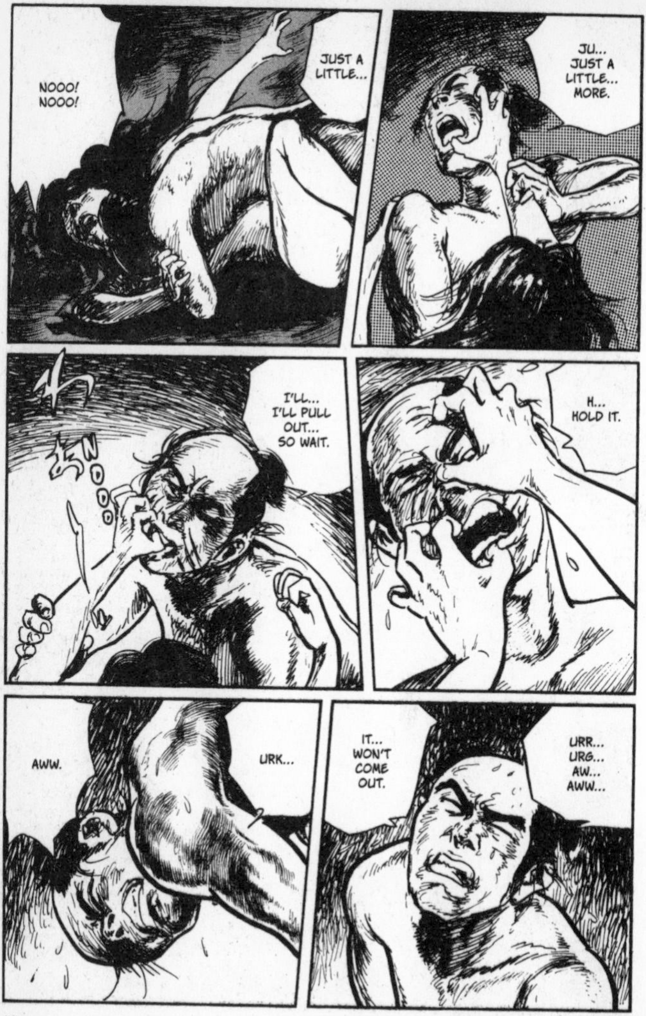
JU... JUST A LITTLE... MORE.
JUST A LITTLE...
NOOO! NOOO!
H... HOLD IT.
I'LL... I'LL PULL OUT... SO WAIT.
NDDD
URR... URG... AW... AWW...
IT... WON'T COME OUT.
URK...
AWW.

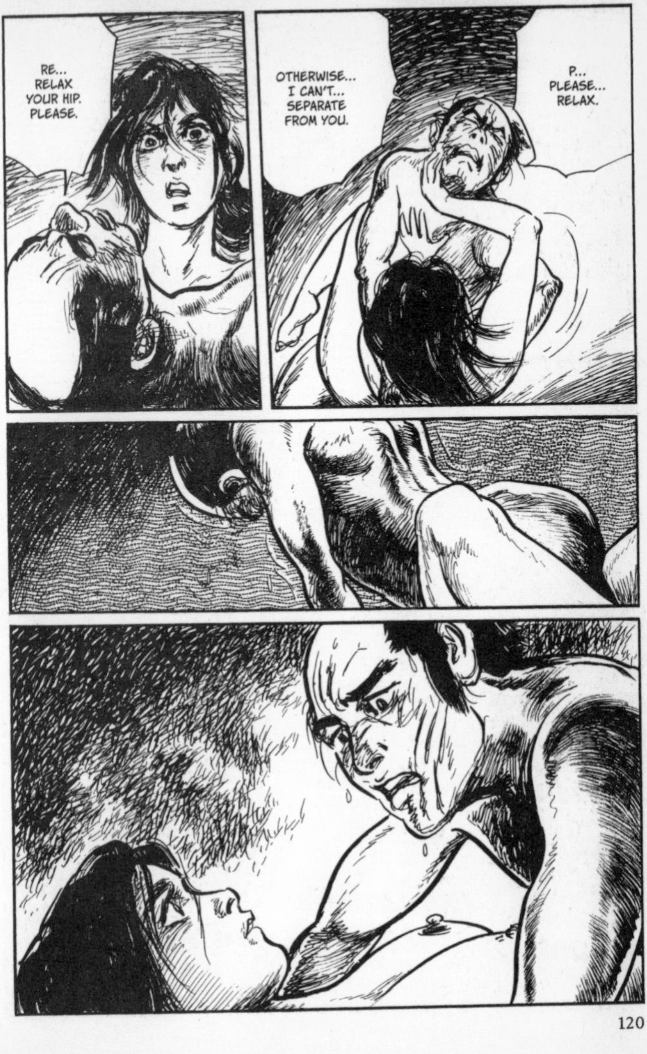
P... PLEASE... RELAX.
OTHERWISE... I CAN'T... SEPARATE FROM YOU.
RE... RELAX YOUR HIP. PLEASE.

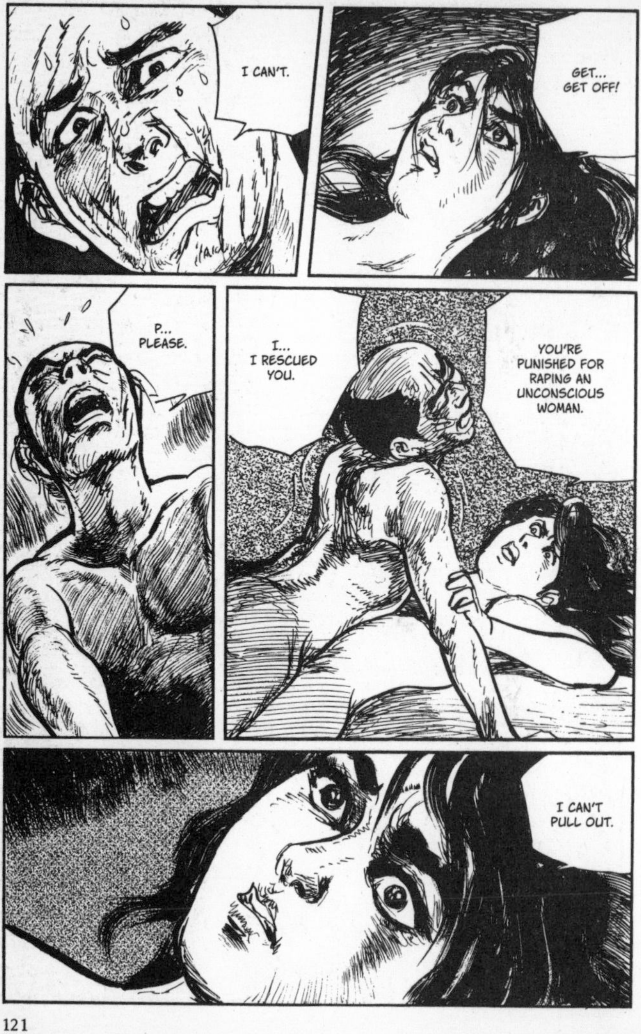
GET... GET OFF!
I CAN'T.
YOU'RE PUNISHED FOR RAPING AN UNCONSCIOUS WOMAN.
I... I RESCUED YOU.
P... PLEASE.
I CAN'T PULL OUT.

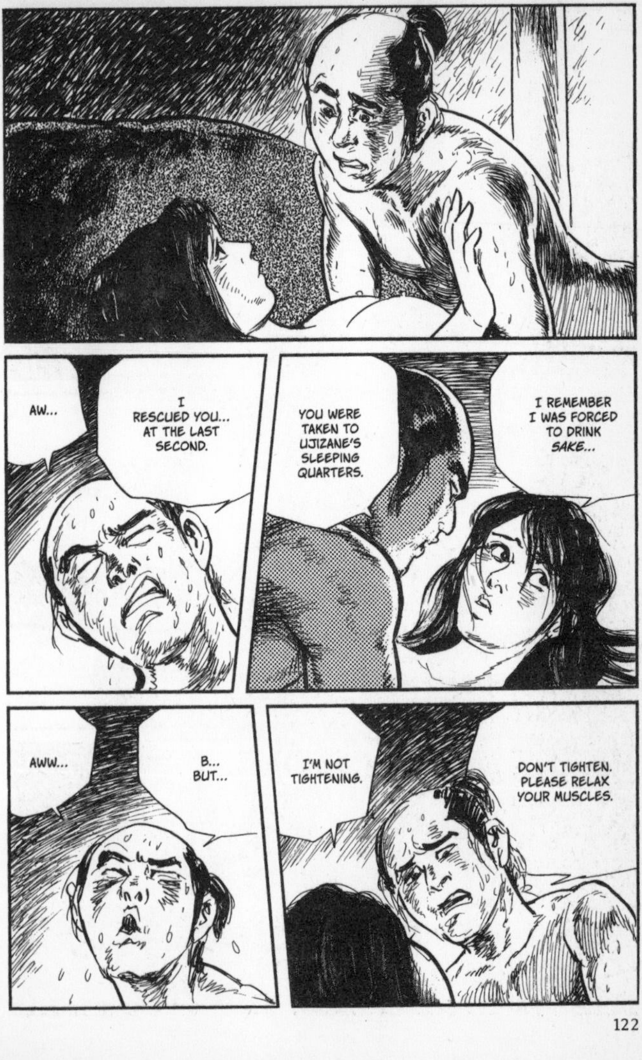
I REMEMBER I WAS FORCED TO DRINK *SAKE*...
YOU WERE TAKEN TO UJIZANE'S SLEEPING QUARTERS.
I RESCUED YOU... AT THE LAST SECOND.
AW...
DON'T TIGHTEN. PLEASE RELAX YOUR MUSCLES.
I'M NOT TIGHTENING.
B... BUT...
AWW...

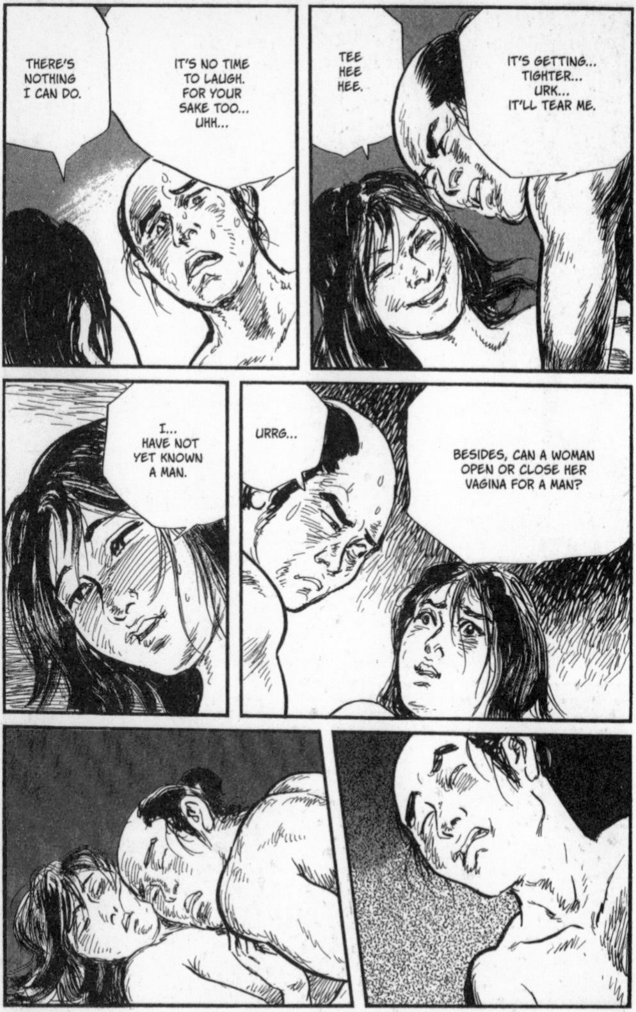
IT'S GETTING... TIGHTER... URK... IT'LL TEAR ME.
TEE HEE HEE.
IT'S NO TIME TO LAUGH. FOR YOUR SAKE TOO... UHH...
THERE'S NOTHING I CAN DO.
BESIDES, CAN A WOMAN OPEN OR CLOSE HER VAGINA FOR A MAN?
URRG...
I... HAVE NOT YET KNOWN A MAN.

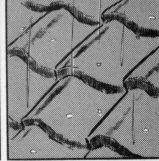

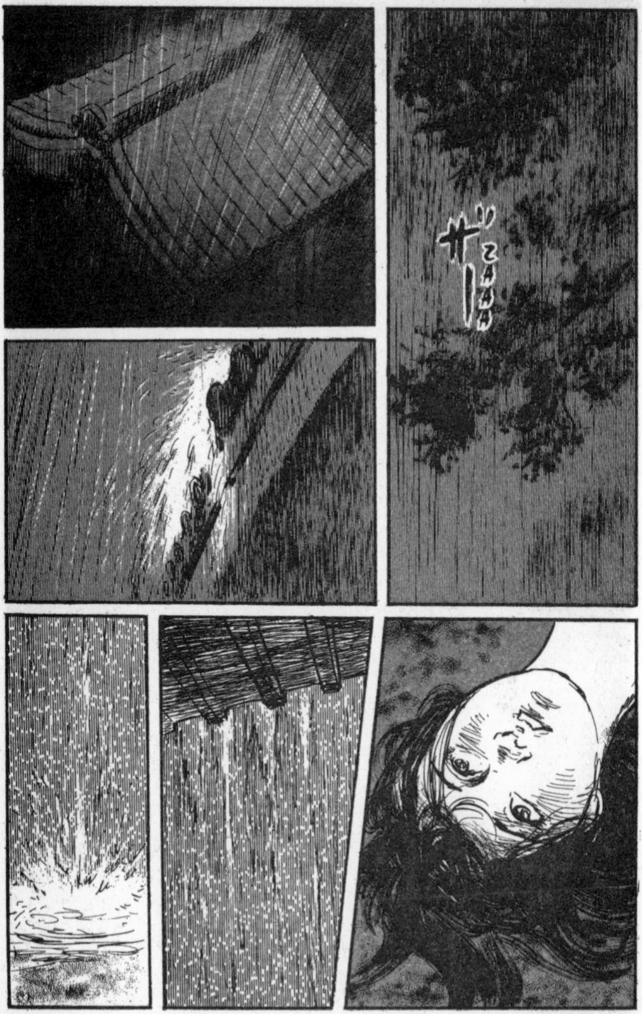
ザー
ZAAA

I'M
COLD...

YEAH.

YOU ARE
COLD.

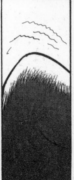

IT'S...
RAINING.

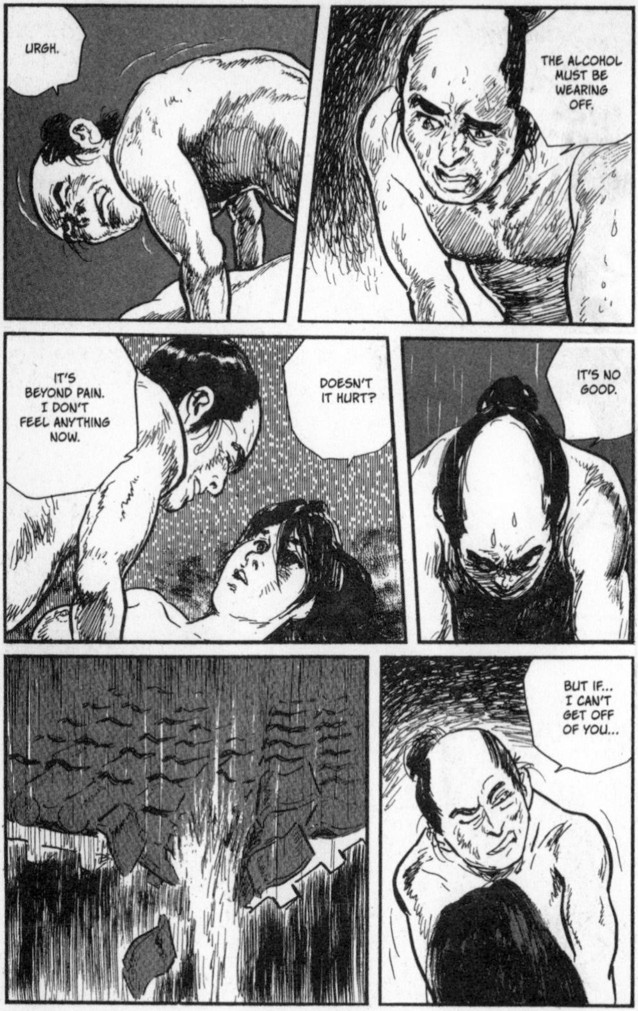
THE ALCOHOL MUST BE WEARING OFF.
URGH.
IT'S NO GOOD.
DOESN'T IT HURT?
IT'S BEYOND PAIN. I DON'T FEEL ANYTHING NOW.
BUT IF... I CAN'T GET OFF OF YOU...

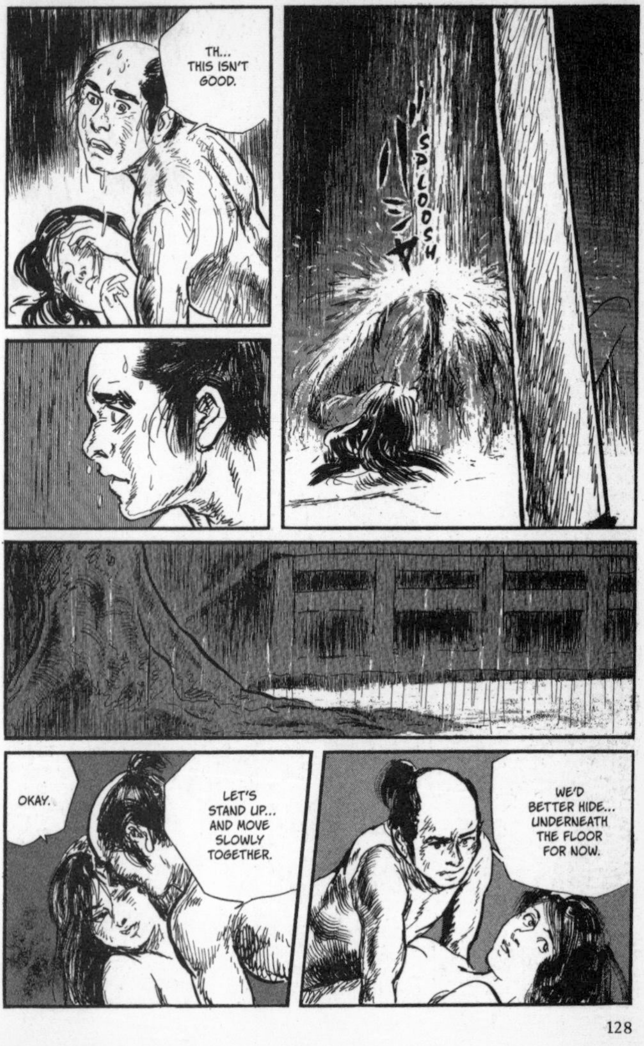
SPLOOSH
TH... THIS ISN'T GOOD.
WE'D BETTER HIDE... UNDERNEATH THE FLOOR FOR NOW.
LET'S STAND UP... AND MOVE SLOWLY TOGETHER.
OKAY.

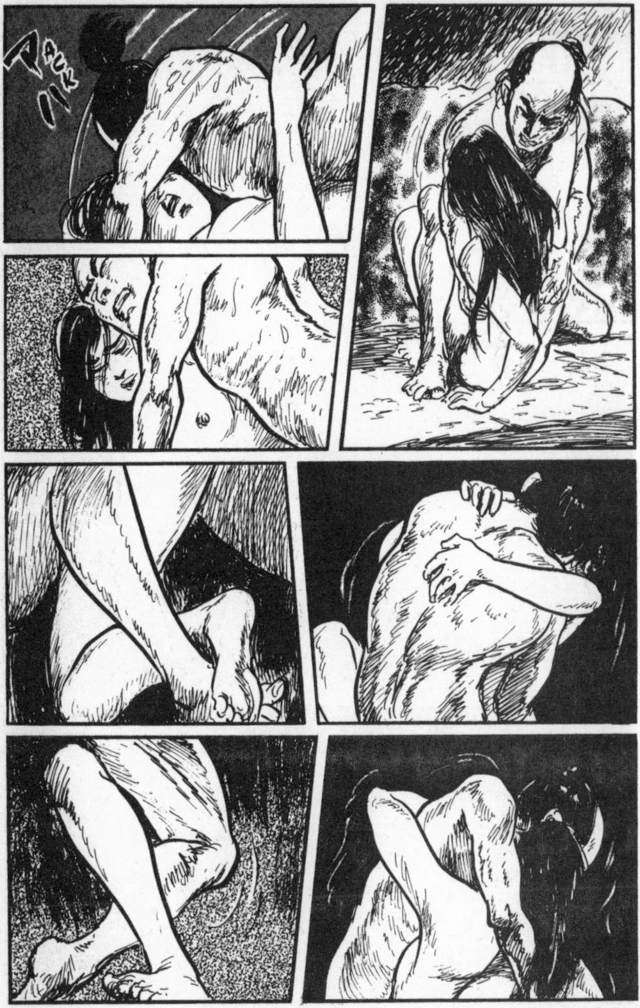
PAUK!!

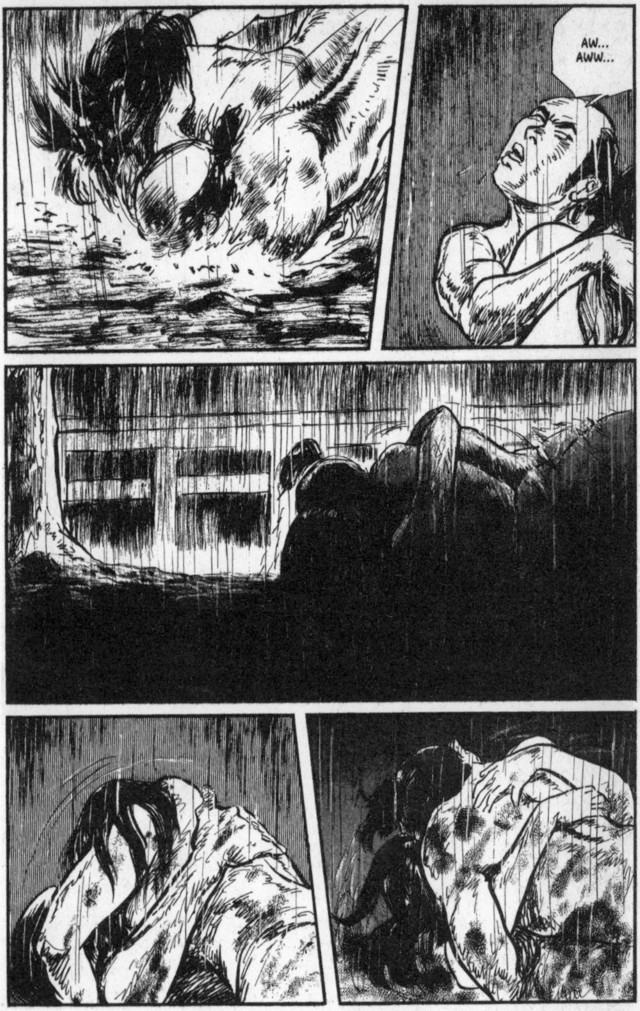
AW...
AWW...

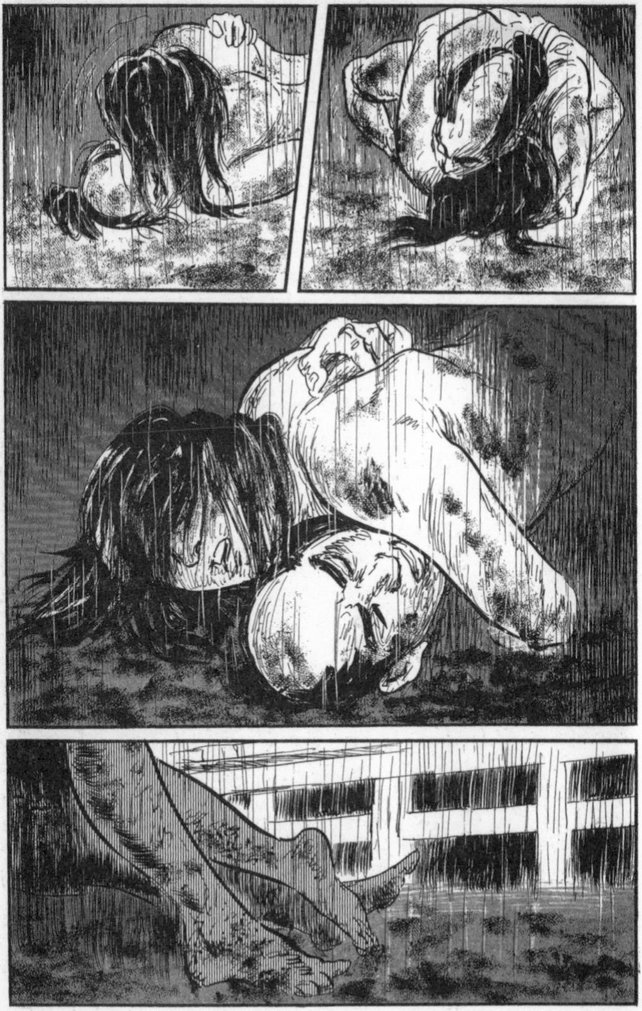

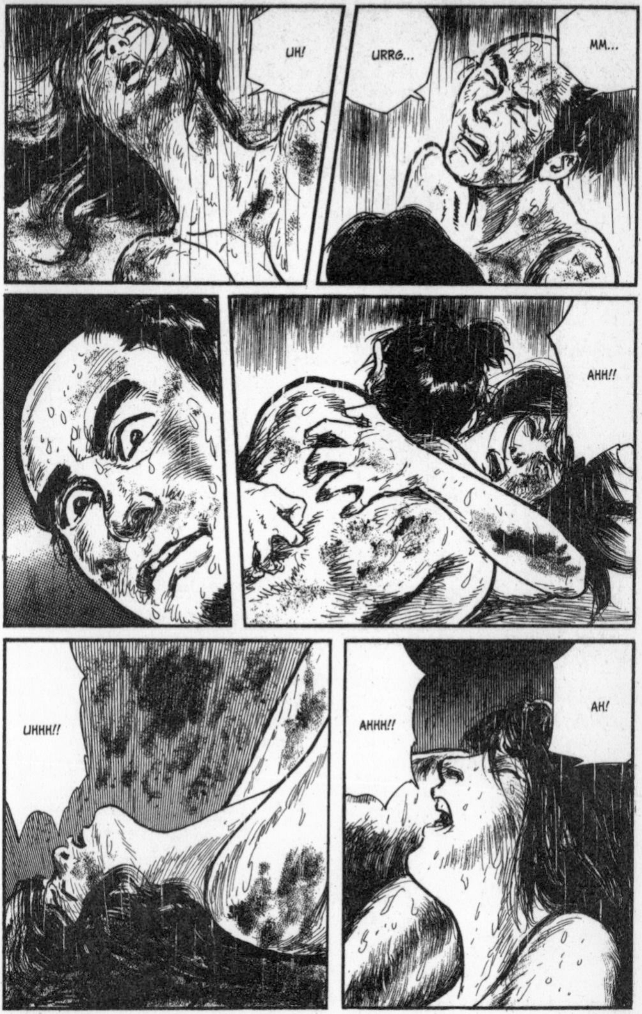
MM...
URRG...
UH!
AHH!!
AH!
AHHH!!
UHHH!!

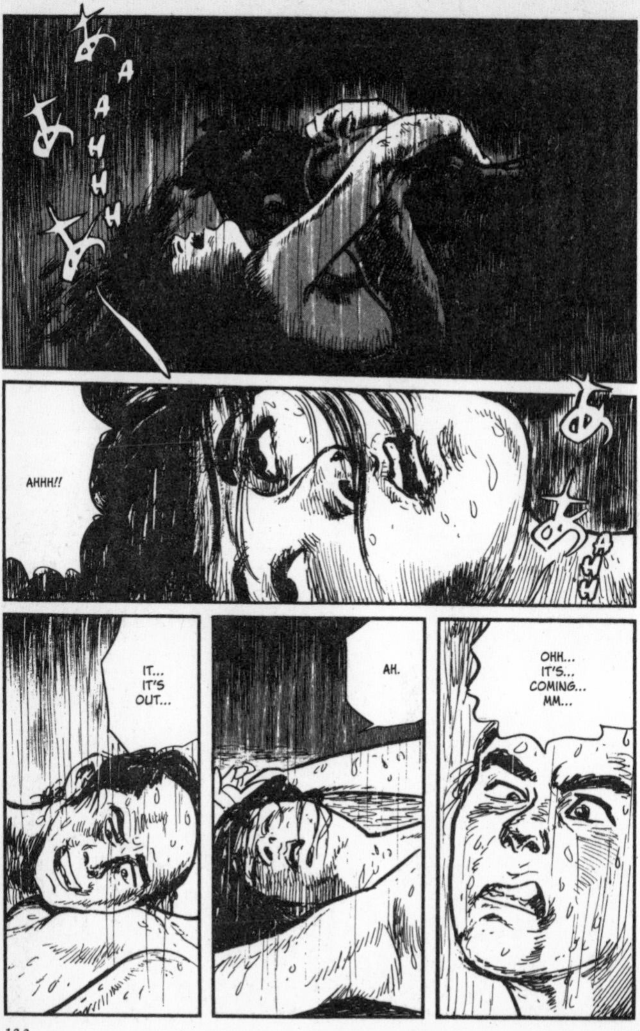
A
AHHHH
AHH
AHHH!!
OHH... IT'S... COMING... MM...
AH.
IT... IT'S OUT...

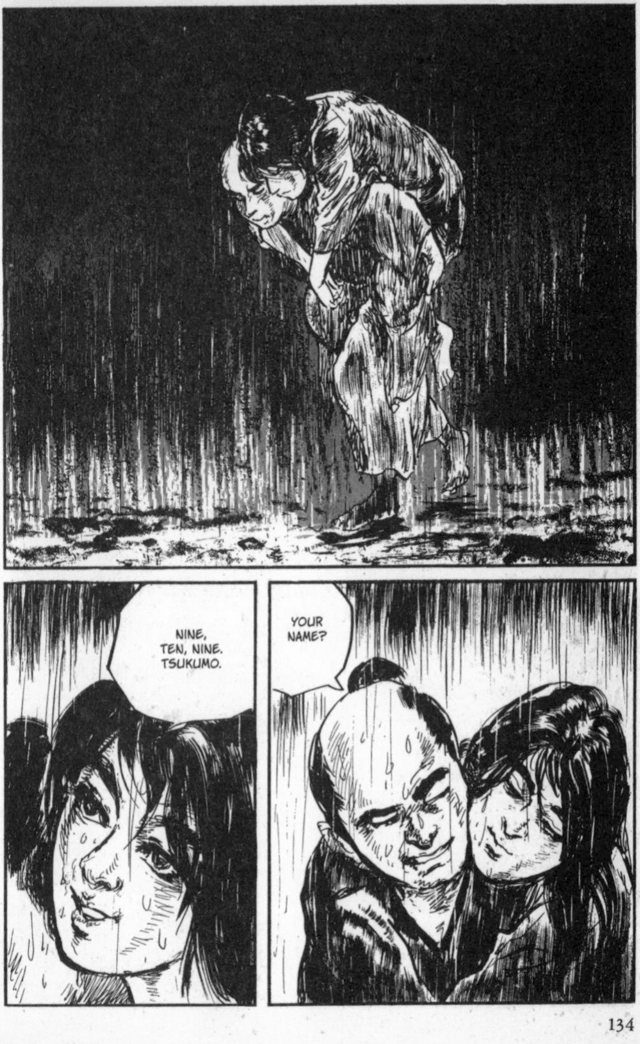
YOUR NAME?
NINE, TEN, NINE. TSUKUMO.

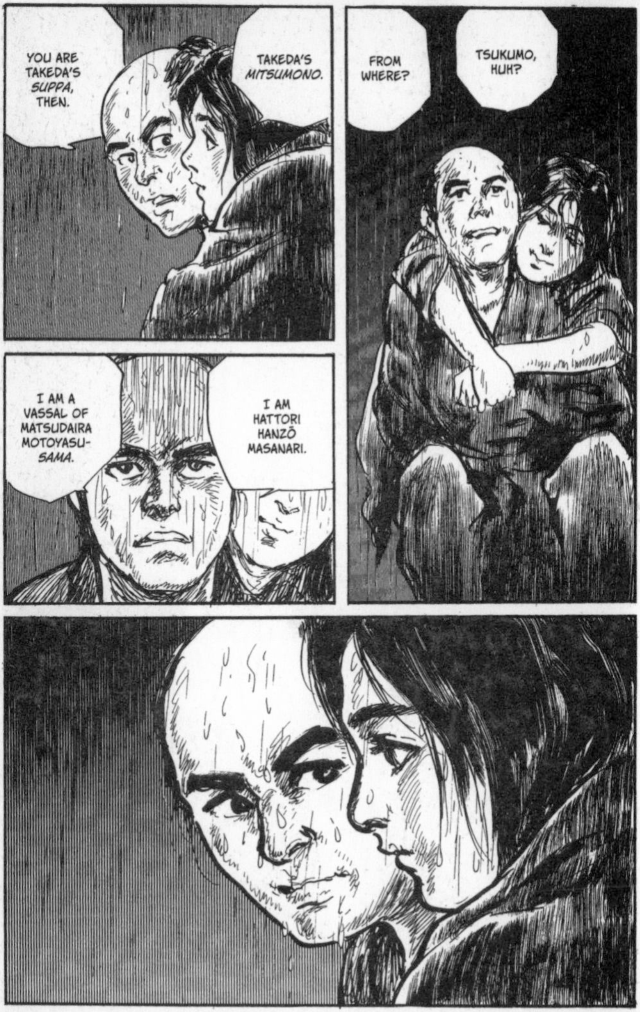
TSUKUMO, HUH?
FROM WHERE?
TAKEDA'S *MITSUMONO.*
YOU ARE TAKEDA'S *SUPPA,* THEN.
I AM HATTORI HANZŌ MASANARI.
I AM A VASSAL OF MATSUDAIRA MOTOYASU-*SAMA.*

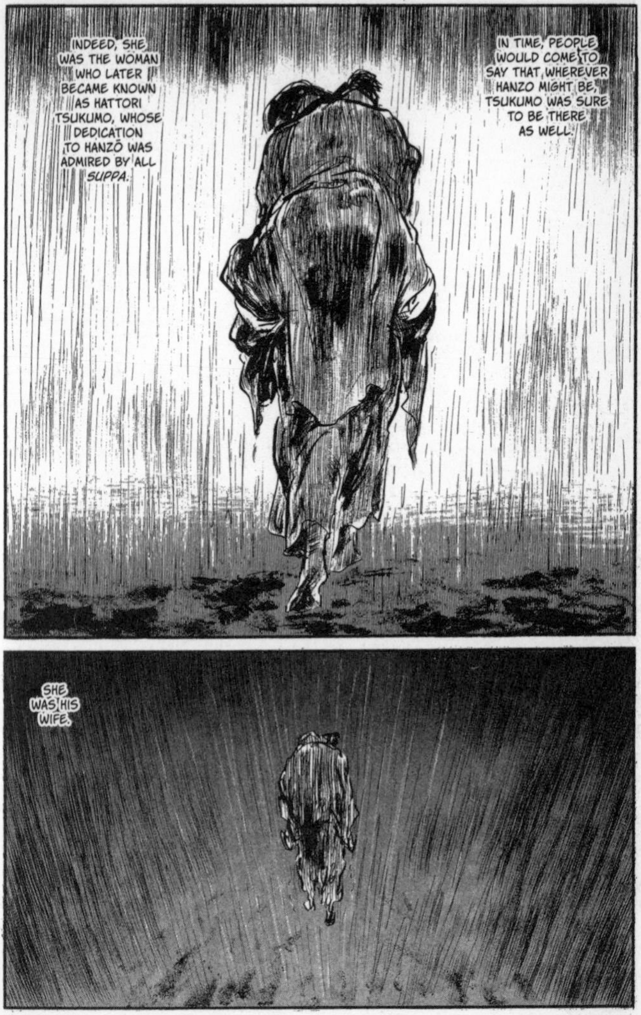
IN TIME, PEOPLE WOULD COME TO SAY THAT, WHEREVER HANZO MIGHT BE, TSUKUMO WAS SURE TO BE THERE AS WELL.
INDEED, SHE WAS THE WOMAN WHO LATER BECAME KNOWN AS HATTORI TSUKUMO, WHOSE DEDICATION TO HANZŌ WAS ADMIRED BY ALL *SUPPA*.
SHE WAS HIS WIFE.

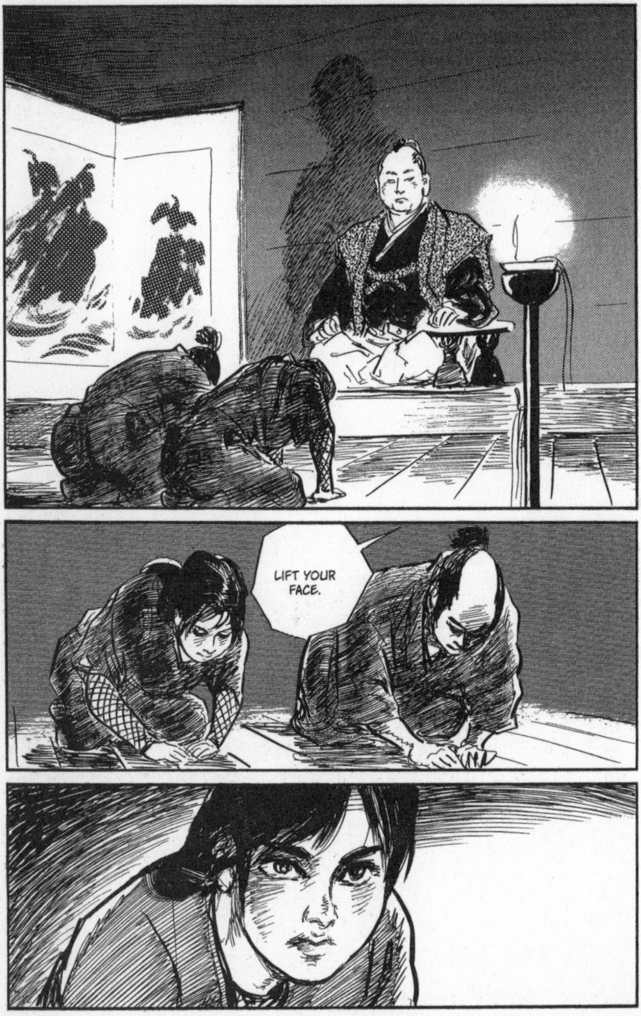
LIFT YOUR FACE.

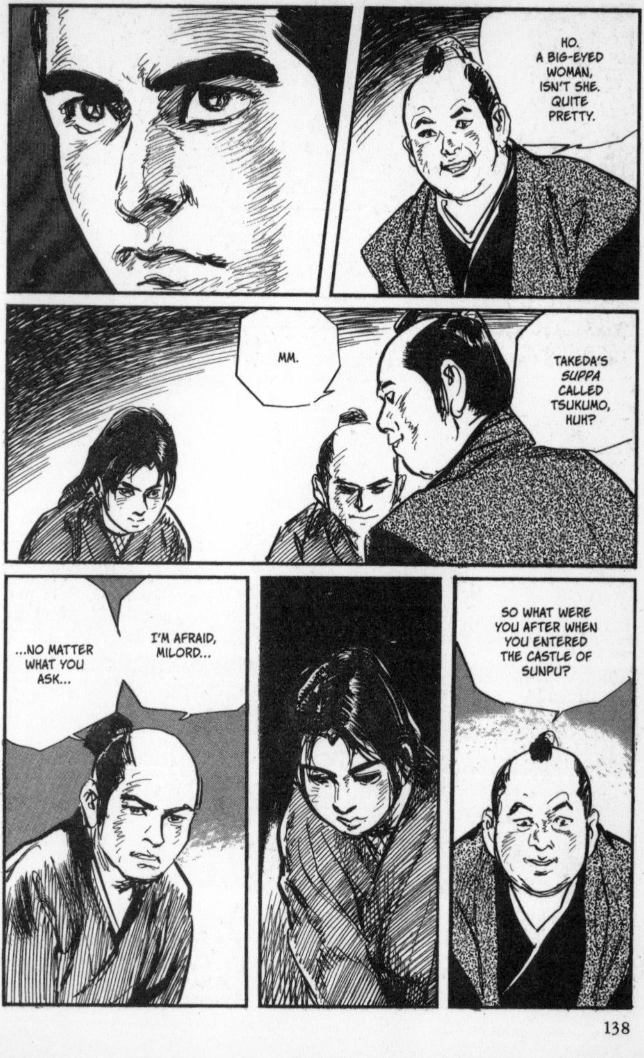
HO. A BIG-EYED WOMAN, ISN'T SHE. QUITE PRETTY.
TAKEDA'S *SUPPA* CALLED TSUKUMO, HUH?
MM.
SO WHAT WERE YOU AFTER WHEN YOU ENTERED THE CASTLE OF SUNPU?
I'M AFRAID, MILORD...
...NO MATTER WHAT YOU ASK...

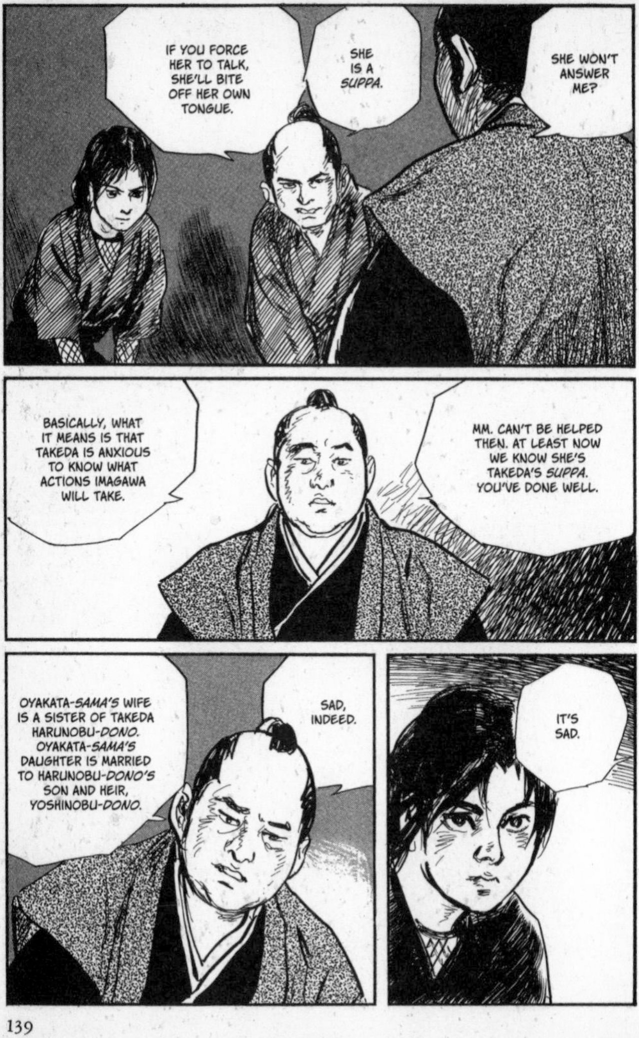
SHE WON'T ANSWER ME?
SHE IS A *SUPPA*.
IF YOU FORCE HER TO TALK, SHE'LL BITE OFF HER OWN TONGUE.
MM. CAN'T BE HELPED THEN. AT LEAST NOW WE KNOW SHE'S TAKEDA'S *SUPPA*. YOU'VE DONE WELL.
BASICALLY, WHAT IT MEANS IS THAT TAKEDA IS ANXIOUS TO KNOW WHAT ACTIONS IMAGAWA WILL TAKE.
IT'S SAD.
SAD, INDEED.
OYAKATA-*SAMA'S* WIFE IS A SISTER OF TAKEDA HARUNOBU-*DONO*. OYAKATA-*SAMA'S* DAUGHTER IS MARRIED TO HARUNOBU-*DONO'S* SON AND HEIR, YOSHINOBU-*DONO*.

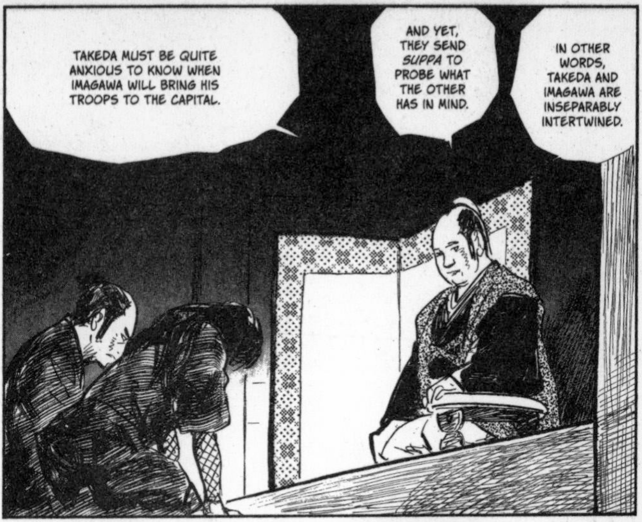
IN OTHER WORDS, TAKEDA AND IMAGAWA ARE INSEPARABLY INTERTWINED.
AND YET, THEY SEND *SUPPA* TO PROBE WHAT THE OTHER HAS IN MIND.
TAKEDA MUST BE QUITE ANXIOUS TO KNOW WHEN IMAGAWA WILL BRING HIS TROOPS TO THE CAPITAL.

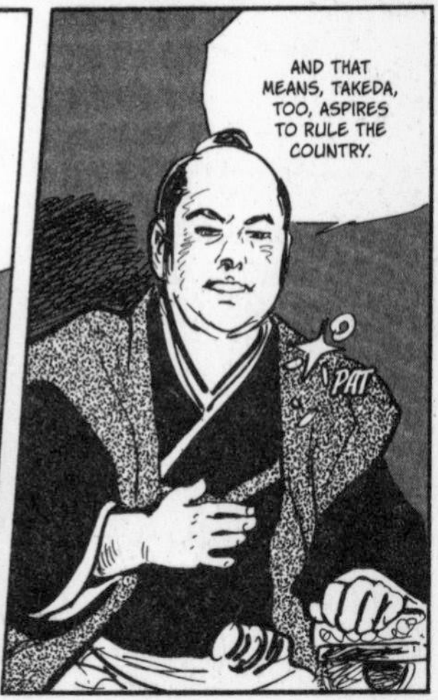
AND THAT MEANS, TAKEDA, TOO, ASPIRES TO RULE THE COUNTRY.
PAT

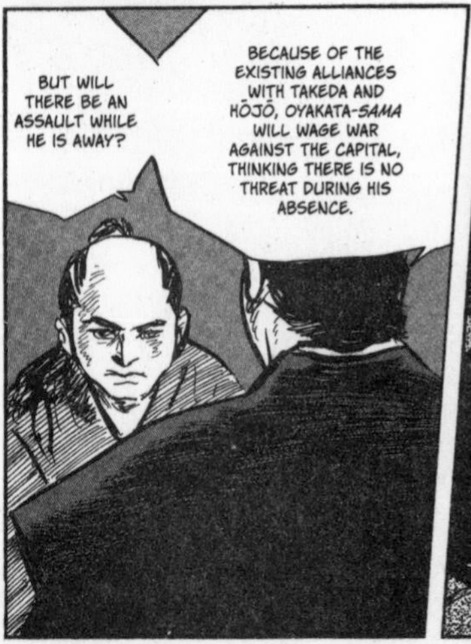
BECAUSE OF THE EXISTING ALLIANCES WITH TAKEDA AND HŌJŌ, OYAKATA-*SAMA* WILL WAGE WAR AGAINST THE CAPITAL, THINKING THERE IS NO THREAT DURING HIS ABSENCE.
BUT WILL THERE BE AN ASSAULT WHILE HE IS AWAY?

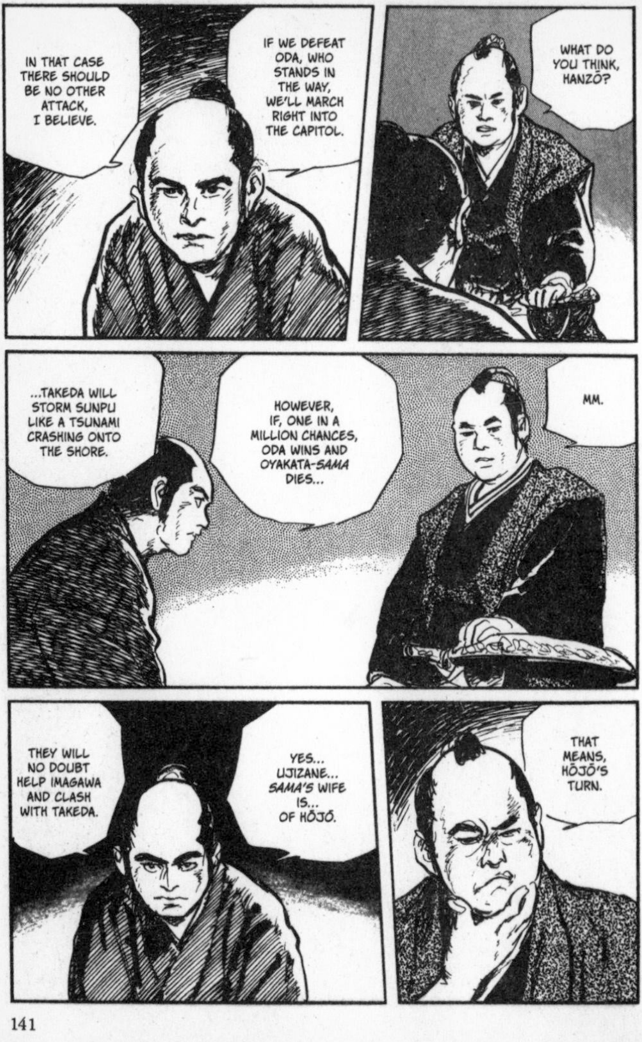
WHAT DO YOU THINK, HANZŌ?
IF WE DEFEAT ODA, WHO STANDS IN THE WAY, WE'LL MARCH RIGHT INTO THE CAPITOL.
IN THAT CASE THERE SHOULD BE NO OTHER ATTACK, I BELIEVE.
MM.
HOWEVER, IF, ONE IN A MILLION CHANCES, ODA WINS AND OYAKATA-*SAMA* DIES...
...TAKEDA WILL STORM SUNPU LIKE A TSUNAMI CRASHING ONTO THE SHORE.
THAT MEANS, HŌJŌ'S TURN.
YES... UJIZANE... *SAMA'S* WIFE IS... OF HŌJŌ.
THEY WILL NO DOUBT HELP IMAGAWA AND CLASH WITH TAKEDA.

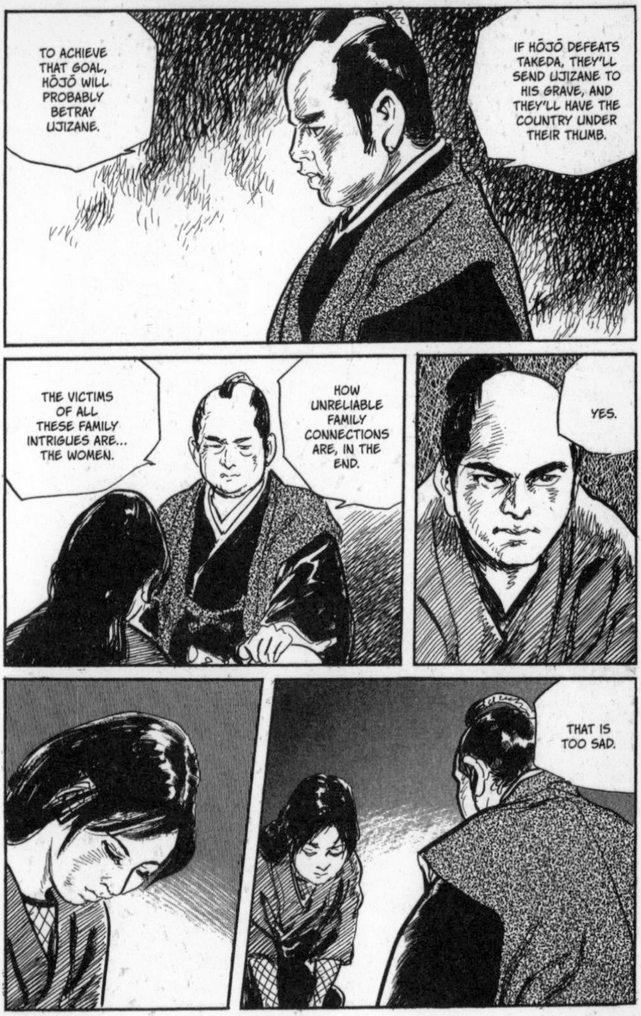
IF HŌJŌ DEFEATS TAKEDA, THEY'LL SEND UJIZANE TO HIS GRAVE, AND THEY'LL HAVE THE COUNTRY UNDER THEIR THUMB.
TO ACHIEVE THAT GOAL, HŌJŌ WILL PROBABLY BETRAY UJIZANE.
YES.
HOW UNRELIABLE FAMILY CONNECTIONS ARE, IN THE END.
THE VICTIMS OF ALL THESE FAMILY INTRIGUES ARE... THE WOMEN.
THAT IS TOO SAD.

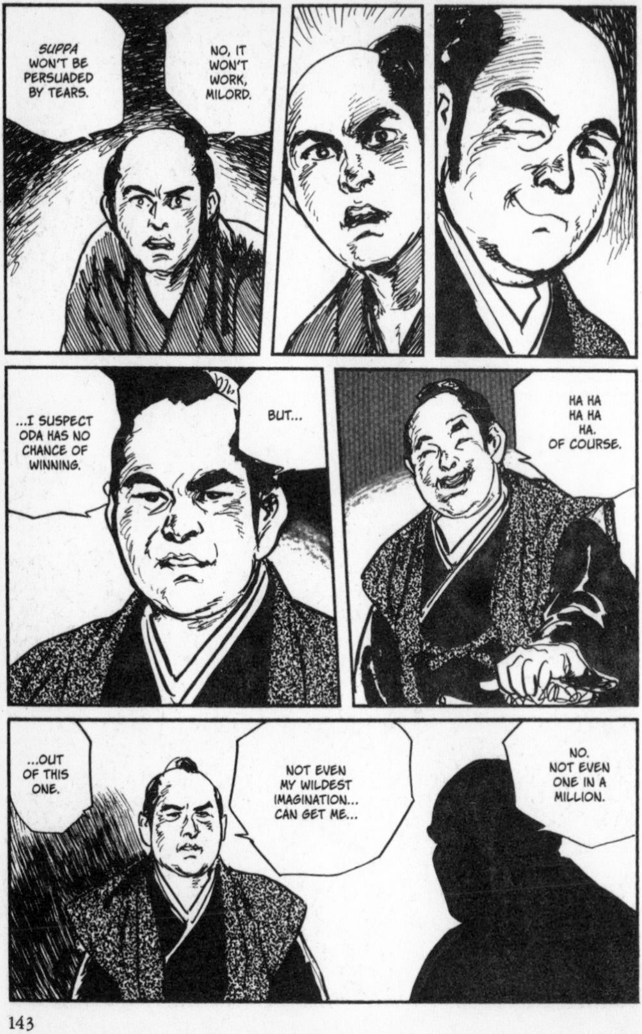
NO, IT WON'T WORK, MILORD.
SUPPA WON'T BE PERSUADED BY TEARS.
HA HA HA HA HA. OF COURSE.
BUT...
...I SUSPECT ODA HAS NO CHANCE OF WINNING.
NO. NOT EVEN ONE IN A MILLION.
NOT EVEN MY WILDEST IMAGINATION... CAN GET ME...
...OUT OF THIS ONE.

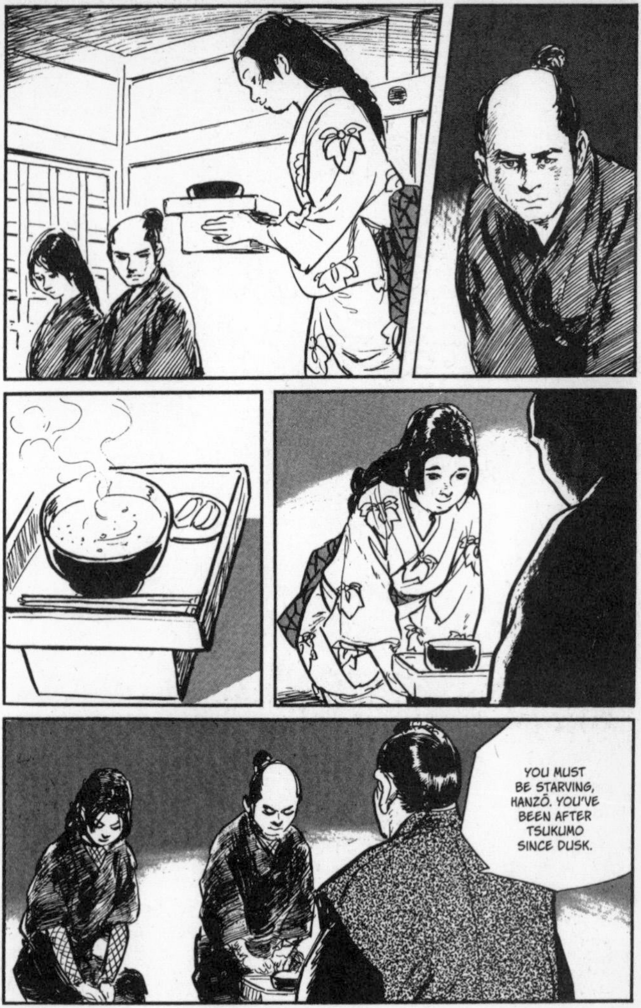
YOU MUST BE STARVING, HANZŌ. YOU'VE BEEN AFTER TSUKUMO SINCE DUSK.

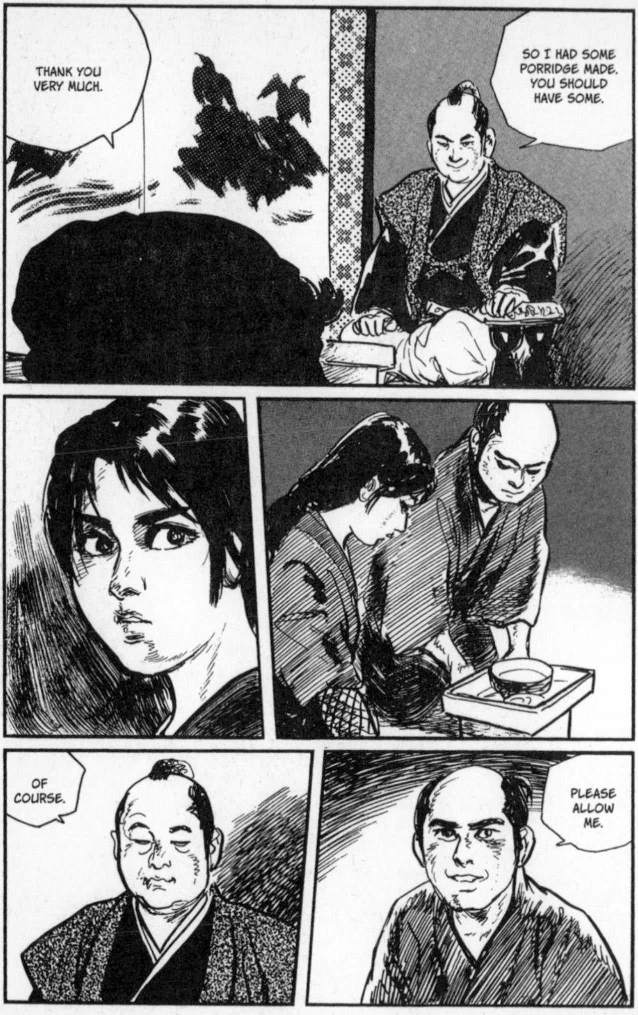
SO I HAD SOME PORRIDGE MADE. YOU SHOULD HAVE SOME.
THANK YOU VERY MUCH.
PLEASE ALLOW ME.
OF COURSE.

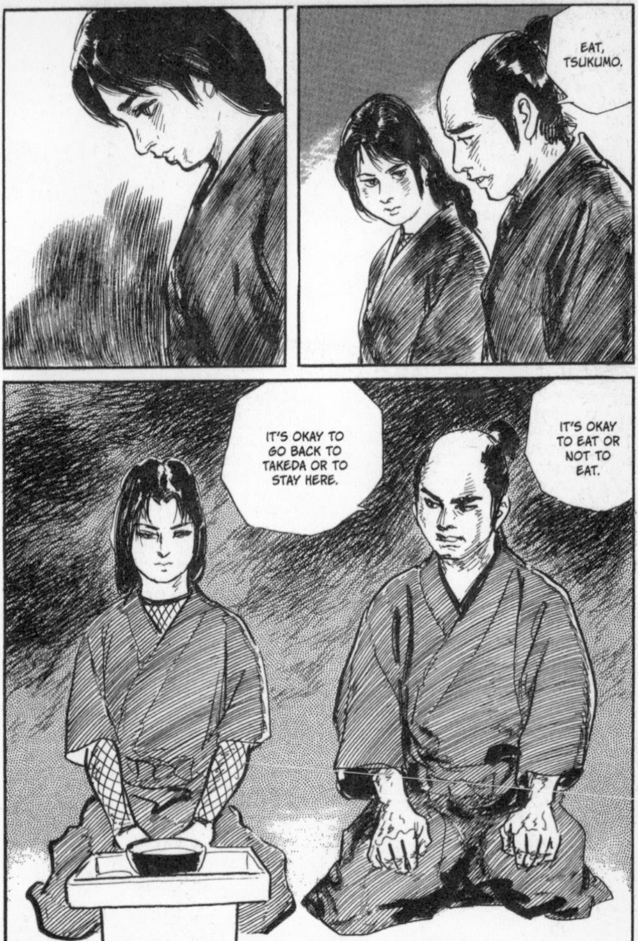
EAT, TSUKUMO.
IT'S OKAY TO EAT OR NOT TO EAT.
IT'S OKAY TO GO BACK TO TAKEDA OR TO STAY HERE.

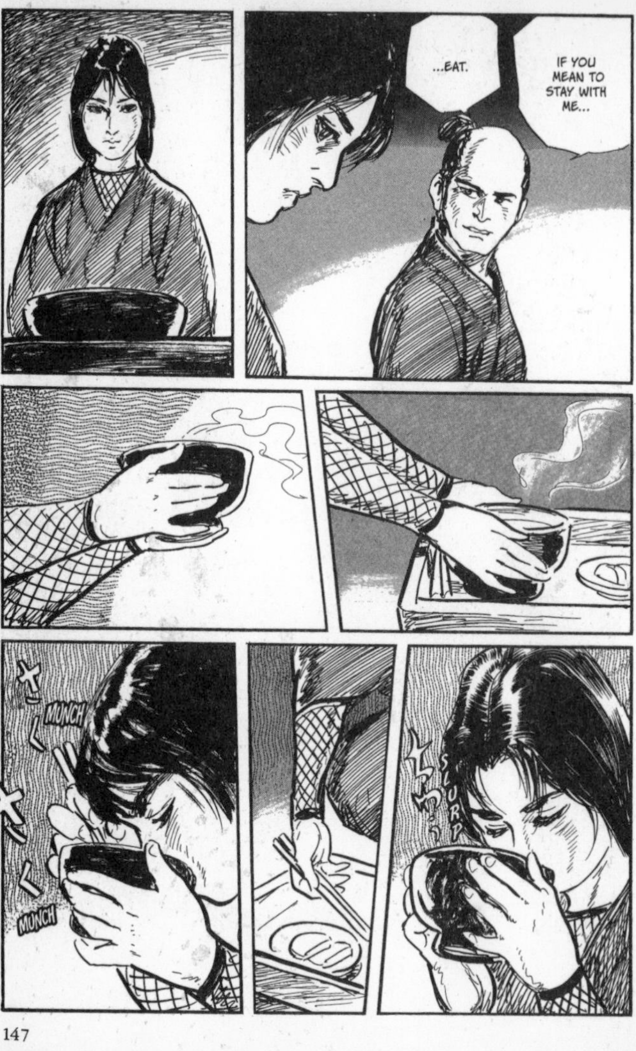
IF YOU MEAN TO STAY WITH ME...
...EAT.
SLURP
MONCH
MONCH

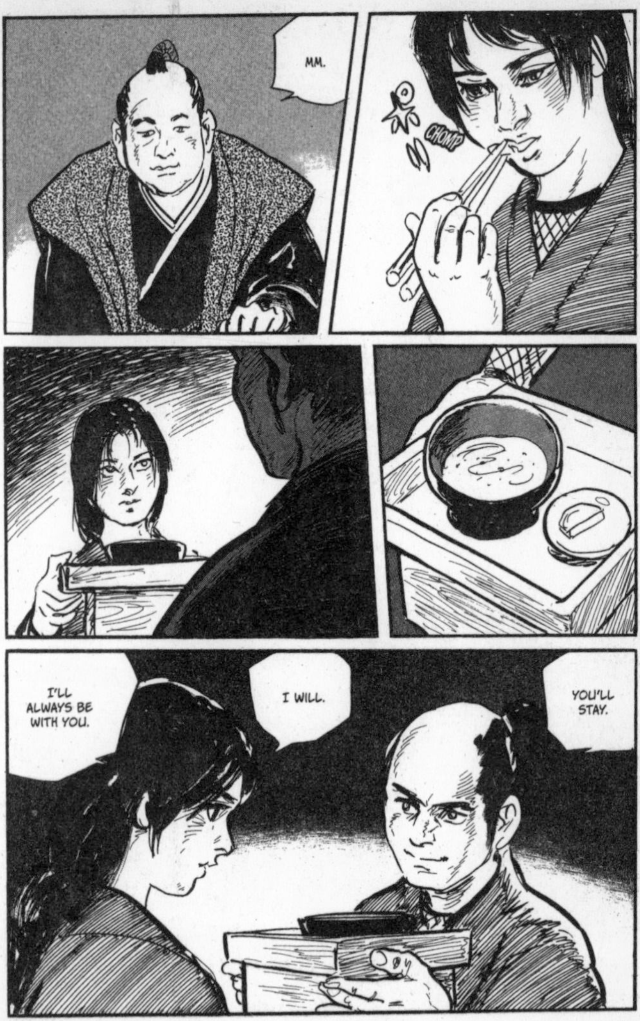
CHOMP
MM.
YOU'LL STAY.
I WILL.
I'LL ALWAYS BE WITH YOU.

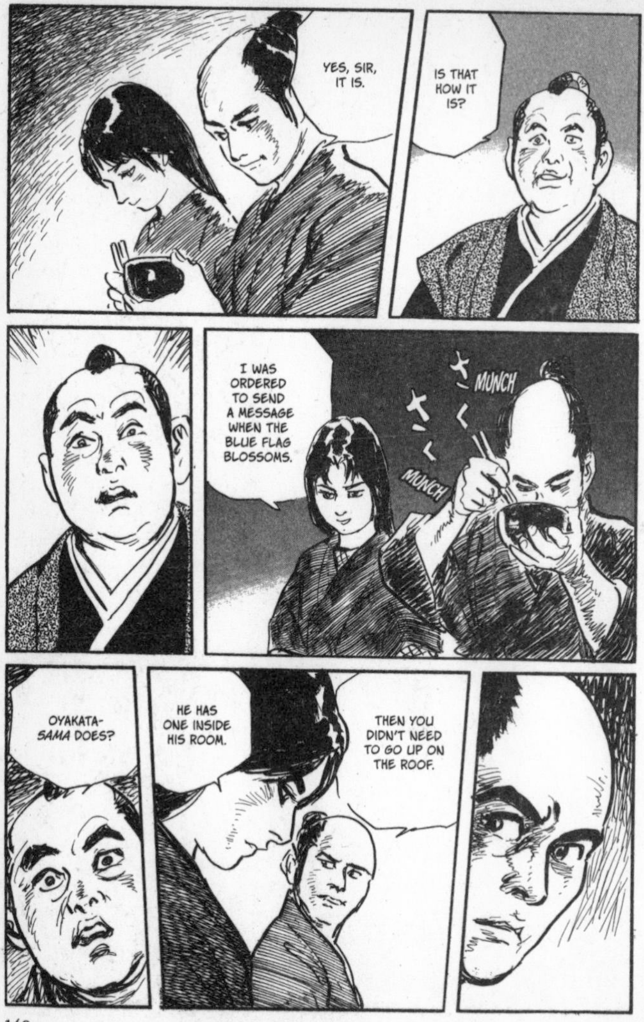
IS THAT HOW IT IS?
YES, SIR, IT IS.
I WAS ORDERED TO SEND A MESSAGE WHEN THE BLUE FLAG BLOSSOMS.
MUNCH
MUNCH
THEN YOU DIDN'T NEED TO GO UP ON THE ROOF.
HE HAS ONE INSIDE HIS ROOM.
OYAKATA-SAMA DOES?

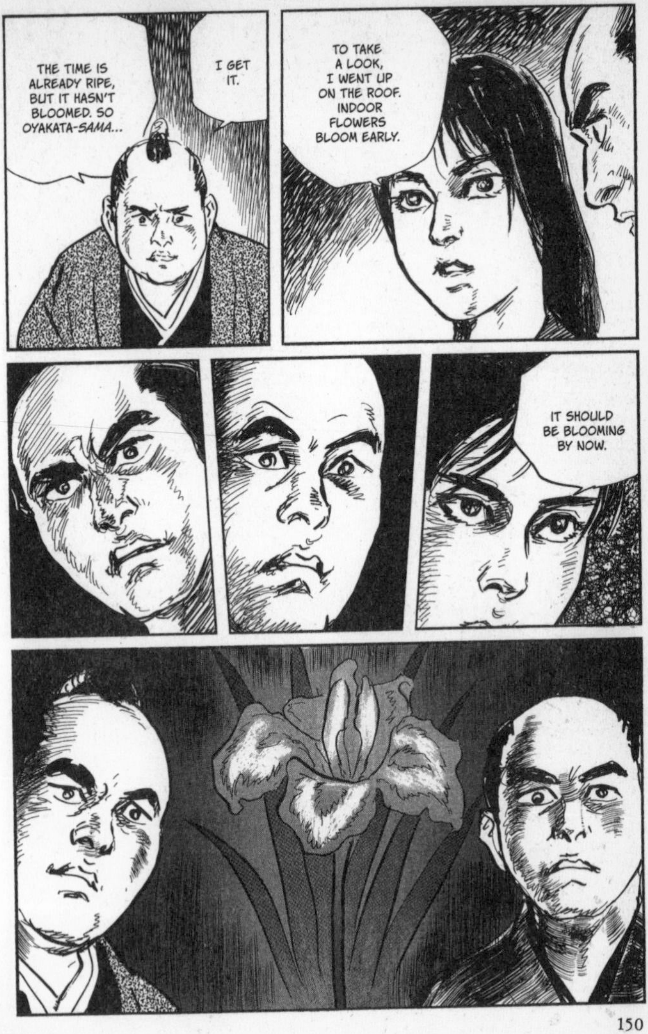
TO TAKE A LOOK, I WENT UP ON THE ROOF. INDOOR FLOWERS BLOOM EARLY.
I GET IT.
THE TIME IS ALREADY RIPE, BUT IT HASN'T BLOOMED. SO OYAKATA-*SAMA*...
IT SHOULD BE BLOOMING BY NOW.

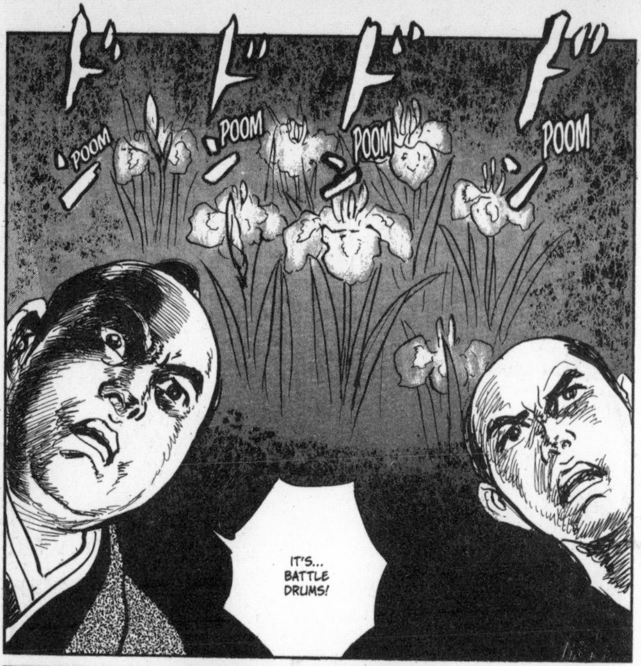
POOM
POOM
POOM
POOM
IT'S... BATTLE DRUMS!

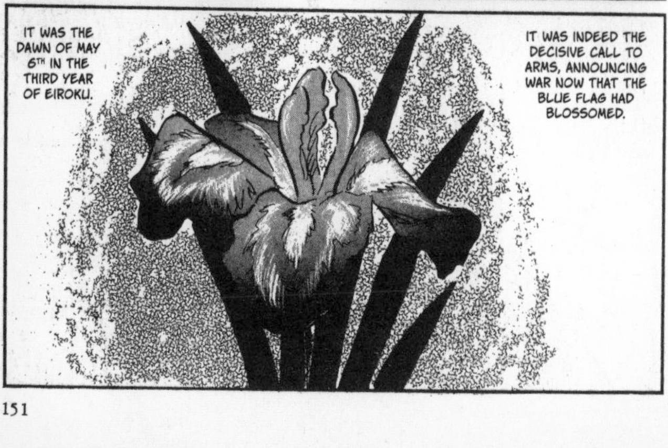
IT WAS THE DAWN OF MAY 6TH IN THE THIRD YEAR OF EIROKU.
IT WAS INDEED THE DECISIVE CALL TO ARMS, ANNOUNCING WAR NOW THAT THE BLUE FLAG HAD BLOSSOMED.

Chapter On Relinquishing Factions

No. 7: Wife's Horse

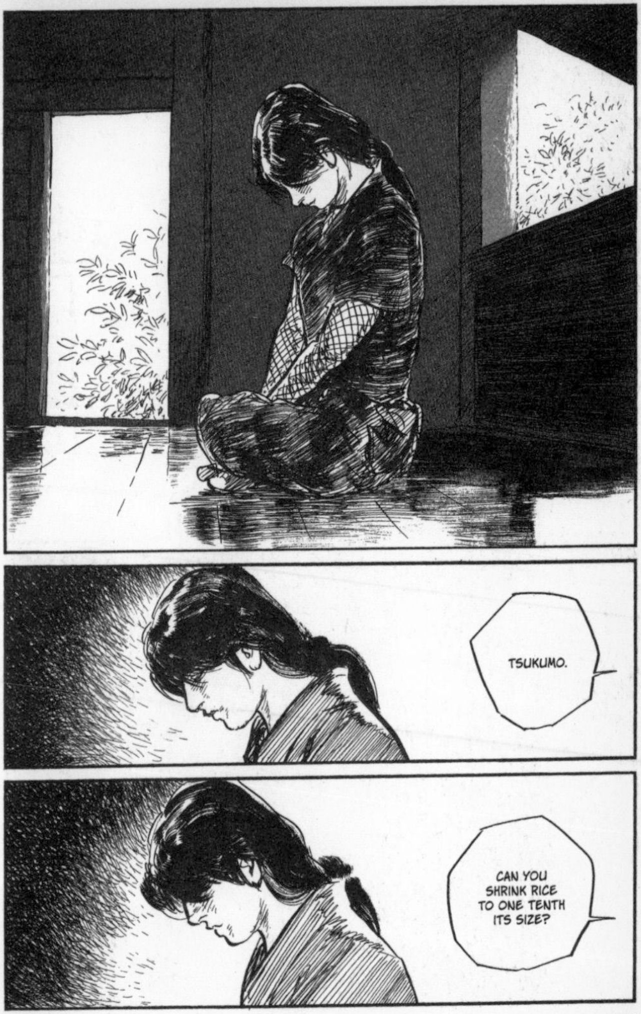
TSUKUMO.
CAN YOU SHRINK RICE TO ONE TENTH ITS SIZE?

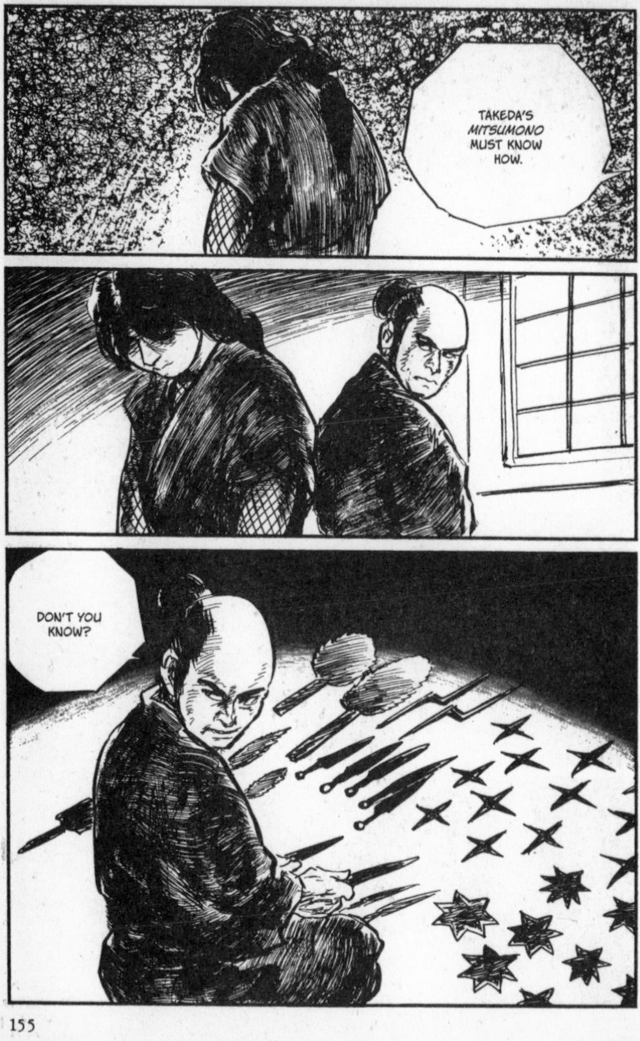
TAKEDA'S *MITSUMONO* MUST KNOW HOW.
DON'T YOU KNOW?

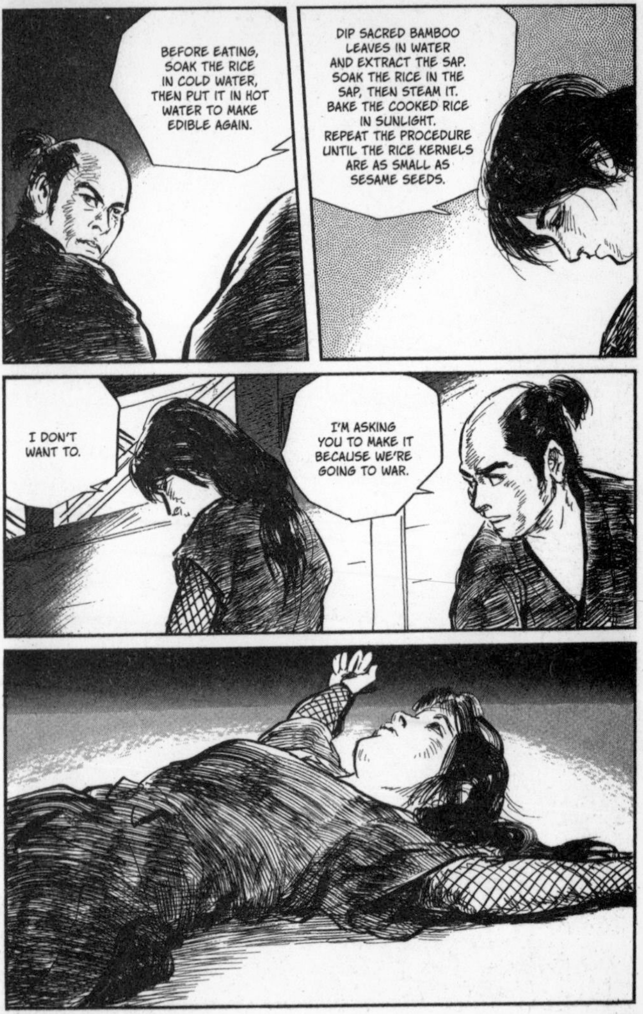
DIP SACRED BAMBOO LEAVES IN WATER AND EXTRACT THE SAP. SOAK THE RICE IN THE SAP, THEN STEAM IT. BAKE THE COOKED RICE IN SUNLIGHT. REPEAT THE PROCEDURE UNTIL THE RICE KERNELS ARE AS SMALL AS SESAME SEEDS.
BEFORE EATING, SOAK THE RICE IN COLD WATER, THEN PUT IT IN HOT WATER TO MAKE EDIBLE AGAIN.
I'M ASKING YOU TO MAKE IT BECAUSE WE'RE GOING TO WAR.
I DON'T WANT TO.

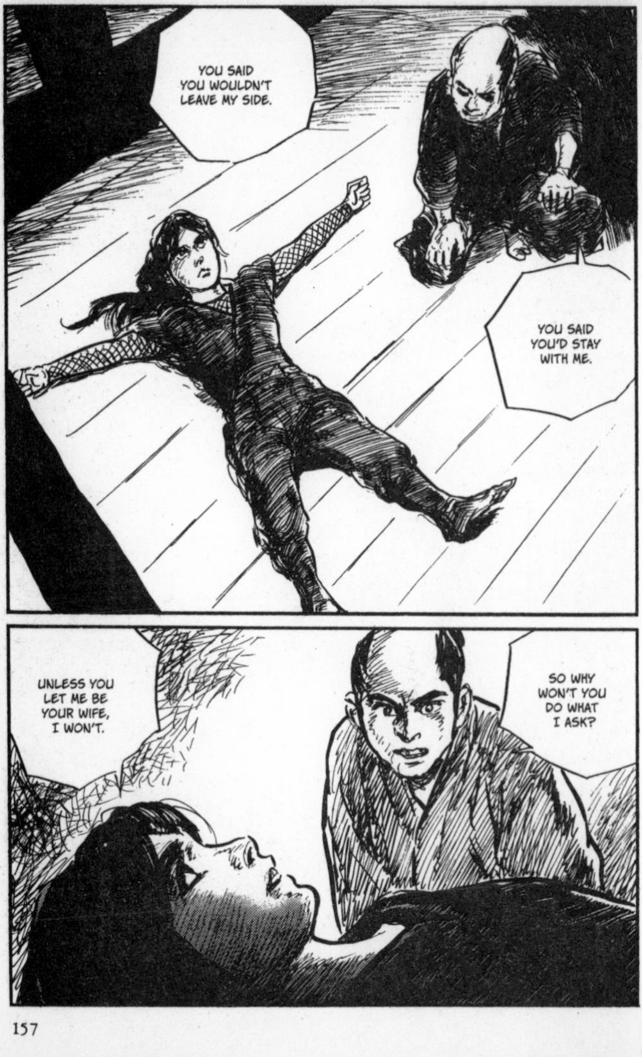
YOU SAID YOU WOULDN'T LEAVE MY SIDE.
YOU SAID YOU'D STAY WITH ME.
SO WHY WON'T YOU DO WHAT I ASK?
UNLESS YOU LET ME BE YOUR WIFE, I WON'T.

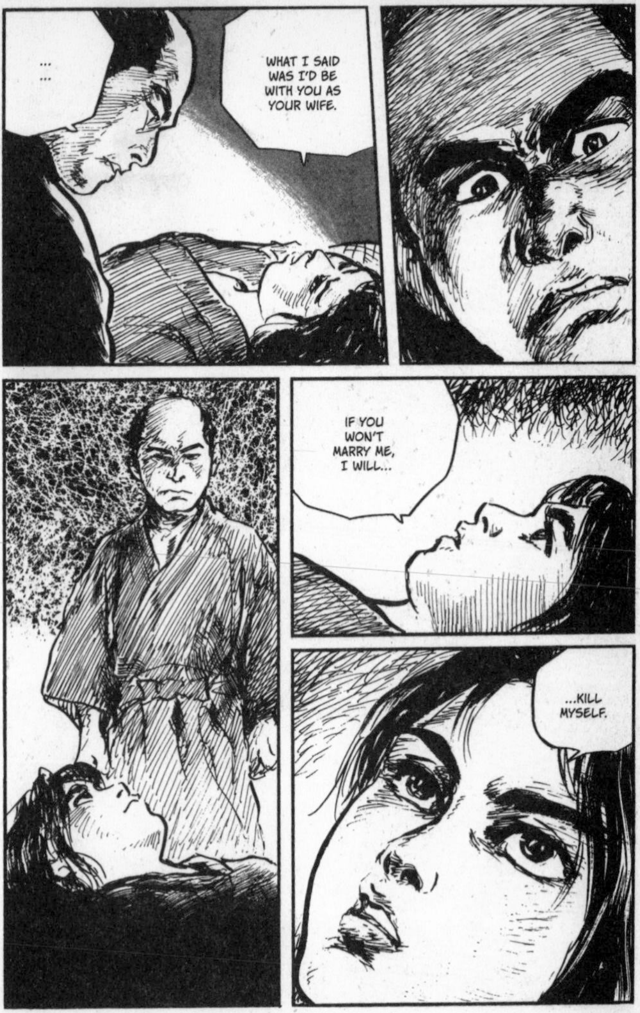
WHAT I SAID WAS I'D BE WITH YOU AS YOUR WIFE.
...
...
IF YOU WON'T MARRY ME, I WILL...
...KILL MYSELF.

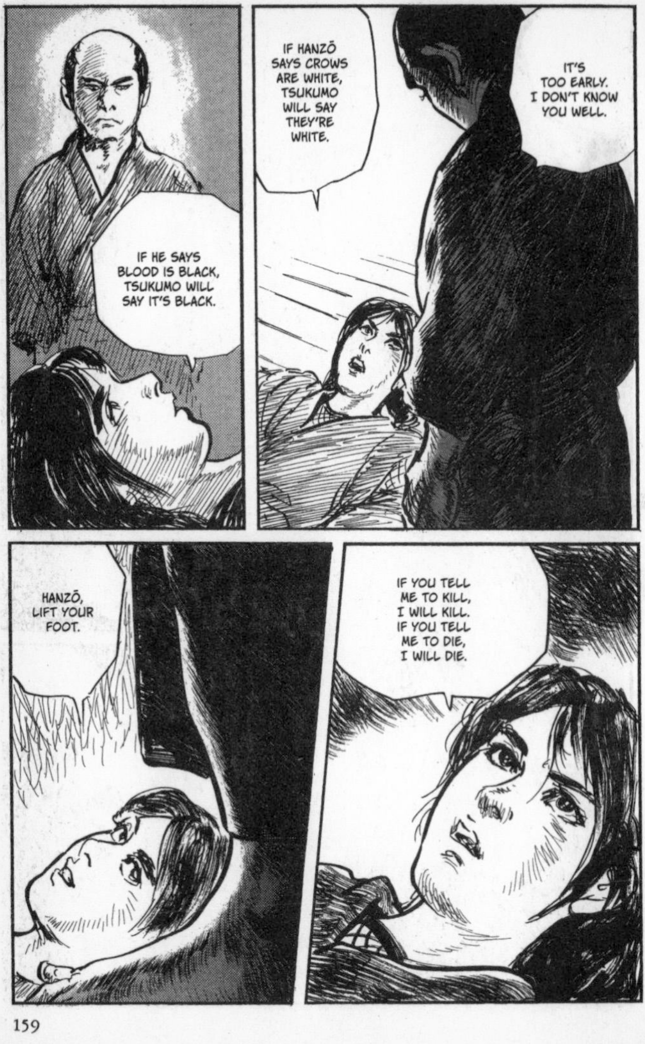
IT'S TOO EARLY. I DON'T KNOW YOU WELL.
IF HANZŌ SAYS CROWS ARE WHITE, TSUKUMO WILL SAY THEY'RE WHITE.
IF HE SAYS BLOOD IS BLACK, TSUKUMO WILL SAY IT'S BLACK.
IF YOU TELL ME TO KILL, I WILL KILL. IF YOU TELL ME TO DIE, I WILL DIE.
HANZŌ, LIFT YOUR FOOT.

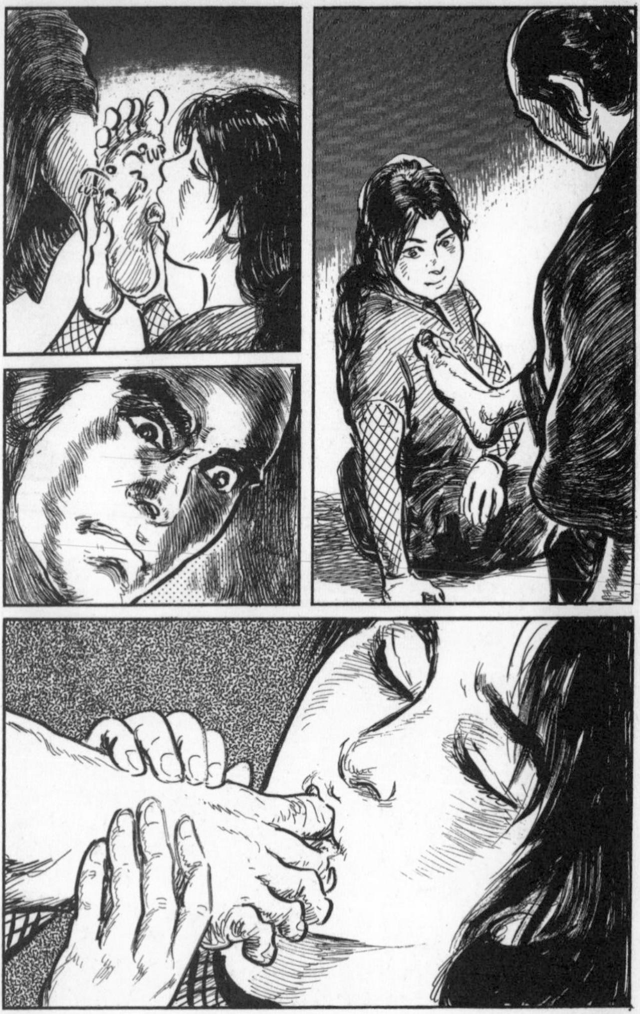
LUP
LUP

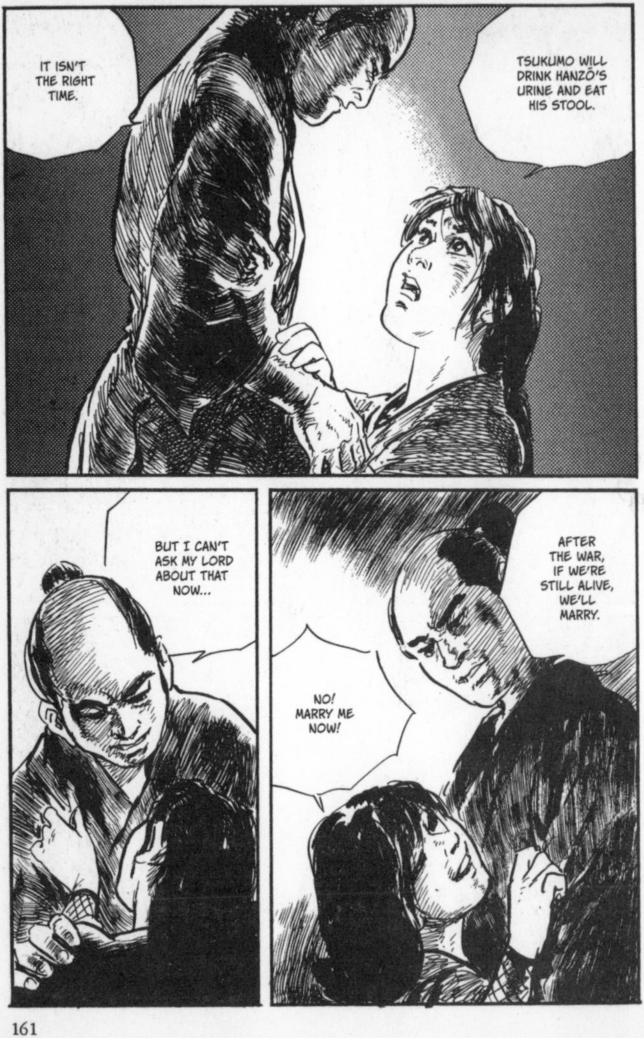
TSUKUMO WILL DRINK HANZŌ'S URINE AND EAT HIS STOOL.
IT ISN'T THE RIGHT TIME.
AFTER THE WAR, IF WE'RE STILL ALIVE, WE'LL MARRY.
NO! MARRY ME NOW!
BUT I CAN'T ASK MY LORD ABOUT THAT NOW...

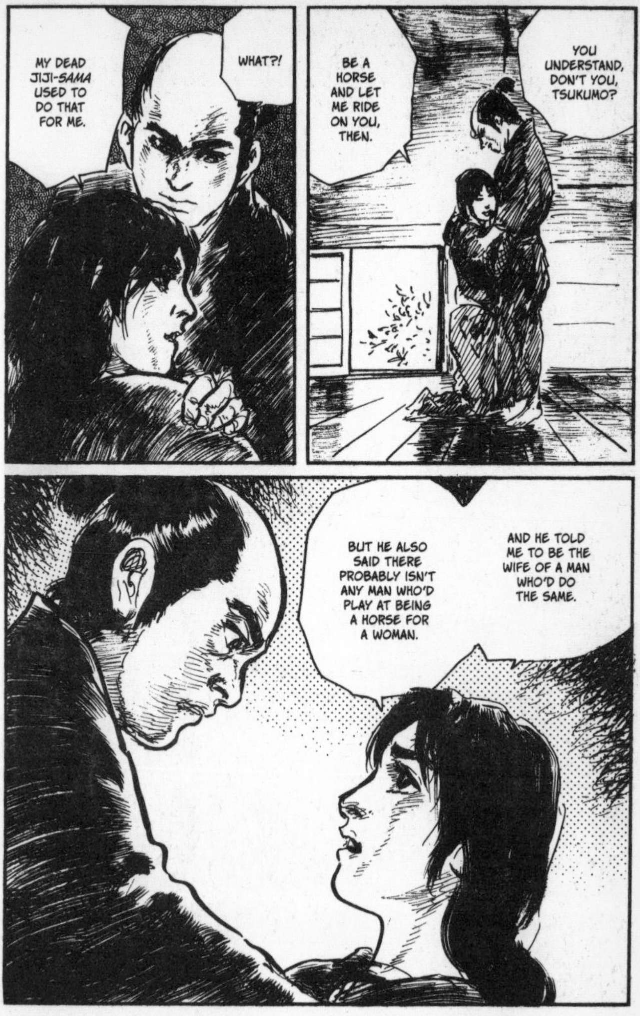
YOU UNDERSTAND, DON'T YOU, TSUKUMO?
BE A HORSE AND LET ME RIDE ON YOU, THEN.
WHAT?!
MY DEAD JIJI-*SAMA* USED TO DO THAT FOR ME.
AND HE TOLD ME TO BE THE WIFE OF A MAN WHO'D DO THE SAME.
BUT HE ALSO SAID THERE PROBABLY ISN'T ANY MAN WHO'D PLAY AT BEING A HORSE FOR A WOMAN.

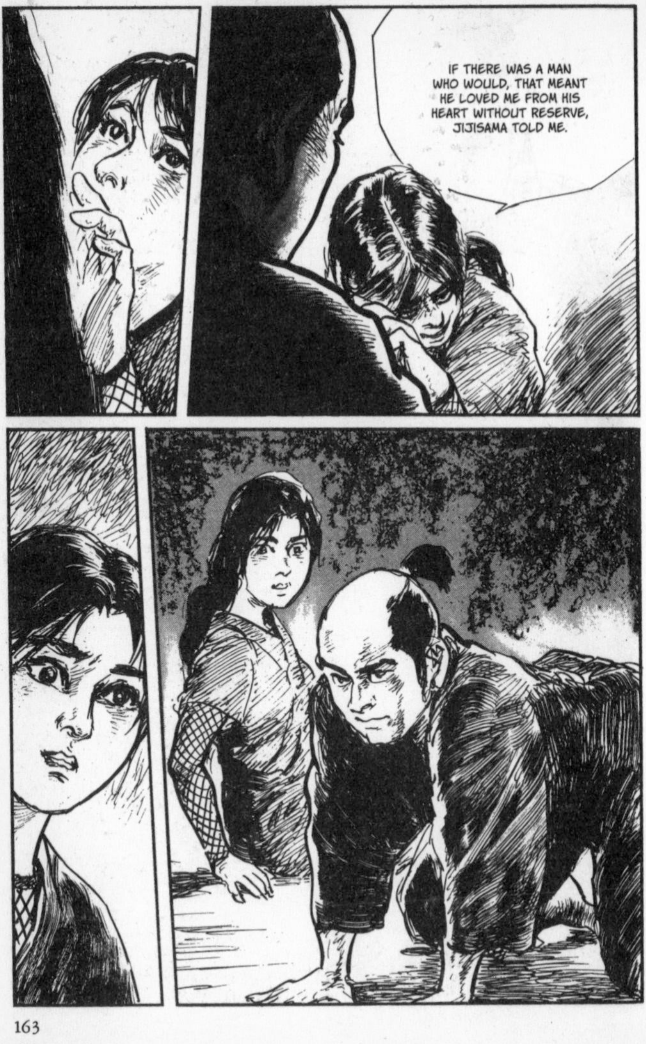
IF THERE WAS A MAN WHO WOULD, THAT MEANT HE LOVED ME FROM HIS HEART WITHOUT RESERVE, JIJISAMA TOLD ME.

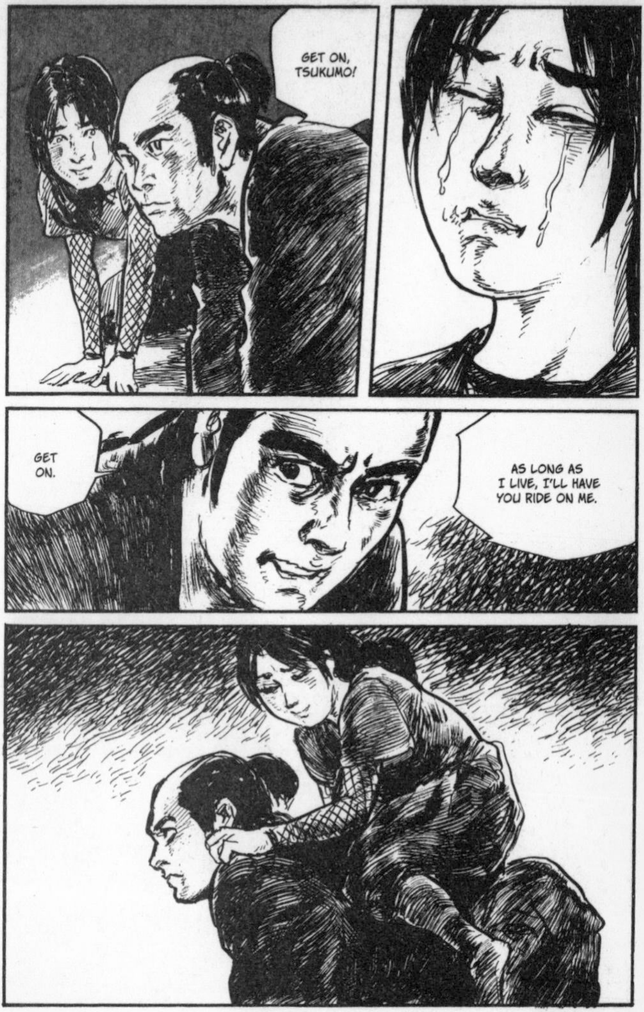
GET ON, TSUKUMO!
AS LONG AS I LIVE, I'LL HAVE YOU RIDE ON ME.
GET ON.

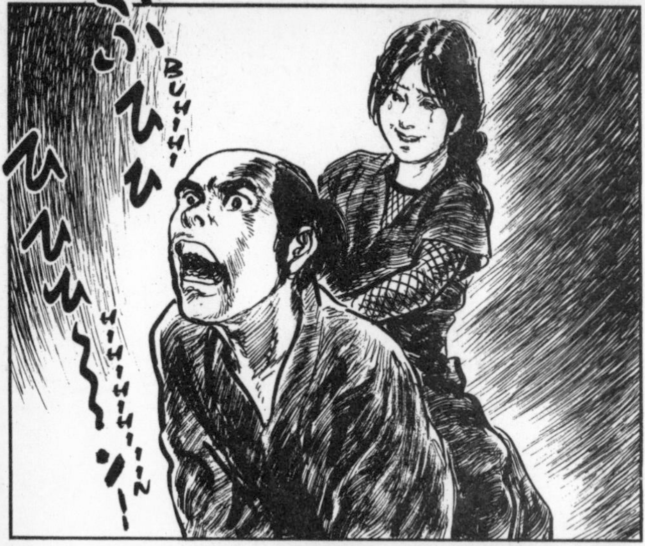
ぶひひ
BUHIHI
ひひひ〜〜ン!
HIHIHIHIIIN

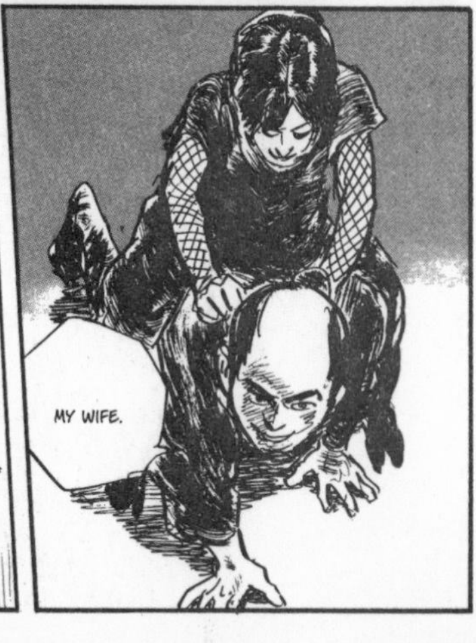
MY WIFE.

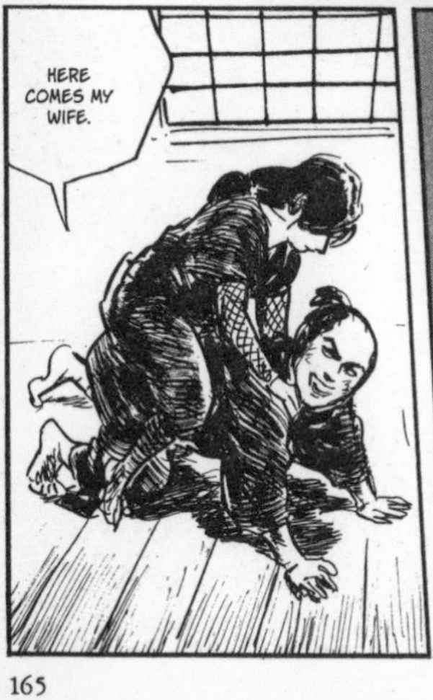
HERE COMES MY WIFE.

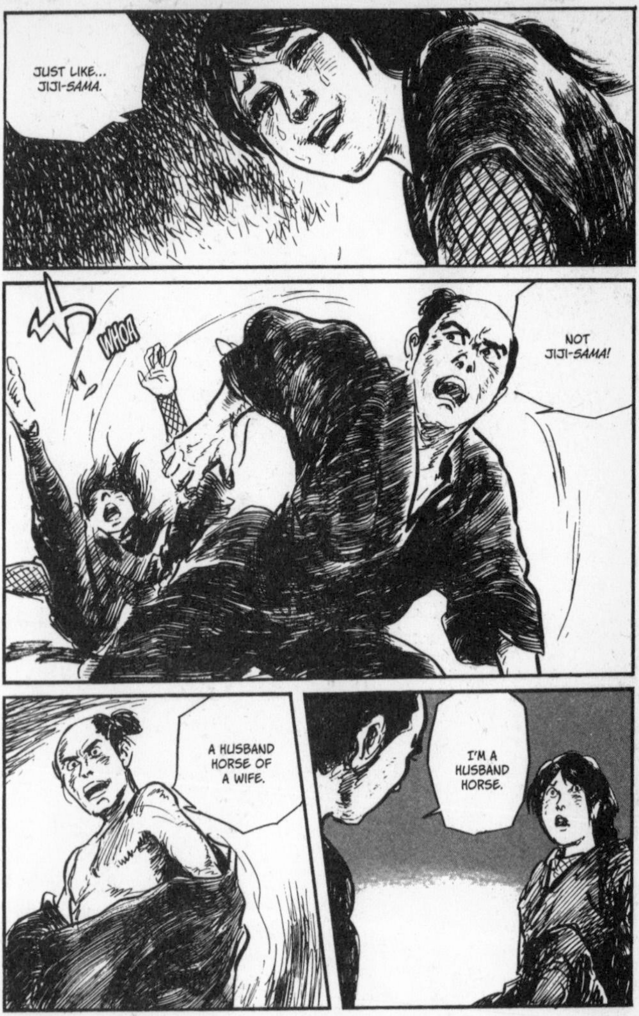
JUST LIKE... JIJI-SAMA.
NOT JIJI-SAMA!
WHOA
I'M A HUSBAND HORSE.
A HUSBAND HORSE OF A WIFE.

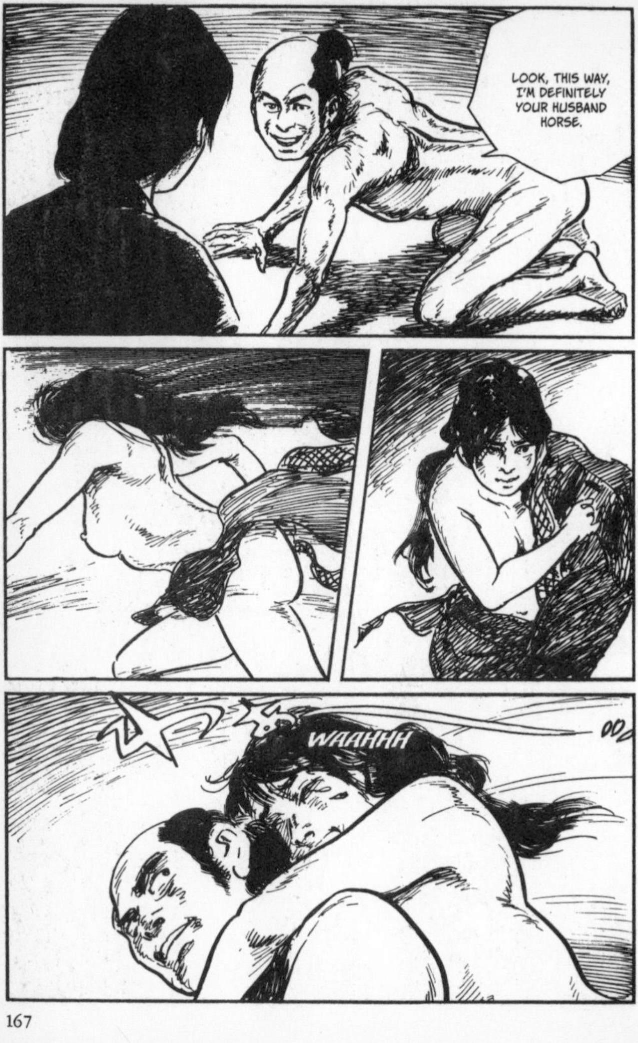
LOOK, THIS WAY, I'M DEFINITELY YOUR HUSBAND HORSE.
WAAHHH

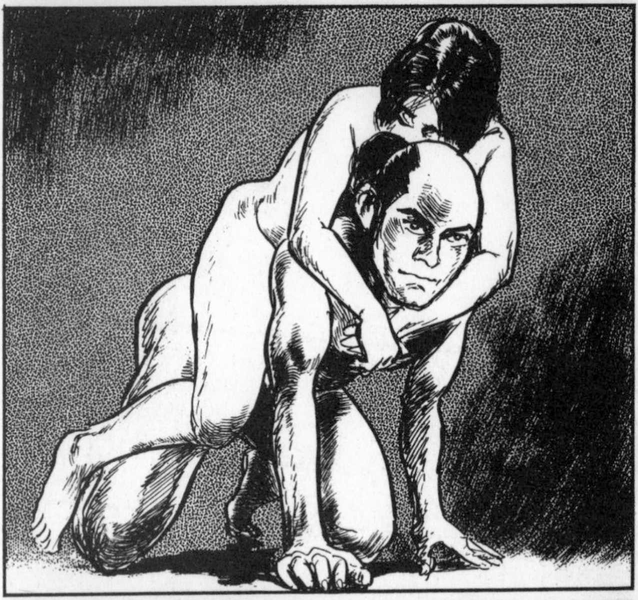

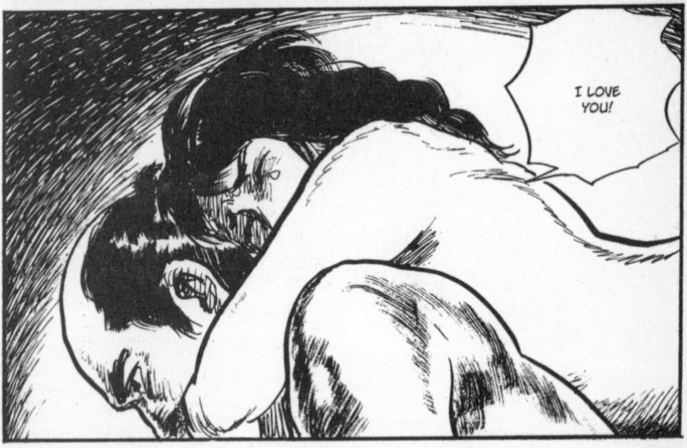
I LOVE YOU!

Chapter On Relinquishing Factions

No. 8: When Bitten by a Mosquito

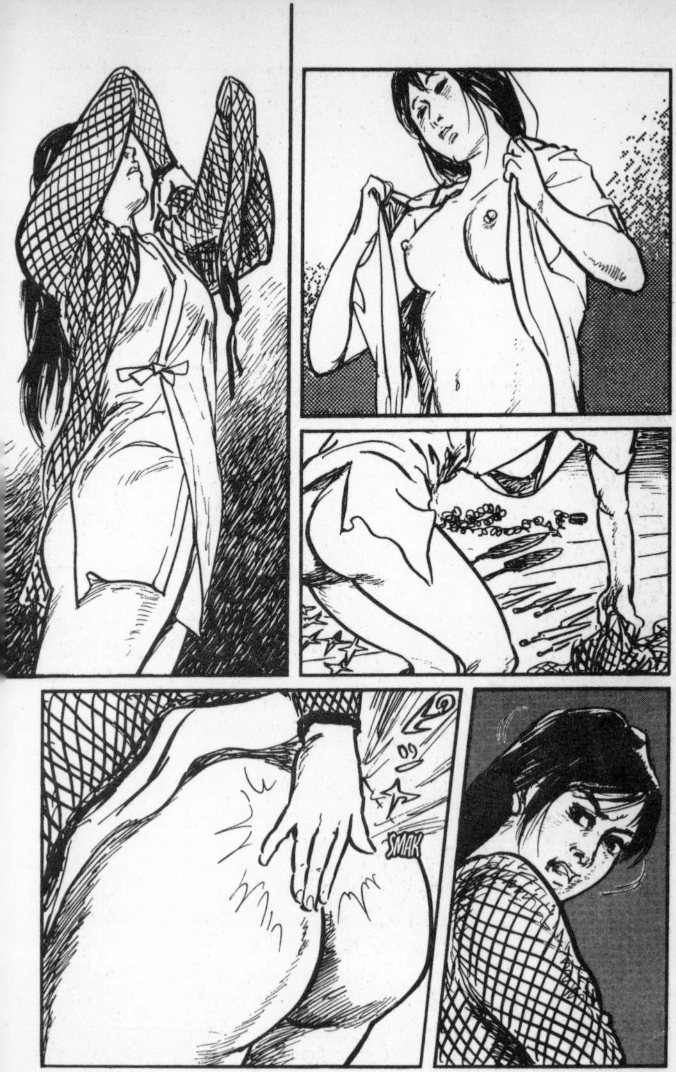
SMAK

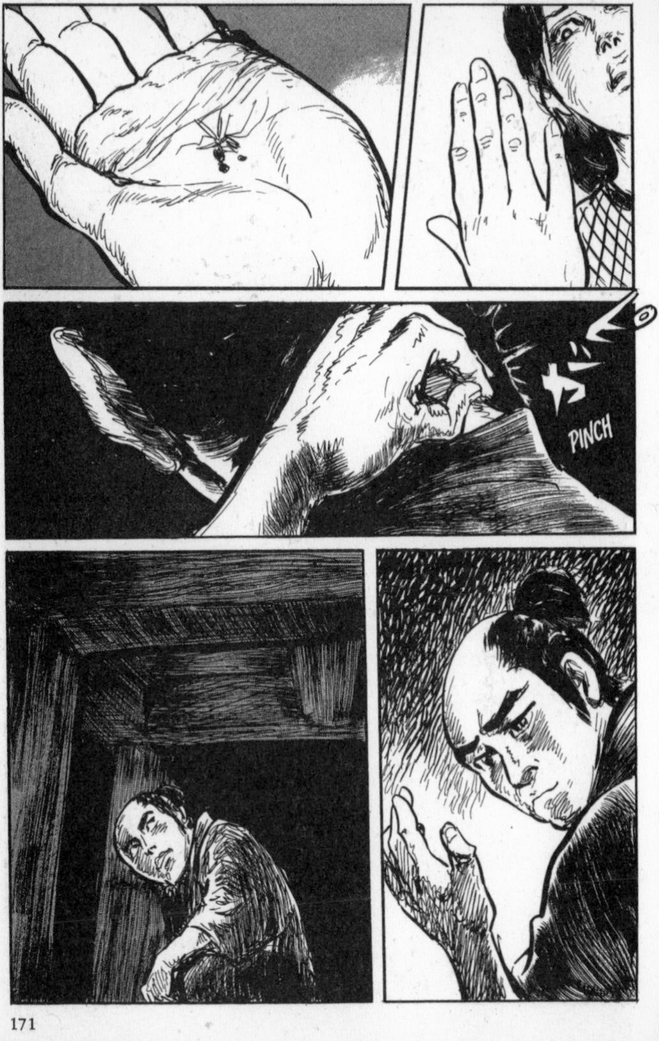
ガッ
PINCH

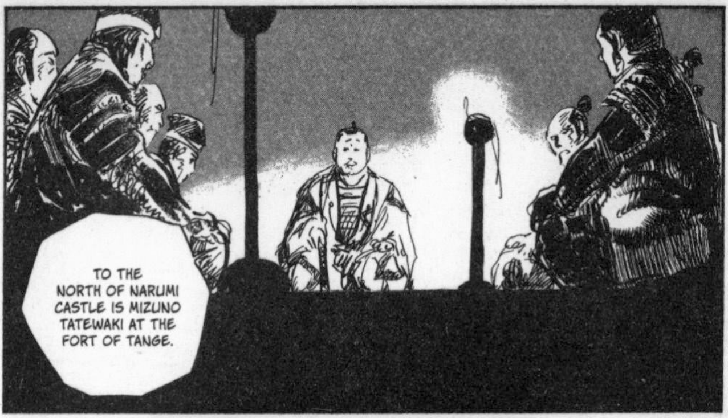
TO THE NORTH OF NARUMI CASTLE IS MIZUNO TATEWAKI AT THE FORT OF TANGE.

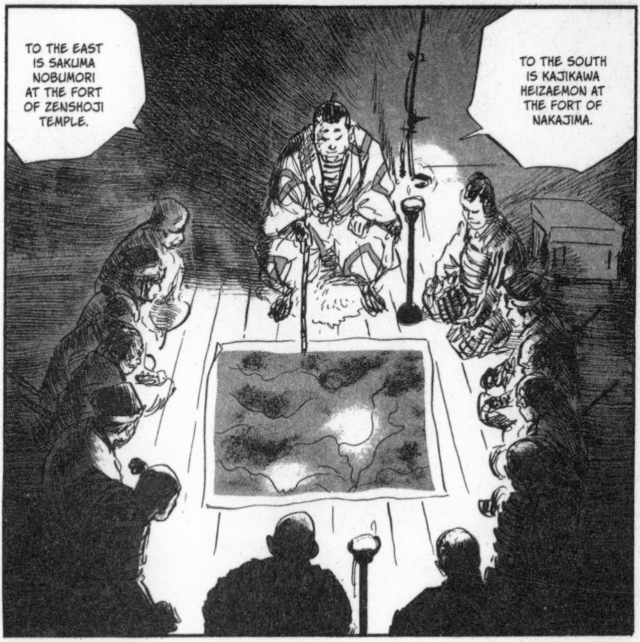
TO THE SOUTH IS KAJIKAWA HEIZAEMON AT THE FORT OF NAKAJIMA.
TO THE EAST IS SAKUMA NOBUMORI AT THE FORT OF ZENSHOJI TEMPLE.

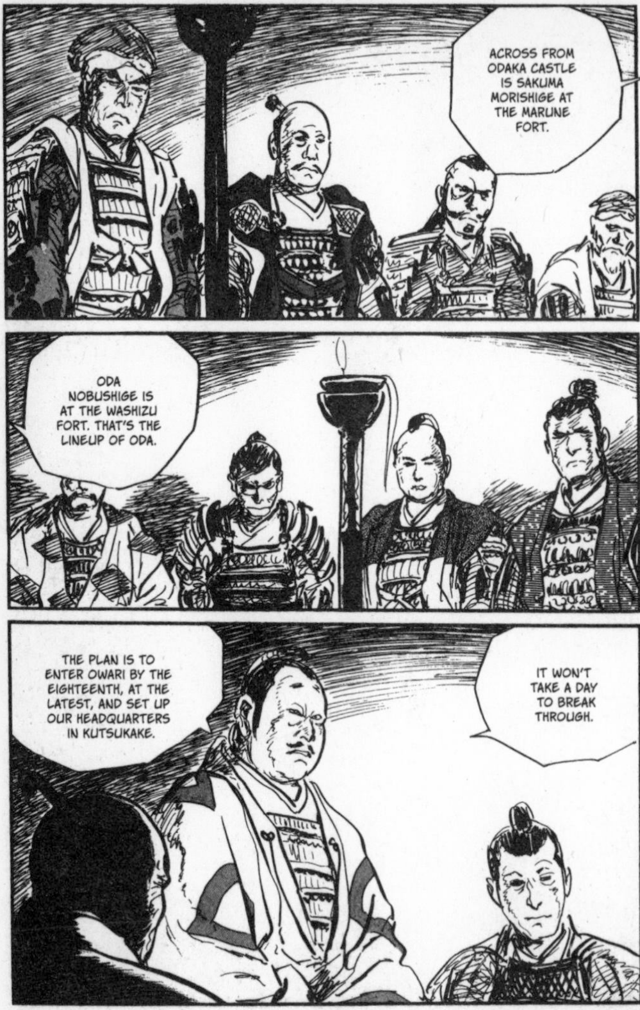
ACROSS FROM ODAKA CASTLE IS SAKUMA MORISHIGE AT THE MARUNE FORT.
ODA NOBUSHIGE IS AT THE WASHIZU FORT. THAT'S THE LINEUP OF ODA.
IT WON'T TAKE A DAY TO BREAK THROUGH.
THE PLAN IS TO ENTER OWARI BY THE EIGHTEENTH, AT THE LATEST, AND SET UP OUR HEADQUARTERS IN KUTSUKAKE.

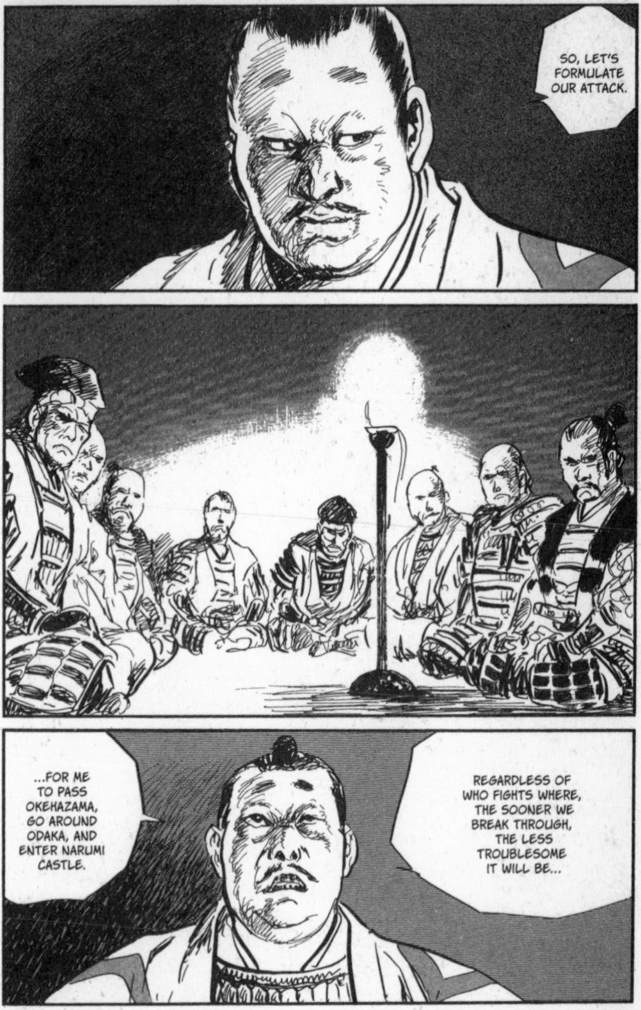
SO, LET'S FORMULATE OUR ATTACK.
REGARDLESS OF WHO FIGHTS WHERE, THE SOONER WE BREAK THROUGH, THE LESS TROUBLESOME IT WILL BE...
...FOR ME TO PASS OKEHAZAMA, GO AROUND ODAKA, AND ENTER NARUMI CASTLE.

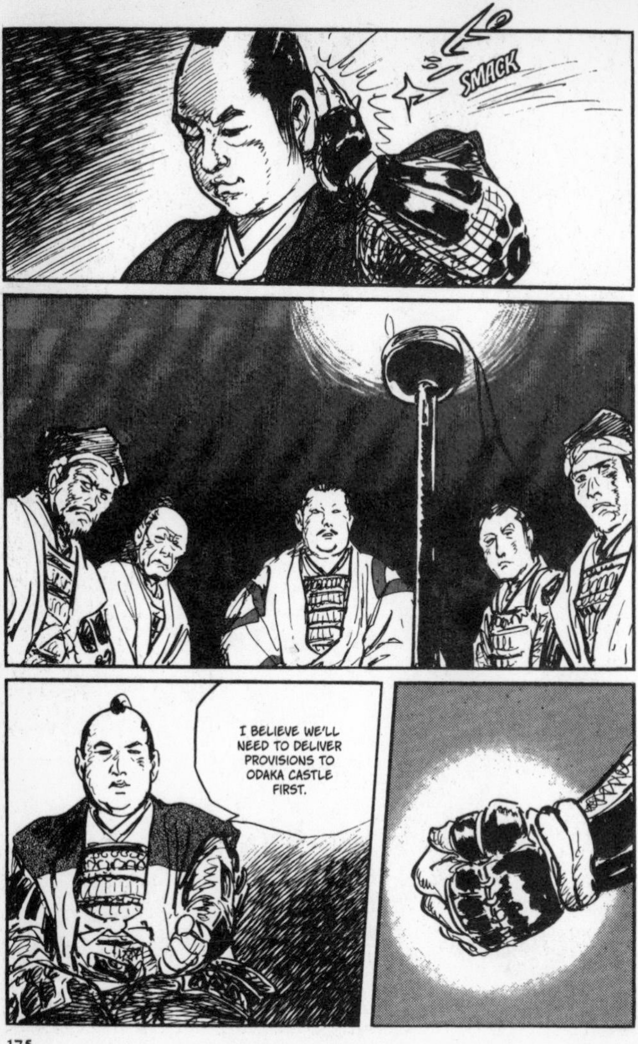
SMACK
I BELIEVE WE'LL NEED TO DELIVER PROVISIONS TO ODAKA CASTLE FIRST.

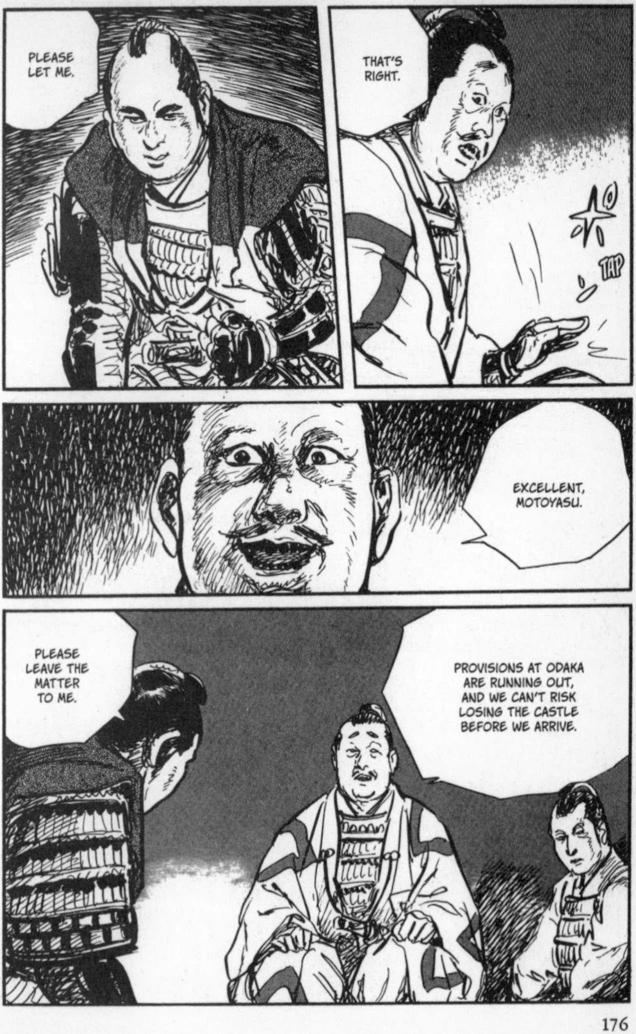
THAT'S RIGHT.
TAP
PLEASE LET ME.
EXCELLENT, MOTOYASU.
PROVISIONS AT ODAKA ARE RUNNING OUT, AND WE CAN'T RISK LOSING THE CASTLE BEFORE WE ARRIVE.
PLEASE LEAVE THE MATTER TO ME.

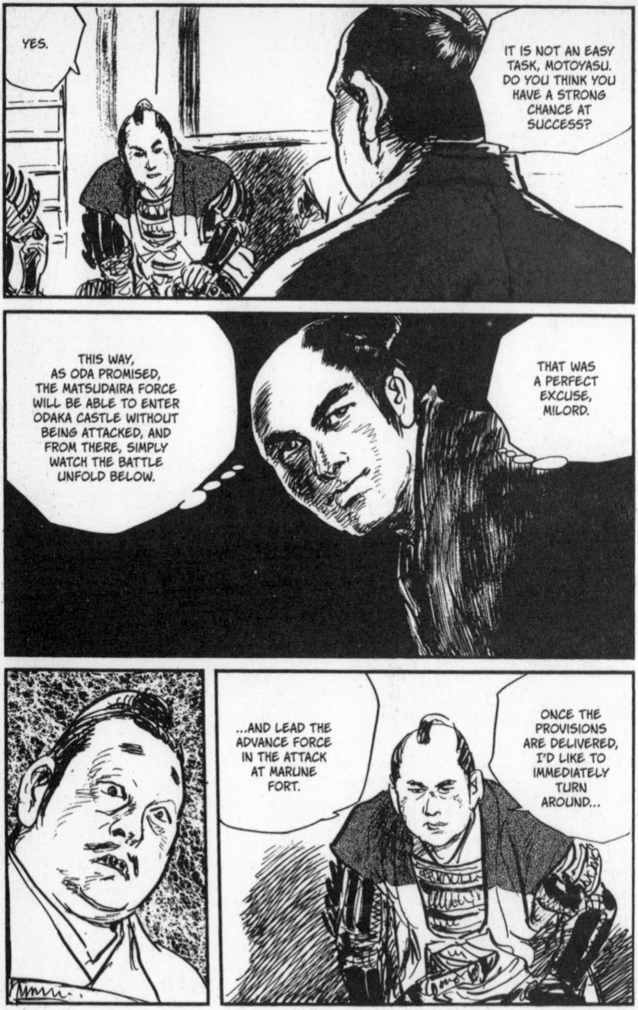
IT IS NOT AN EASY TASK, MOTOYASU. DO YOU THINK YOU HAVE A STRONG CHANCE AT SUCCESS?
YES.
THAT WAS A PERFECT EXCUSE, MILORD.
THIS WAY, AS ODA PROMISED, THE MATSUDAIRA FORCE WILL BE ABLE TO ENTER ODAKA CASTLE WITHOUT BEING ATTACKED, AND FROM THERE, SIMPLY WATCH THE BATTLE UNFOLD BELOW.
ONCE THE PROVISIONS ARE DELIVERED, I'D LIKE TO IMMEDIATELY TURN AROUND...
...AND LEAD THE ADVANCE FORCE IN THE ATTACK AT MARUNE FORT.

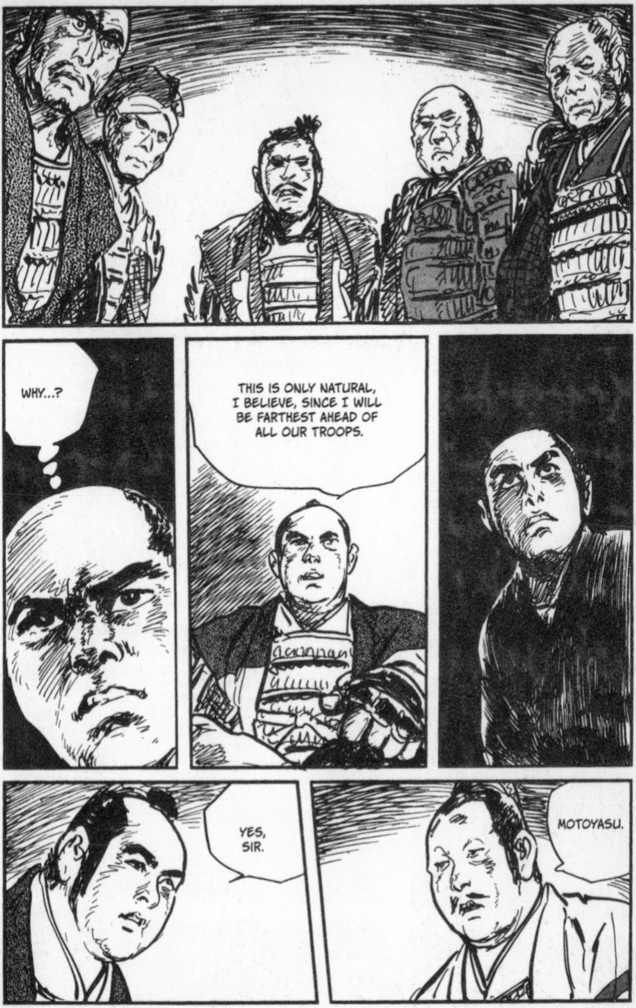
THIS IS ONLY NATURAL, I BELIEVE, SINCE I WILL BE FARTHEST AHEAD OF ALL OUR TROOPS.
WHY...?
MOTOYASU.
YES, SIR.

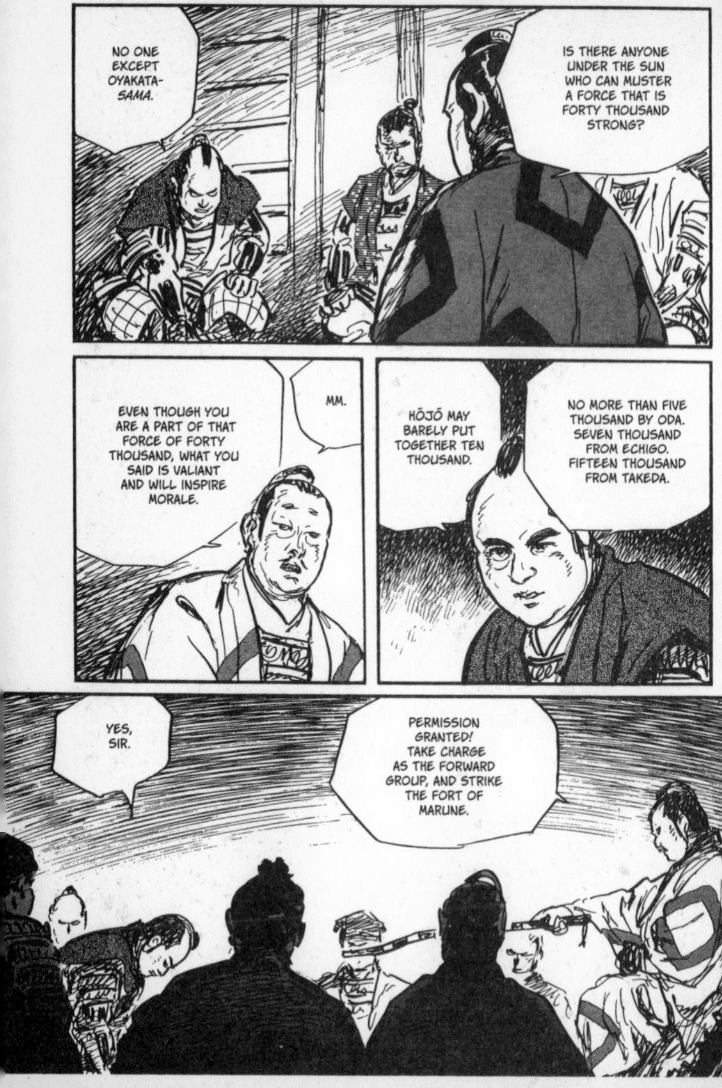
IS THERE ANYONE UNDER THE SUN WHO CAN MUSTER A FORCE THAT IS FORTY THOUSAND STRONG?
NO ONE EXCEPT OYAKATA-SAMA.
NO MORE THAN FIVE THOUSAND BY ODA. SEVEN THOUSAND FROM ECHIGO. FIFTEEN THOUSAND FROM TAKEDA.
HŌJŌ MAY BARELY PUT TOGETHER TEN THOUSAND.
MM.
EVEN THOUGH YOU ARE A PART OF THAT FORCE OF FORTY THOUSAND, WHAT YOU SAID IS VALIANT AND WILL INSPIRE MORALE.
PERMISSION GRANTED! TAKE CHARGE AS THE FORWARD GROUP, AND STRIKE THE FORT OF MARUNE.
YES, SIR.

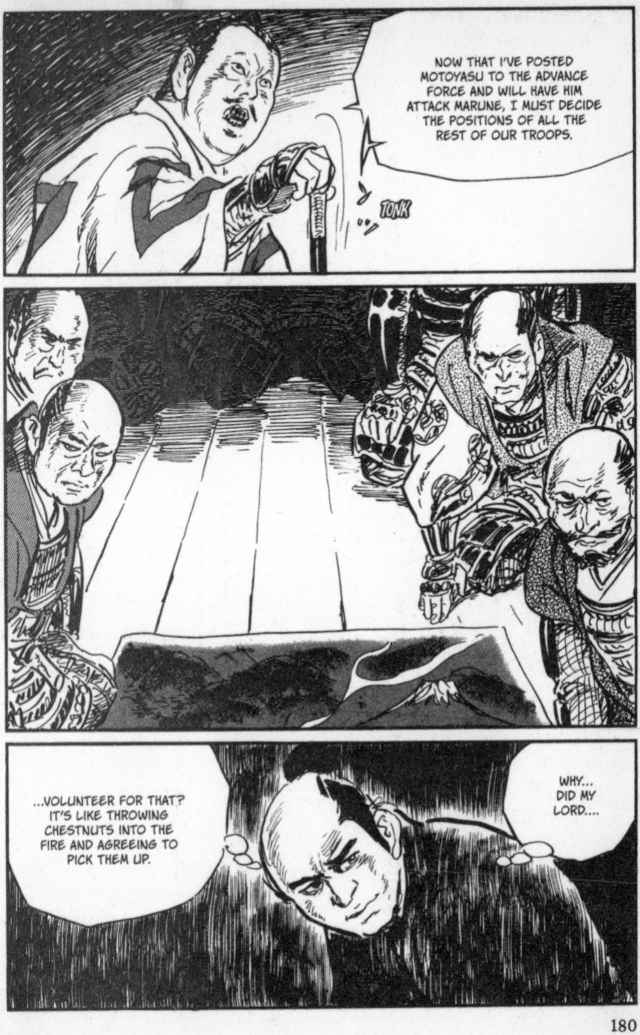
NOW THAT I'VE POSTED MOTOYASU TO THE ADVANCE FORCE AND WILL HAVE HIM ATTACK MARUNE, I MUST DECIDE THE POSITIONS OF ALL THE REST OF OUR TROOPS.
TONK
WHY... DID MY LORD....
...VOLUNTEER FOR THAT? IT'S LIKE THROWING CHESTNUTS INTO THE FIRE AND AGREEING TO PICK THEM UP.

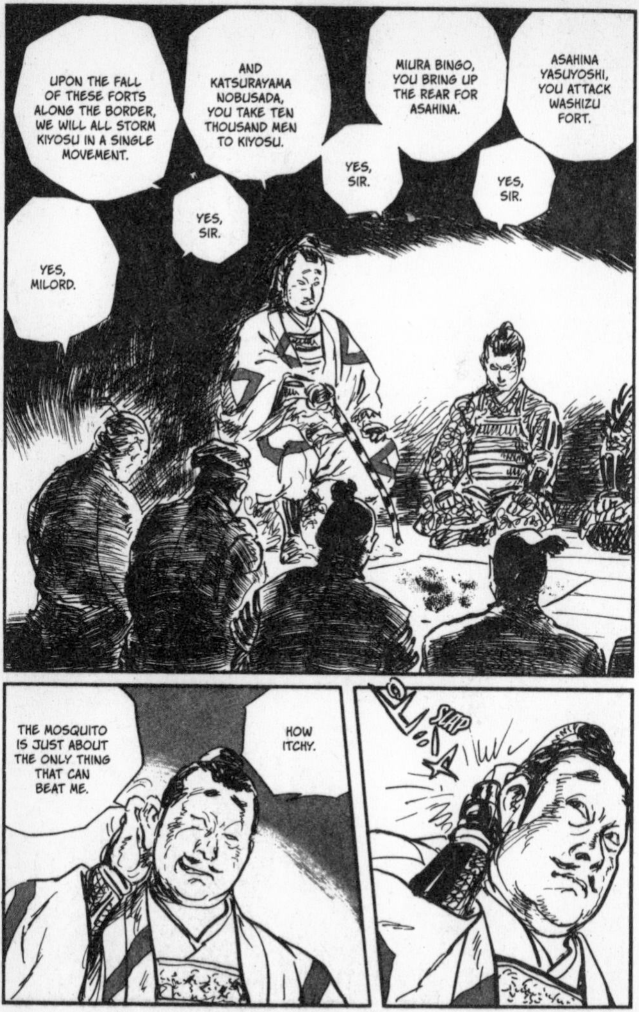
ASAHINA YASUYOSHI, YOU ATTACK WASHIZU FORT.
YES, SIR.
MIURA BINGO, YOU BRING UP THE REAR FOR ASAHINA.
YES, SIR.
AND KATSURAYAMA NOBUSADA, YOU TAKE TEN THOUSAND MEN TO KIYOSU.
YES, SIR.
UPON THE FALL OF THESE FORTS ALONG THE BORDER, WE WILL ALL STORM KIYOSU IN A SINGLE MOVEMENT.
YES, MILORD.
SLAP
HOW ITCHY.
THE MOSQUITO IS JUST ABOUT THE ONLY THING THAT CAN BEAT ME.

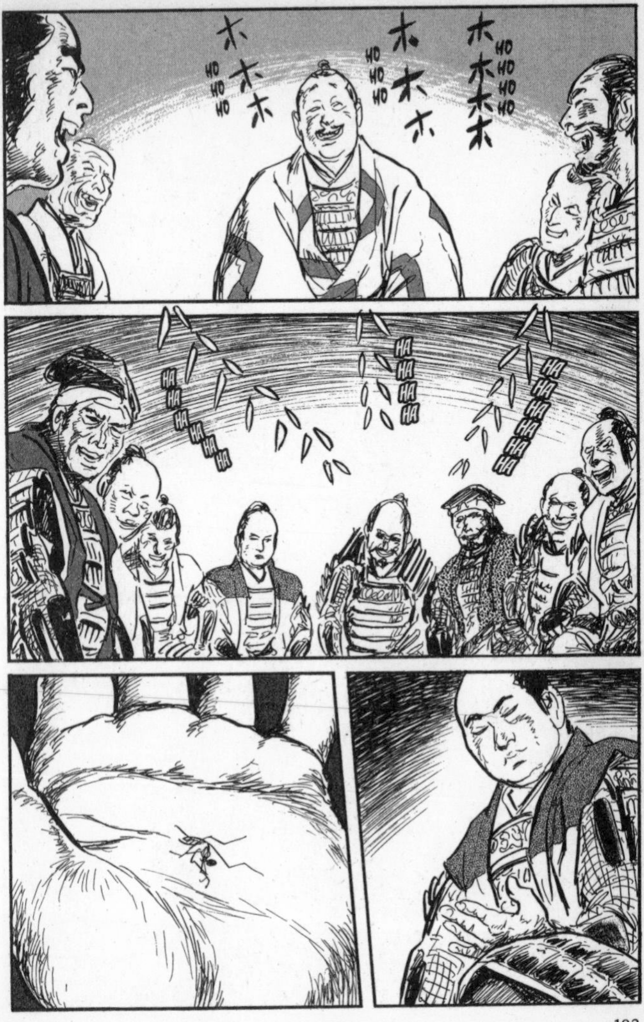
ホホホホホ
HO HO HO HO
ホホホ
HO HO HO
ホホホ
HO HO HO
HA HA HA HA HA HA
HA HA HA HA
HA HA HA HA HA HA

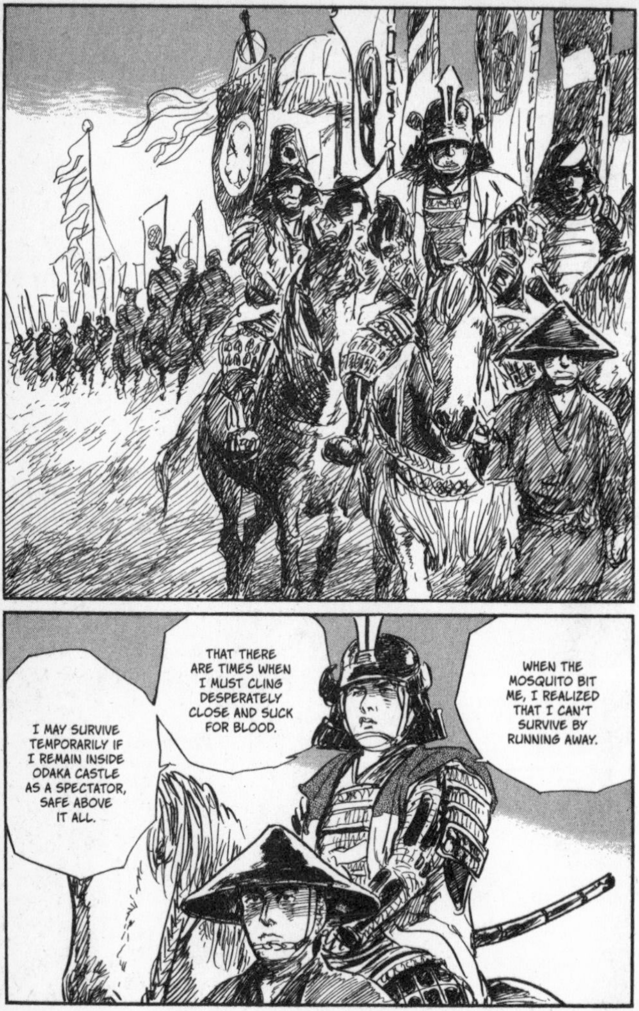
WHEN THE MOSQUITO BIT ME, I REALIZED THAT I CAN'T SURVIVE BY RUNNING AWAY.
THAT THERE ARE TIMES WHEN I MUST CLING DESPERATELY CLOSE AND SUCK FOR BLOOD.
I MAY SURVIVE TEMPORARILY IF I REMAIN INSIDE ODAKA CASTLE AS A SPECTATOR, SAFE ABOVE IT ALL.

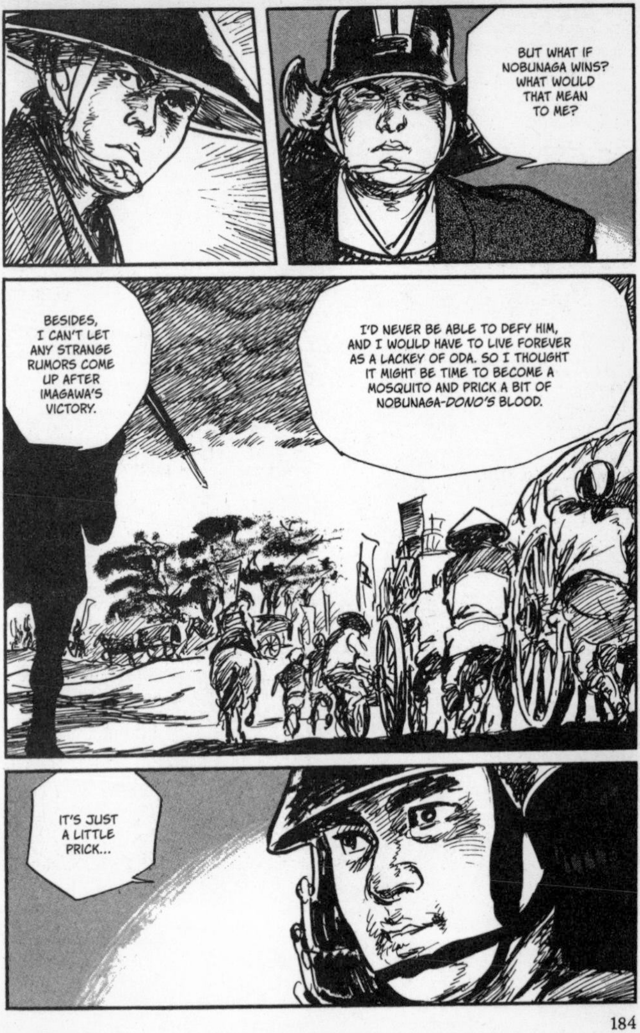
BUT WHAT IF NOBUNAGA WINS? WHAT WOULD THAT MEAN TO ME?
I'D NEVER BE ABLE TO DEFY HIM, AND I WOULD HAVE TO LIVE FOREVER AS A LACKEY OF ODA. SO I THOUGHT IT MIGHT BE TIME TO BECOME A MOSQUITO AND PRICK A BIT OF NOBUNAGA-*DONO*'S BLOOD.
BESIDES, I CAN'T LET ANY STRANGE RUMORS COME UP AFTER IMAGAWA'S VICTORY.
IT'S JUST A LITTLE PRICK...

Chapter On Relinquishing Factions

No. 9:
Comparison
of a
Man

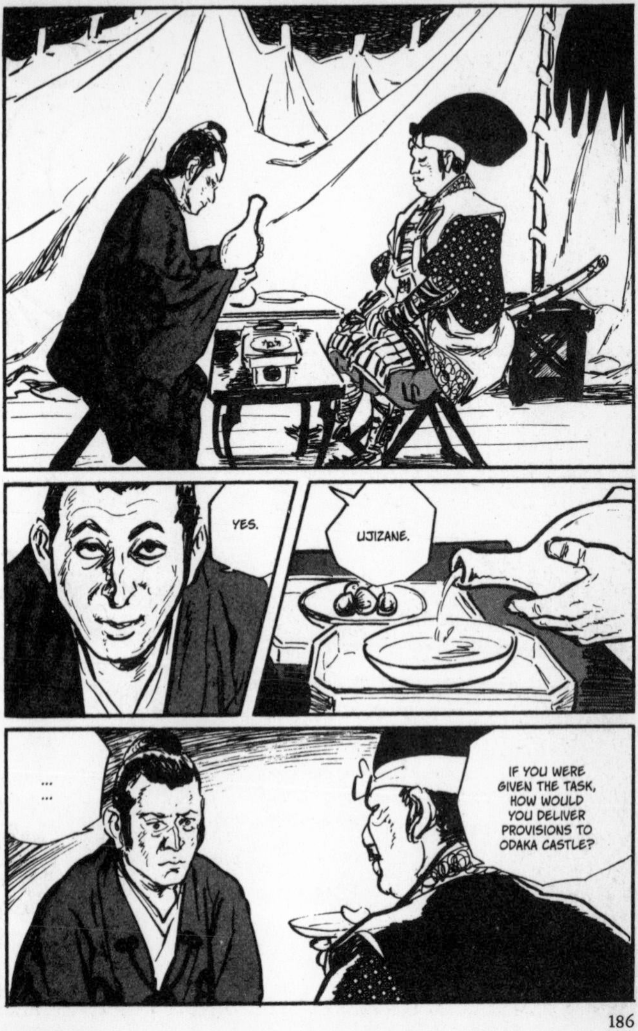
UJIZANE.
YES.
IF YOU WERE GIVEN THE TASK, HOW WOULD YOU DELIVER PROVISIONS TO ODAKA CASTLE?
... ...

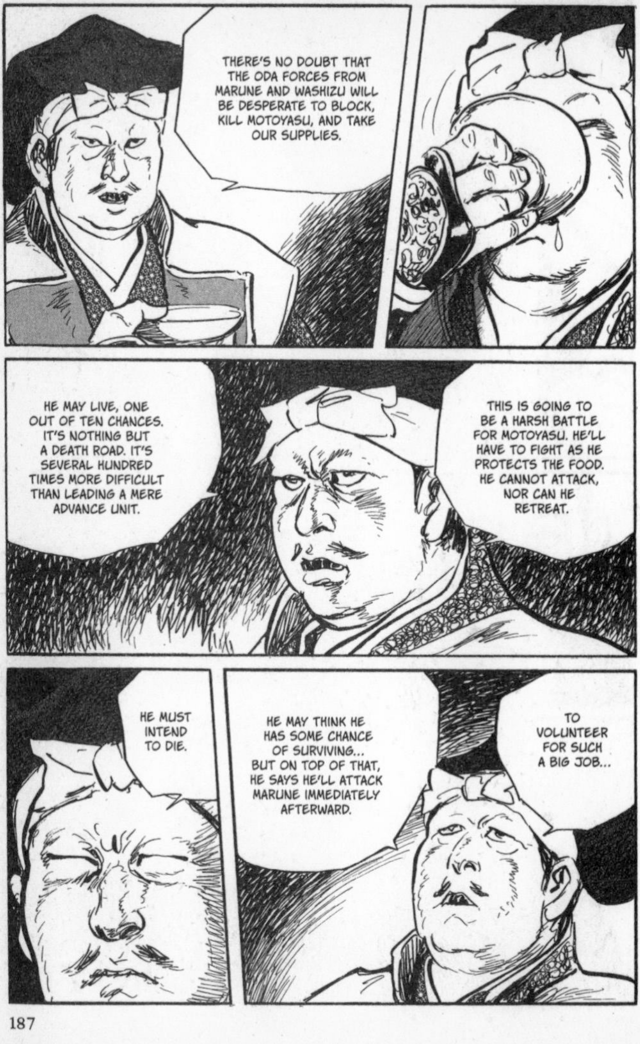
THERE'S NO DOUBT THAT THE ODA FORCES FROM MARUNE AND WASHIZU WILL BE DESPERATE TO BLOCK, KILL MOTOYASU, AND TAKE OUR SUPPLIES.
THIS IS GOING TO BE A HARSH BATTLE FOR MOTOYASU. HE'LL HAVE TO FIGHT AS HE PROTECTS THE FOOD. HE CANNOT ATTACK, NOR CAN HE RETREAT.
HE MAY LIVE, ONE OUT OF TEN CHANCES. IT'S NOTHING BUT A DEATH ROAD. IT'S SEVERAL HUNDRED TIMES MORE DIFFICULT THAN LEADING A MERE ADVANCE UNIT.
TO VOLUNTEER FOR SUCH A BIG JOB...
HE MAY THINK HE HAS SOME CHANCE OF SURVIVING... BUT ON TOP OF THAT, HE SAYS HE'LL ATTACK MARUNE IMMEDIATELY AFTERWARD.
HE MUST INTEND TO DIE.

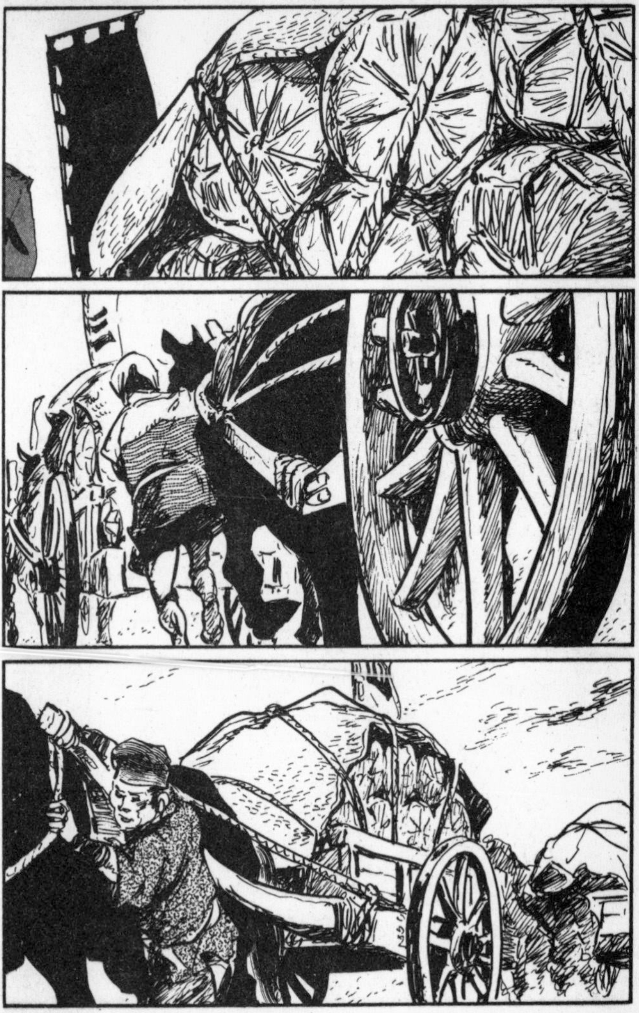

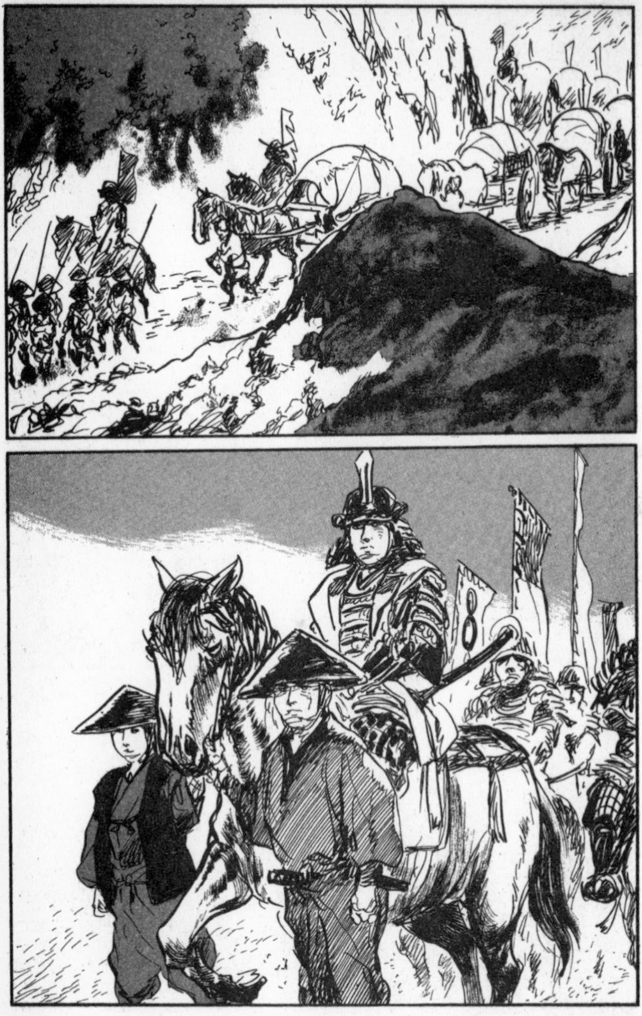

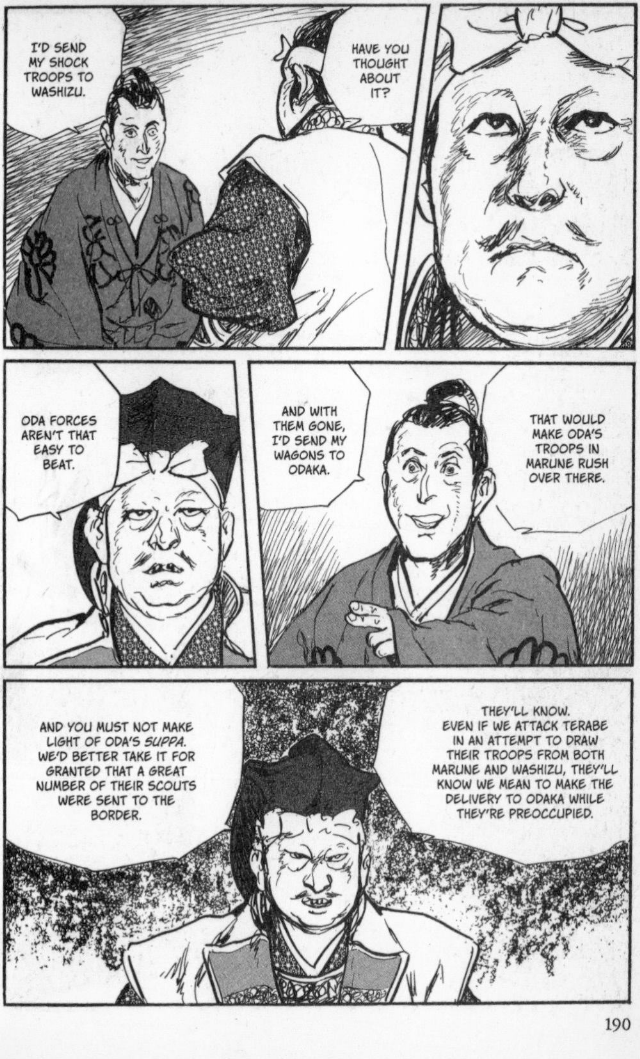
HAVE YOU THOUGHT ABOUT IT?
I'D SEND MY SHOCK TROOPS TO WASHIZU.
THAT WOULD MAKE ODA'S TROOPS IN MARUNE RUSH OVER THERE.
AND WITH THEM GONE, I'D SEND MY WAGONS TO ODAKA.
ODA FORCES AREN'T THAT EASY TO BEAT.
THEY'LL KNOW. EVEN IF WE ATTACK TERABE IN AN ATTEMPT TO DRAW THEIR TROOPS FROM BOTH MARUNE AND WASHIZU, THEY'LL KNOW WE MEAN TO MAKE THE DELIVERY TO ODAKA WHILE THEY'RE PREOCCUPIED.
AND YOU MUST NOT MAKE LIGHT OF ODA'S *SUPPA*. WE'D BETTER TAKE IT FOR GRANTED THAT A GREAT NUMBER OF THEIR SCOUTS WERE SENT TO THE BORDER.

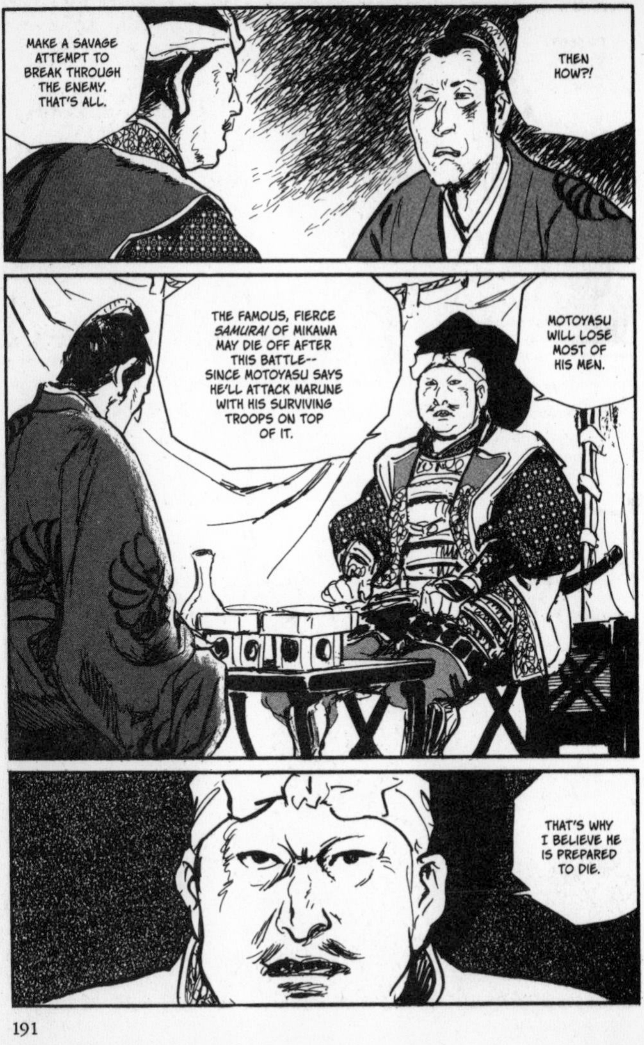
THEN HOW?!
MAKE A SAVAGE ATTEMPT TO BREAK THROUGH THE ENEMY. THAT'S ALL.
MOTOYASU WILL LOSE MOST OF HIS MEN.
THE FAMOUS, FIERCE *SAMURAI* OF MIKAWA MAY DIE OFF AFTER THIS BATTLE-- SINCE MOTOYASU SAYS HE'LL ATTACK MARUNE WITH HIS SURVIVING TROOPS ON TOP OF IT.
THAT'S WHY I BELIEVE HE IS PREPARED TO DIE.

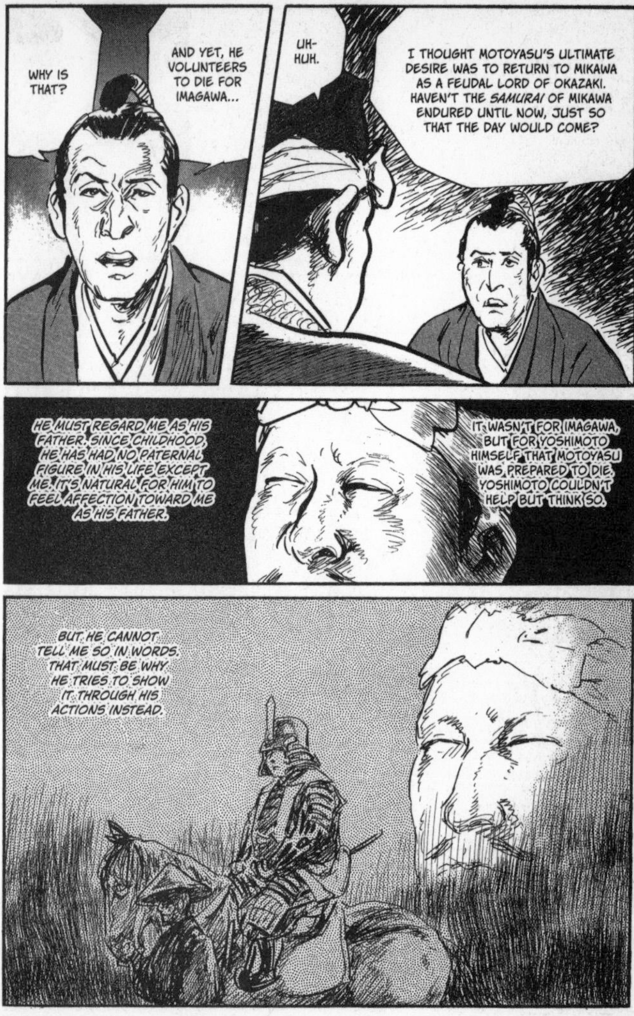
I THOUGHT MOTOYASU'S ULTIMATE DESIRE WAS TO RETURN TO MIKAWA AS A FEUDAL LORD OF OKAZAKI. HAVEN'T THE *SAMURAI* OF MIKAWA ENDURED UNTIL NOW, JUST SO THAT THE DAY WOULD COME?
UH-HUH.
AND YET, HE VOLUNTEERS TO DIE FOR IMAGAWA...
WHY IS THAT?
IT WASN'T FOR IMAGAWA, BUT FOR YOSHIMOTO HIMSELF THAT MOTOYASU WAS PREPARED TO DIE. YOSHIMOTO COULDN'T HELP BUT THINK SO.
HE MUST REGARD ME AS HIS FATHER. SINCE CHILDHOOD, HE HAS HAD NO PATERNAL FIGURE IN HIS LIFE EXCEPT ME. IT'S NATURAL FOR HIM TO FEEL AFFECTION TOWARD ME AS HIS FATHER.
BUT HE CANNOT TELL ME SO IN WORDS. THAT MUST BE WHY HE TRIES TO SHOW IT THROUGH HIS ACTIONS INSTEAD.

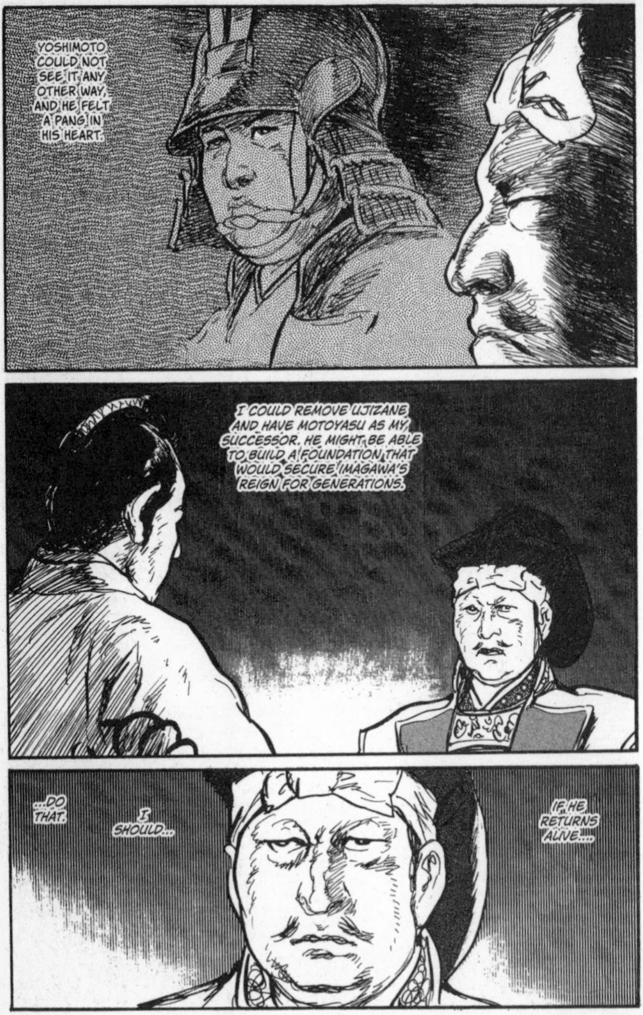
YOSHIMOTO COULD NOT SEE IT ANY OTHER WAY, AND HE FELT A PANG IN HIS HEART.
I COULD REMOVE UJIZANE AND HAVE MOTOYASU AS MY SUCCESSOR. HE MIGHT BE ABLE TO BUILD A FOUNDATION THAT WOULD SECURE IMAGAWA'S REIGN FOR GENERATIONS.
IF HE RETURNS ALIVE....
I SHOULD...
...DO THAT.

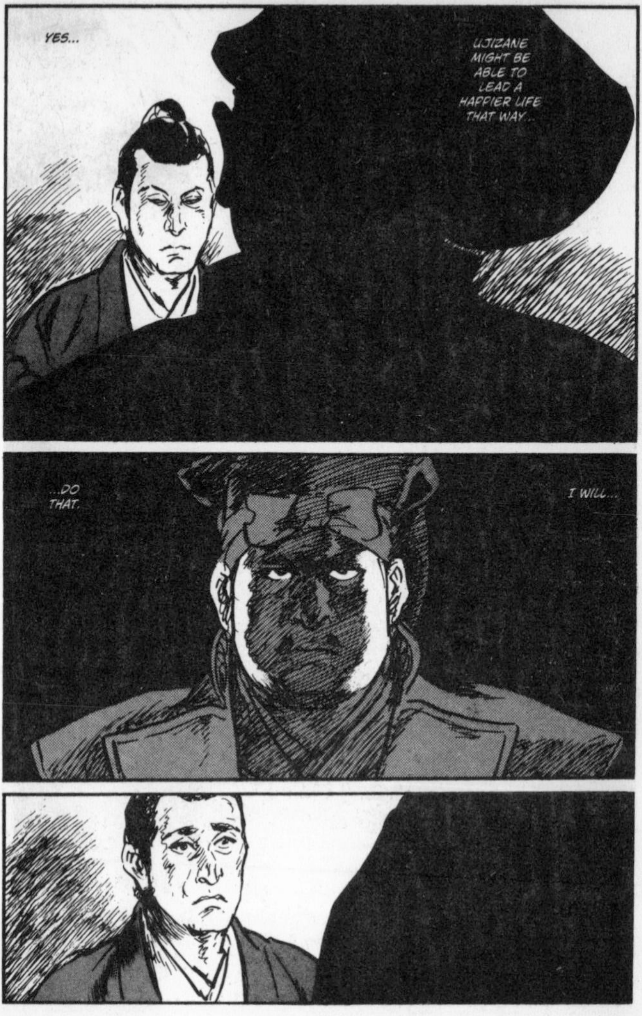
UJIZANE MIGHT BE ABLE TO LEAD A HAPPIER LIFE THAT WAY...
YES...
I WILL...
...DO THAT.

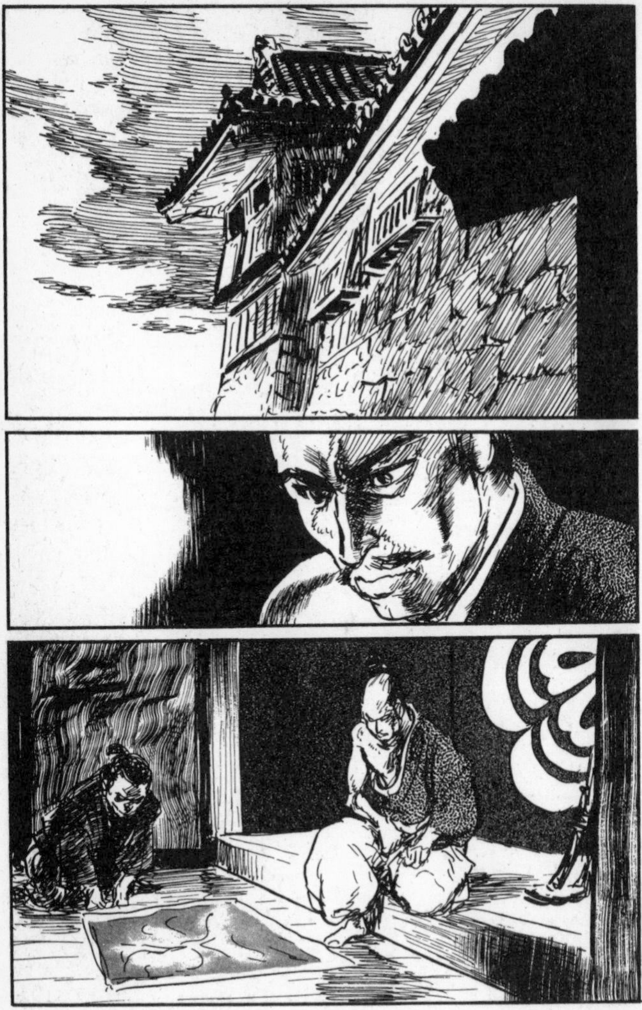

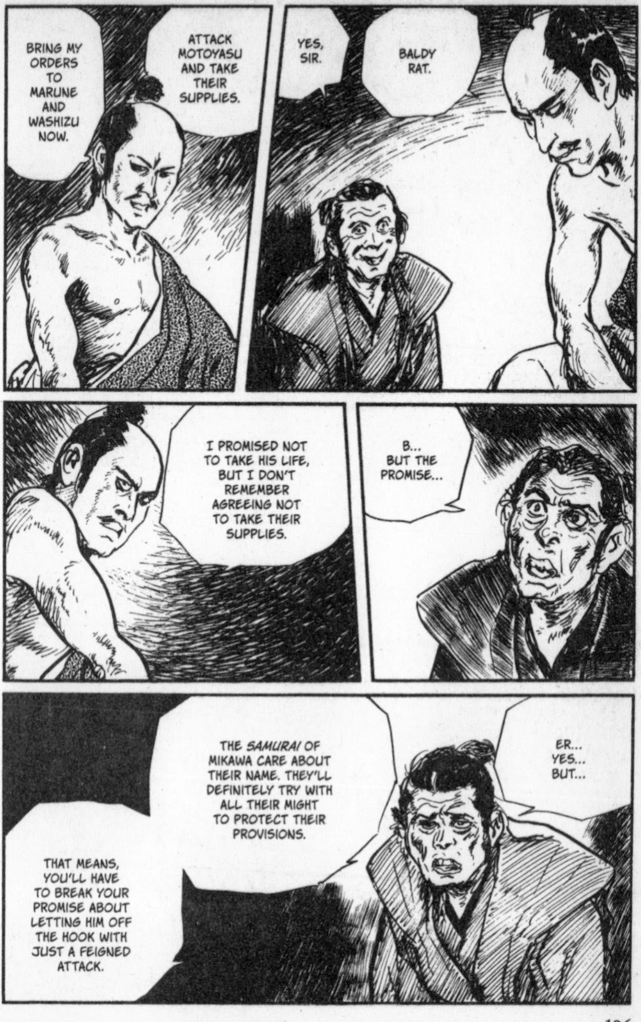
BALDY RAT.
YES, SIR.
ATTACK MOTOYASU AND TAKE THEIR SUPPLIES.
BRING MY ORDERS TO MARUNE AND WASHIZU NOW.
B... BUT THE PROMISE...
I PROMISED NOT TO TAKE HIS LIFE, BUT I DON'T REMEMBER AGREEING NOT TO TAKE THEIR SUPPLIES.
ER... YES... BUT...
THE *SAMURAI* OF MIKAWA CARE ABOUT THEIR NAME. THEY'LL DEFINITELY TRY WITH ALL THEIR MIGHT TO PROTECT THEIR PROVISIONS.
THAT MEANS, YOU'LL HAVE TO BREAK YOUR PROMISE ABOUT LETTING HIM OFF THE HOOK WITH JUST A FEIGNED ATTACK.

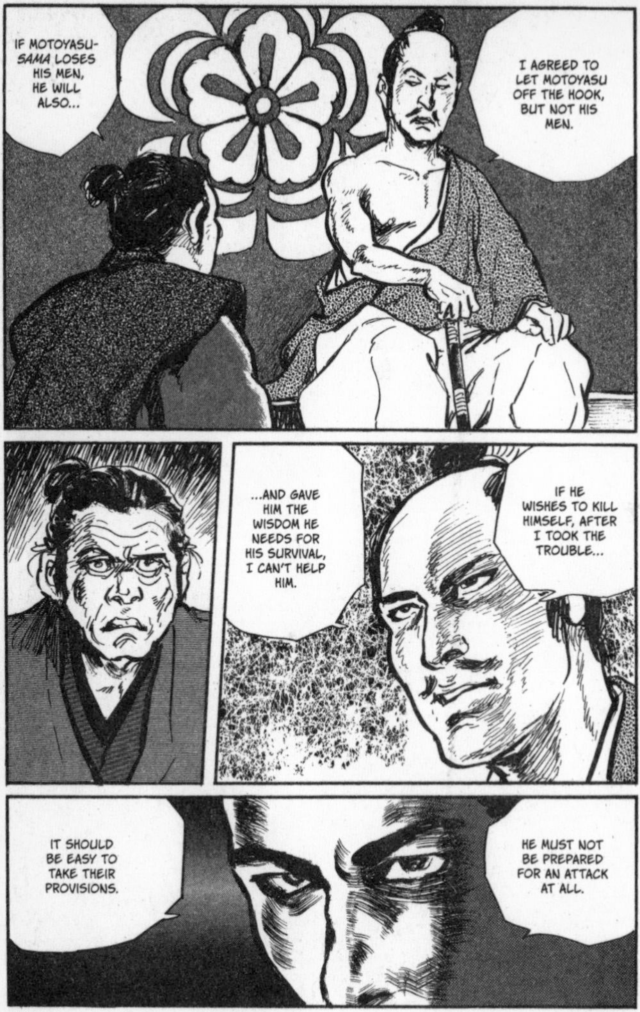
I AGREED TO LET MOTOYASU OFF THE HOOK, BUT NOT HIS MEN.
IF MOTOYASU-SAMA LOSES HIS MEN, HE WILL ALSO...
IF HE WISHES TO KILL HIMSELF, AFTER I TOOK THE TROUBLE...
...AND GAVE HIM THE WISDOM HE NEEDS FOR HIS SURVIVAL, I CAN'T HELP HIM.
HE MUST NOT BE PREPARED FOR AN ATTACK AT ALL.
IT SHOULD BE EASY TO TAKE THEIR PROVISIONS.

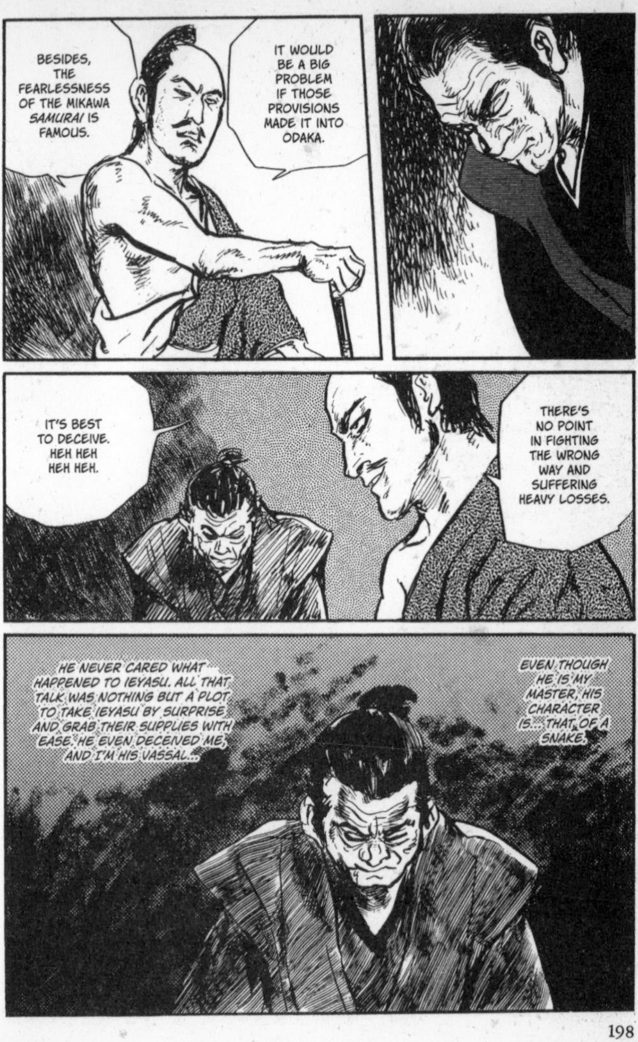
IT WOULD BE A BIG PROBLEM IF THOSE PROVISIONS MADE IT INTO ODAKA.
BESIDES, THE FEARLESSNESS OF THE MIKAWA *SAMURAI* IS FAMOUS.
THERE'S NO POINT IN FIGHTING THE WRONG WAY AND SUFFERING HEAVY LOSSES.
IT'S BEST TO DECEIVE. HEH HEH HEH HEH.
EVEN THOUGH HE IS MY MASTER, HIS CHARACTER IS... THAT OF A SNAKE.
HE NEVER CARED WHAT HAPPENED TO IEYASU. ALL THAT TALK WAS NOTHING BUT A PLOT TO TAKE IEYASU BY SURPRISE AND GRAB THEIR SUPPLIES WITH EASE. HE EVEN DECEIVED ME, AND I'M HIS VASSAL...

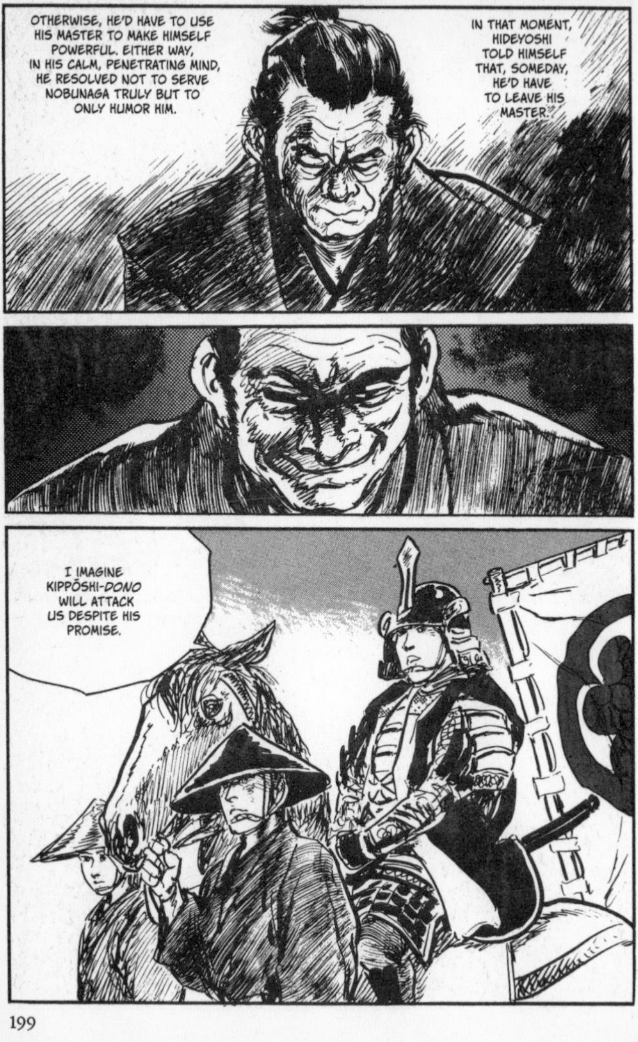
IN THAT MOMENT, HIDEYOSHI TOLD HIMSELF THAT, SOMEDAY, HE'D HAVE TO LEAVE HIS MASTER.
OTHERWISE, HE'D HAVE TO USE HIS MASTER TO MAKE HIMSELF POWERFUL. EITHER WAY, IN HIS CALM, PENETRATING MIND, HE RESOLVED NOT TO SERVE NOBUNAGA TRULY BUT TO ONLY HUMOR HIM.
I IMAGINE KIPPŌSHI-*DONO* WILL ATTACK US DESPITE HIS PROMISE.

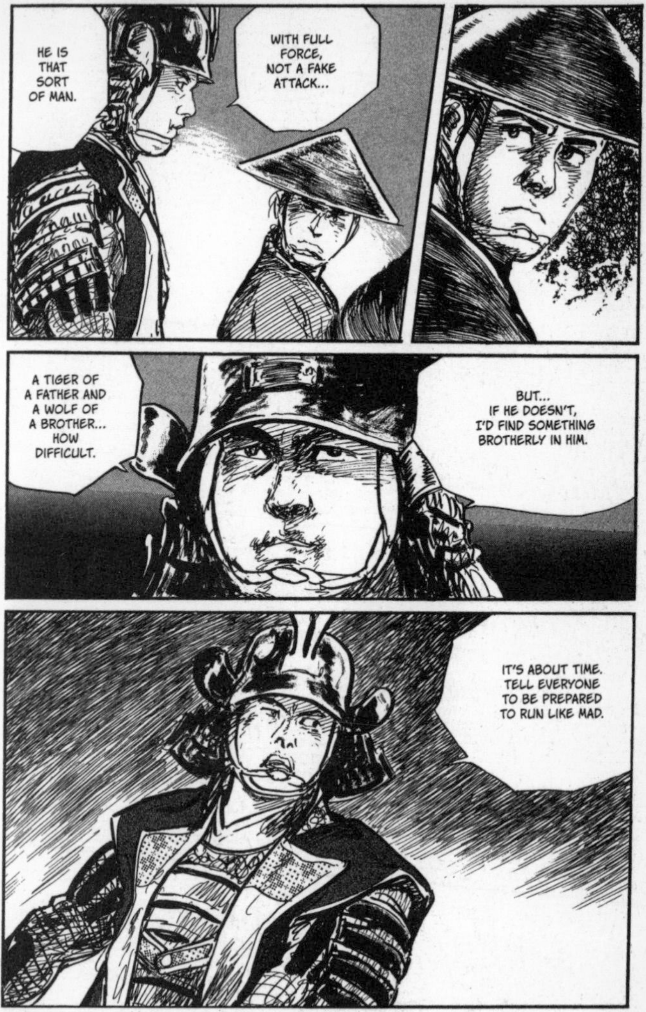
WITH FULL FORCE, NOT A FAKE ATTACK...
HE IS THAT SORT OF MAN.
BUT... IF HE DOESN'T, I'D FIND SOMETHING BROTHERLY IN HIM.
A TIGER OF A FATHER AND A WOLF OF A BROTHER... HOW DIFFICULT.
IT'S ABOUT TIME. TELL EVERYONE TO BE PREPARED TO RUN LIKE MAD.

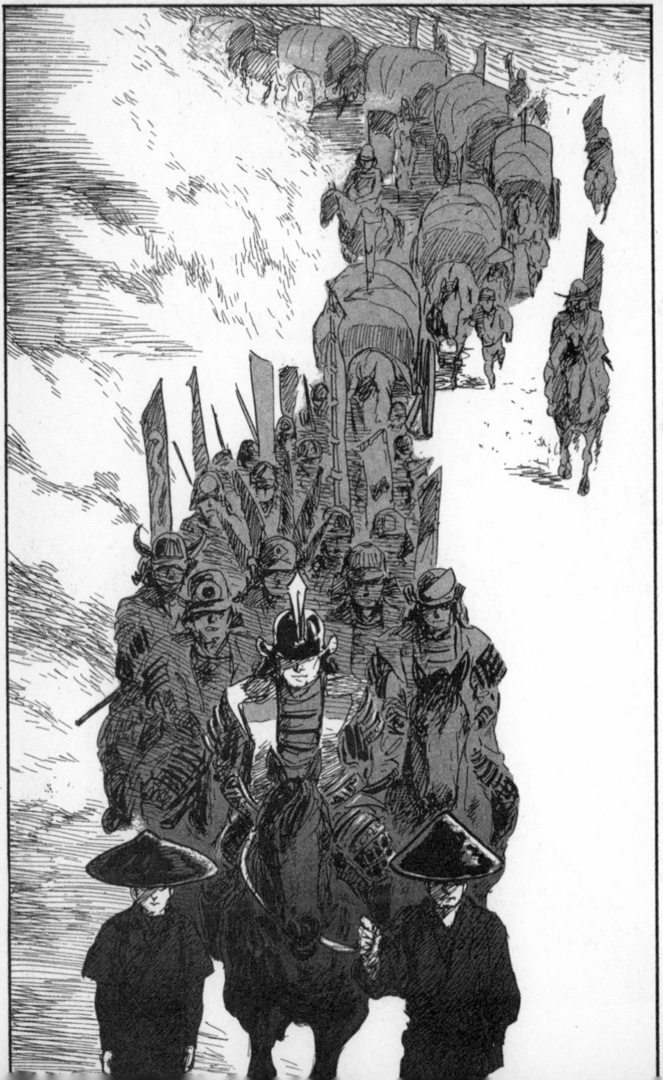

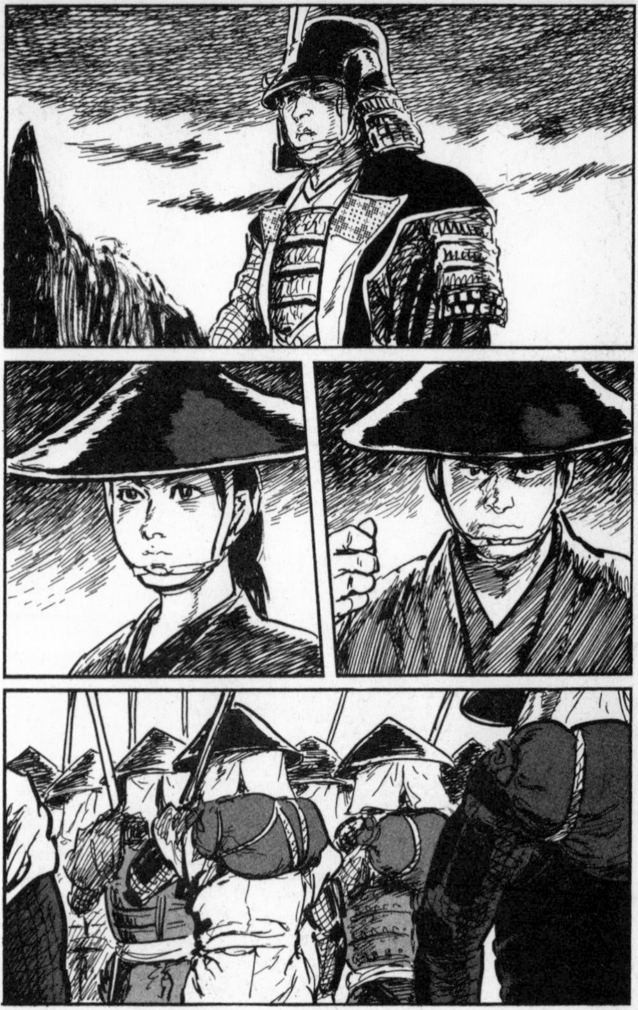

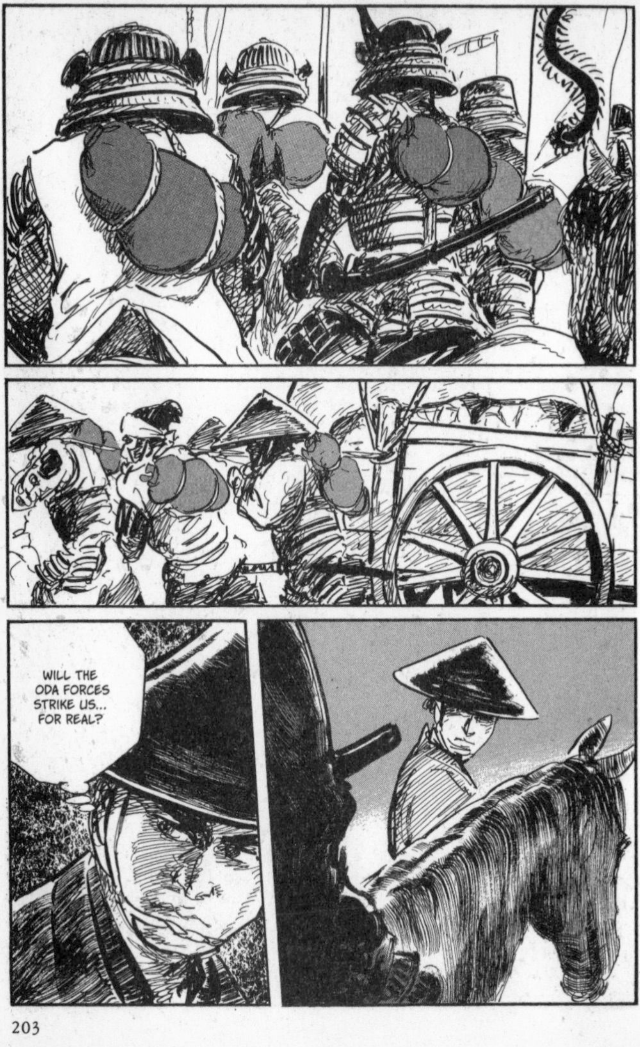
WILL THE ODA FORCES STRIKE US... FOR REAL?

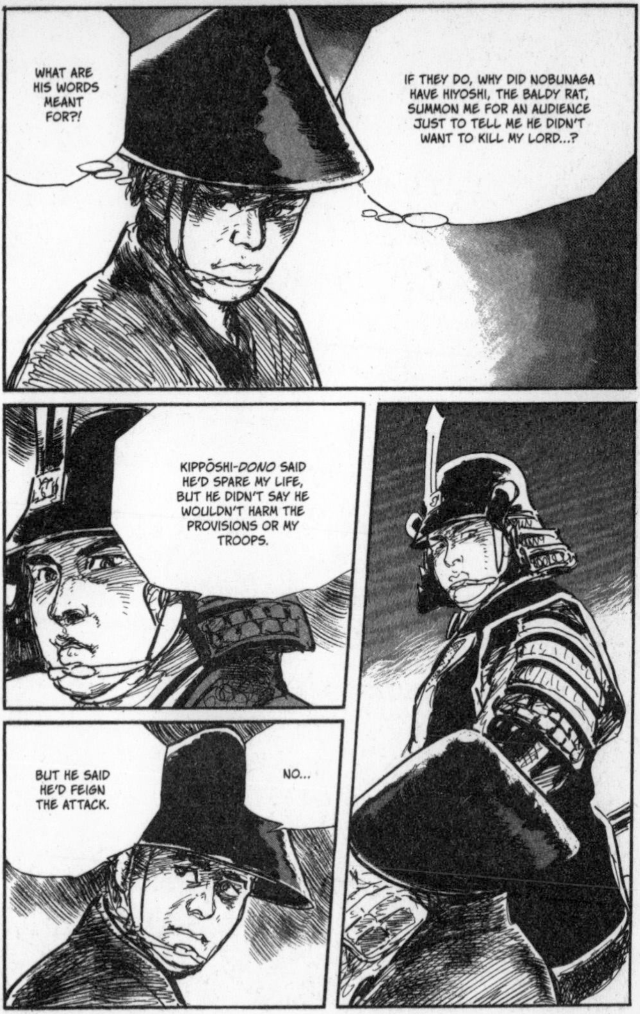
IF THEY DO, WHY DID NOBUNAGA HAVE HIYOSHI, THE BALDY RAT, SUMMON ME FOR AN AUDIENCE JUST TO TELL ME HE DIDN'T WANT TO KILL MY LORD...?
WHAT ARE HIS WORDS MEANT FOR?!
KIPPŌSHI-*DONO* SAID HE'D SPARE MY LIFE, BUT HE DIDN'T SAY HE WOULDN'T HARM THE PROVISIONS OR MY TROOPS.
NO...
BUT HE SAID HE'D FEIGN THE ATTACK.

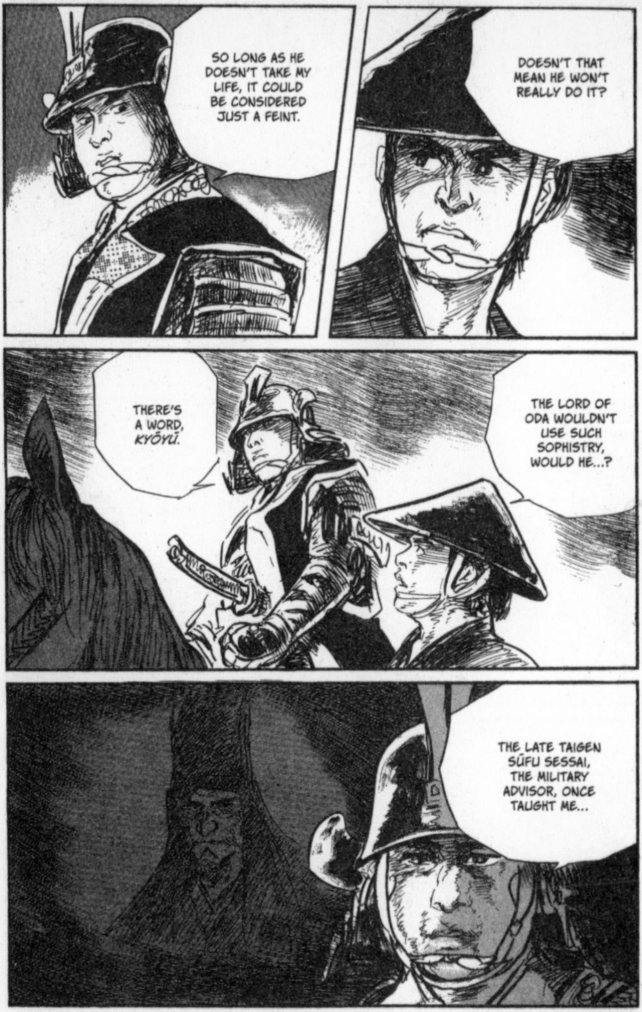
DOESN'T THAT MEAN HE WON'T REALLY DO IT?
SO LONG AS HE DOESN'T TAKE MY LIFE, IT COULD BE CONSIDERED JUST A FEINT.
THE LORD OF ODA WOULDN'T USE SUCH SOPHISTRY, WOULD HE...?
THERE'S A WORD, *KYŌYŪ*.
THE LATE TAIGEN SŪFU SESSAI, THE MILITARY ADVISOR, ONCE TAUGHT ME...

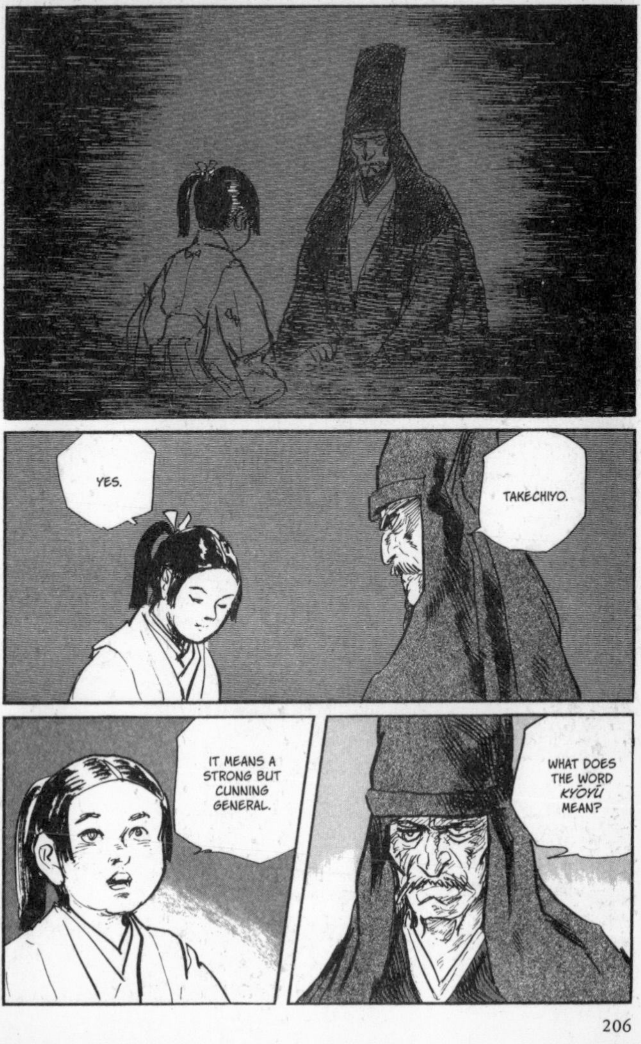
TAKECHIYO.
YES.
WHAT DOES THE WORD *KYŌYŪ* MEAN?
IT MEANS A STRONG BUT CUNNING GENERAL.

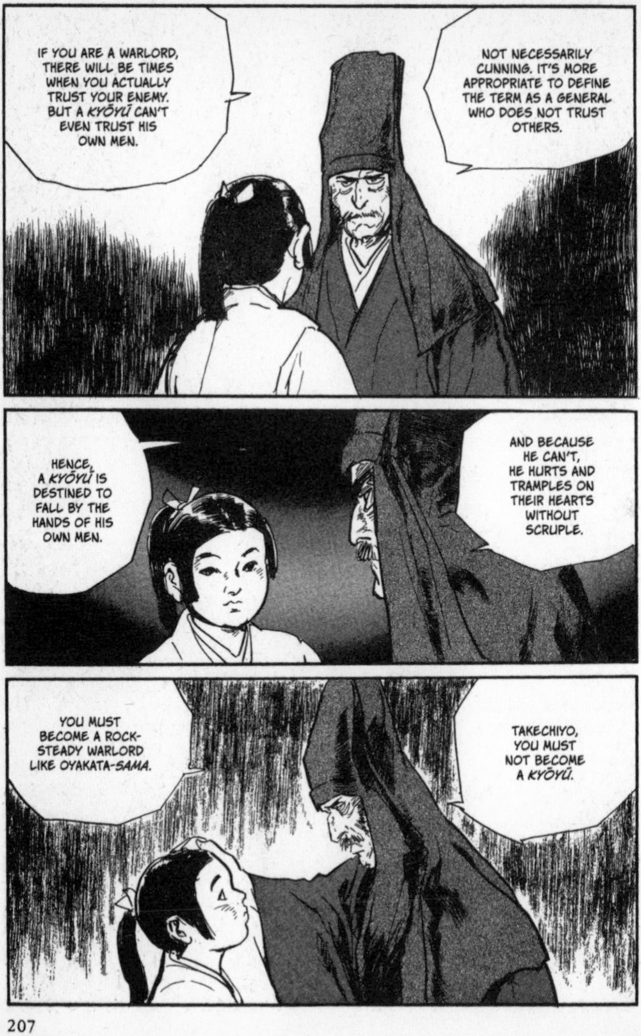
NOT NECESSARILY CUNNING. IT'S MORE APPROPRIATE TO DEFINE THE TERM AS A GENERAL WHO DOES NOT TRUST OTHERS.
IF YOU ARE A WARLORD, THERE WILL BE TIMES WHEN YOU ACTUALLY TRUST YOUR ENEMY. BUT A *KYŌYŪ* CAN'T EVEN TRUST HIS OWN MEN.
AND BECAUSE HE CAN'T, HE HURTS AND TRAMPLES ON THEIR HEARTS WITHOUT SCRUPLE.
HENCE, A *KYŌYŪ* IS DESTINED TO FALL BY THE HANDS OF HIS OWN MEN.
TAKECHIYO, YOU MUST NOT BECOME A *KYŌYŪ*.
YOU MUST BECOME A ROCK-STEADY WARLORD LIKE OYAKATA-*SAMA*.

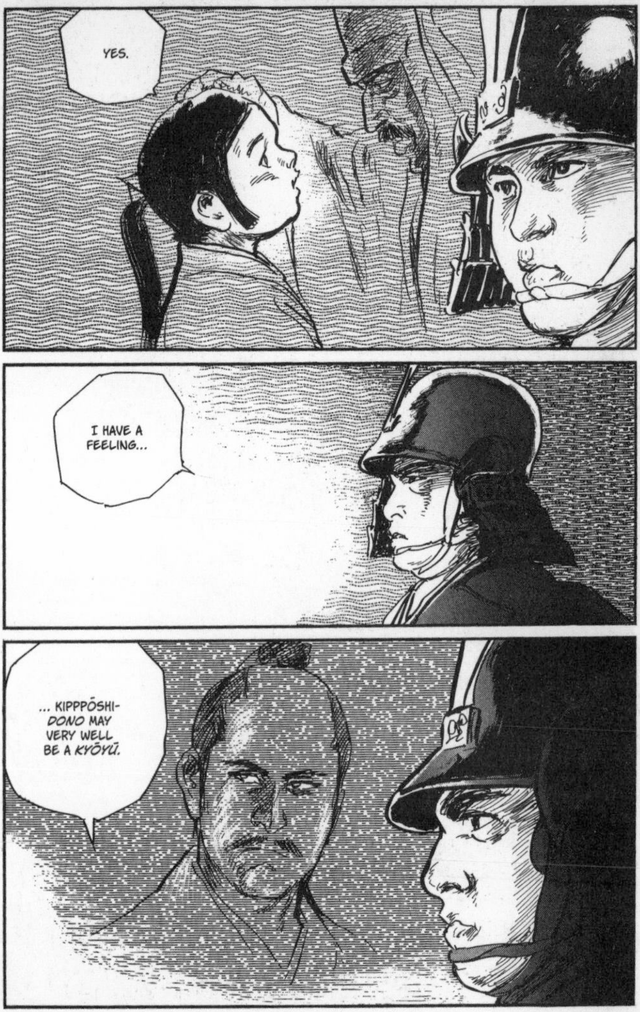
YES.
I HAVE A FEELING...
... KIPPPŌSHI-DONO MAY VERY WELL BE A KYŌYŪ.

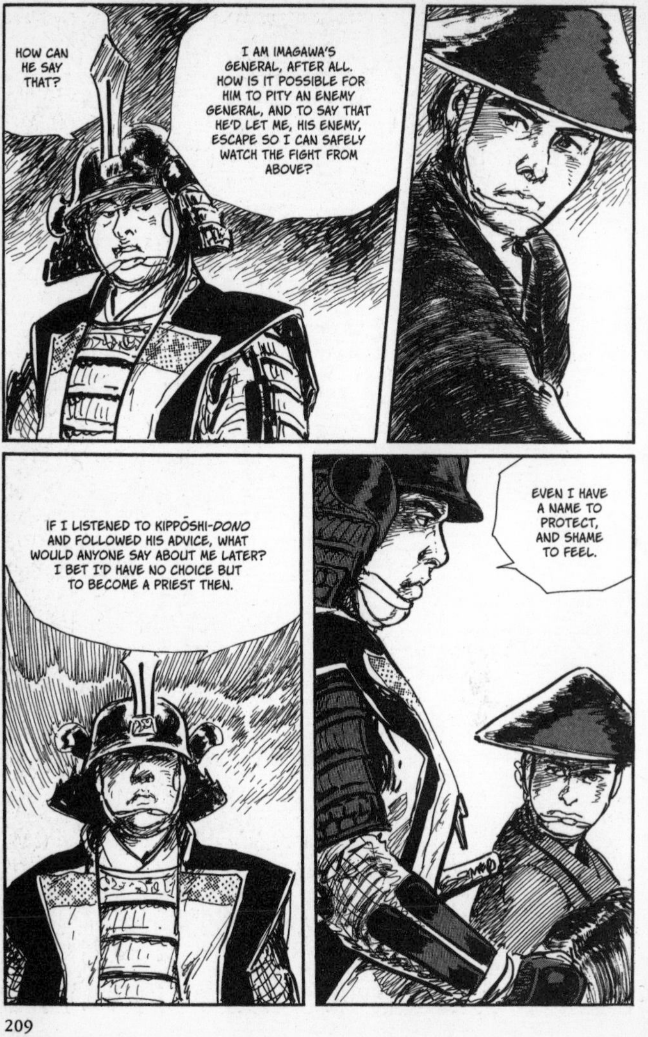
I AM IMAGAWA'S GENERAL, AFTER ALL. HOW IS IT POSSIBLE FOR HIM TO PITY AN ENEMY GENERAL, AND TO SAY THAT HE'D LET ME, HIS ENEMY, ESCAPE SO I CAN SAFELY WATCH THE FIGHT FROM ABOVE?
HOW CAN HE SAY THAT?
EVEN I HAVE A NAME TO PROTECT, AND SHAME TO FEEL.
IF I LISTENED TO KIPPŌSHI-*DONO* AND FOLLOWED HIS ADVICE, WHAT WOULD ANYONE SAY ABOUT ME LATER? I BET I'D HAVE NO CHOICE BUT TO BECOME A PRIEST THEN.

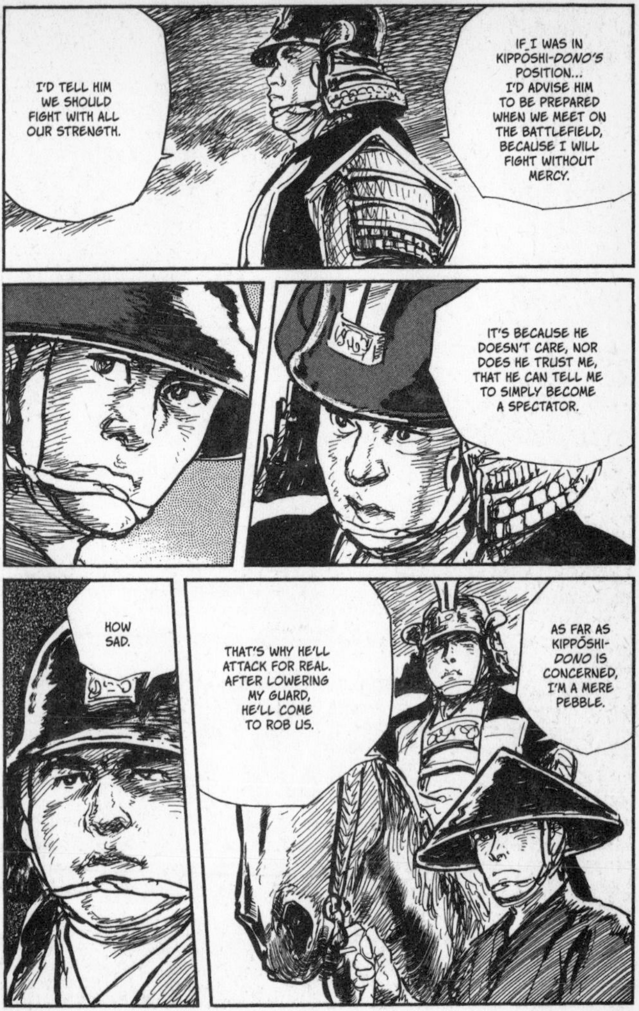
IF I WAS IN KIPPŌSHI-*DONO'S* POSITION... I'D ADVISE HIM TO BE PREPARED WHEN WE MEET ON THE BATTLEFIELD, BECAUSE I WILL FIGHT WITHOUT MERCY.
I'D TELL HIM WE SHOULD FIGHT WITH ALL OUR STRENGTH.
IT'S BECAUSE HE DOESN'T CARE, NOR DOES HE TRUST ME, THAT HE CAN TELL ME TO SIMPLY BECOME A SPECTATOR.
AS FAR AS KIPPŌSHI-*DONO* IS CONCERNED, I'M A MERE PEBBLE.
THAT'S WHY HE'LL ATTACK FOR REAL. AFTER LOWERING MY GUARD, HE'LL COME TO ROB US.
HOW SAD.

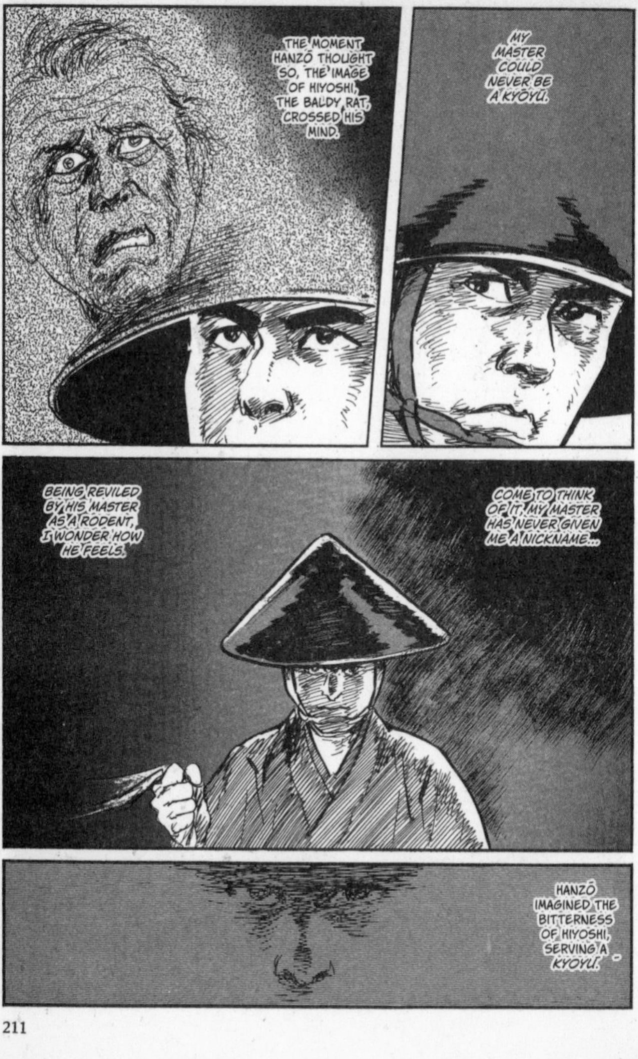
MY MASTER COULD NEVER BE A KYŌYŪ.
THE MOMENT HANZŌ THOUGHT SO, THE IMAGE OF HIYOSHI, THE BALDY RAT, CROSSED HIS MIND.
COME TO THINK OF IT, MY MASTER HAS NEVER GIVEN ME A NICKNAME...
BEING REVILED BY HIS MASTER AS A RODENT, I WONDER HOW HE FEELS.
HANZŌ IMAGINED THE BITTERNESS OF HIYOSHI, SERVING A KYŌYŪ.

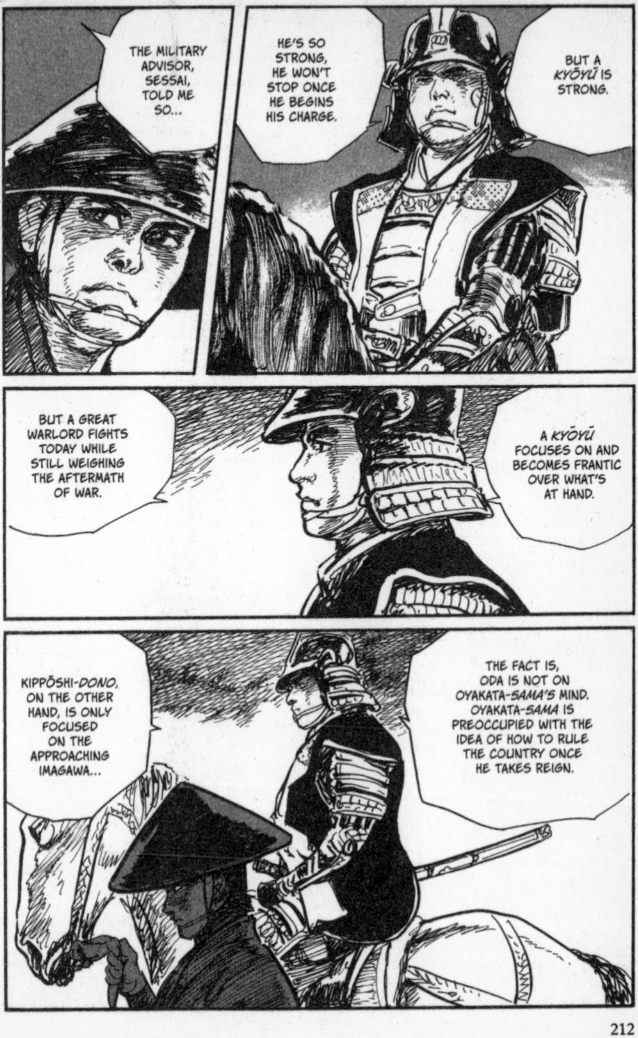
BUT A *KYŌYŪ* IS STRONG.
HE'S SO STRONG, HE WON'T STOP ONCE HE BEGINS HIS CHARGE.
THE MILITARY ADVISOR, SESSAI, TOLD ME SO...
A *KYŌYŪ* FOCUSES ON AND BECOMES FRANTIC OVER WHAT'S AT HAND.
BUT A GREAT WARLORD FIGHTS TODAY WHILE STILL WEIGHING THE AFTERMATH OF WAR.
THE FACT IS, ODA IS NOT ON OYAKATA-*SAMA'S* MIND. OYAKATA-*SAMA* IS PREOCCUPIED WITH THE IDEA OF HOW TO RULE THE COUNTRY ONCE HE TAKES REIGN.
KIPPŌSHI-*DONO*, ON THE OTHER HAND, IS ONLY FOCUSED ON THE APPROACHING IMAGAWA...

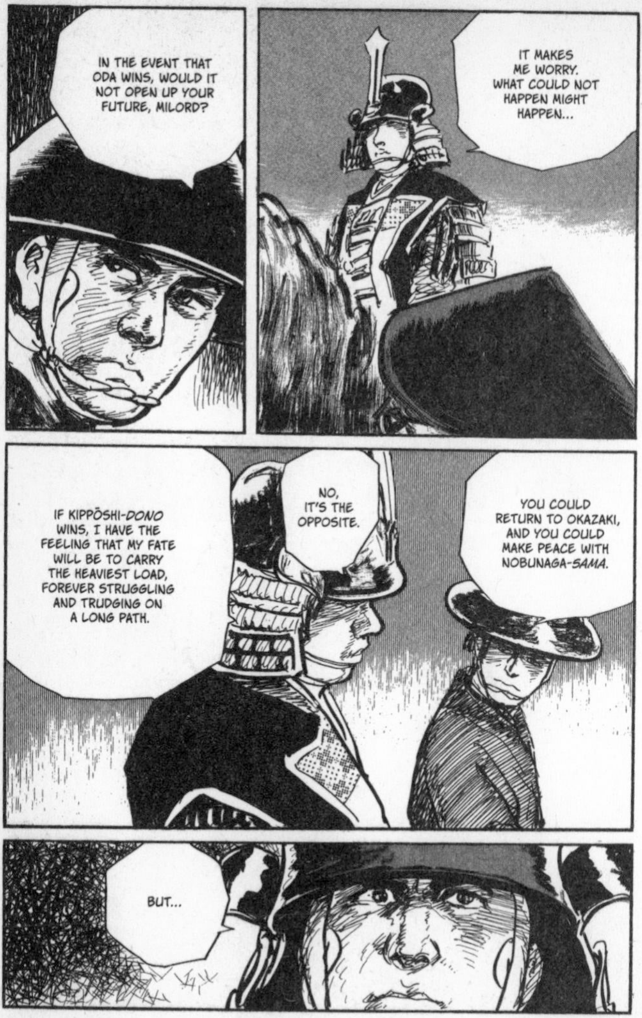
IT MAKES ME WORRY. WHAT COULD NOT HAPPEN MIGHT HAPPEN...
IN THE EVENT THAT ODA WINS, WOULD IT NOT OPEN UP YOUR FUTURE, MILORD?
YOU COULD RETURN TO OKAZAKI, AND YOU COULD MAKE PEACE WITH NOBUNAGA-*SAMA*.
NO, IT'S THE OPPOSITE.
IF KIPPŌSHI-*DONO* WINS, I HAVE THE FEELING THAT MY FATE WILL BE TO CARRY THE HEAVIEST LOAD, FOREVER STRUGGLING AND TRUDGING ON A LONG PATH.
BUT...

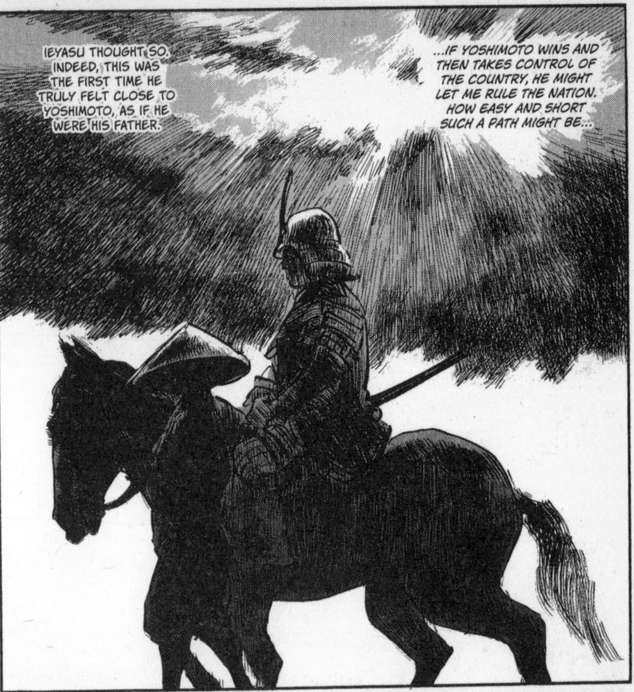
...IF YOSHIMOTO WINS AND THEN TAKES CONTROL OF THE COUNTRY, HE MIGHT LET ME RULE THE NATION. HOW EASY AND SHORT SUCH A PATH MIGHT BE...
IEYASU THOUGHT SO. INDEED, THIS WAS THE FIRST TIME HE TRULY FELT CLOSE TO YOSHIMOTO, AS IF HE WERE HIS FATHER.
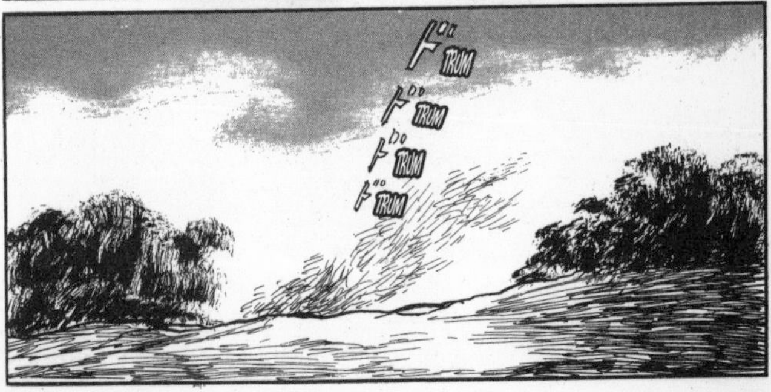
ド TRUM
ド TRUM
ド TRUM
ド TRUM

ODA IS COMING!!
BE PREPARED!!
ド TRUM
ド TRUM
ド TRUM

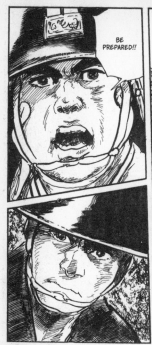

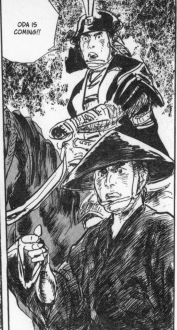

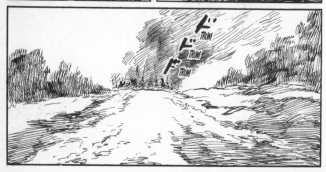

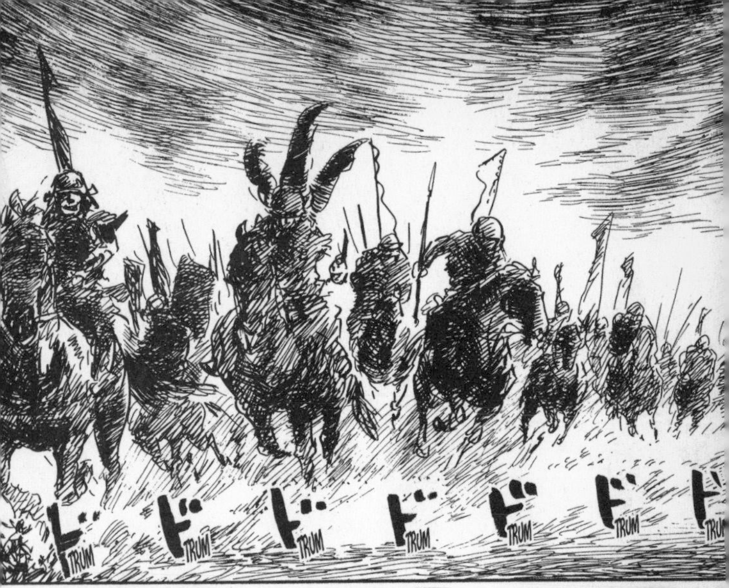
ド TRUM
ド TRUM
ド TRUM
ド TRUM
ド TRUM
ド TRUM
ド
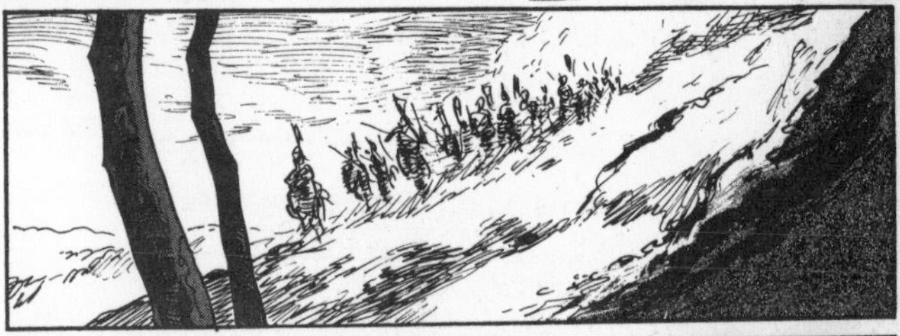
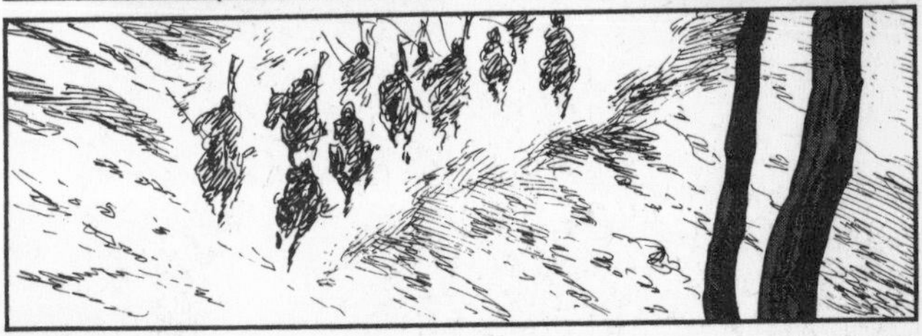

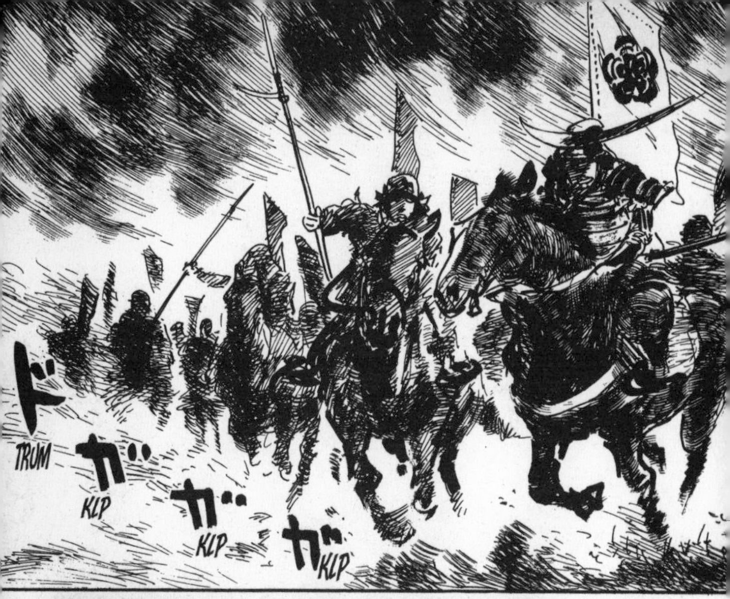
ド
TRUM
ガ
KLP
ガ
KLP
ガ
KLP

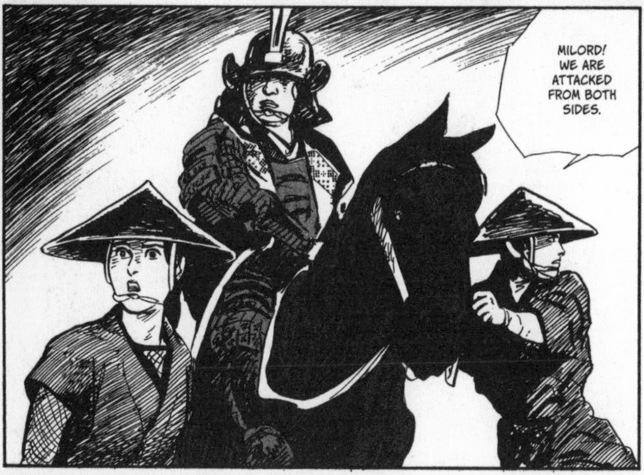
MILORD! WE ARE ATTACKED FROM BOTH SIDES.

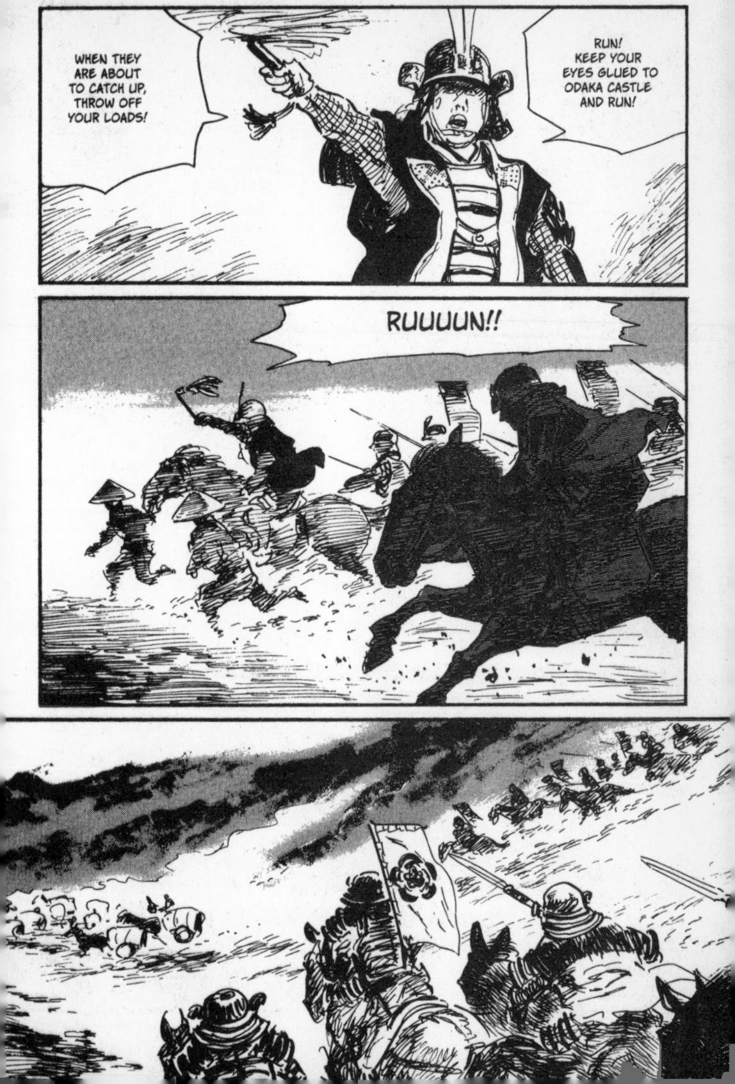
RUN! KEEP YOUR EYES GLUED TO ODAKA CASTLE AND RUN!
WHEN THEY ARE ABOUT TO CATCH UP, THROW OFF YOUR LOADS!
RUUUUN!!

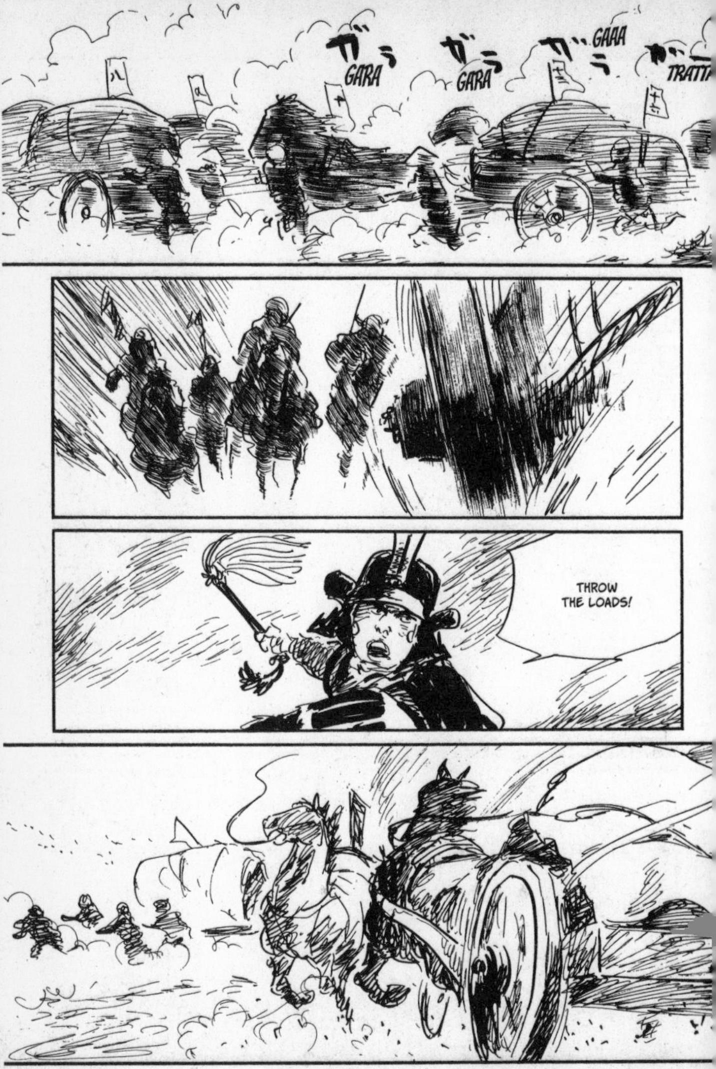
TRATTA
GAAA
GARA
GARA
THROW THE LOADS!

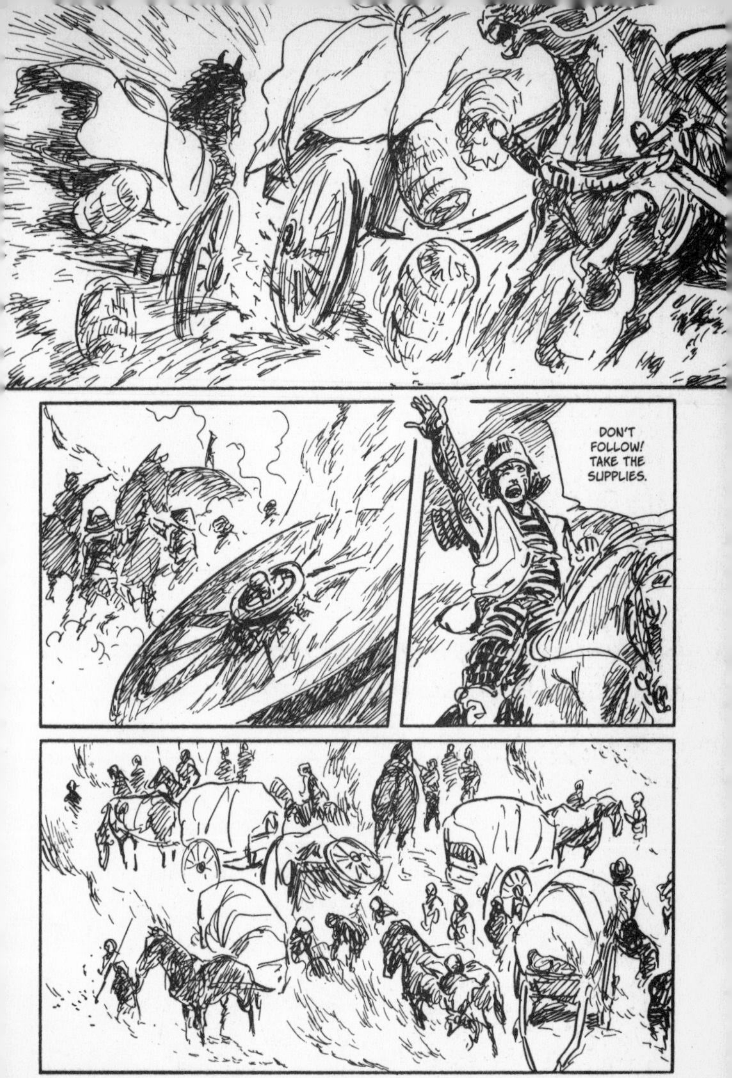
DON'T FOLLOW! TAKE THE SUPPLIES.

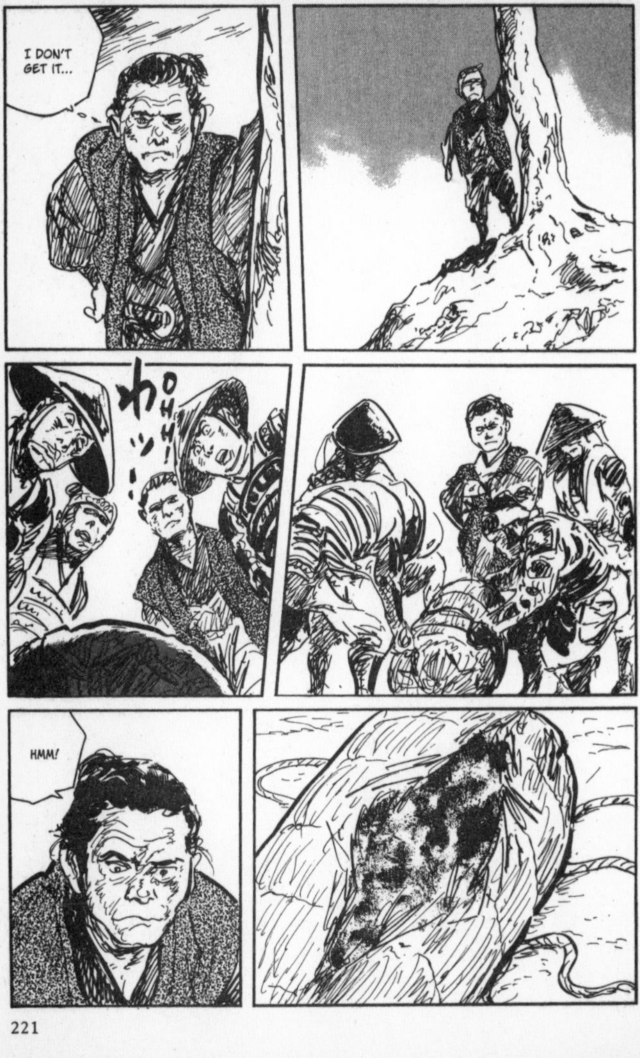
I DON'T GET IT...
わッ!!
OHHH!
HMM!

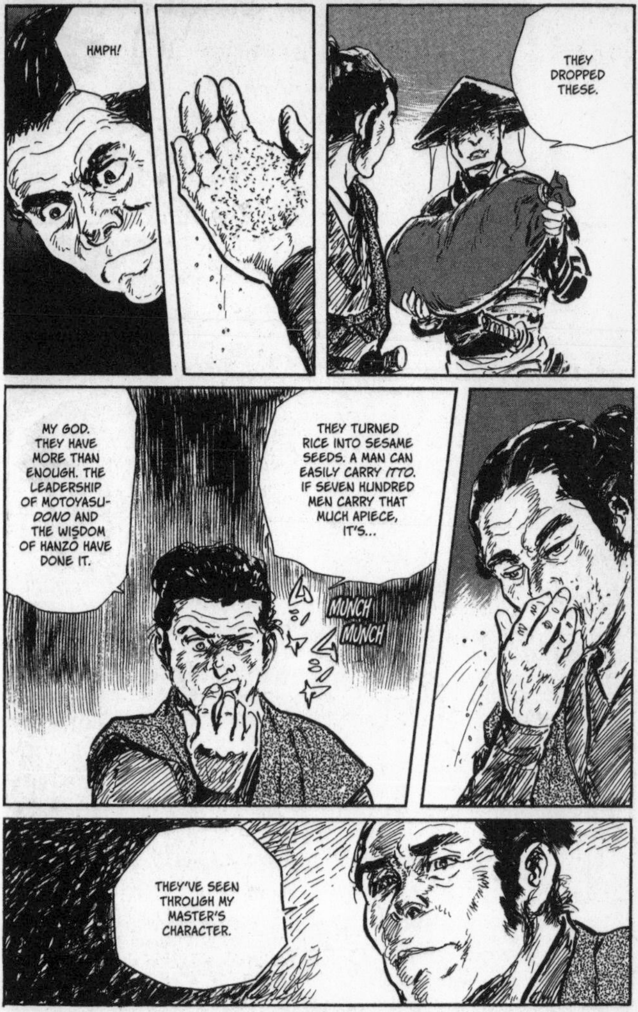
THEY DROPPED THESE.
HMPH!
THEY TURNED RICE INTO SESAME SEEDS. A MAN CAN EASILY CARRY *ITTO*. IF SEVEN HUNDRED MEN CARRY THAT MUCH APIECE, IT'S...
MY GOD. THEY HAVE MORE THAN ENOUGH. THE LEADERSHIP OF MOTOYASU-*DONO* AND THE WISDOM OF HANZŌ HAVE DONE IT.
MUNCH MUNCH
THEY'VE SEEN THROUGH MY MASTER'S CHARACTER.

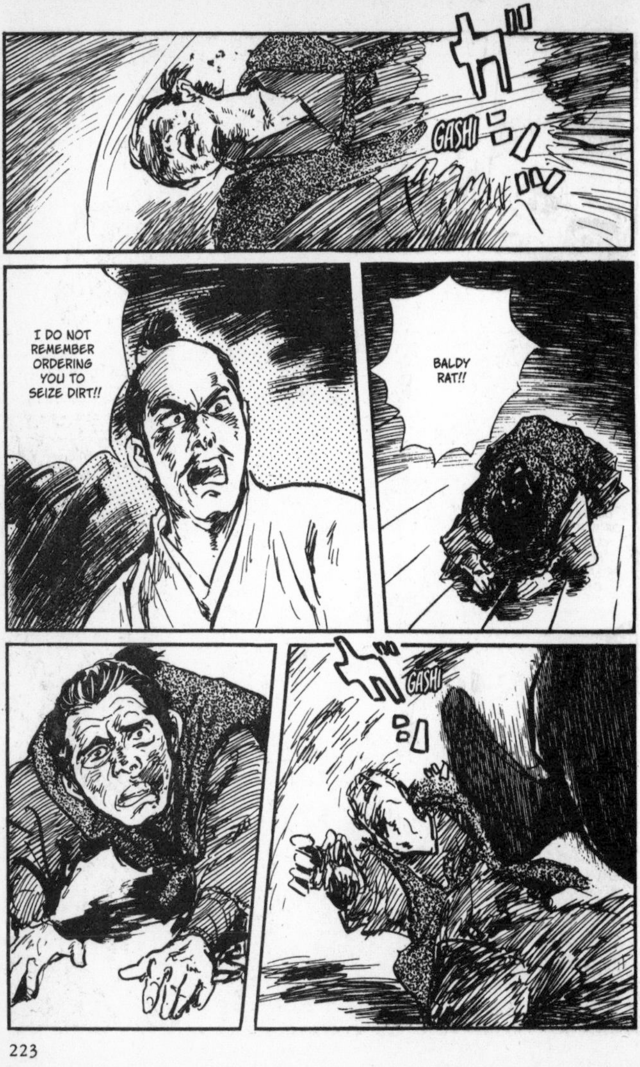
GASHI
BALDY RAT!!
I DO NOT REMEMBER ORDERING YOU TO SEIZE DIRT!!
GASHI

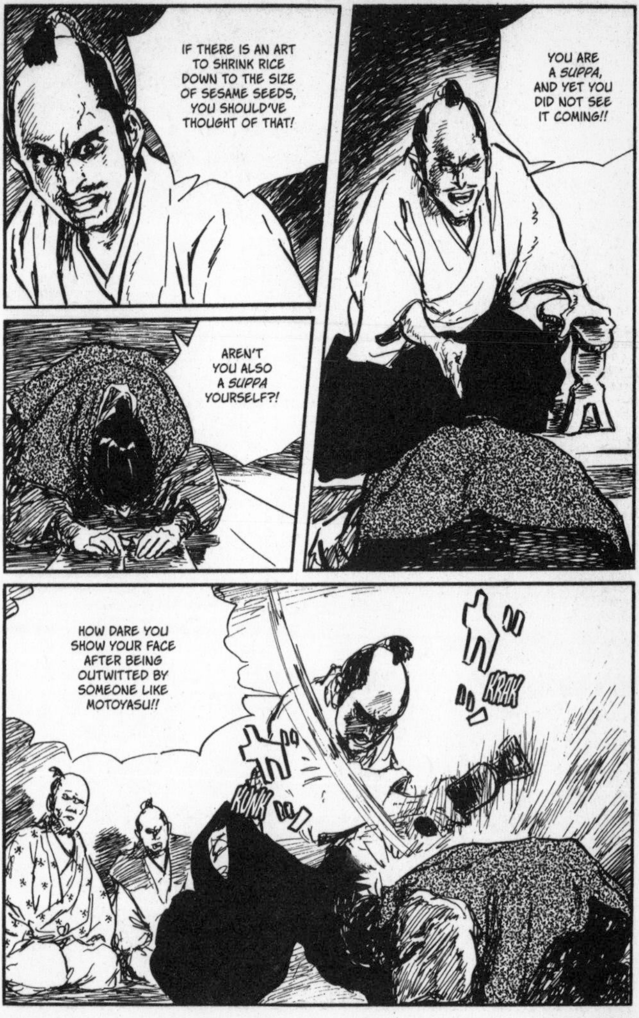
YOU ARE A *SUPPA*, AND YET YOU DID NOT SEE IT COMING!!
IF THERE IS AN ART TO SHRINK RICE DOWN TO THE SIZE OF SESAME SEEDS, YOU SHOULD'VE THOUGHT OF THAT!
AREN'T YOU ALSO A *SUPPA* YOURSELF?!
KRAK
HOW DARE YOU SHOW YOUR FACE AFTER BEING OUTWITTED BY SOMEONE LIKE MOTOYASU!!
KONK

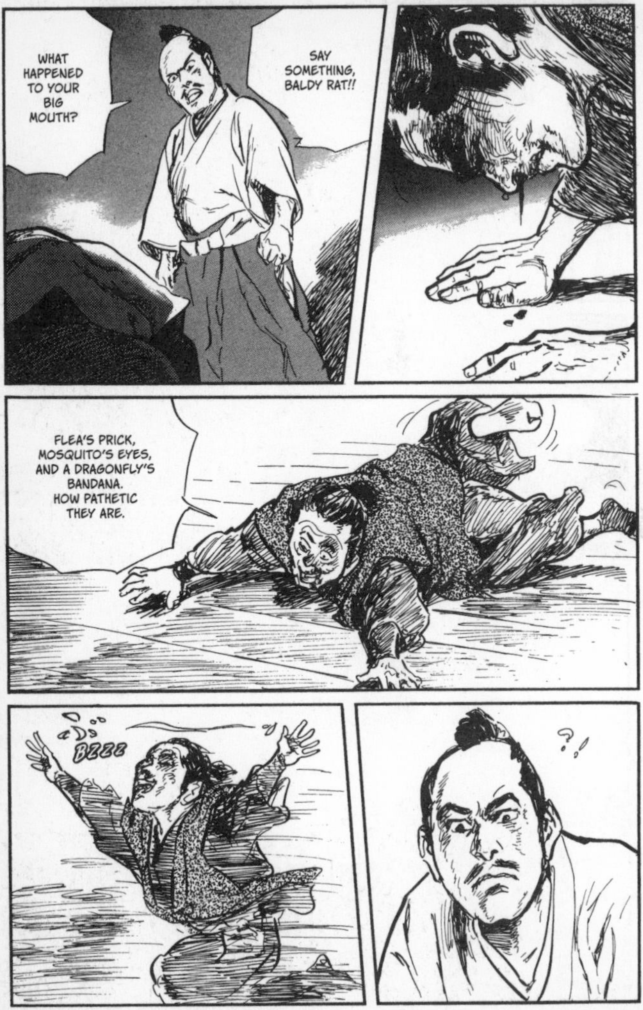
SAY SOMETHING, BALDY RAT!!
WHAT HAPPENED TO YOUR BIG MOUTH?
FLEA'S PRICK, MOSQUITO'S EYES, AND A DRAGONFLY'S BANDANA. HOW PATHETIC THEY ARE.
?!
BZZZ

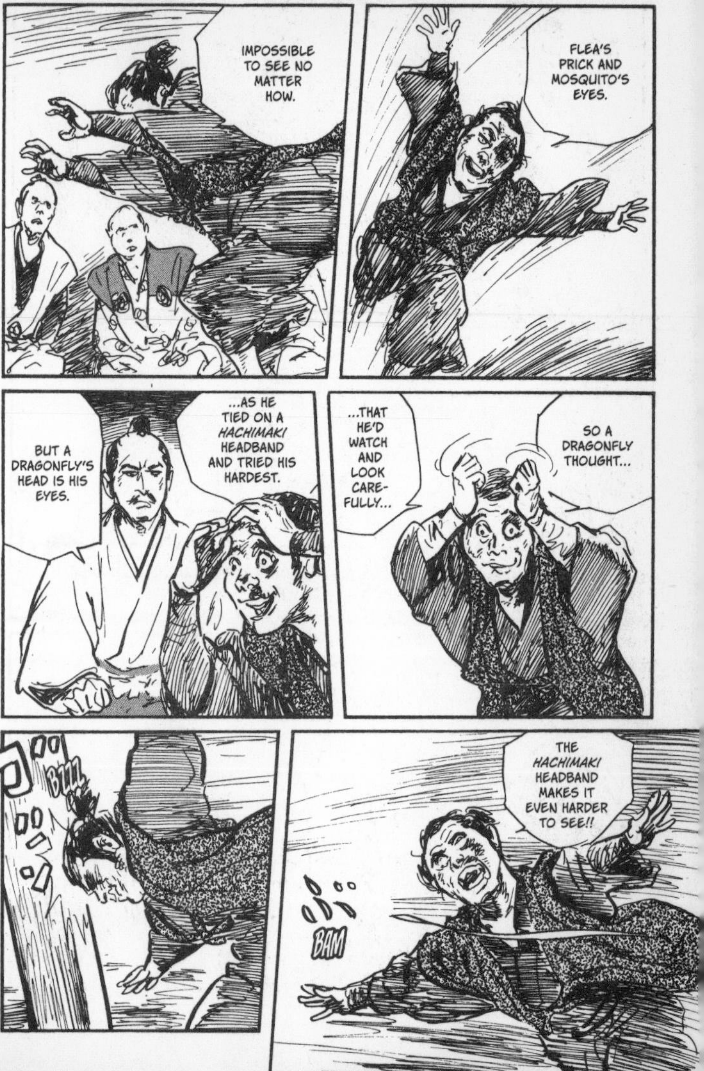
FLEA'S PRICK AND MOSQUITO'S EYES.
IMPOSSIBLE TO SEE NO MATTER HOW.
SO A DRAGONFLY THOUGHT...
...THAT HE'D WATCH AND LOOK CARE-FULLY...
...AS HE TIED ON A *HACHIMAKI* HEADBAND AND TRIED HIS HARDEST.
BUT A DRAGONFLY'S HEAD IS HIS EYES.
THE *HACHIMAKI* HEADBAND MAKES IT EVEN HARDER TO SEE!!
BAM
BZZZ

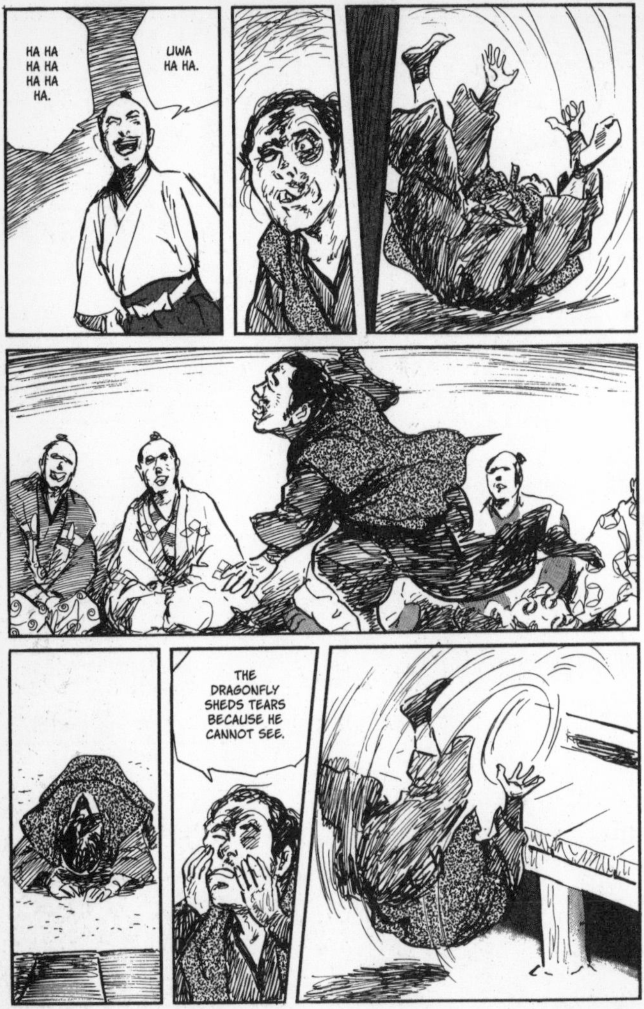
UWA HA HA.
HA HA HA HA HA HA HA.
THE DRAGONFLY SHEDS TEARS BECAUSE HE CANNOT SEE.

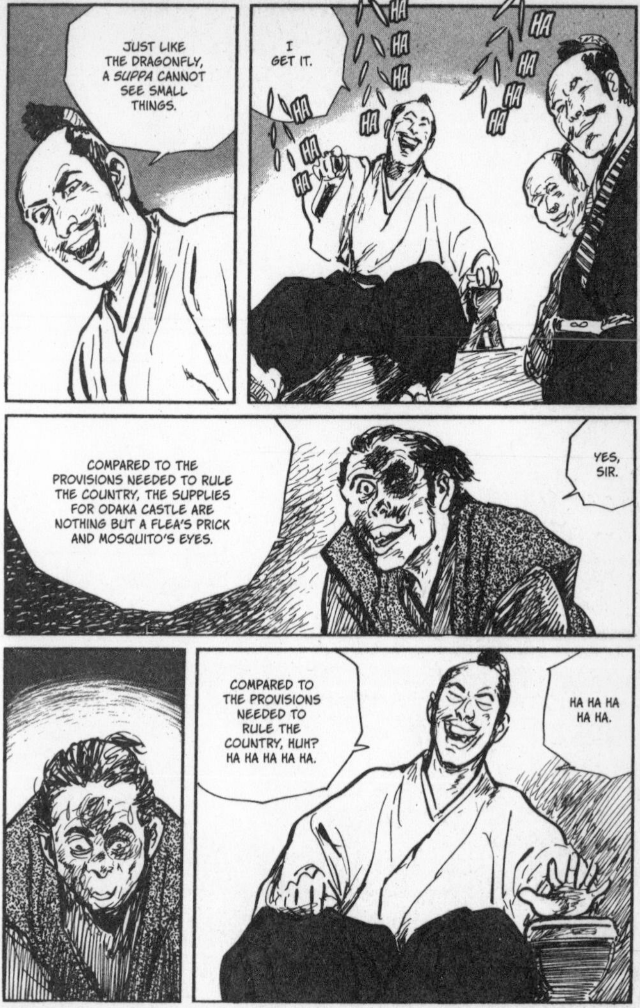
HA HA HA HA HA HA
HA HA HA HA
I GET IT.
HA HA HA
JUST LIKE THE DRAGONFLY, A *SUPPA* CANNOT SEE SMALL THINGS.
YES, SIR.
COMPARED TO THE PROVISIONS NEEDED TO RULE THE COUNTRY, THE SUPPLIES FOR ODAKA CASTLE ARE NOTHING BUT A FLEA'S PRICK AND MOSQUITO'S EYES.
HA HA HA HA HA.
COMPARED TO THE PROVISIONS NEEDED TO RULE THE COUNTRY, HUH? HA HA HA HA HA.

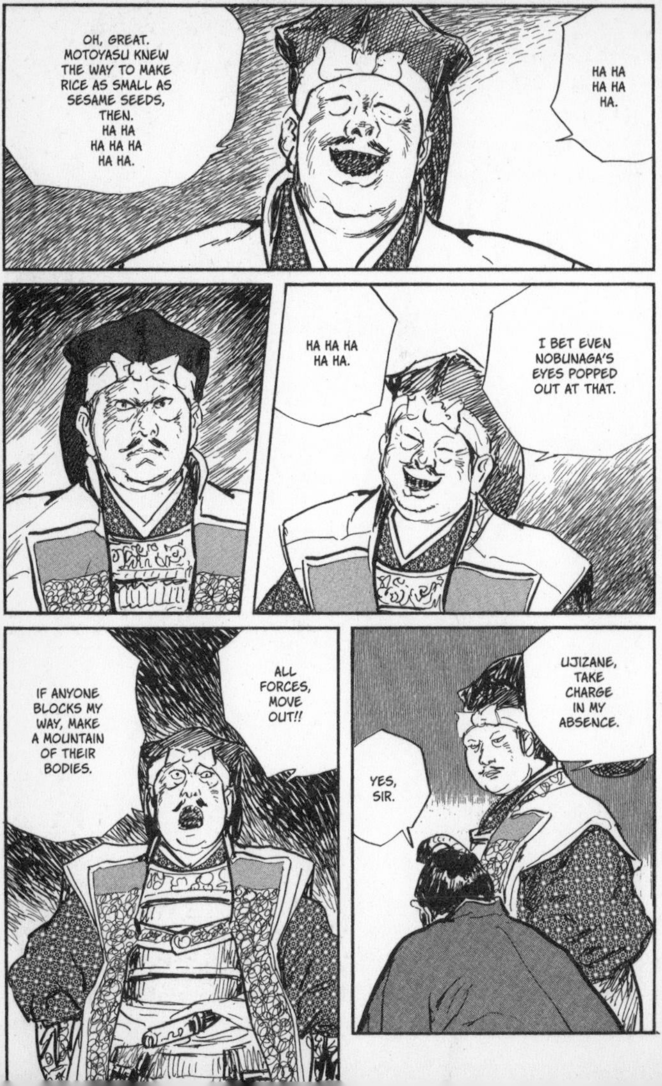
OH, GREAT. MOTOYASU KNEW THE WAY TO MAKE RICE AS SMALL AS SESAME SEEDS, THEN. HA HA HA HA HA HA HA.
HA HA HA HA HA.
I BET EVEN NOBUNAGA'S EYES POPPED OUT AT THAT.
HA HA HA HA HA.
UJIZANE, TAKE CHARGE IN MY ABSENCE.
YES, SIR.
ALL FORCES, MOVE OUT!!
IF ANYONE BLOCKS MY WAY, MAKE A MOUNTAIN OF THEIR BODIES.

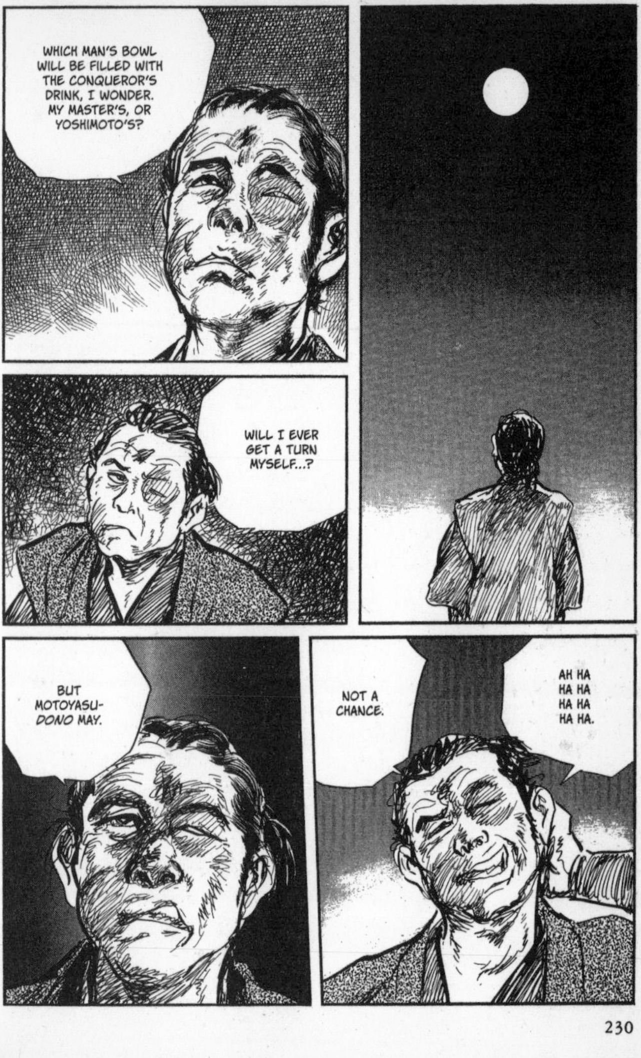
WHICH MAN'S BOWL WILL BE FILLED WITH THE CONQUEROR'S DRINK, I WONDER. MY MASTER'S, OR YOSHIMOTO'S?
WILL I EVER GET A TURN MYSELF...?
AH HA HA HA HA HA HA HA.
NOT A CHANCE.
BUT MOTOYASU-DONO MAY.

Chapter On Relinquishing Death

No. 1: Straw Sandals for Conqueror's Horses

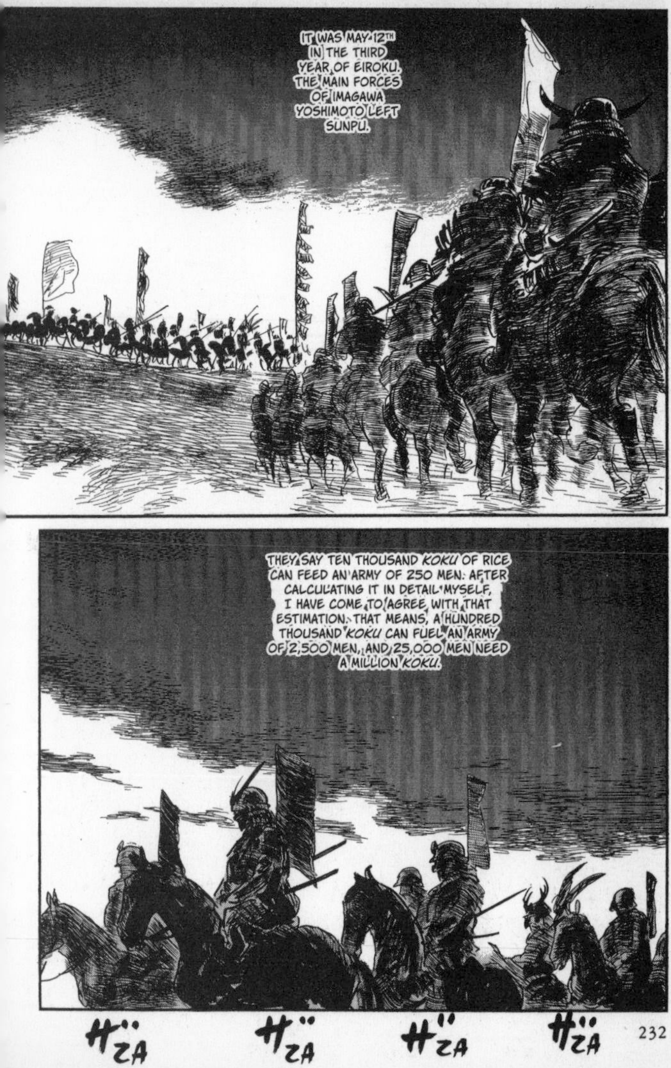
IT WAS MAY 12TH IN THE THIRD YEAR OF EIROKU. THE MAIN FORCES OF IMAGAWA YOSHIMOTO LEFT SUNPU.
THEY SAY TEN THOUSAND *KOKU* OF RICE CAN FEED AN ARMY OF 250 MEN. AFTER CALCULATING IT IN DETAIL MYSELF, I HAVE COME TO AGREE WITH THAT ESTIMATION. THAT MEANS, A HUNDRED THOUSAND *KOKU* CAN FUEL AN ARMY OF 2,500 MEN, AND 25,000 MEN NEED A MILLION *KOKU*.
ZA
ZA
ZA
ZA

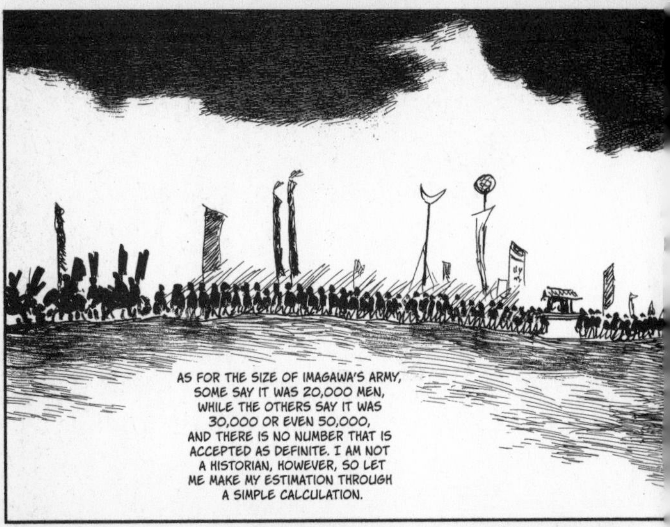
AS FOR THE SIZE OF IMAGAWA'S ARMY, SOME SAY IT WAS 20,000 MEN, WHILE THE OTHERS SAY IT WAS 30,000 OR EVEN 50,000, AND THERE IS NO NUMBER THAT IS ACCEPTED AS DEFINITE. I AM NOT A HISTORIAN, HOWEVER, SO LET ME MAKE MY ESTIMATION THROUGH A SIMPLE CALCULATION.

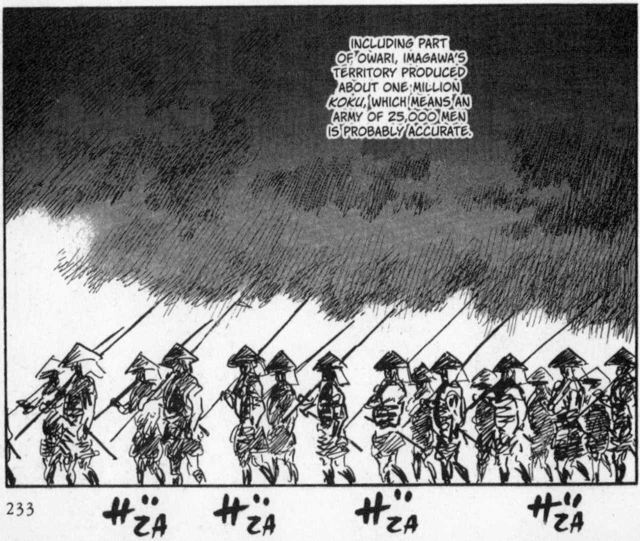
INCLUDING PART OF OWARI, IMAGAWA'S TERRITORY PRODUCED ABOUT ONE MILLION *KOKU*, WHICH MEANS AN ARMY OF 25,000 MEN IS PROBABLY ACCURATE.
ZA
ZA
ZA
ZA

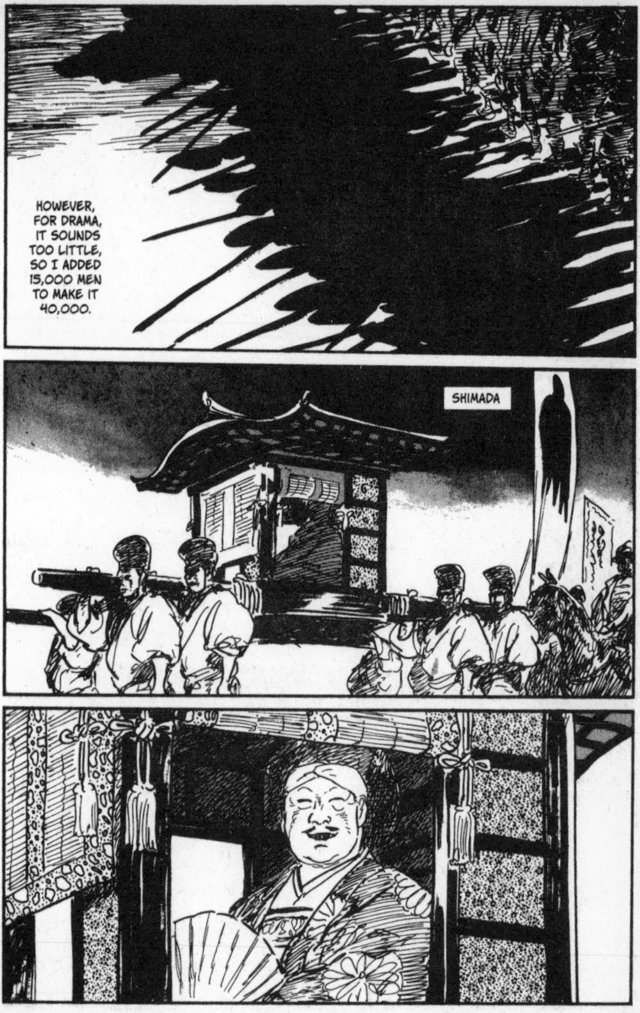
HOWEVER, FOR DRAMA, IT SOUNDS TOO LITTLE, SO I ADDED 15,000 MEN TO MAKE IT 40,000.
SHIMADA

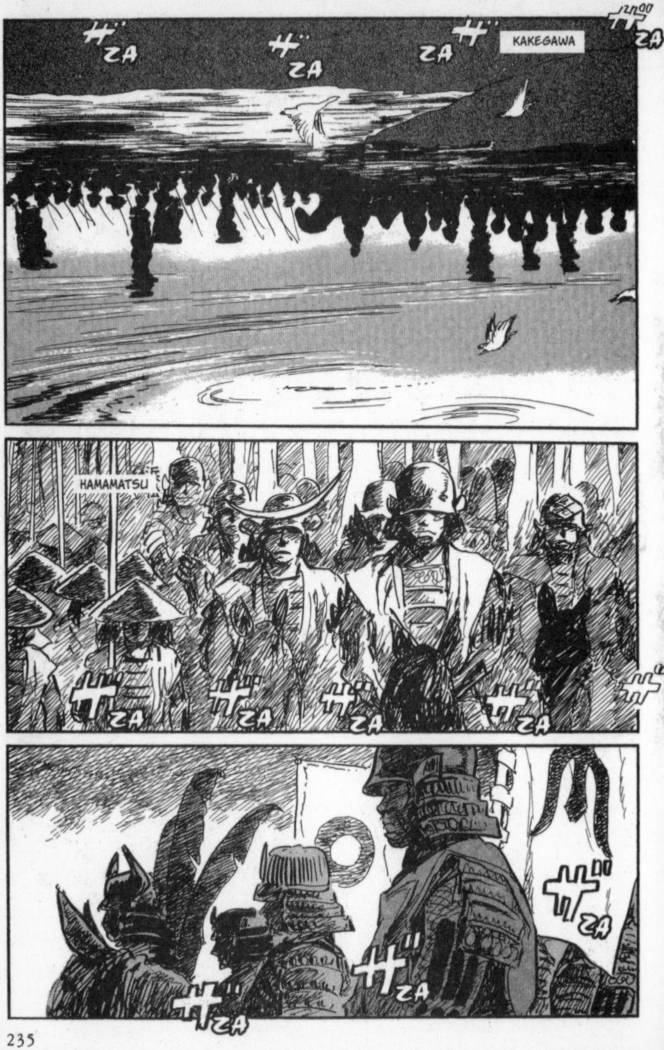
KAKEGAWA
ZA
ZA
ZA
ZA
HAMAMATSU
ZA
ZA
ZA
ZA
ZA
ZA
ZA

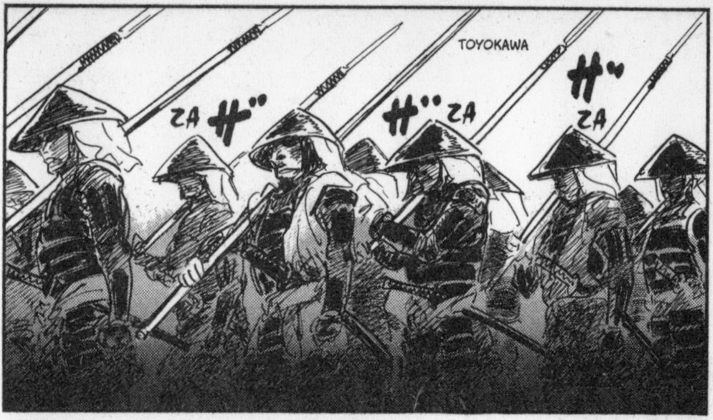
TOYOKAWA
ザ ZA
ザ ZA
ZA ザ

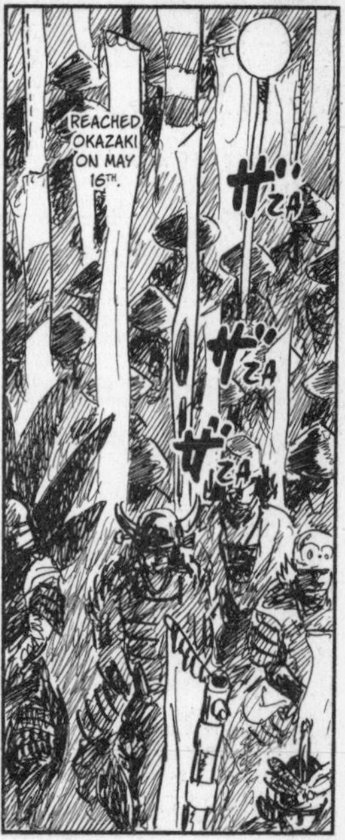
REACHED OKAZAKI ON MAY 16TH.
ザ ZA
ザ ZA
ザ ZA

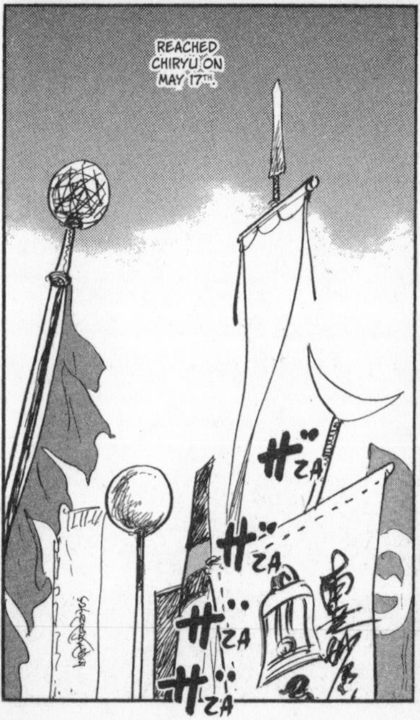
REACHED CHIRYU ON MAY 17TH.
ザ ZA
ザ ZA
ザ ZA
ザ ZA

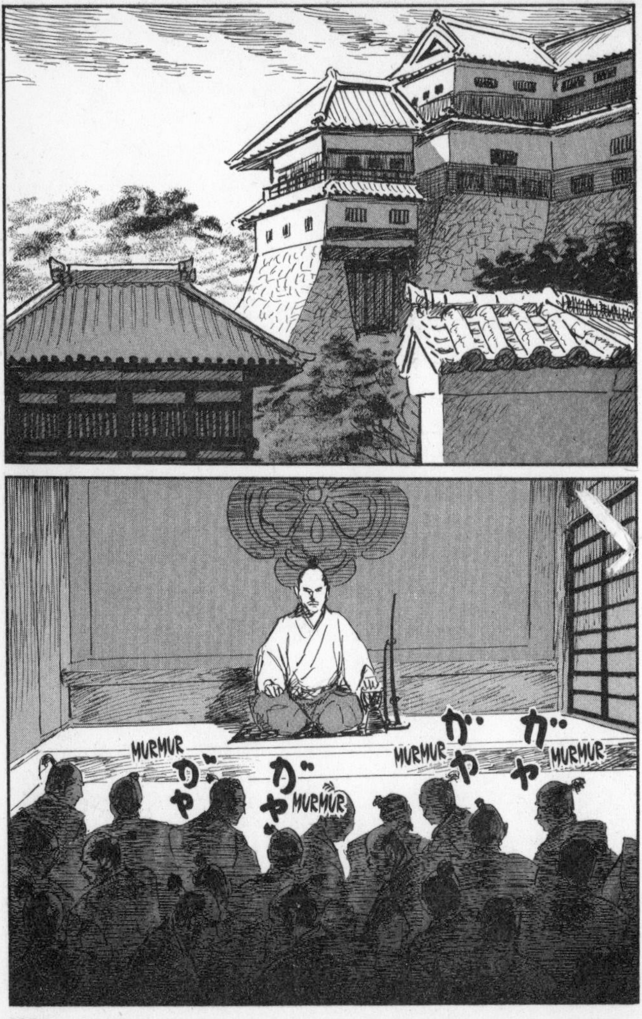
MURMUR
ガャ
がや
MURMUR
MURMUR
がや
MURMUR
がや

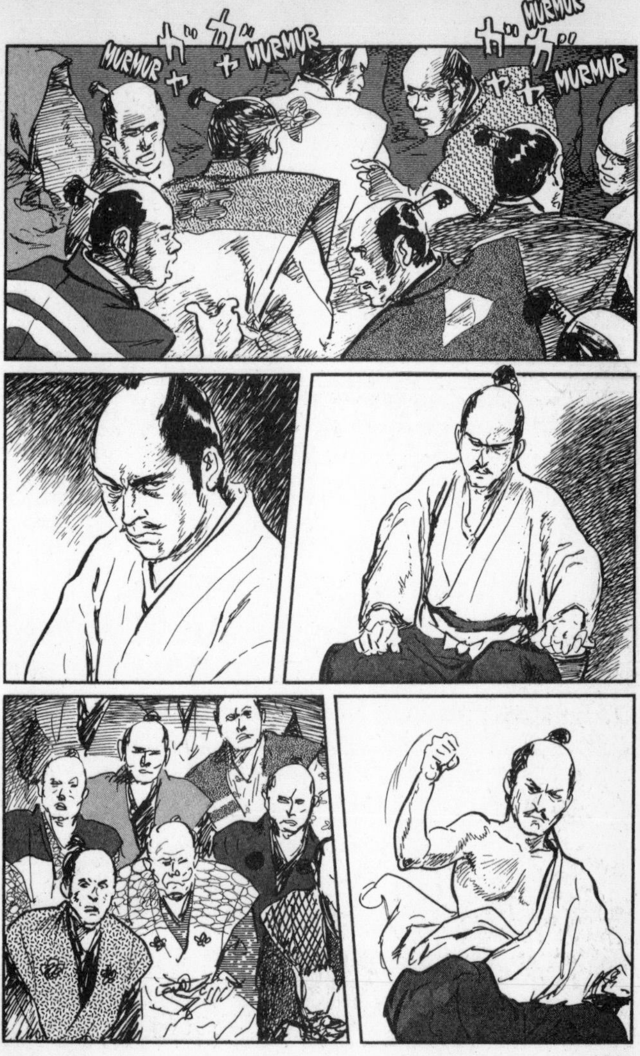
MURMUR
ガヤガヤ
MURMUR
MURMUR
ガヤガヤ
MURMUR

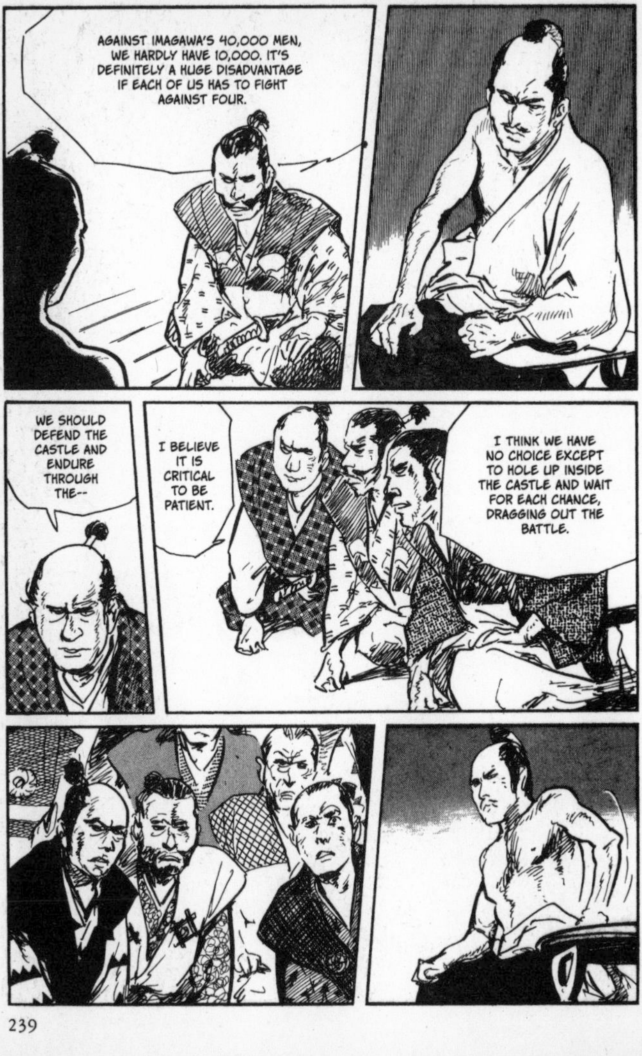
AGAINST IMAGAWA'S 40,000 MEN, WE HARDLY HAVE 10,000. IT'S DEFINITELY A HUGE DISADVANTAGE IF EACH OF US HAS TO FIGHT AGAINST FOUR.
I THINK WE HAVE NO CHOICE EXCEPT TO HOLE UP INSIDE THE CASTLE AND WAIT FOR EACH CHANCE, DRAGGING OUT THE BATTLE.
I BELIEVE IT IS CRITICAL TO BE PATIENT.
WE SHOULD DEFEND THE CASTLE AND ENDURE THROUGH THE--

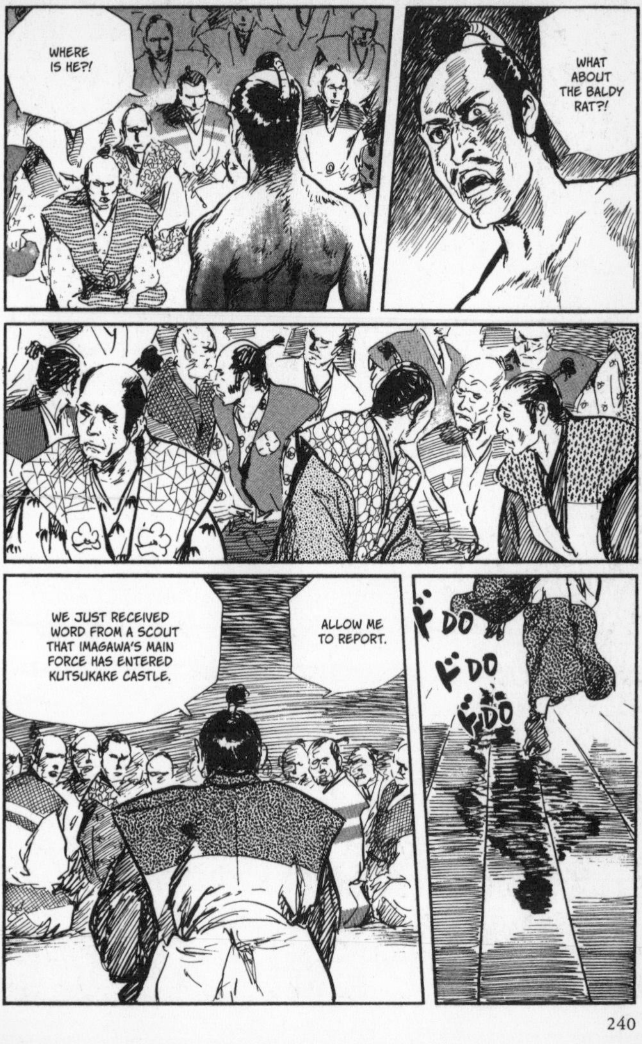
WHAT ABOUT THE BALDY RAT?!
WHERE IS HE?!
ドDO
ドDO
ドDO
ALLOW ME TO REPORT.
WE JUST RECEIVED WORD FROM A SCOUT THAT IMAGAWA'S MAIN FORCE HAS ENTERED KUTSUKAKE CASTLE.

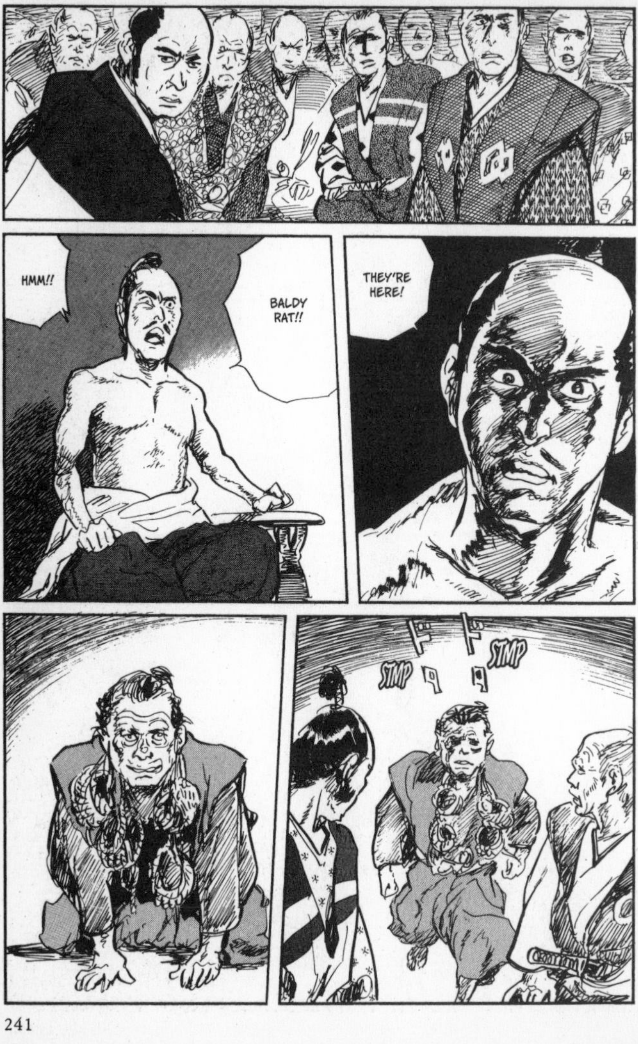
THEY'RE HERE!
BALDY RAT!!
HMM!!
STMP
STMP

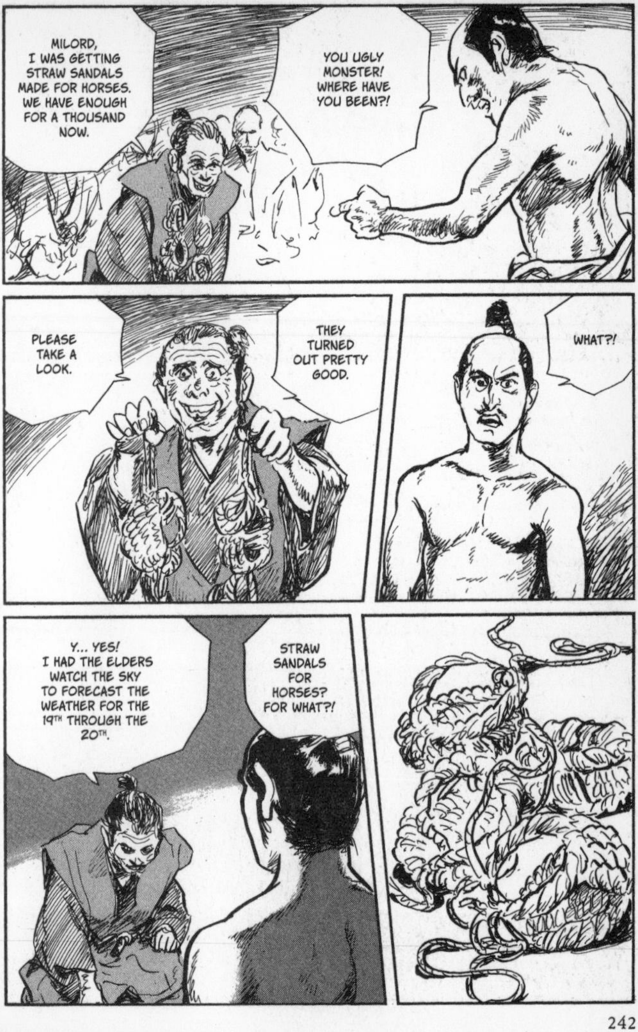
YOU UGLY MONSTER! WHERE HAVE YOU BEEN?!
MILORD, I WAS GETTING STRAW SANDALS MADE FOR HORSES. WE HAVE ENOUGH FOR A THOUSAND NOW.
WHAT?!
THEY TURNED OUT PRETTY GOOD.
PLEASE TAKE A LOOK.
STRAW SANDALS FOR HORSES? FOR WHAT?!
Y... YES! I HAD THE ELDERS WATCH THE SKY TO FORECAST THE WEATHER FOR THE 19TH THROUGH THE 20TH.

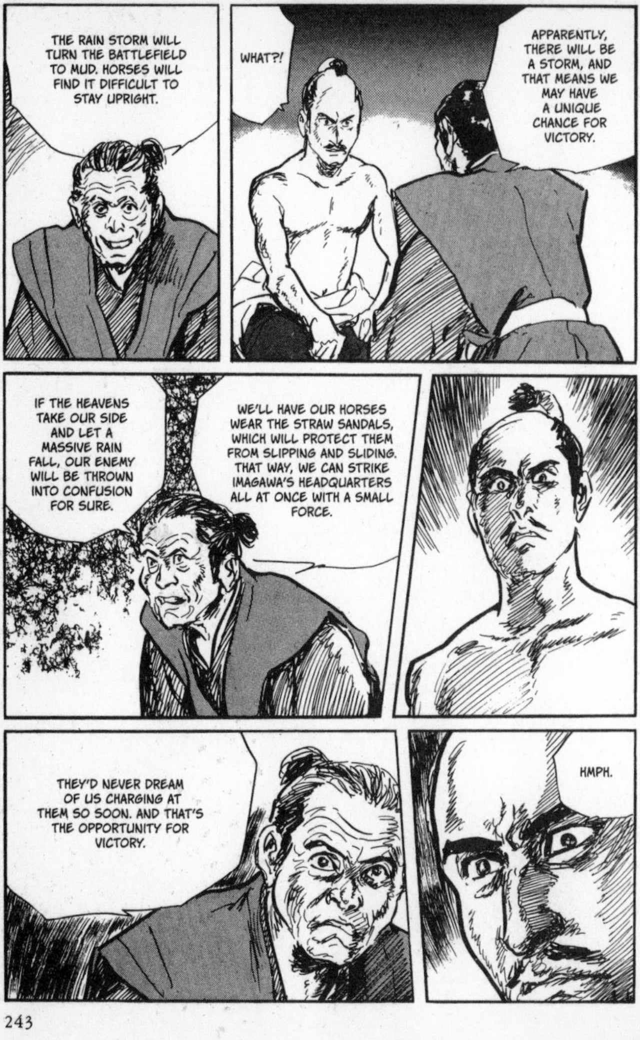
APPARENTLY, THERE WILL BE A STORM, AND THAT MEANS WE MAY HAVE A UNIQUE CHANCE FOR VICTORY.
WHAT?!
THE RAIN STORM WILL TURN THE BATTLEFIELD TO MUD. HORSES WILL FIND IT DIFFICULT TO STAY UPRIGHT.
WE'LL HAVE OUR HORSES WEAR THE STRAW SANDALS, WHICH WILL PROTECT THEM FROM SLIPPING AND SLIDING. THAT WAY, WE CAN STRIKE IMAGAWA'S HEADQUARTERS ALL AT ONCE WITH A SMALL FORCE.
IF THE HEAVENS TAKE OUR SIDE AND LET A MASSIVE RAIN FALL, OUR ENEMY WILL BE THROWN INTO CONFUSION FOR SURE.
HMPH.
THEY'D NEVER DREAM OF US CHARGING AT THEM SO SOON. AND THAT'S THE OPPORTUNITY FOR VICTORY.

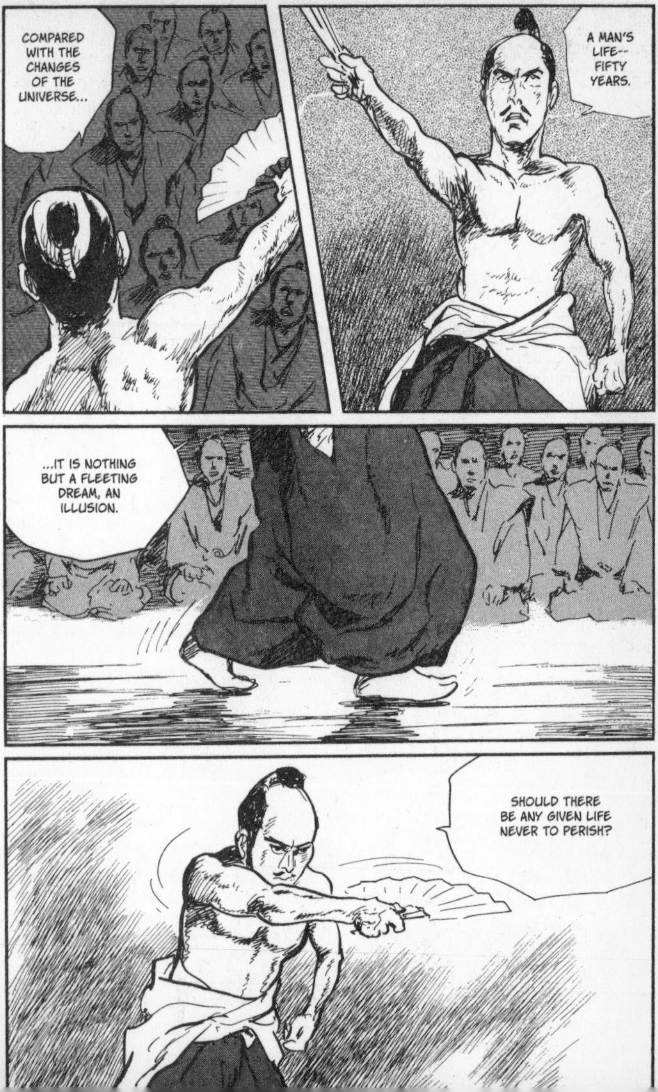
A MAN'S LIFE-- FIFTY YEARS.
COMPARED WITH THE CHANGES OF THE UNIVERSE...
...IT IS NOTHING BUT A FLEETING DREAM, AN ILLUSION.
SHOULD THERE BE ANY GIVEN LIFE NEVER TO PERISH?

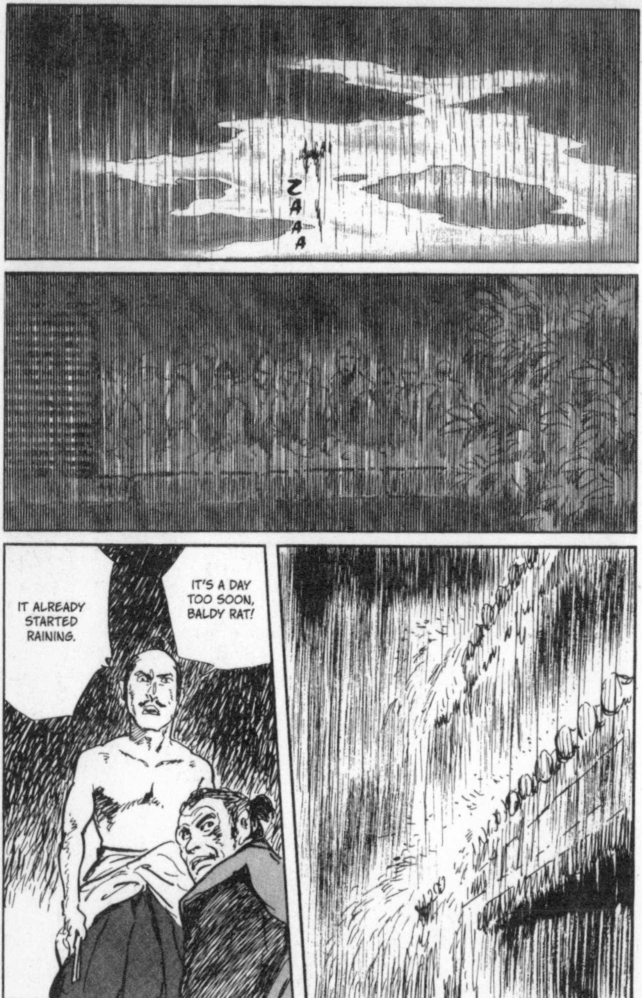
ZAAA
IT'S A DAY TOO SOON, BALDY RAT!
IT ALREADY STARTED RAINING.

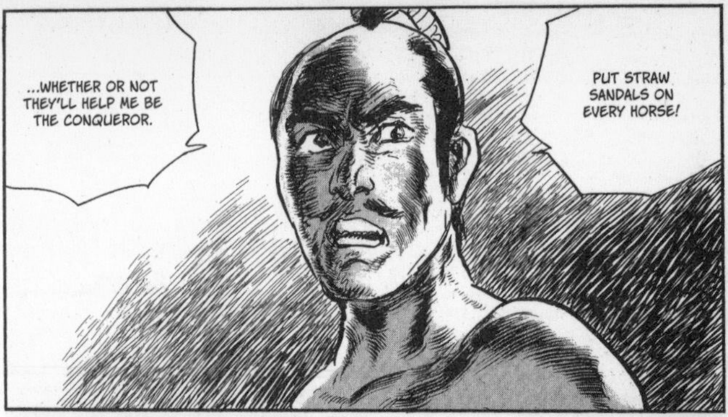
PUT STRAW SANDALS ON EVERY HORSE!
...WHETHER OR NOT THEY'LL HELP ME BE THE CONQUEROR.

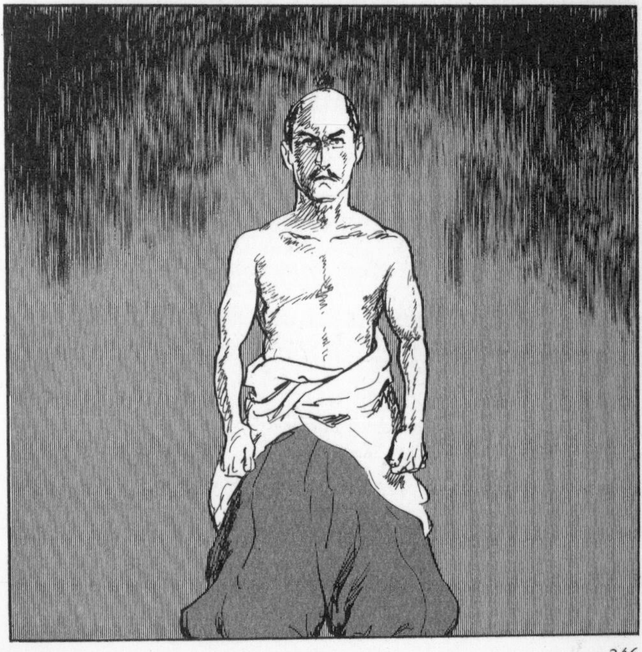

Chapter On Relinquishing Death

No. 2: Hard Crossroad on the Plain, Part 1

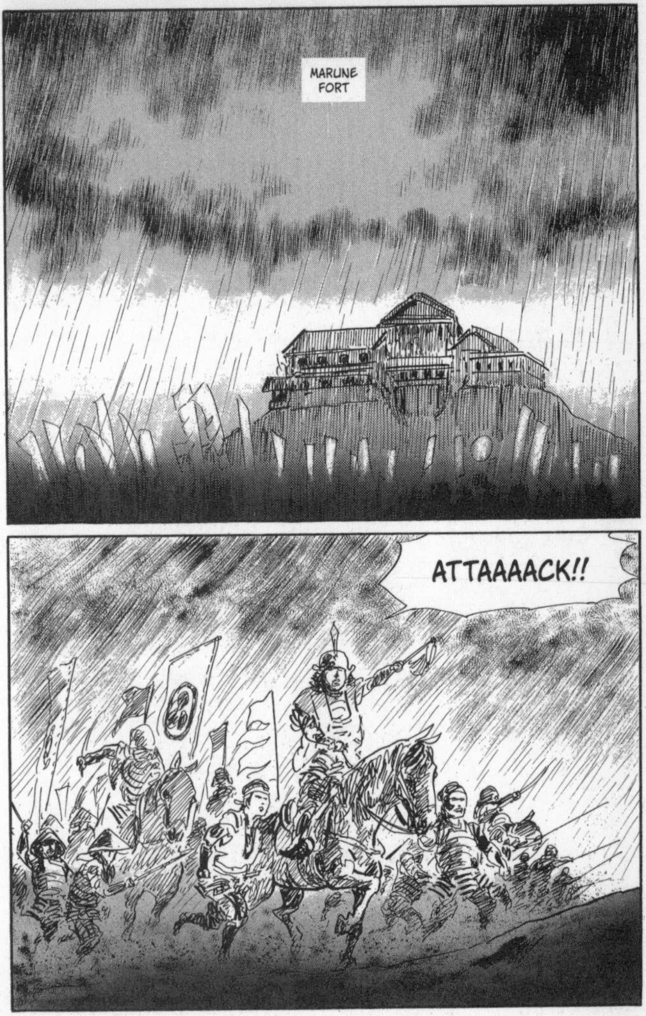
MARUNE FORT
ATTAAAACK!!

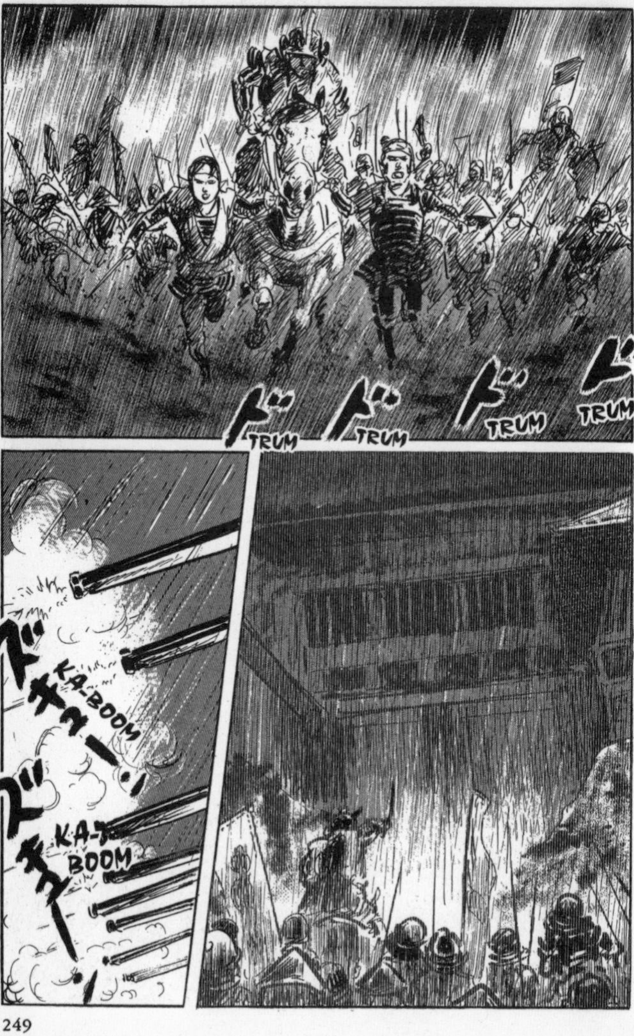
ド TRUM
ド TRUM
ド TRUM
ド TRUM
KA-BOOM
KA-BOOM

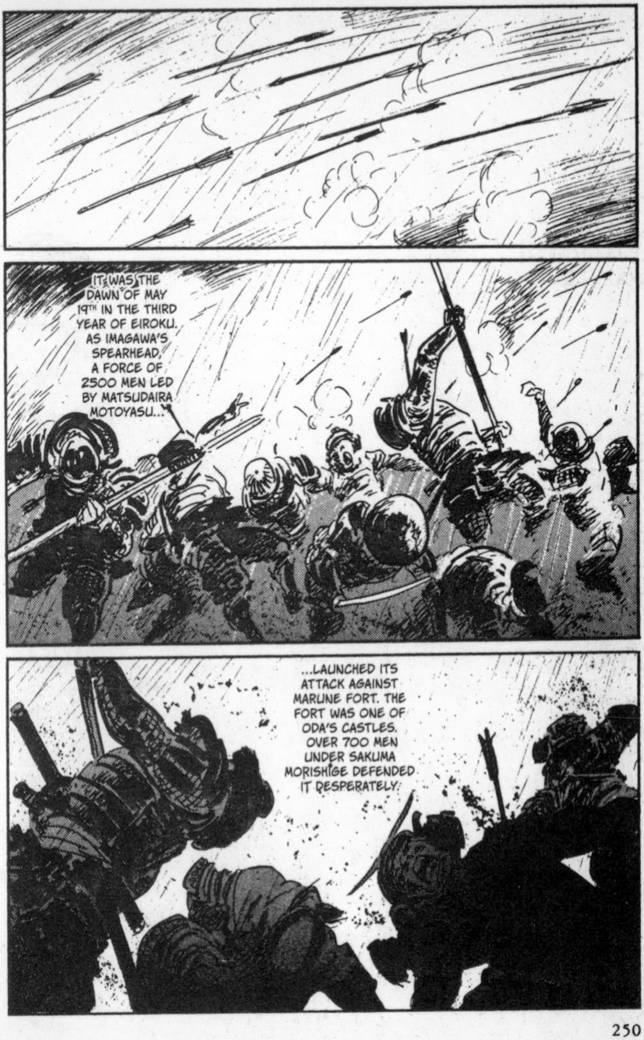
IT WAS THE DAWN OF MAY 19TH IN THE THIRD YEAR OF EIROKU. AS IMAGAWA'S SPEARHEAD, A FORCE OF 2500 MEN LED BY MATSUDAIRA MOTOYASU...
...LAUNCHED ITS ATTACK AGAINST MARUNE FORT. THE FORT WAS ONE OF ODA'S CASTLES. OVER 700 MEN UNDER SAKUMA MORISHIGE DEFENDED IT DESPERATELY.

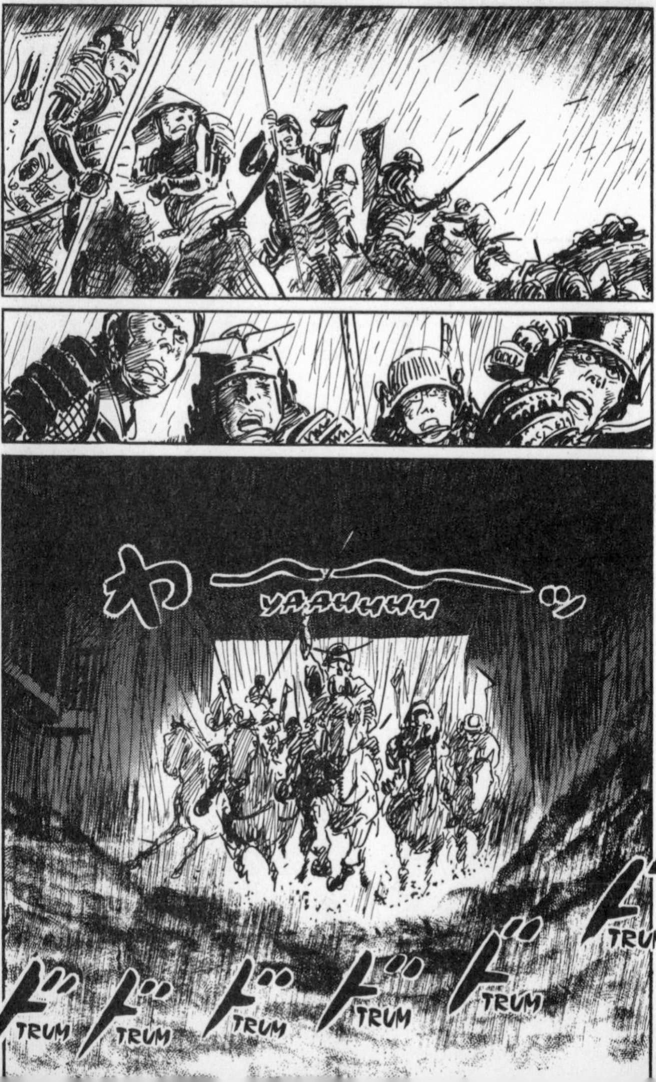
わーーーッ
YAAHHHH
ド
TRUM
ド
TRUM
ド
TRUM
ド
TRUM
ド
TRUM
ド
TRUM

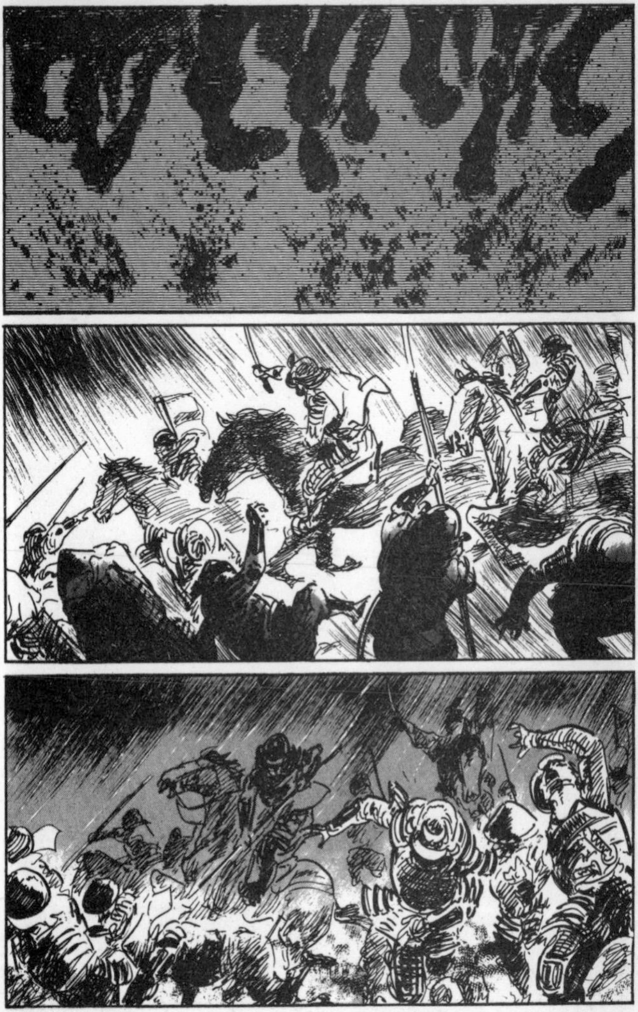

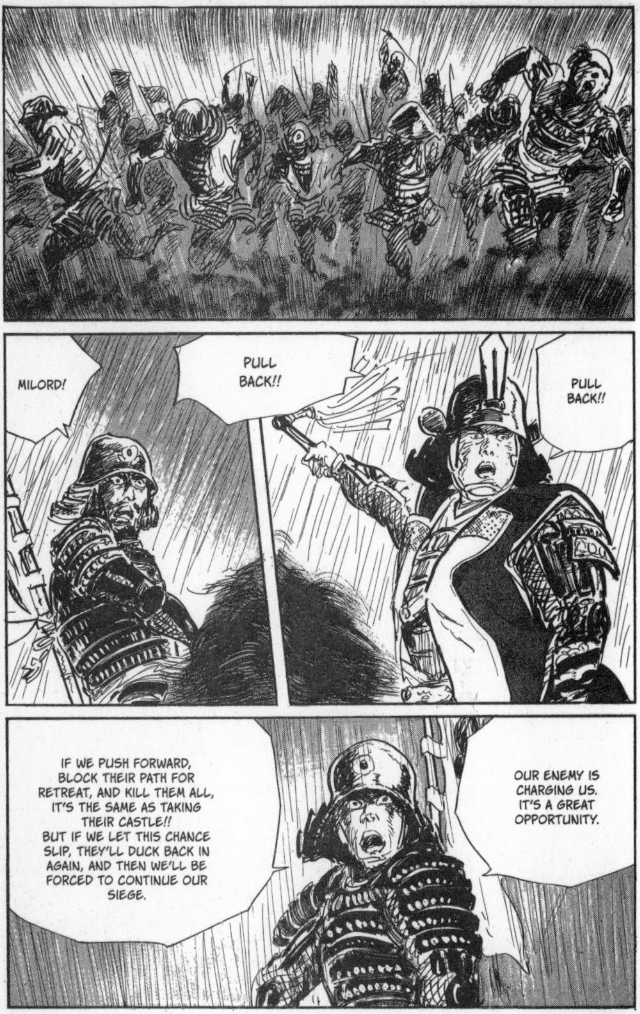
PULL BACK!!
PULL BACK!!
MILORD!
OUR ENEMY IS CHARGING US. IT'S A GREAT OPPORTUNITY.
IF WE PUSH FORWARD, BLOCK THEIR PATH FOR RETREAT, AND KILL THEM ALL, IT'S THE SAME AS TAKING THEIR CASTLE!! BUT IF WE LET THIS CHANCE SLIP, THEY'LL DUCK BACK IN AGAIN, AND THEN WE'LL BE FORCED TO CONTINUE OUR SIEGE.

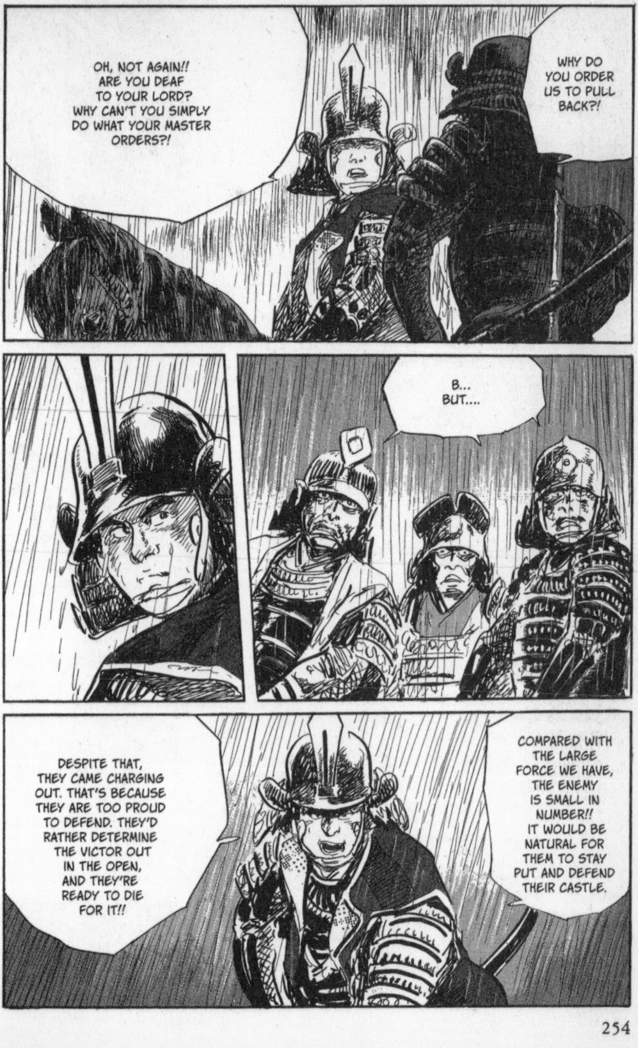
WHY DO YOU ORDER US TO PULL BACK?!
OH, NOT AGAIN!! ARE YOU DEAF TO YOUR LORD? WHY CAN'T YOU SIMPLY DO WHAT YOUR MASTER ORDERS?!
B... BUT....
COMPARED WITH THE LARGE FORCE WE HAVE, THE ENEMY IS SMALL IN NUMBER!! IT WOULD BE NATURAL FOR THEM TO STAY PUT AND DEFEND THEIR CASTLE.
DESPITE THAT, THEY CAME CHARGING OUT. THAT'S BECAUSE THEY ARE TOO PROUD TO DEFEND. THEY'D RATHER DETERMINE THE VICTOR OUT IN THE OPEN, AND THEY'RE READY TO DIE FOR IT!!

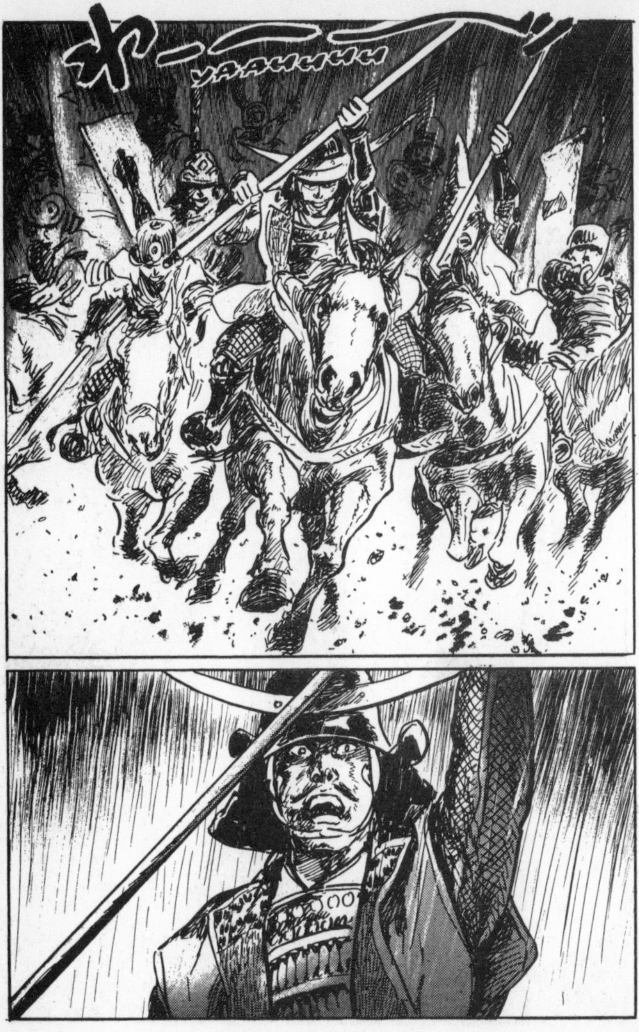
オーーーッ
YAAHHHH

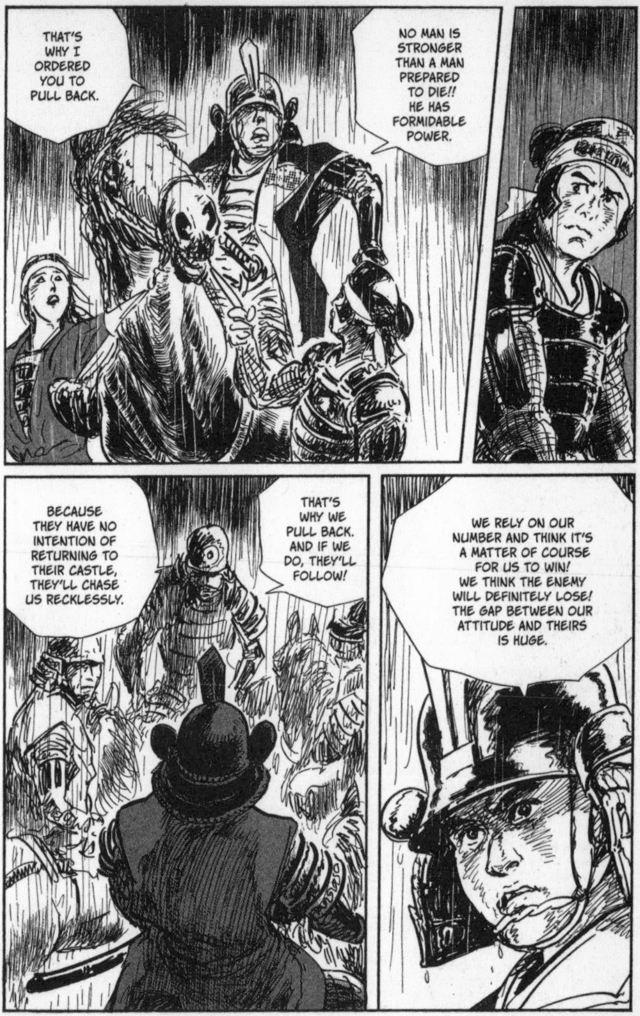
NO MAN IS STRONGER THAN A MAN PREPARED TO DIE!! HE HAS FORMIDABLE POWER.
THAT'S WHY I ORDERED YOU TO PULL BACK.
WE RELY ON OUR NUMBER AND THINK IT'S A MATTER OF COURSE FOR US TO WIN! WE THINK THE ENEMY WILL DEFINITELY LOSE! THE GAP BETWEEN OUR ATTITUDE AND THEIRS IS HUGE.
THAT'S WHY WE PULL BACK. AND IF WE DO, THEY'LL FOLLOW!
BECAUSE THEY HAVE NO INTENTION OF RETURNING TO THEIR CASTLE, THEY'LL CHASE US RECKLESSLY.

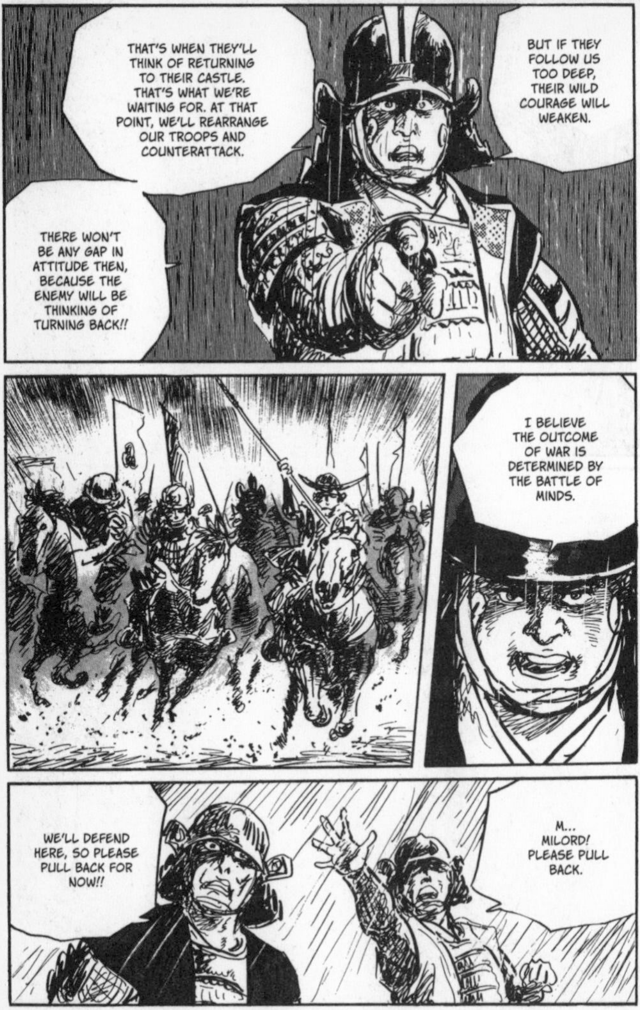
BUT IF THEY FOLLOW US TOO DEEP, THEIR WILD COURAGE WILL WEAKEN.
THAT'S WHEN THEY'LL THINK OF RETURNING TO THEIR CASTLE. THAT'S WHAT WE'RE WAITING FOR. AT THAT POINT, WE'LL REARRANGE OUR TROOPS AND COUNTERATTACK.
THERE WON'T BE ANY GAP IN ATTITUDE THEN, BECAUSE THE ENEMY WILL BE THINKING OF TURNING BACK!!
I BELIEVE THE OUTCOME OF WAR IS DETERMINED BY THE BATTLE OF MINDS.
M... MILORD! PLEASE PULL BACK.
WE'LL DEFEND HERE, SO PLEASE PULL BACK FOR NOW!!

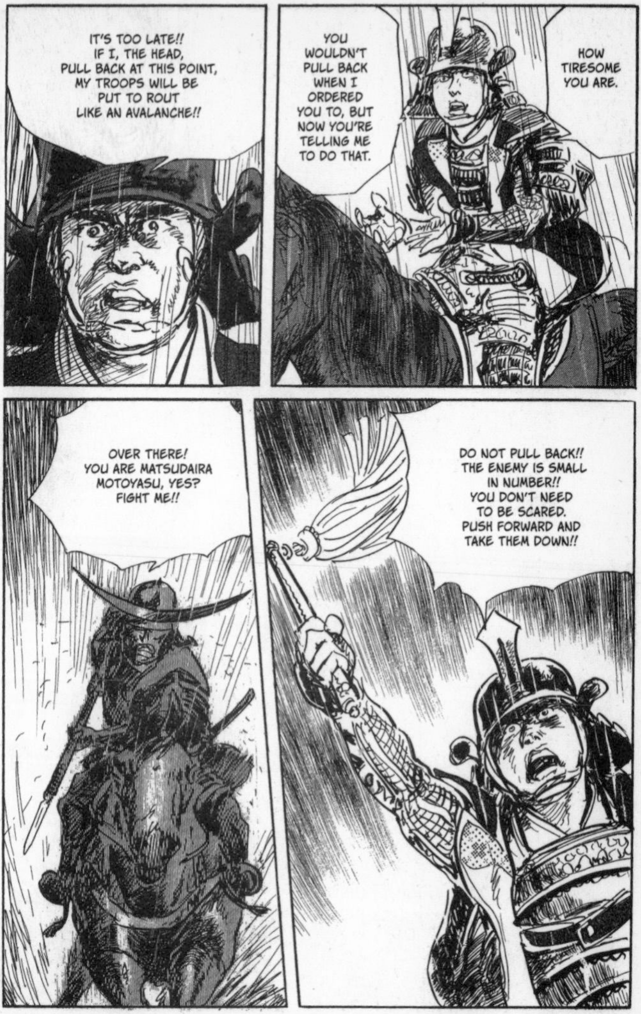
YOU WOULDN'T PULL BACK WHEN I ORDERED YOU TO, BUT NOW YOU'RE TELLING ME TO DO THAT.
HOW TIRESOME YOU ARE.
IT'S TOO LATE!! IF I, THE HEAD, PULL BACK AT THIS POINT, MY TROOPS WILL BE PUT TO ROUT LIKE AN AVALANCHE!!
DO NOT PULL BACK!! THE ENEMY IS SMALL IN NUMBER!! YOU DON'T NEED TO BE SCARED. PUSH FORWARD AND TAKE THEM DOWN!!
OVER THERE! YOU ARE MATSUDAIRA MOTOYASU, YES? FIGHT ME!!

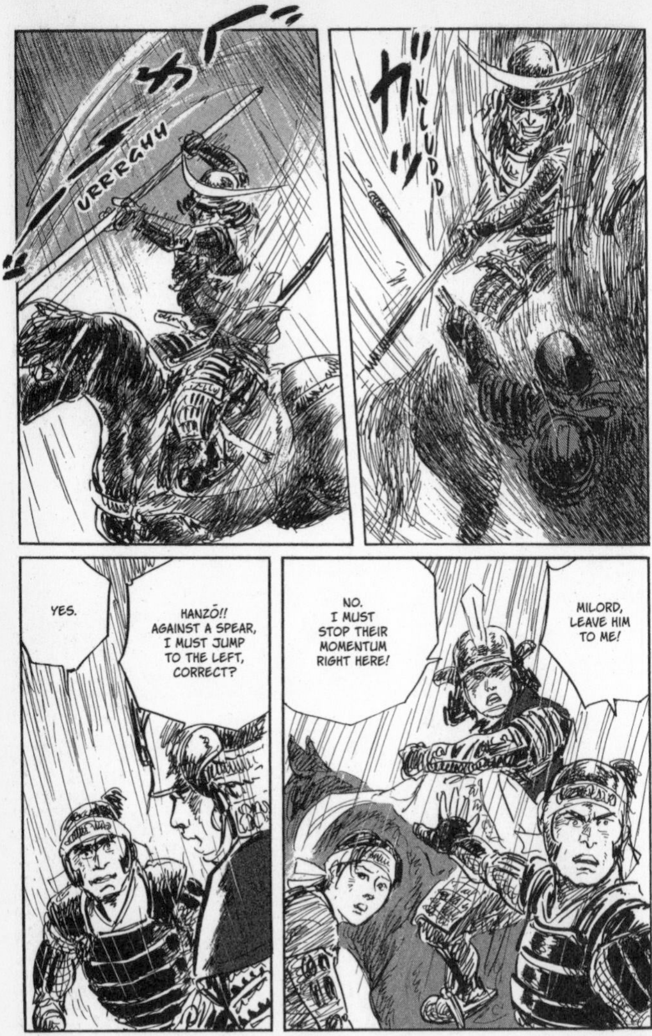
KLUDDD
URR'RGHH
MILORD, LEAVE HIM TO ME!
NO. I MUST STOP THEIR MOMENTUM RIGHT HERE!
HANZŌ!! AGAINST A SPEAR, I MUST JUMP TO THE LEFT, CORRECT?
YES.

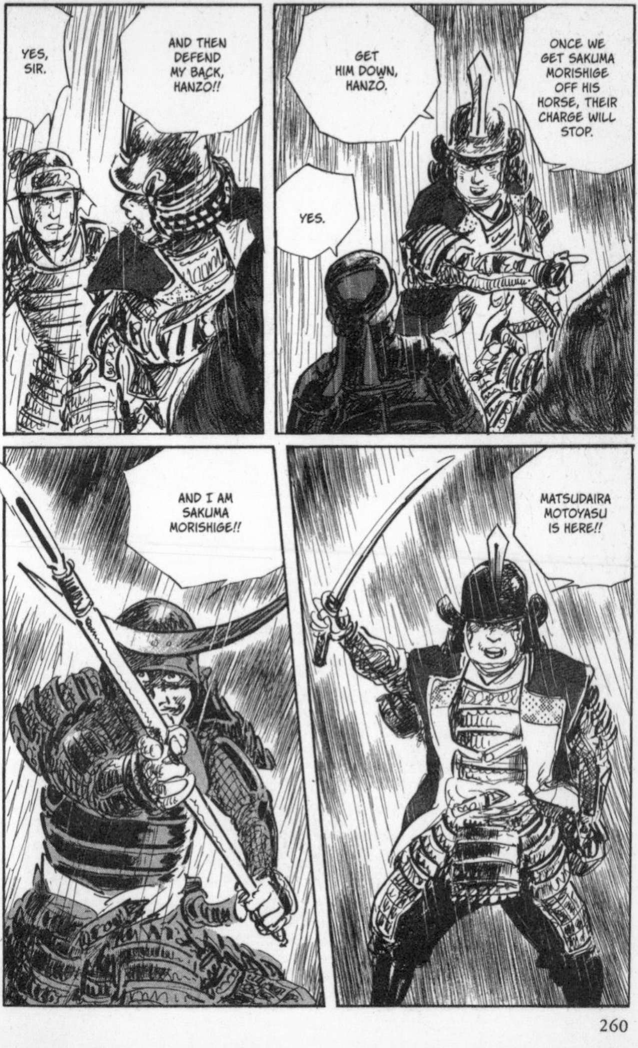
ONCE WE GET SAKUMA MORISHIGE OFF HIS HORSE, THEIR CHARGE WILL STOP.
GET HIM DOWN, HANZŌ.
YES.
AND THEN DEFEND MY BACK, HANZO!!
YES, SIR.
MATSUDAIRA MOTOYASU IS HERE!!
AND I AM SAKUMA MORISHIGE!!

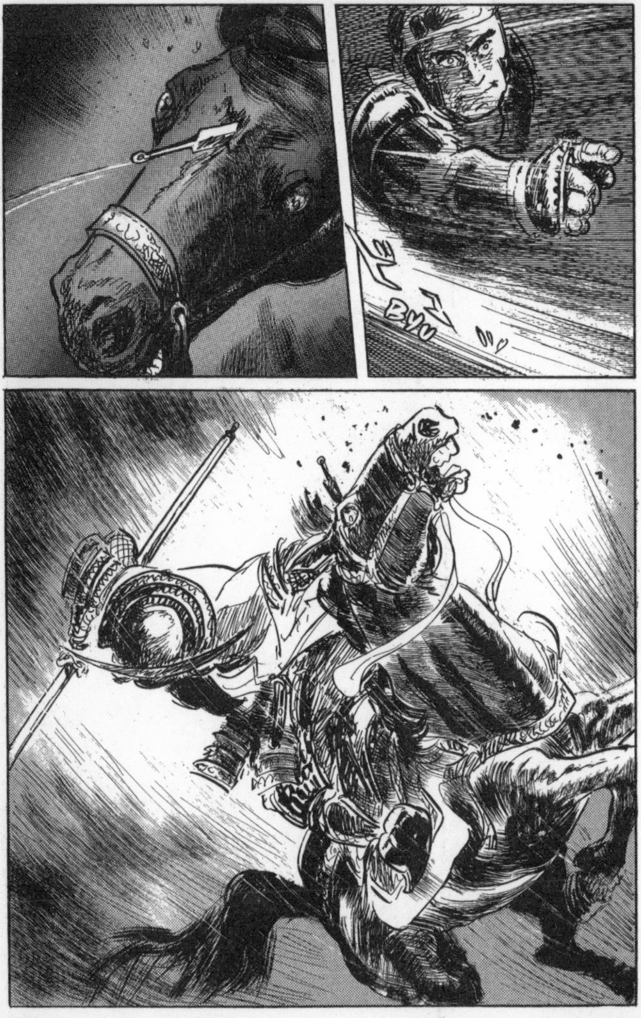
BYU

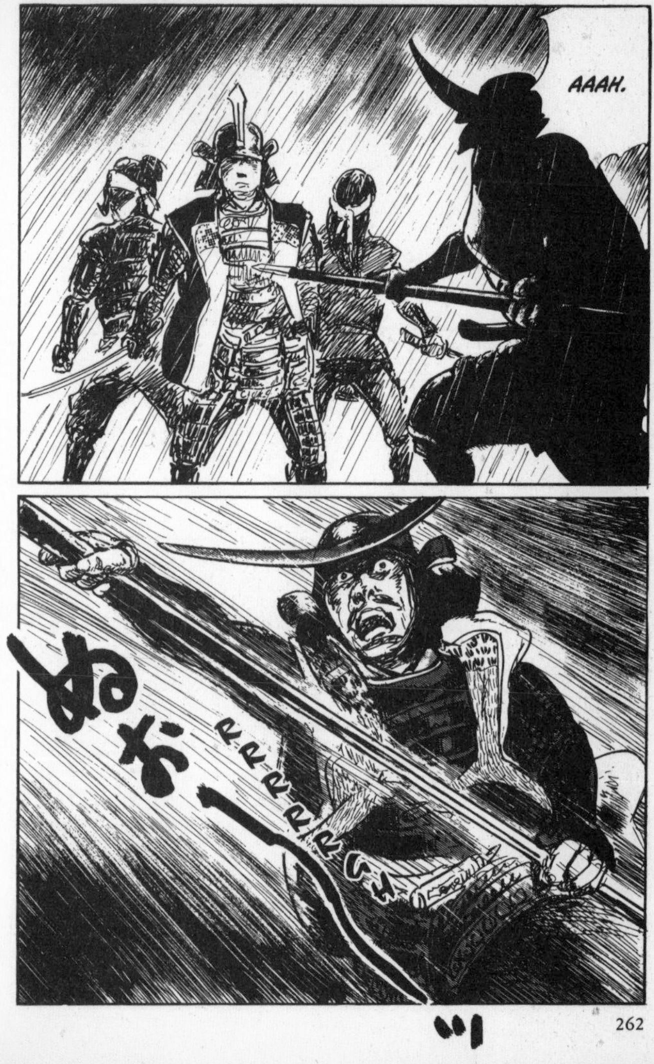
AAAH.
ぬおーッ
RRRRRGH

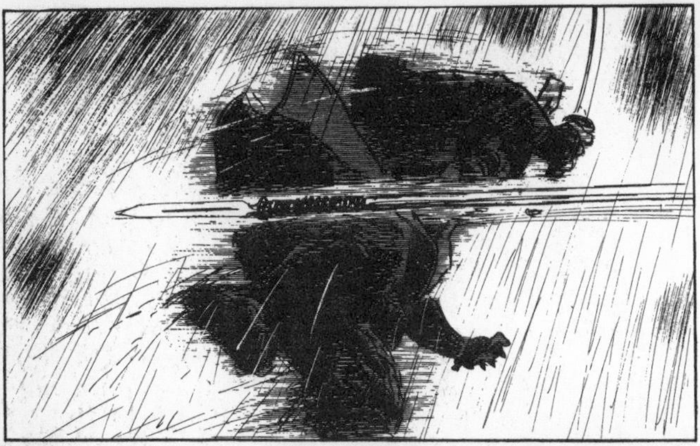

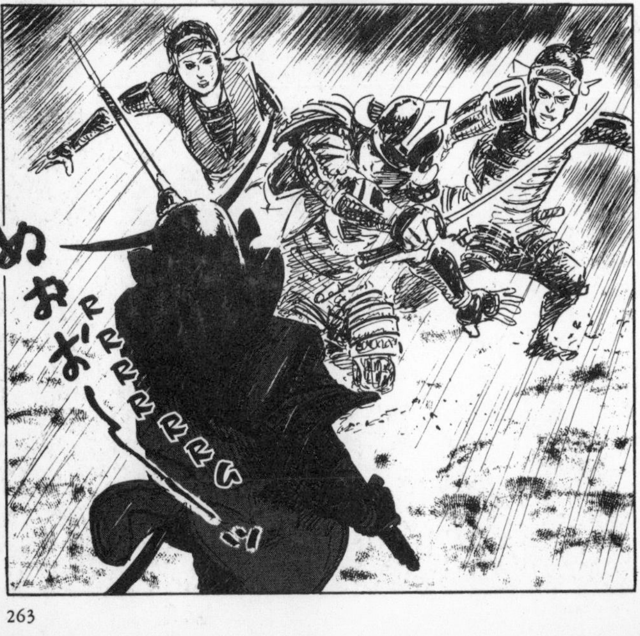
ぬおおーRRRRRRG!!

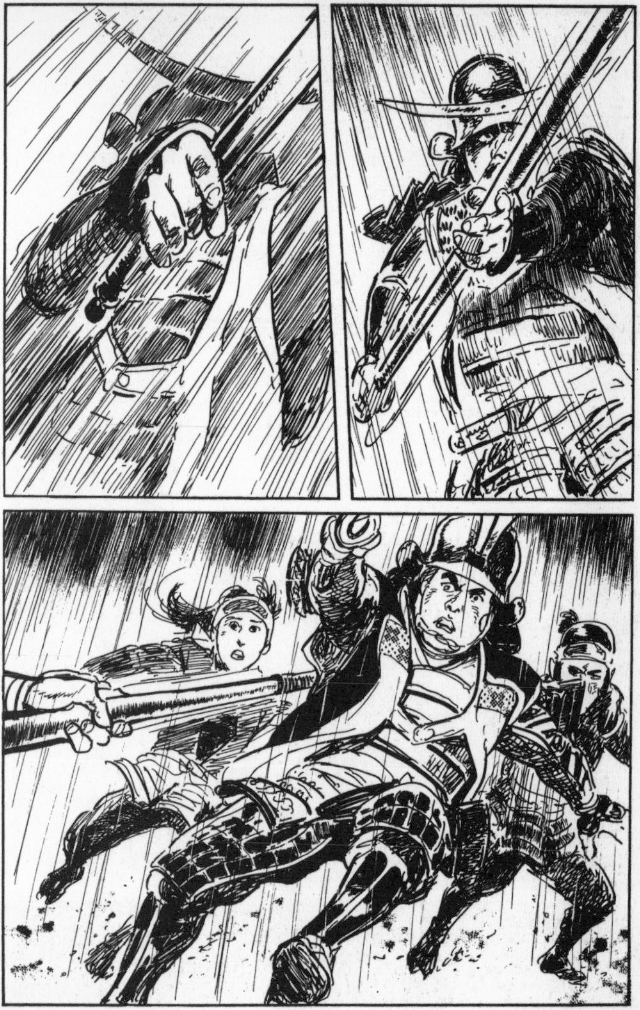

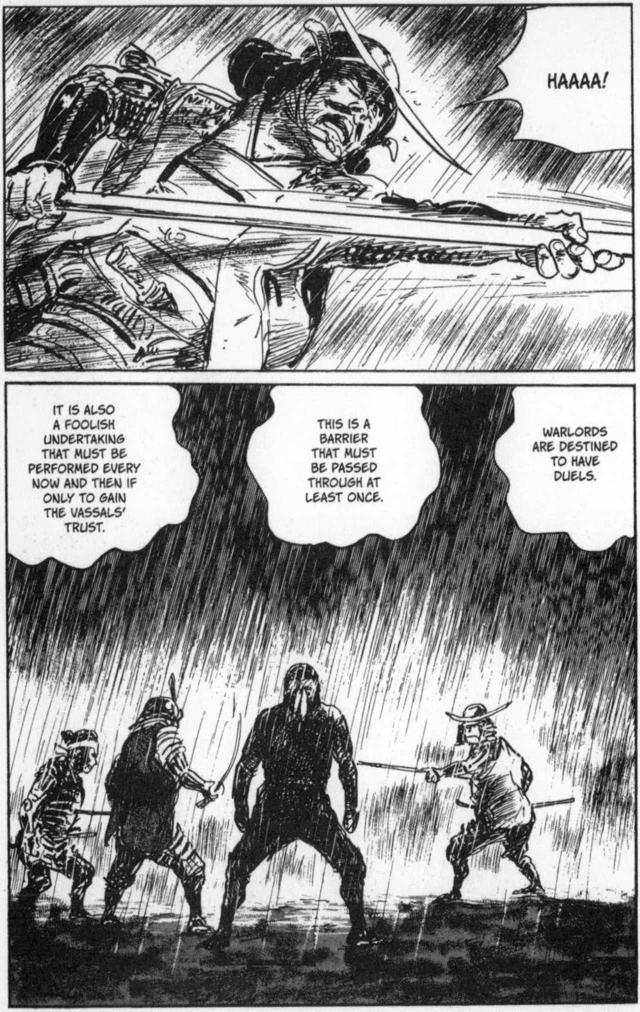
HAAAA!
WARLORDS ARE DESTINED TO HAVE DUELS.
THIS IS A BARRIER THAT MUST BE PASSED THROUGH AT LEAST ONCE.
IT IS ALSO A FOOLISH UNDERTAKING THAT MUST BE PERFORMED EVERY NOW AND THEN IF ONLY TO GAIN THE VASSALS' TRUST.

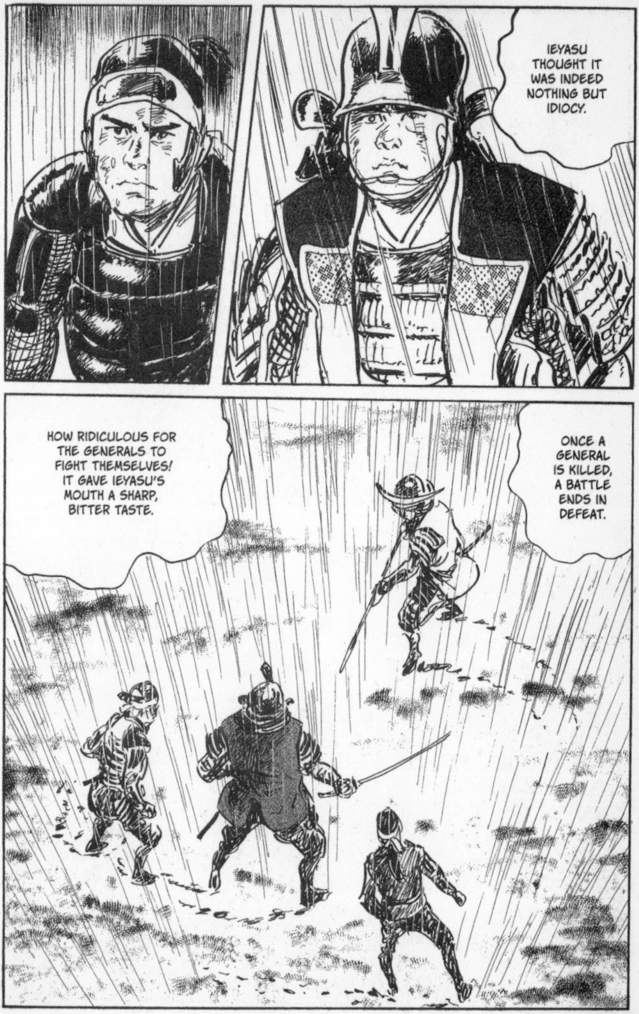
IEYASU THOUGHT IT WAS INDEED NOTHING BUT IDIOCY.
ONCE A GENERAL IS KILLED, A BATTLE ENDS IN DEFEAT.
HOW RIDICULOUS FOR THE GENERALS TO FIGHT THEMSELVES! IT GAVE IEYASU'S MOUTH A SHARP, BITTER TASTE.

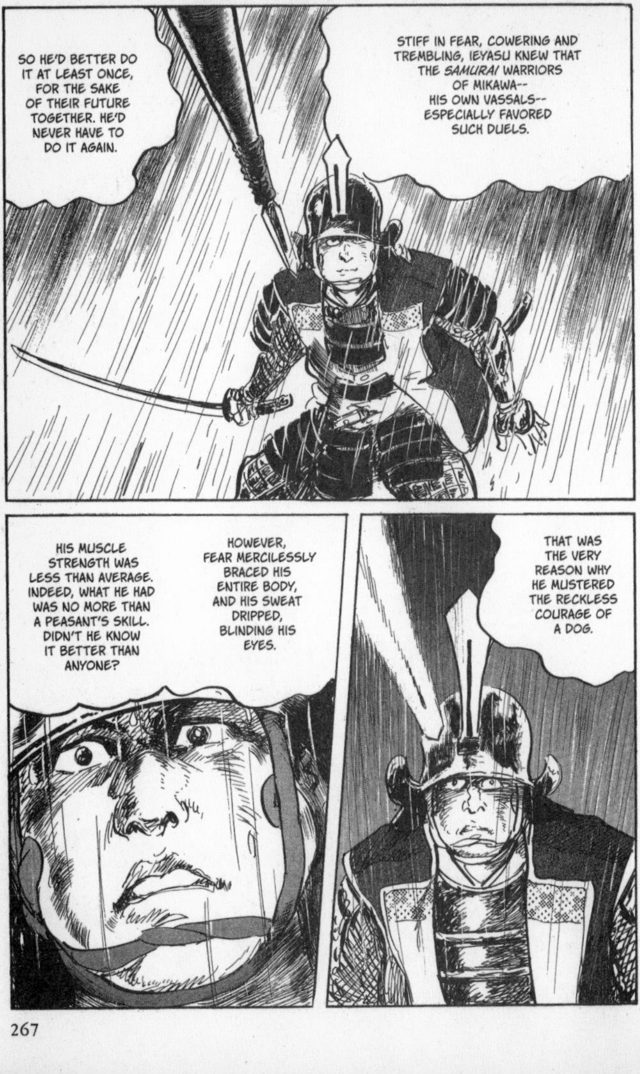
STIFF IN FEAR, COWERING AND TREMBLING, IEYASU KNEW THAT THE *SAMURAI* WARRIORS OF MIKAWA-- HIS OWN VASSALS-- ESPECIALLY FAVORED SUCH DUELS.
SO HE'D BETTER DO IT AT LEAST ONCE, FOR THE SAKE OF THEIR FUTURE TOGETHER. HE'D NEVER HAVE TO DO IT AGAIN.
THAT WAS THE VERY REASON WHY HE MUSTERED THE RECKLESS COURAGE OF A DOG.
HOWEVER, FEAR MERCILESSLY BRACED HIS ENTIRE BODY, AND HIS SWEAT DRIPPED, BLINDING HIS EYES.
HIS MUSCLE STRENGTH WAS LESS THAN AVERAGE. INDEED, WHAT HE HAD WAS NO MORE THAN A PEASANT'S SKILL. DIDN'T HE KNOW IT BETTER THAN ANYONE?

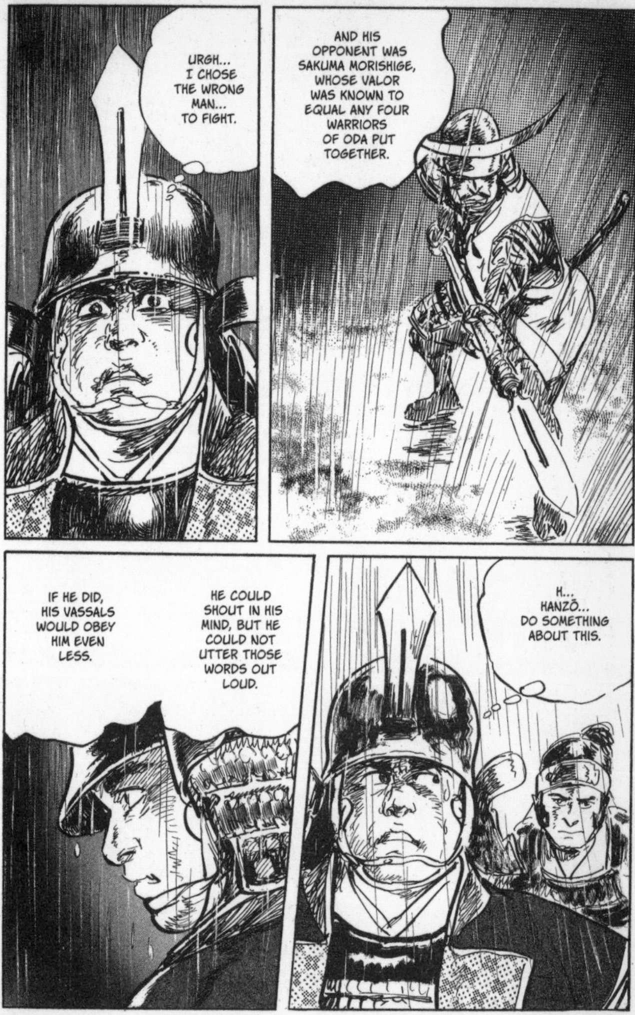
AND HIS OPPONENT WAS SAKUMA MORISHIGE, WHOSE VALOR WAS KNOWN TO EQUAL ANY FOUR WARRIORS OF ODA PUT TOGETHER.
URGH... I CHOSE THE WRONG MAN... TO FIGHT.
H... HANZŌ... DO SOMETHING ABOUT THIS.
HE COULD SHOUT IN HIS MIND, BUT HE COULD NOT UTTER THOSE WORDS OUT LOUD.
IF HE DID, HIS VASSALS WOULD OBEY HIM EVEN LESS.

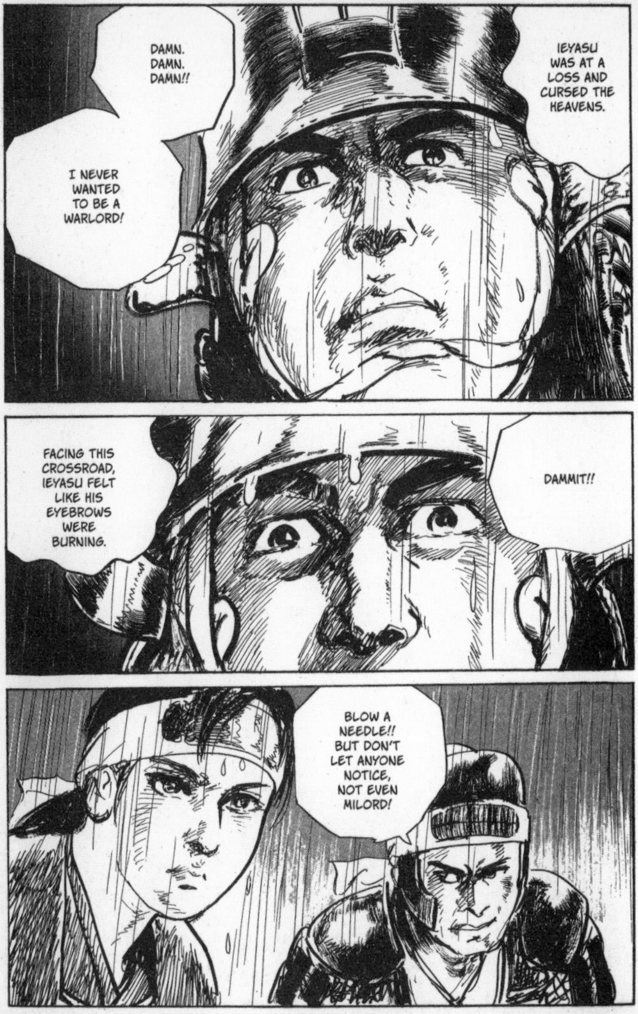
IEYASU WAS AT A LOSS AND CURSED THE HEAVENS.
DAMN. DAMN. DAMN!!
I NEVER WANTED TO BE A WARLORD!
DAMMIT!!
FACING THIS CROSSROAD, IEYASU FELT LIKE HIS EYEBROWS WERE BURNING.
BLOW A NEEDLE!! BUT DON'T LET ANYONE NOTICE, NOT EVEN MILORD!

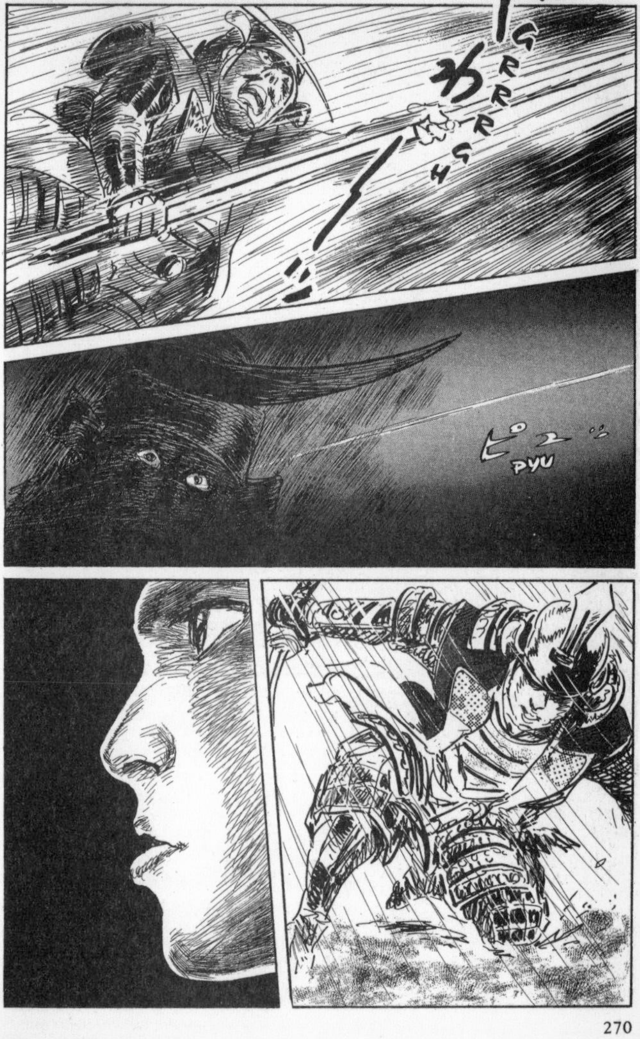
ぐわー!!
GRRRGH
ピュッ
PYU

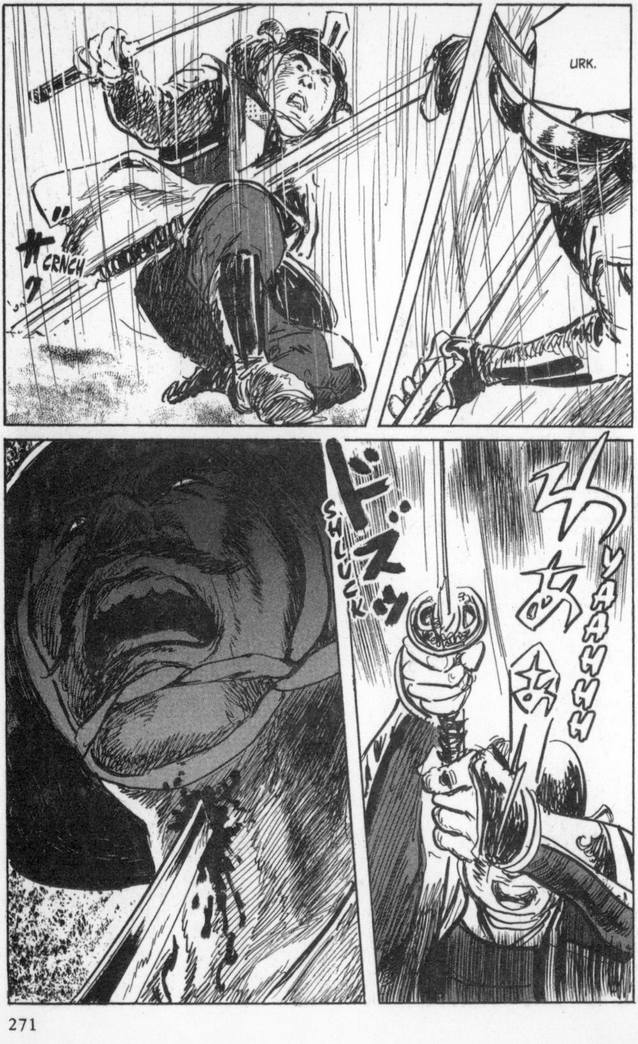
URK.
ザク
CRNCH
YAAHHHH
ドズッ
SHLUCK

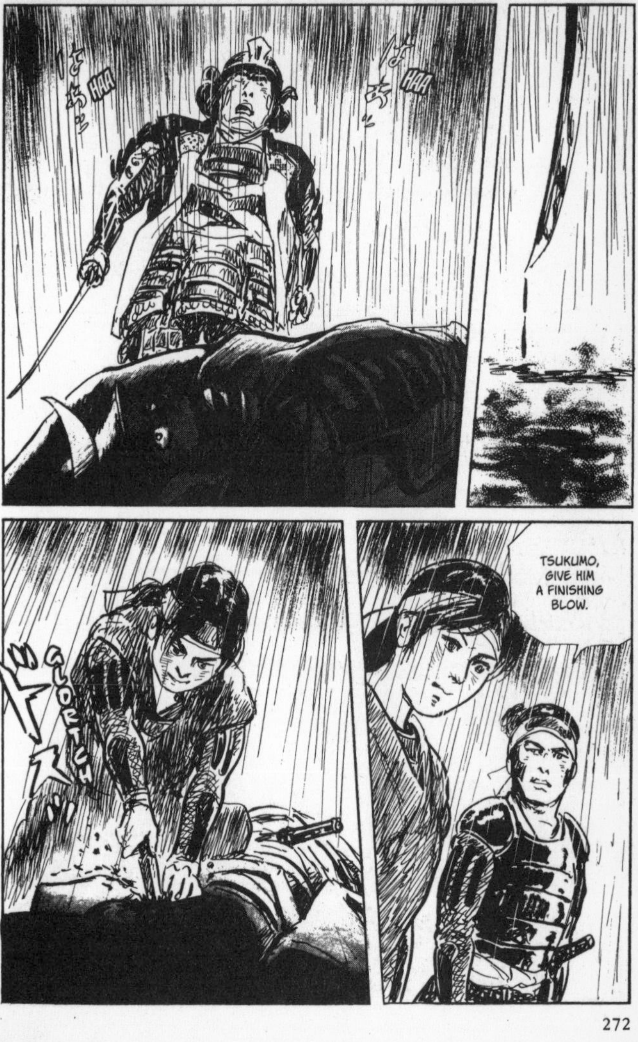
HAA
HAA
TSUKUMO, GIVE HIM A FINISHING BLOW.
GLORTCH

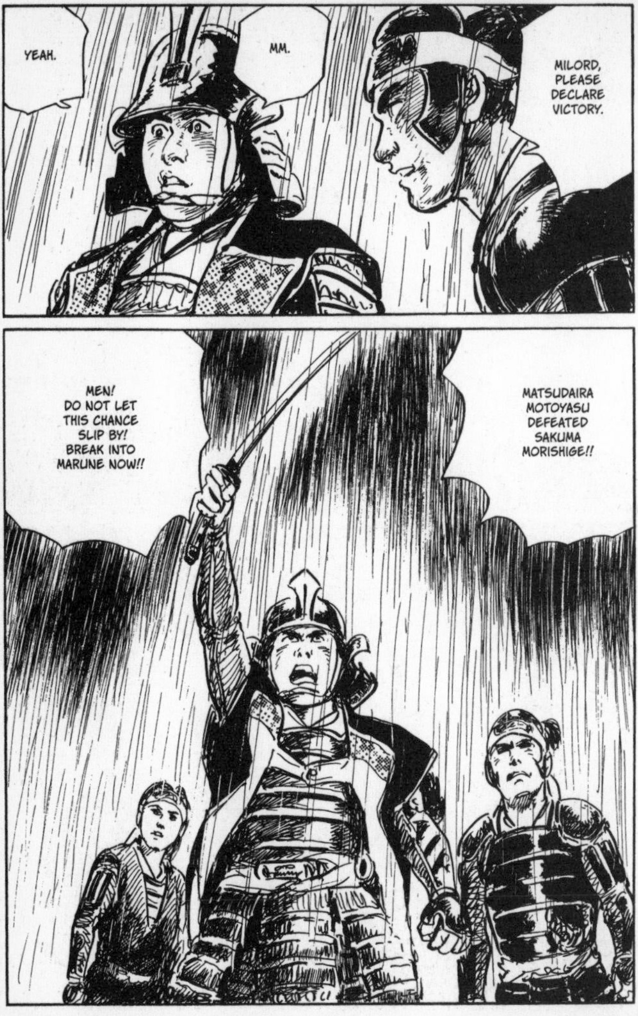
MILORD, PLEASE DECLARE VICTORY.
MM.
YEAH.
MATSUDAIRA MOTOYASU DEFEATED SAKUMA MORISHIGE!!
MEN! DO NOT LET THIS CHANCE SLIP BY! BREAK INTO MARUNE NOW!!

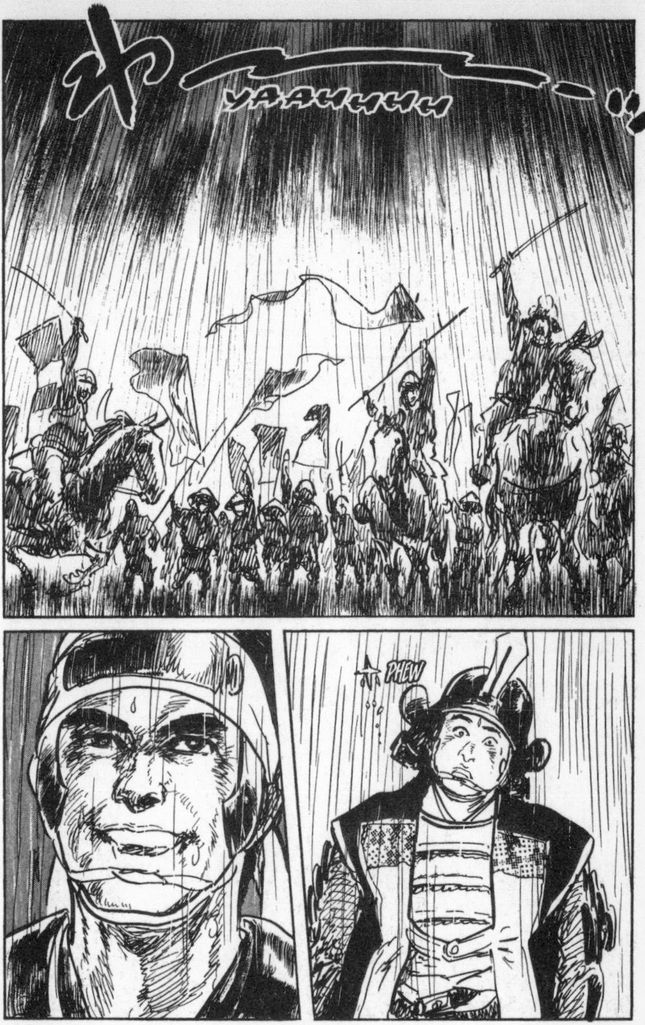
YAAHHHHH
PHEW

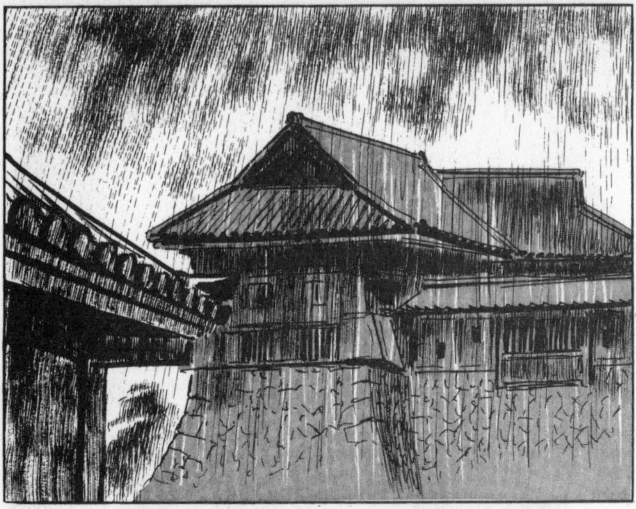
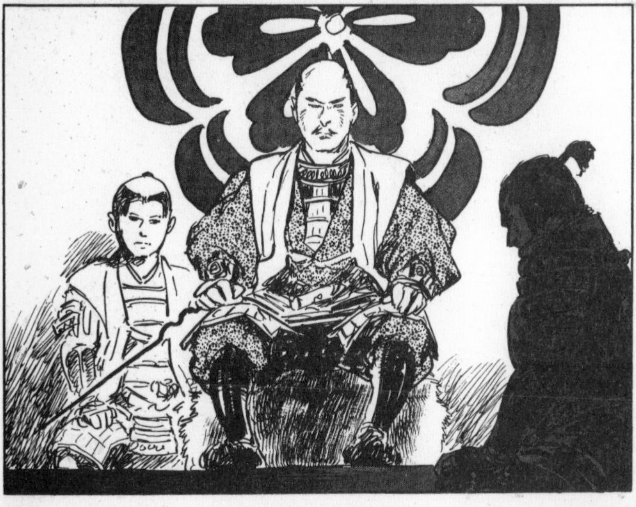

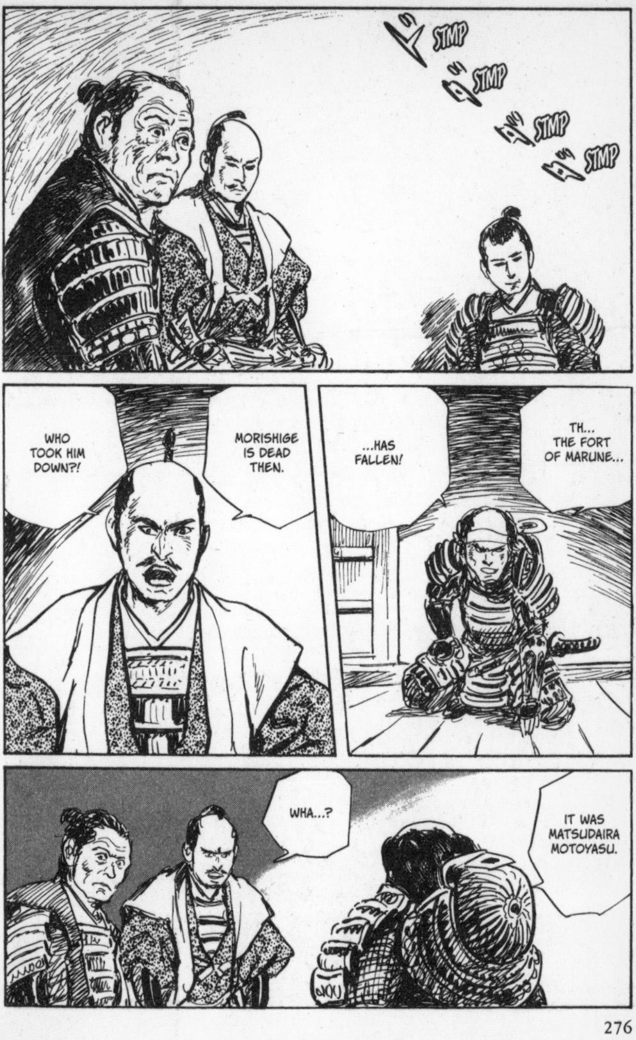
STMP
STMP
STMP
STMP
TH... THE FORT OF MARUNE...
...HAS FALLEN!
MORISHIGE IS DEAD THEN.
WHO TOOK HIM DOWN?!
IT WAS MATSUDAIRA MOTOYASU.
WHA...?

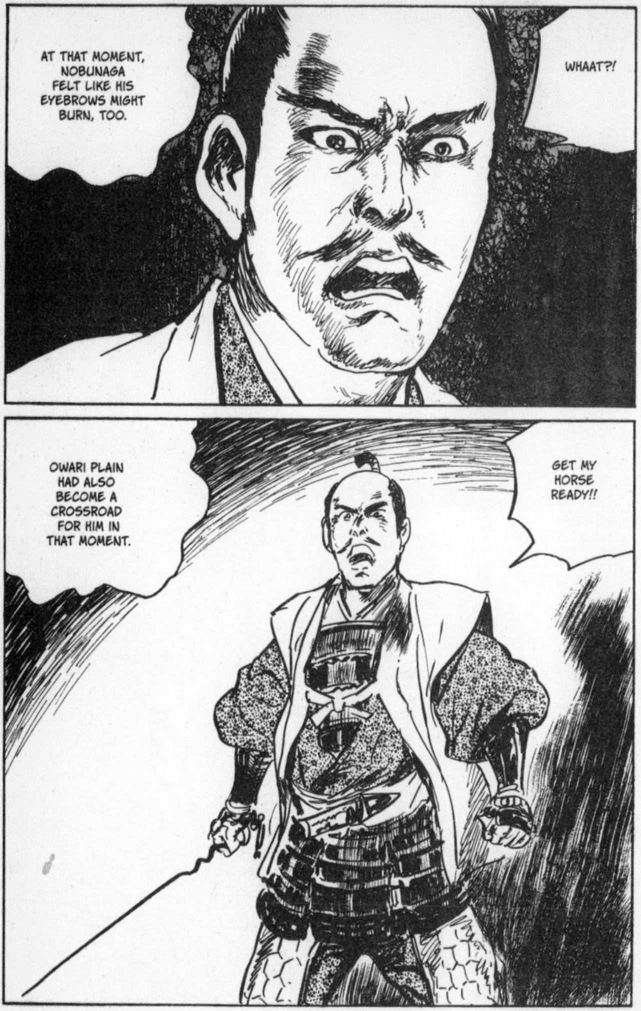
WHAAT?!
AT THAT MOMENT, NOBUNAGA FELT LIKE HIS EYEBROWS MIGHT BURN, TOO.
GET MY HORSE READY!!
OWARI PLAIN HAD ALSO BECOME A CROSSROAD FOR HIM IN THAT MOMENT.

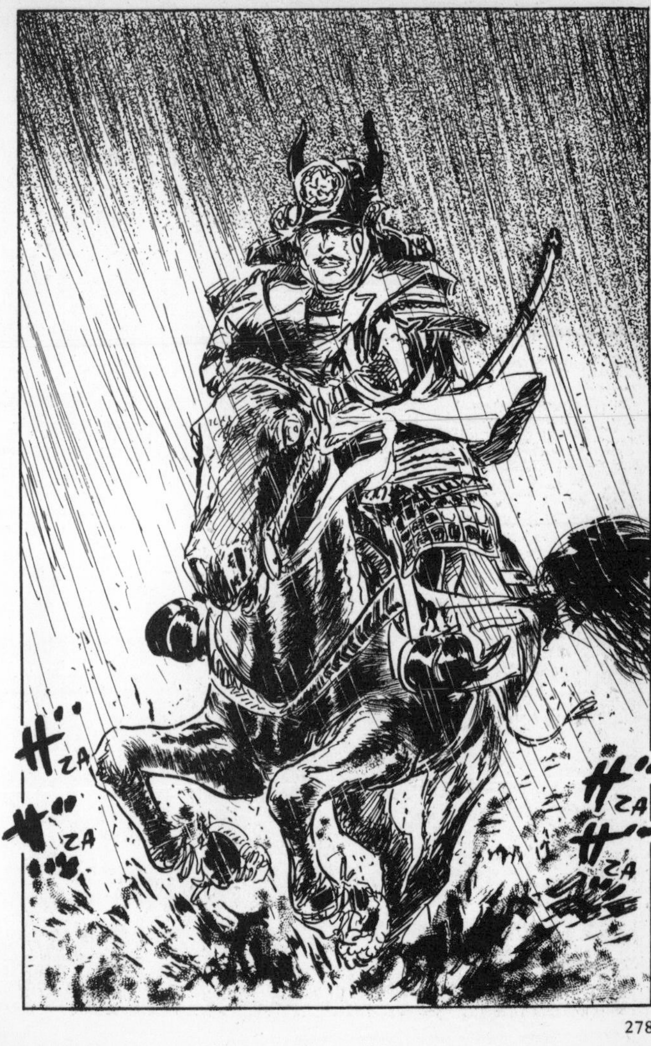

ザ ZA
ザ ZA
ザ ZA
ザ ZA

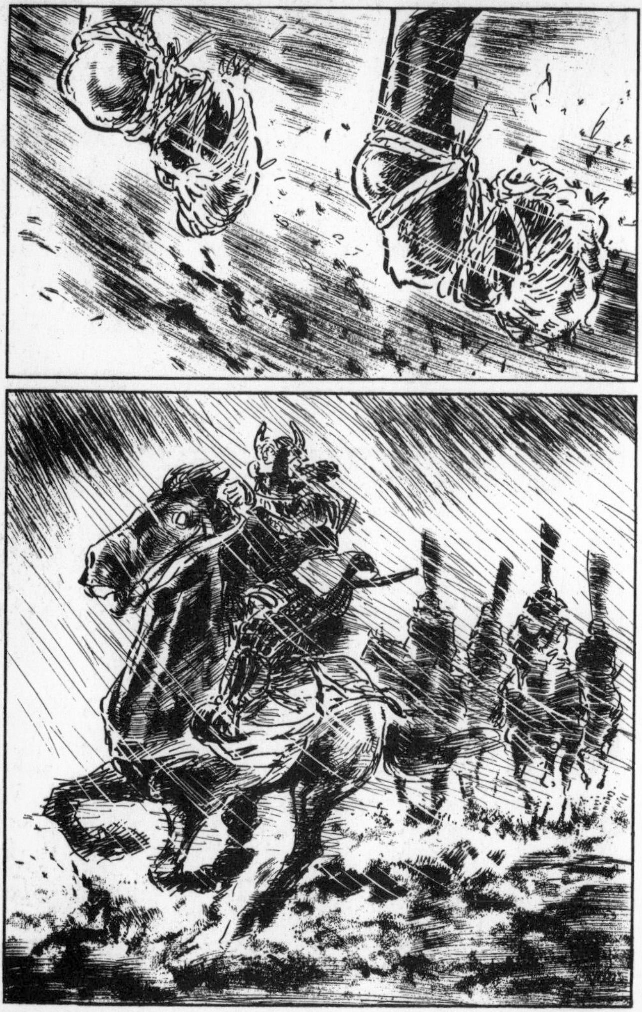

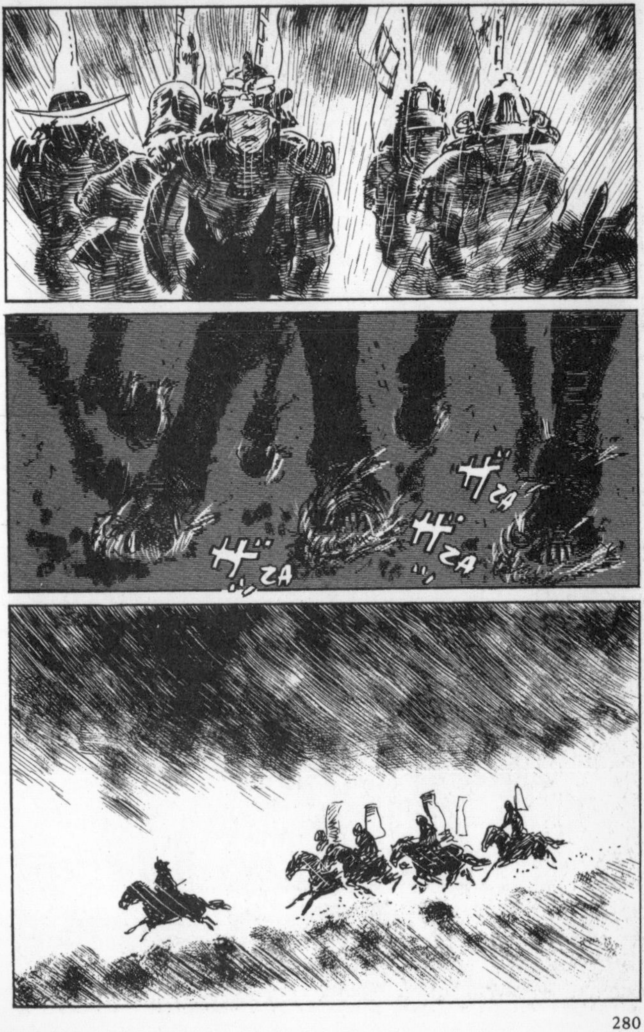
ZA
ZA
ZA

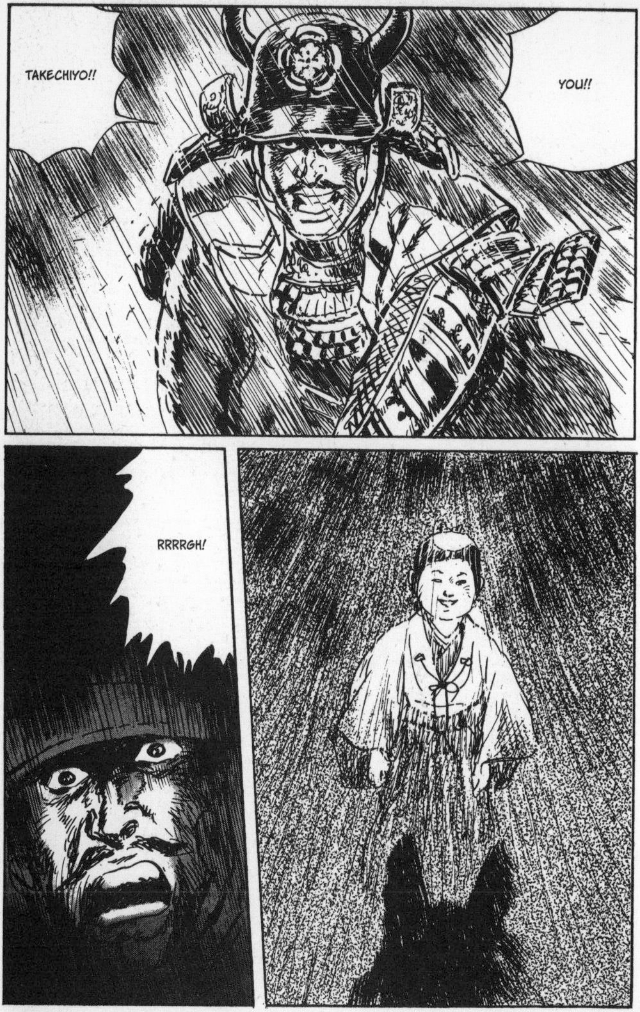
YOU!!
TAKECHIYO!!
RRRRGH!

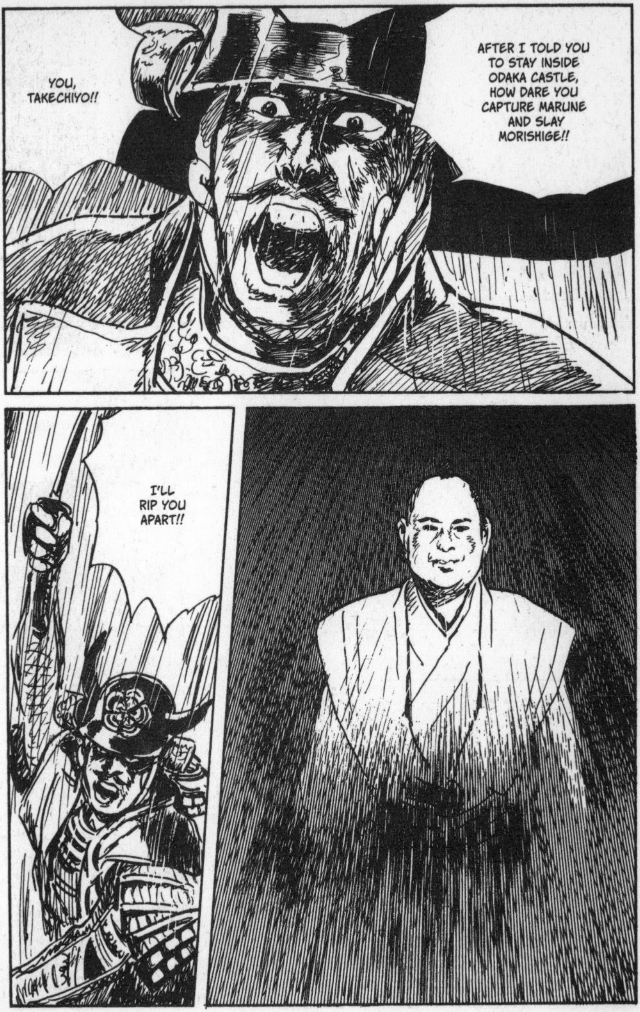
AFTER I TOLD YOU TO STAY INSIDE ODAKA CASTLE, HOW DARE YOU CAPTURE MARUNE AND SLAY MORISHIGE!!
YOU, TAKECHIYO!!
I'LL RIP YOU APART!!

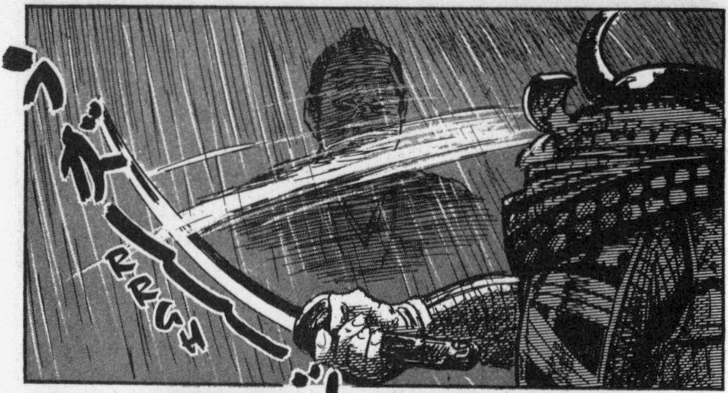
RRUGH

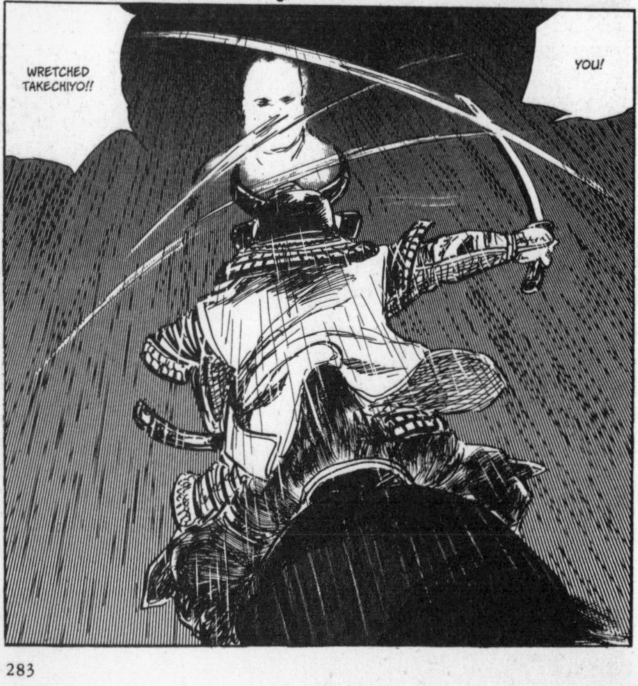
YOU!
WRETCHED TAKECHIYO!!

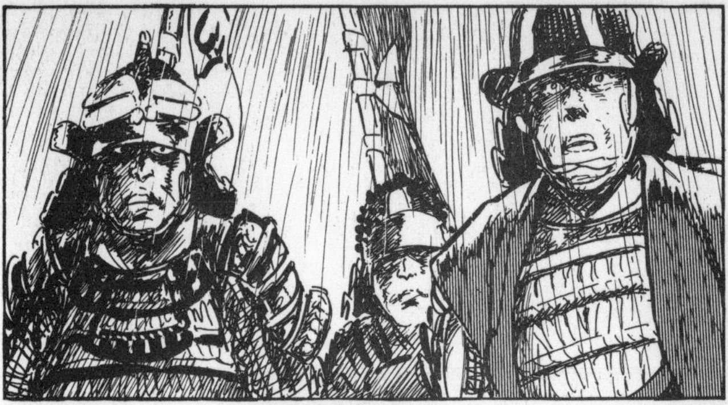

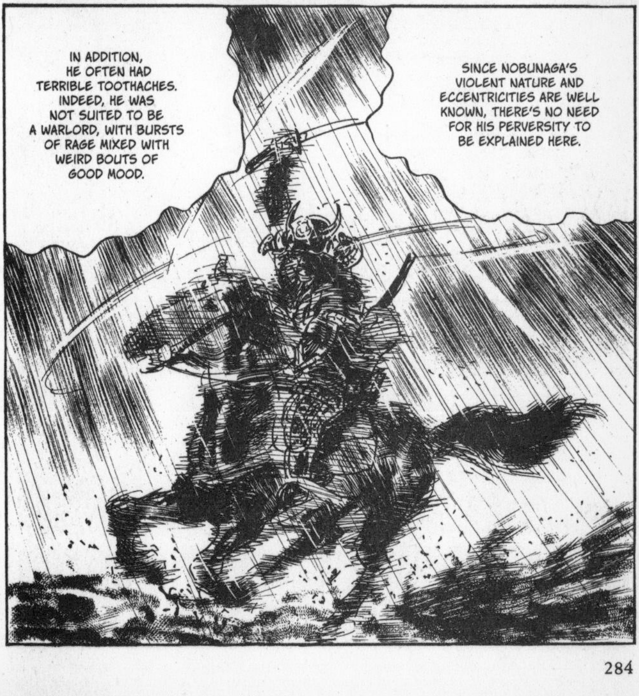
SINCE NOBUNAGA'S VIOLENT NATURE AND ECCENTRICITIES ARE WELL KNOWN, THERE'S NO NEED FOR HIS PERVERSITY TO BE EXPLAINED HERE.
IN ADDITION, HE OFTEN HAD TERRIBLE TOOTHACHES. INDEED, HE WAS NOT SUITED TO BE A WARLORD, WITH BURSTS OF RAGE MIXED WITH WEIRD BOUTS OF GOOD MOOD.

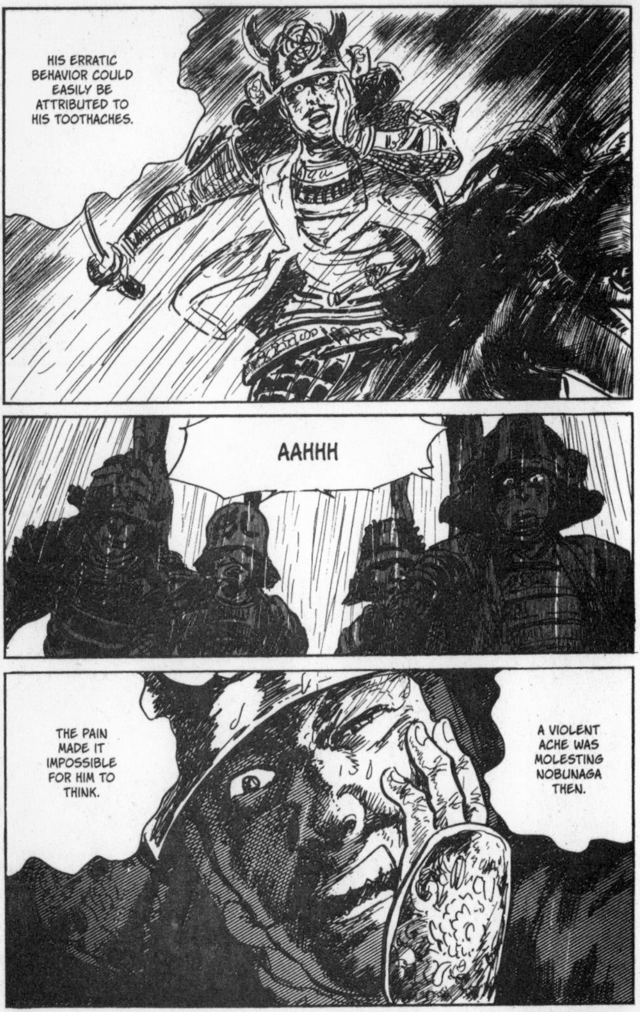
HIS ERRATIC BEHAVIOR COULD EASILY BE ATTRIBUTED TO HIS TOOTHACHES.
AAHHH
A VIOLENT ACHE WAS MOLESTING NOBUNAGA THEN.
THE PAIN MADE IT IMPOSSIBLE FOR HIM TO THINK.

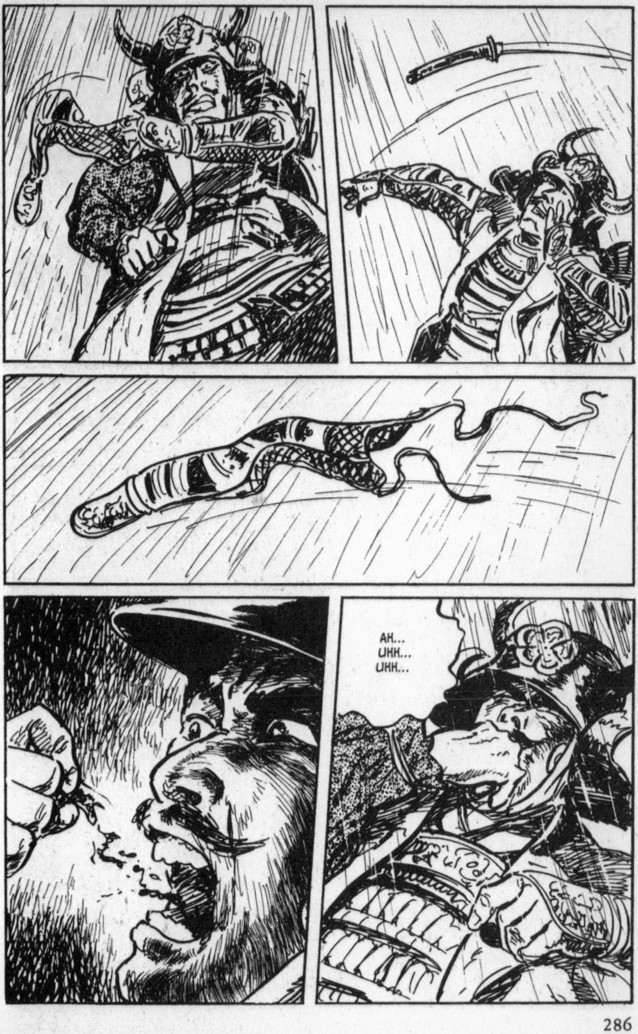
AH...
UHH...
UHH...

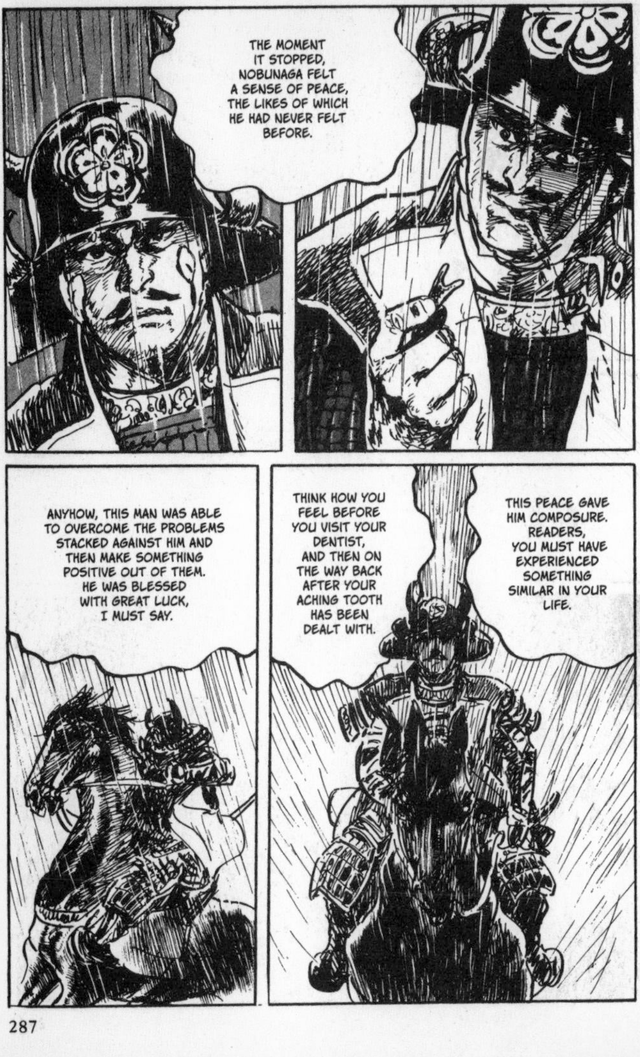
THE MOMENT IT STOPPED, NOBUNAGA FELT A SENSE OF PEACE, THE LIKES OF WHICH HE HAD NEVER FELT BEFORE.
THIS PEACE GAVE HIM COMPOSURE. READERS, YOU MUST HAVE EXPERIENCED SOMETHING SIMILAR IN YOUR LIFE.
THINK HOW YOU FEEL BEFORE YOU VISIT YOUR DENTIST, AND THEN ON THE WAY BACK AFTER YOUR ACHING TOOTH HAS BEEN DEALT WITH.
ANYHOW, THIS MAN WAS ABLE TO OVERCOME THE PROBLEMS STACKED AGAINST HIM AND THEN MAKE SOMETHING POSITIVE OUT OF THEM. HE WAS BLESSED WITH GREAT LUCK, I MUST SAY.

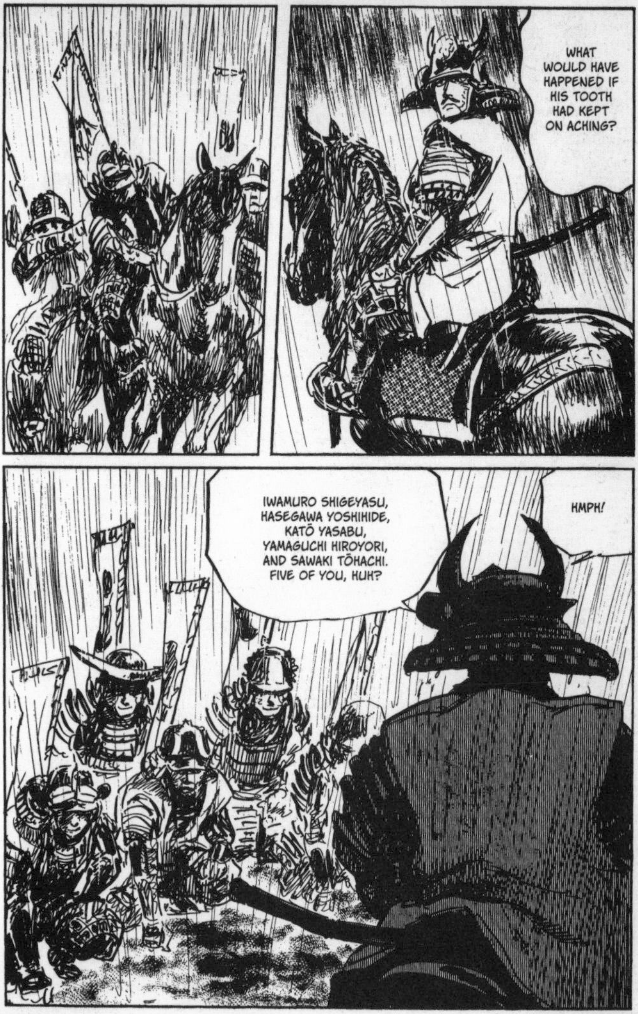
WHAT WOULD HAVE HAPPENED IF HIS TOOTH HAD KEPT ON ACHING?
HMPH!
IWAMURO SHIGEYASU, HASEGAWA YOSHIHIDE, KATŌ YASABU, YAMAGUCHI HIROYORI, AND SAWAKI TŌHACHI. FIVE OF YOU, HUH?

YES,
SIR.

HA HA HA
HA HA HA
HA HA HA
HA HA HA.

ONLY FIVE MEN
COULD KEEP UP
WITH MY GODLY
SPEED.

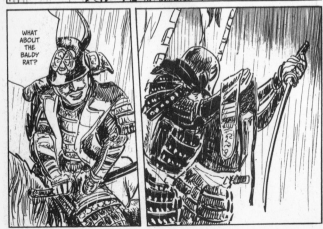

WHAT
ABOUT
THE
BALDY
RAT?

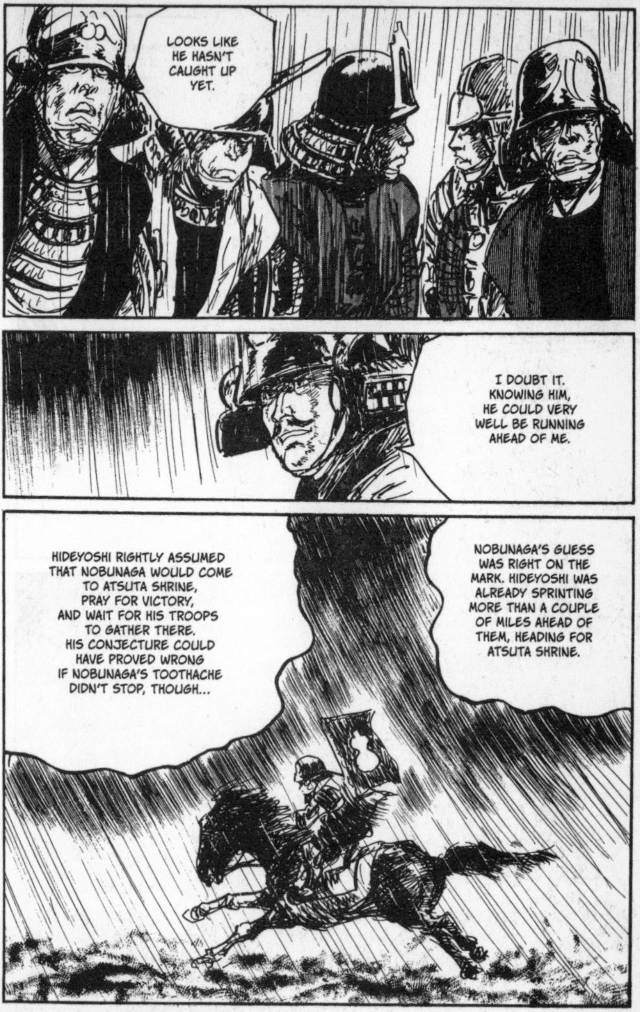
LOOKS LIKE HE HASN'T CAUGHT UP YET.
I DOUBT IT. KNOWING HIM, HE COULD VERY WELL BE RUNNING AHEAD OF ME.
NOBUNAGA'S GUESS WAS RIGHT ON THE MARK. HIDEYOSHI WAS ALREADY SPRINTING MORE THAN A COUPLE OF MILES AHEAD OF THEM, HEADING FOR ATSUTA SHRINE.
HIDEYOSHI RIGHTLY ASSUMED THAT NOBUNAGA WOULD COME TO ATSUTA SHRINE, PRAY FOR VICTORY, AND WAIT FOR HIS TROOPS TO GATHER THERE. HIS CONJECTURE COULD HAVE PROVED WRONG IF NOBUNAGA'S TOOTHACHE DIDN'T STOP, THOUGH...

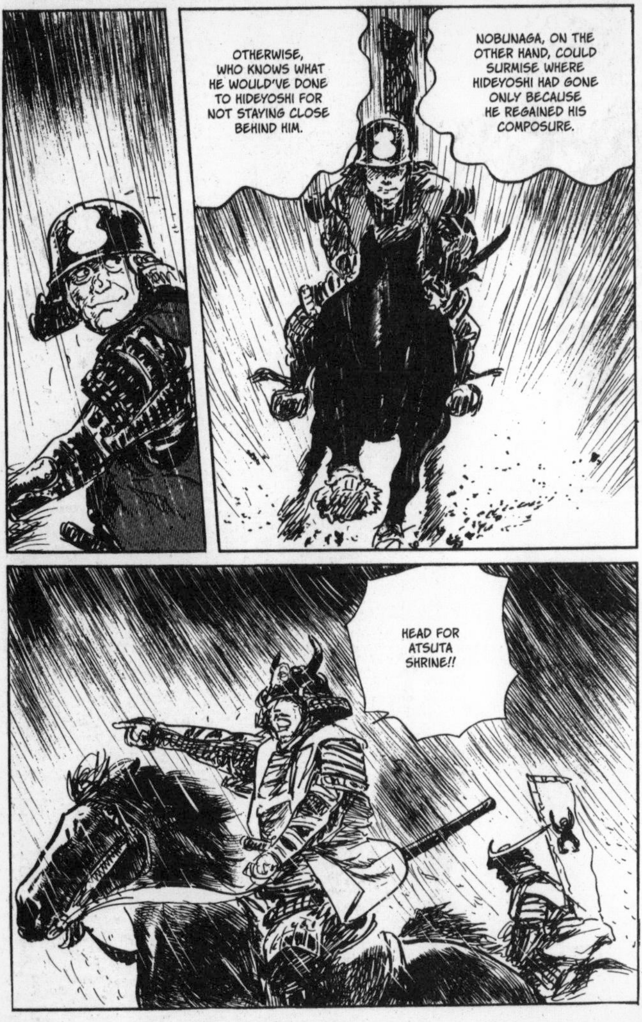
NOBUNAGA, ON THE OTHER HAND, COULD SURMISE WHERE HIDEYOSHI HAD GONE ONLY BECAUSE HE REGAINED HIS COMPOSURE.
OTHERWISE, WHO KNOWS WHAT HE WOULD'VE DONE TO HIDEYOSHI FOR NOT STAYING CLOSE BEHIND HIM.
HEAD FOR ATSUTA SHRINE!!

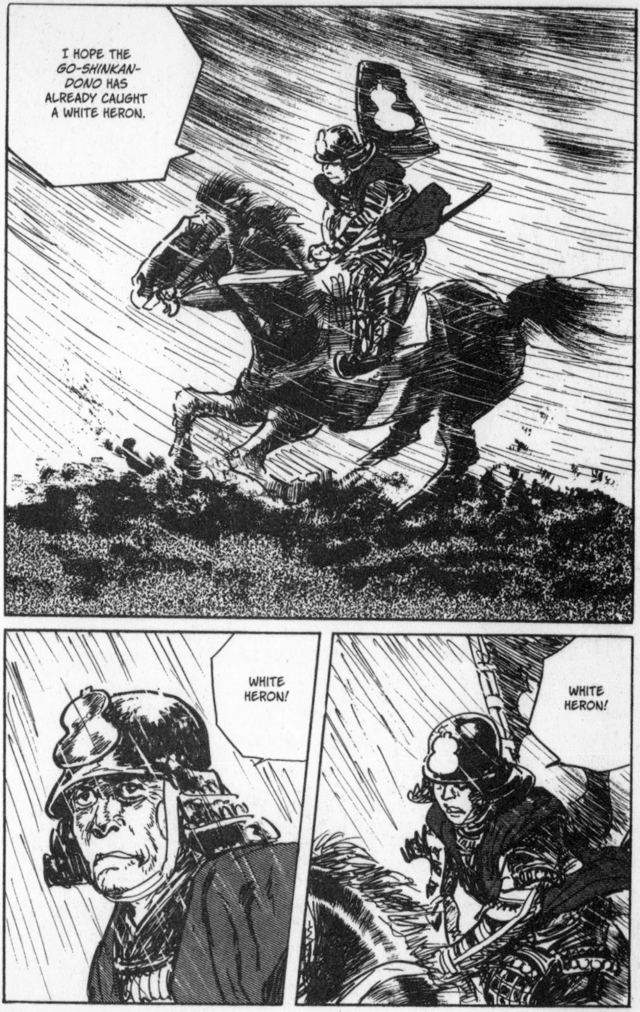
I HOPE THE *GO-SHINKAN-DONO* HAS ALREADY CAUGHT A WHITE HERON.
WHITE HERON!
WHITE HERON!

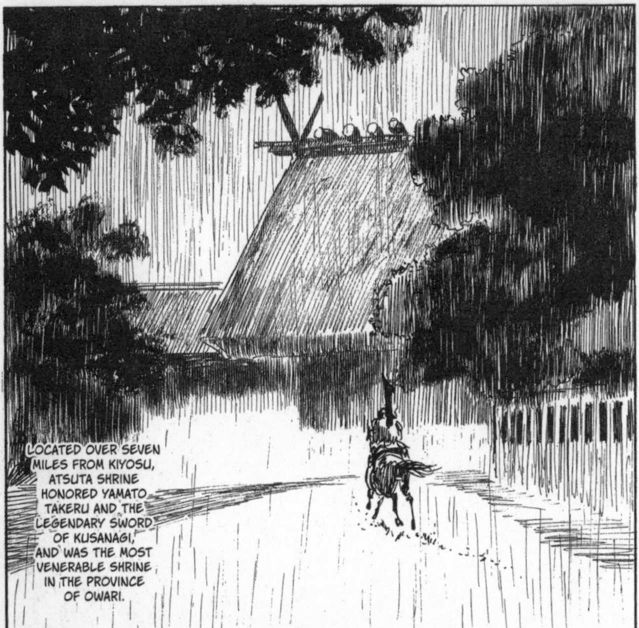
LOCATED OVER SEVEN MILES FROM KIYOSU, ATSUTA SHRINE HONORED YAMATO TAKERU AND THE LEGENDARY SWORD OF KUSANAGI, AND WAS THE MOST VENERABLE SHRINE IN THE PROVINCE OF OWARI.

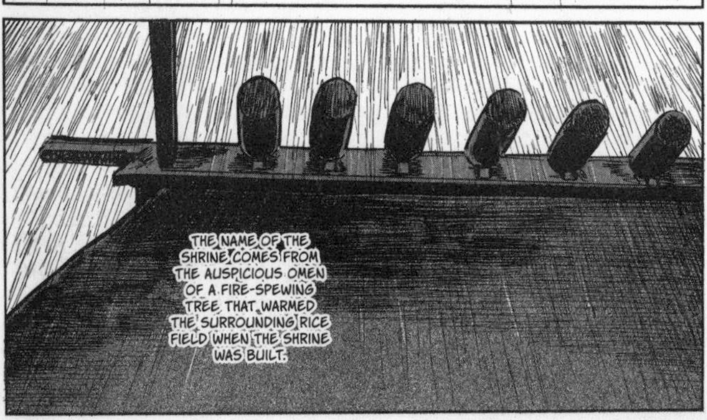
THE NAME OF THE SHRINE COMES FROM THE AUSPICIOUS OMEN OF A FIRE-SPEWING TREE THAT WARMED THE SURROUNDING RICE FIELD WHEN THE SHRINE WAS BUILT.

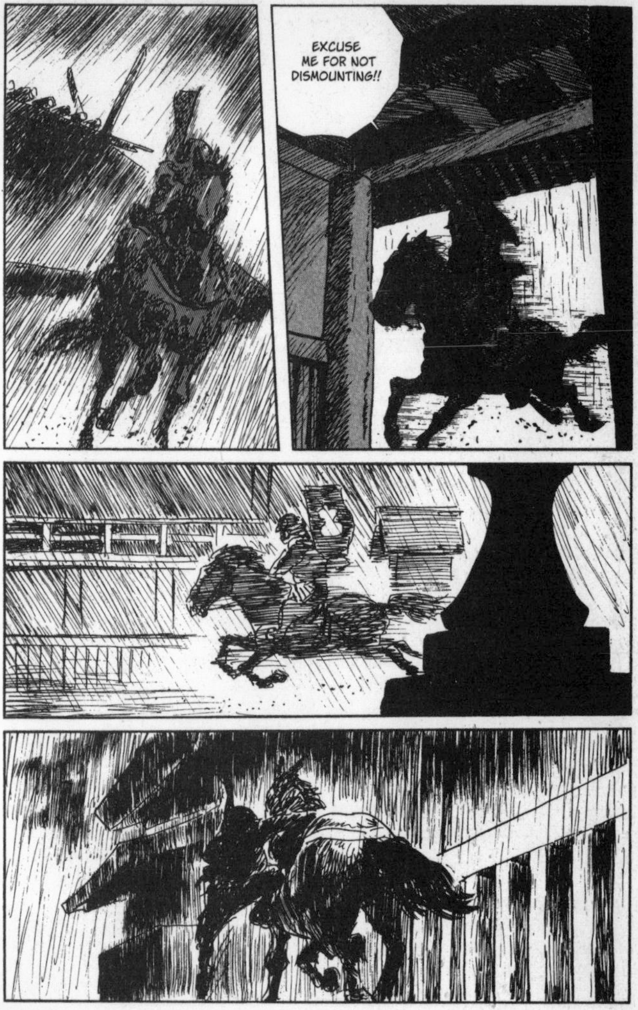
EXCUSE ME FOR NOT DISMOUNTING!!

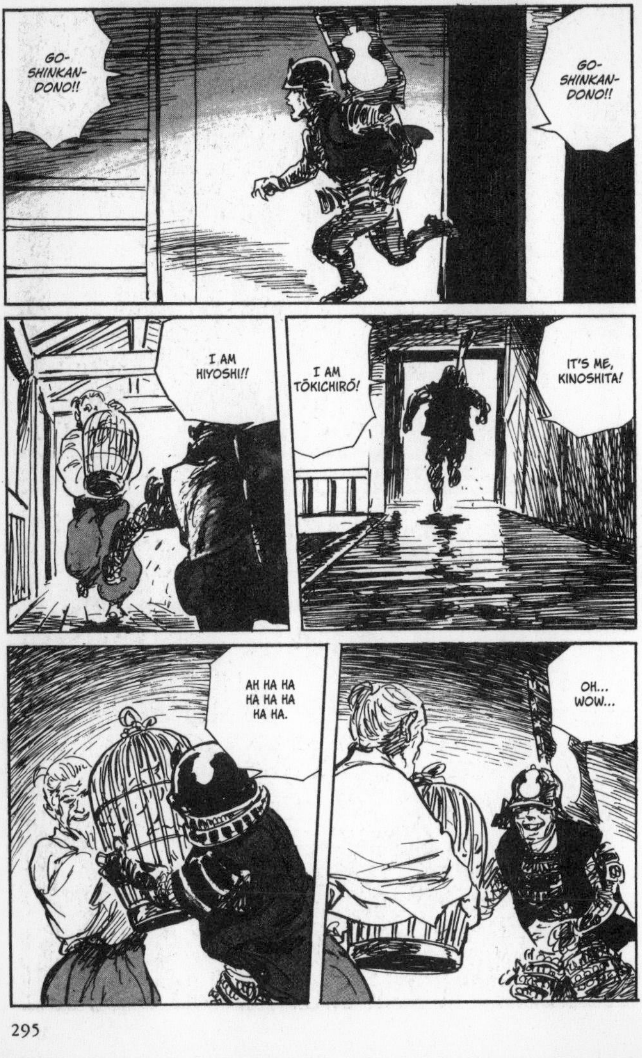
GO-SHINKAN-DONO!!
GO-SHINKAN-DONO!!
IT'S ME, KINOSHITA!
I AM TŌKICHIRŌ!
I AM HIYOSHI!!
OH... WOW...
AH HA HA HA HA HA HA HA.

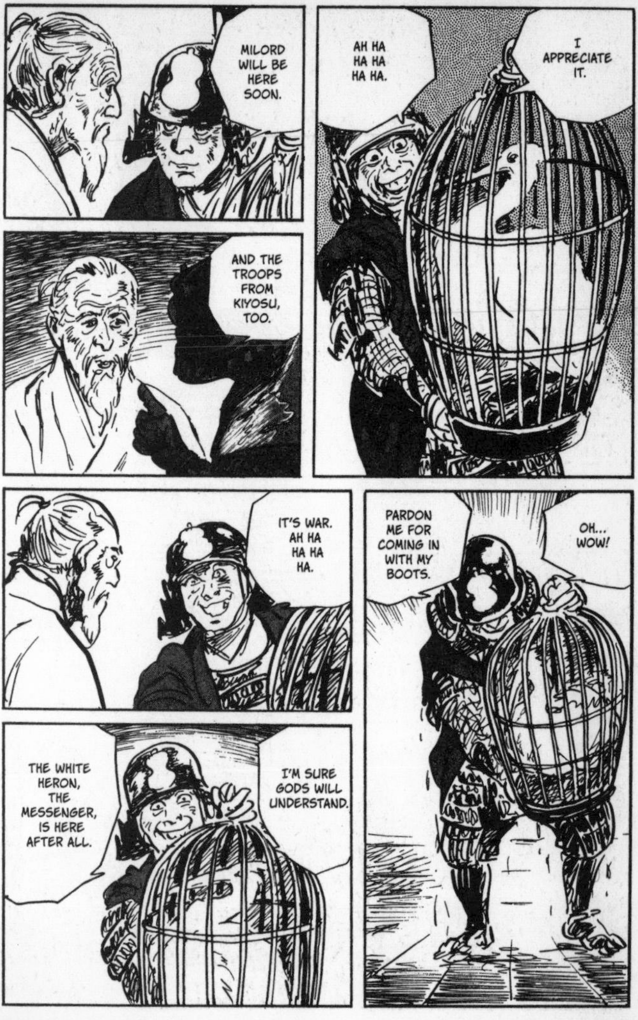
I APPRECIATE IT.
AH HA HA HA HA HA.
MILORD WILL BE HERE SOON.
AND THE TROOPS FROM KIYOSU, TOO.
OH... WOW!
PARDON ME FOR COMING IN WITH MY BOOTS.
IT'S WAR. AH HA HA HA HA.
I'M SURE GODS WILL UNDERSTAND.
THE WHITE HERON, THE MESSENGER, IS HERE AFTER ALL.

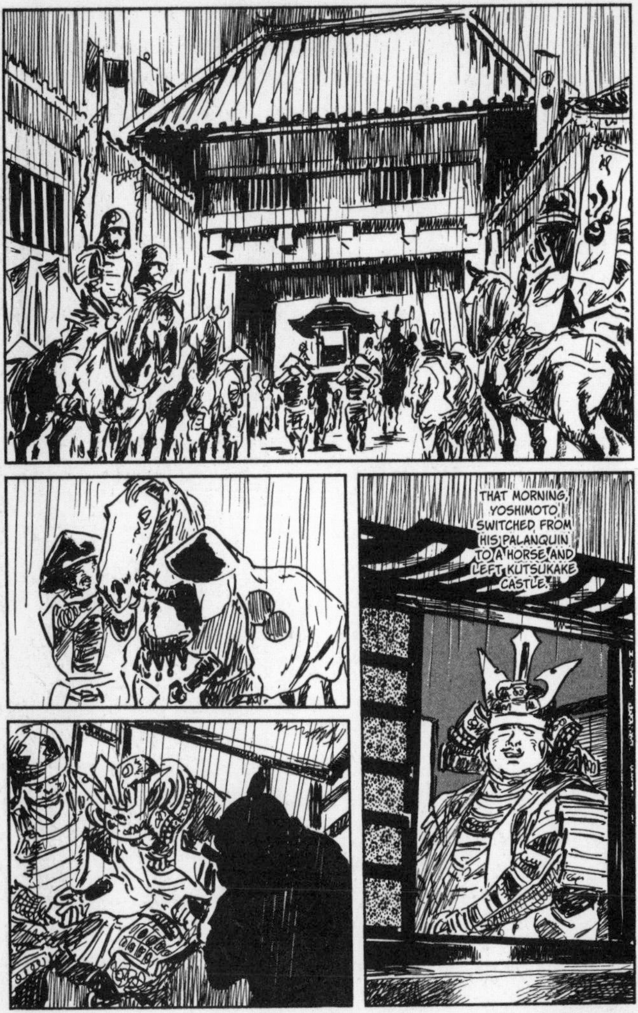
THAT MORNING, YOSHIMOTO SWITCHED FROM HIS PALANQUIN TO A HORSE AND LEFT KUTSUKAKE CASTLE.

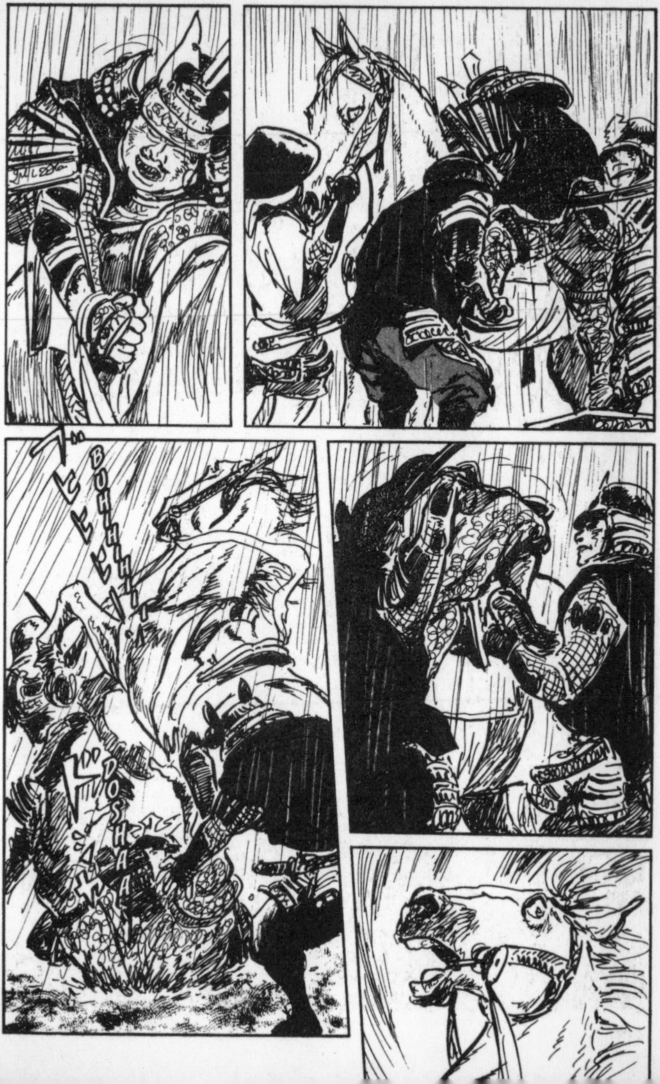
BUHIHIHII
DOSHAAA

OYAKATA-
SAMA!

MILORD!

AWW!!

THAT SHOULD
DRIVE AWAY THE
EVIL SPIRITS.
HO HO HO HO.
WHO KNEW THE
GODS COULD BE
SO JEALOUS...

TEE HEE
HO HO HO
HO HO HO
HO HO.

...ABOUT OUR
INCREDIBLE
SUCCESS?
TEE HEE HO
HO HO HO HO.

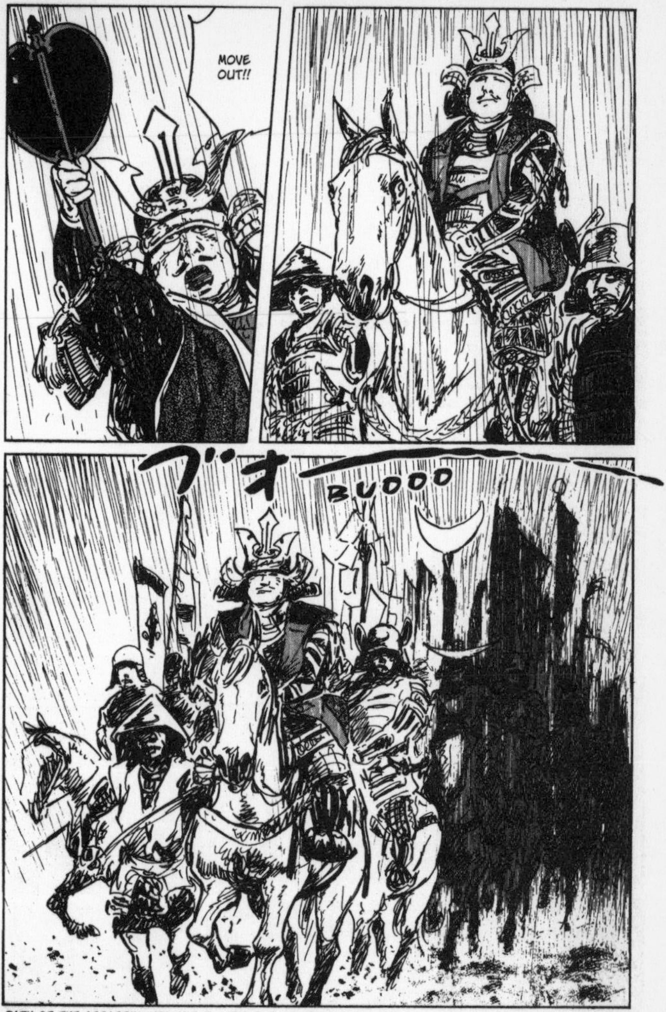
MOVE OUT!!
ブオー
BUOOO

PATH OF THE ASSASSIN, VOLUME 3 / THE END (TO BE CONTINUED)

koku
180 liters.

mitsumono
A system of three types of warriors who specialized in information gathering established by Takeda Shingen.

moto-moto yasui
Cheap by nature.

Nagao
The Nagao clan was a family of daimyo, feudal lords who built and controlled Kasugayama castle and the surrounding fief, in what is now Niigata prefecture.

Nobumori, Sakuma
(1527- 1581) A retainer of Oda clan. He has been also called Dewa no Suke and Uemon no I.

oyakatasama
A term used to address the head of the clan by the clan members. It translates to "house lord."

shinkan
Shrine priest.

Sūfu Sessai, Taigen
(d. 1557) Also known as Taigen Sessai, a Japanese abbot and mountain ascetic. He was the uncle of Imagawa Yoshimoto, and served him as military advisor and as commander of Imagawa's forces, despite his lack of any formal battle training or experience.

Takechiyo
Motoyasu's infant/childhood name.

tsukumo
"Tsu" means "nine," "ku" means "ten," and "mo" also means "nine."

tsuru
Crane.

Ujizane
(1538-1614) Son of Yoshimoto Imagawa. After Yoshimoto's death he was attacked by Shingen and Ieyasu. Ujizane later retaliated at the Takeda army by stopping their supply of salt. This had little effect and only resulted in the downfall of the Imagawa clan. Like his father he also enjoyed playing kemari.

yoroidoshi
A dagger-like thrusting blade, long enough to penetrate armor and reach a vital organ, inflicting a killing blow.

GLOSSARY

Atsuta
Located in Nagoya city, Aichi prefecture.

Atsuta shrine
A Japanese Shinto shrine in Atsuta-ku, Nagoya. It is known as the second-most venerable shrine in Japan.

Blue Flag
Known as *ayame* in Japanese, a member of the genus iris of the iridaceae. Its scientific name is iris Virginica.

Chiryu
A city in Aichi prefecture.

hachimaki
A hachimaki is a stylized headband, usually made of red or white cloth, worn as a symbol of perseverance or effort, originating in Japan.

honorifics
Japan is a class and status society, and proper forms of address are critical. Common markers of respect are the prefixes *o* and *go*, and a wide range of suffixes. Some of the suffixes you will encounter in *Path of the Assassin*:
chan – for children, young women, and close friends
dono – archaic; used for higher-ranked or highly respected figures
san – the most common, used among equals or near-equals
sama – used for superiors
sensei – used for teachers, masters, respected entertainers, and politicians.

itto
Approximately eighteen liters, which is about four gallons.

jijisama
Grandfather.

Kakegawa
A river that runs through the west part of Shizuoka prefecture. It is also the name of a city located in Shizuoka prefecture.

kame
Turtle.

kemari
Kemari is a so-called sport that was popular in Japan and China in the Heian period. The object of kemari is to keep a small, deerskin ball in the air, with all players cooperating to do so.

Kippōshi
Oda Nobunaga's first given name (i.e., his infant/childhood name) before he changed his name to Nobunaga.

GOSEKI KOJIMA

Goseki Kojima was born on November 3, 1928, the very same day as the godfather of Japanese comics, Osamu Tezuka. Art was a Kojima family tradition, his own father an amateur portrait artist and his great-great-grandfather a sculptor.

In 1950, Kojima moved to Tokyo, where the postwar devastation had given rise to special manga forms for audiences too poor to buy the new manga magazines just starting to reach the newsstands. Kojima created art for *kami-shibai*, or "paperplay" narrators, who would use manga story sheets to present narrated street plays, and later moved on to creating works for the *kashi-bon* market, bookstores that rented out books, magazines, and manga to mostly low-income readers.

In 1967, Kojima broke into the magazine market with his ninja adventure, *Dojinki*. As the manga magazine market grew and diversified, he turned out a steady stream of popular samurai manga series.

In 1970, in collaboration with Kazuo Koike, Kojima began the work that would seal his reputation, *Kozure Okami* (*Lone Wolf and Cub*). Many additional series would follow, including *Path of the Assassin* and *Samurai Executioner*.

In his final years, Kojima turned to creating original graphic novels based on the movies of his favorite director, the great Akira Kurosawa. Kojima passed away on January 5, 2000 at the age of seventy-one.

KAZUO KOIKE

Though widely respected as a powerful writer of graphic fiction, Kazuo Koike has spent a lifetime reaching beyond the bounds of the comics medium. Aside from co-creating and writing such classic manga as *Lone Wolf and Cub* and *Crying Freeman*, Koike has hosted the popular *Shibi Golf Weekly* instructional television program; founded the *Albatross View* golf magazine; produced movies; written popular fiction, poetry, and screenplays; and mentored some of Japan's best manga talent.

Koike started the *Gekiga Sonjuku*, a college course aimed at helping talented writers and artists—such as *Ranma 1/2* creator Rumiko Takahashi—break into the comics field. His methods and teachings continue to influence new generations of manga creators, not to mention artists and writers around the world. Examples of Koike's influence range from the comics works of Frank Miller and Stan Sakai to the films of Quentin Tarantino.

The driving focus of Koike's narrative is character development, and his commitment to the character is clear: "Comics are carried by characters. If a character is well-created, the comic becomes a hit." Kazuo Koike's continued success in comics and literature has proven this philosophy true.

Kazuo Koike continues to work in the entertainment media to this very day, consistently diversifying his work and forging new paths across the rough roads of Edo-period history and the green swaths of today's golfing world.

ALSO AVAILABLE FROM DARK HORSE BOOKS

Lady Snowblood
Volumes 1-4

From Kazuo Koike and Kazuo Kamimura, comes *Lady Snowblood*, the tale of a daughter born of a singular purpose, to avenge the death of her family at the hands of a gang of thugs, a purpose woven into her soul from the time of her gestation. Beautifully drafted and full of bloody, sexy action, *Lady Snowblood* lives up to its title and reputation.

Crying Freeman
Volumes 1-2

Written by the legendary Kazuo Koike and illustrated by the incomparable Ryoichi Ikegami, *Crying Freeman* is adult manga at its most challenging: dark, violent, morally complex, erotically charged, and regarded worldwide as one of the classics of adult graphic fiction.